CAPITAL PUNISHMENT

Theory and Practice of the Ultimate Penalty

Virginia Leigh Hatch
Boise State University

Anthony Walsh
Boise State University

NEW YORK   OXFORD
OXFORD UNIVERSITY PRESS

Oxford University Press is a department of the University of Oxford.
It furthers the University's objective of excellence in research,
scholarship, and education by publishing worldwide.

Oxford   New York
Auckland   Cape Town   Dar es Salaam   Hong Kong   Karachi
Kuala Lumpur   Madrid   Melbourne   Mexico City   Nairobi
New Delhi   Shanghai   Taipei   Toronto

With offices in
Argentina   Austria   Brazil   Chile   Czech Republic   France   Greece
Guatemala   Hungary   Italy   Japan   Poland   Portugal   Singapore
South Korea   Switzerland   Thailand   Turkey   Ukraine   Vietnam

Copyright © 2016 by Oxford University Press

For titles covered by Section 112 of the US Higher Education
Opportunity Act, please visit www.oup.com/us/he for the
latest information about pricing and alternate formats.

Published by Oxford University Press
198 Madison Avenue, New York,
New York 10016
http://www.oup.com

Oxford is a registered trademark of Oxford University Press

All rights reserved. No part of this publication may be reproduced,
stored in a retrieval system, or transmitted, in any form or by any means,
electronic, mechanical, photocopying, recording, or otherwise,
without the prior permission of Oxford University Press.

The CIP data is on-file at the Library of Congress.

ISBN: 978-0-19-021268-1

Printing number: 9 8 7 6 5 4 3 2 1

Printed in the United States of America
on acid-free paper

Dedicated to my wonderful husband, Jim; my son, Jackson; my parents, Richard and Denise; my departed colleague, Dr. Michael Blankenship; Anita and Sarah; and the public defenders who work tirelessly to preserve the rights of their clients.

Virginia Hatch

Dedicated to my drop-dead gorgeous wife, Grace; my sons, Robert and Michael; my stepdaughters, Heidi and Kasey; my grandchildren, Robbie, Ryan, Mikey, Randy, Christopher, Ashlyn, Morgan, Stevie, Vivien, and Frankie; and my great-grandchildren, Kaelyn, Logan, Keagan, Caleb, Lucas, and Brayden. I should not forget the spouses that made this all possible: Patricia, Dianna, Sharon, Karen, Collette, Marcus, Michael, Amy, and Jenna.

Anthony Walsh

CONTENTS

PREFACE   x
ACKNOWLEDGMENTS   xv

CHAPTER 1   **WHY DO WE PUNISH: THE ORIGIN AND PURPOSE OF PUNISHMENT**   1
    The Evolutionary Origins of Punishment   2
    Religion, Emotion, Social Order, and Punishment   3
    The Co-Evolution of Punishment and Social Cooperation   5
    Second- and Third-Party Punishment   8
    From Primitive Vengeance to Modern Law   9
    The Assumptions about Human Nature and Punishment Justifications   12
    Free Will, Determinism, and the Law   13
    Punishment Justifications   15
        Deterrence   16
        Incapacitation   16
        Rehabilitation   17
        Reintegration   18
        Retribution   18
    Kantian Retribution: The Major Justification of Capital Punishment   19
        Retribution and Emotion   20
        Reconciliation and Reintegration   21

CHAPTER 2   **HISTORY OF THE DEATH PENALTY IN THE UNITED STATES: PAST AND PRESENT**   29
    Capital Punishment in Antiquity   30
    The History of the Death Penalty in America   31
    Pre-Modern Era/Pre-*Furman*   32
        Seventeenth and Eighteenth Centuries   32
        Religion   33

Deterrence		35
Retribution		37
Nineteenth Century/Abolitionist Movement		38
*Twentieth Century/Pre-*Furman		42
Furman v. Georgia *(1972)*		44
Modern Era/Post-*Furman*		47

CHAPTER 3 **THE FOUNDATIONAL CASES: *FURMAN* TO *STANFORD*** 53

Furman v. Georgia (1972)	55
Concurring Opinions	56
Dissenting Opinions	58
Gregg v. Georgia (1976)	59
Concurring Opinions	61
Dissenting Opinions	61
Additional Case of Interest	62
Coker v. Georgia (1977)	62
Concurring Opinions	63
Dissenting Opinions	64
Additional Case of Interest	65
Lockett v. Ohio (1978)	65
Concurring Opinions	67
Dissenting Opinion	68
Additional Cases of Interest	68
McCleskey v. Kemp (1987)	68
Concurring Opinions	70
Dissenting Opinions	71
Additional Cases of Interest	72
Stanford v. Kentucky (1989)	72
Concurring Opinions	74
Dissenting Opinions	74
Additional Cases of Interest	76

CHAPTER 4 **THE FOUNDATIONAL CASES: *ATKINS* TO *BAZE*** 81

Atkins v. Virginia (2002)	82
Concurring Opinions	84
Dissenting Opinion	85
Additional Cases of Interest	87

Ring v. Arizona (2002)		88
Concurring Opinions		89
Dissenting Opinion		90
Additional Cases of Interest		91
Roper v. Simmons (2005)		94
Concurring Opinions		96
Dissenting Opinions		97
Additional Cases of Interest		98
Baze and Bowling v. Reez (2008)		98
Concurring Opinions		99
Dissenting Opinion		100
Additional Cases of Interest		100
CHAPTER 5	**THE DEATH PENALTY AND PUBLIC OPINION**	103
	The Ups and Downs of Public Opinion	104
	The Ways that Public Support Maintains the Death Penalty	106
	Attitudinal Model and Political Adjustment Hypothesis	108
	Expression of Public Opinion	109
	The Marshall Hypothesis	115
	Global Perspectives on the Death Penalty	118
CHAPTER 6	**METHODS OF EXECUTION**	125
	The Evolution of Execution Methods	126
	Hanging	127
	Electrocution	130
	Gas Chamber	134
	Firing Squad	142
	Lethal Injection	143
	Three- vs. One-Drug Injection	145
	Drug Availability	148
	Executioners	149
	Last Words and Last Meals	150
CHAPTER 7	**DETERRENCE AND THE DEATH PENALTY**	155
	The Assumptions of Deterrence Theory	156
	Specific and General Deterrence	158

	Three Principles of Punishment	159
	The Death Penalty/Deterrence Debate	161
	Deterrence: Criminologists and Sociologists versus Economists	165
	Does Capital Punishment Have a Brutalizing Effect?	167
	The Inconclusive Conclusion of the Committee on Deterrence and the Death Penalty	168
	What Is Needed to Demonstrate if the Death Penalty Is a Deterrent?	169
	The Opinions of Criminologists and Police Chiefs on the Death Penalty	173
	Pascal's Wager: A "Last Ditch" Effort	175
CHAPTER 8	**THE DEATH PENALTY AND SPECIAL POPULATIONS: RACE, GENDER, AGE, AND MENTAL CAPACITY**	**183**
	Race and the Death Penalty	185
	Racial Disproportionality in Capital Punishment	185
	The Issue of Victim's Race	189
	Dueling Statisticians Redux	191
	Juveniles and the Death Penalty	194
	Women and the Death Penalty	197
	Women Executed Since 1976	198
	The Chivalry Explanation in Female Capital Cases	200
	The Evil Woman Explanation in Females Capital Cases	201
	The Death Penalty and Mental Illness	202
	Mental Disability	205
	Mental Illness	207
CHAPTER 9	**MODERN SCIENCE AND THE DEATH PENALTY**	**215**
	Exoneration and Mitigation	216
	The Innocence Revolution	217
	Science, Agency, Genes, and Culpability	218
	What Are Genes and How Do They Make Us Different?	221
	DNA "Fingerprinting" in a Nutshell	222
	Brain Imaging in a Nutshell	224
	Brain Imaging and the Abolition of the Juvenile Death Penalty	225

	Some Problems with DNA Testing to Consider	230
	Some Problems with fMRI to Consider	232

CHAPTER 10	**WRONGFUL CONVICTIONS AND THE DEATH PENALTY**		239
	Exoneration and Factual Innocence		240
	Due Process versus Crime Control Models of Criminal Justice Systems		243
	The Blackstone Ratio		244
	The "Big Six"		245
		Eyewitness Misidentification	245
		False Confessions	250
		Informant/Snitch Testimony	254
		Bad Science	257
		Ineffective Defense Counsel	260
		Government Misconduct	263
	Post-Exoneration Compensation		265

CHAPTER 11	**THE FINANCIAL BURDEN OF THE DEATH PENALTY AND OTHER COLLATERAL COSTS**	273
	Death Penalty: A Yellow Brick Road	274
	The Timothy McVeigh Federal Murder Trial	275
	The Financial Burden of the Death Penalty	277
	The Financial Cost of Court Proceedings: Death Penalty versus LWOP	277
	Court Costs	281
	Expert Witnesses	284
	Habeas Corpus Petition versus Direct Appeal	286
	Introduction of the Antiterrorism and Effective Death Penalty Act	287
	All Bark and Little Bite	288
	Collateral Costs: Victims' and Defendants' Families	290

CHAPTER 12	**THE DEATH PENALTY: THE FEDERAL, MILITARY, AND INTERNATIONAL PERSPECTIVE**	297
	Why Does the United States Retain the Death Penalty?	298
	Federal Death Penalty	300

The U.S. Military Death Penalty	305
The U.S. Military's Current Death Row Population	307
The Death Penalty on the International Stage	308
The Death Penalty in the Communist World	311
People's Republic of China	311
Democratic People's Republic of Korea (North Korea)	315
The Death Penalty in the Islamic World	317
Kingdom of Saudi Arabia	317
Islamic Republic of Iran	320
Republic of Iraq	322
EPILOGUE	329
Libby the Liberal and Conrad the Conservative Debate the Death Penalty	329
APPENDIX	337
INDEX	339

PREFACE

This book is about what may be the greatest moral issue facing American society—the penalty of death. If it is not the greatest moral issue facing society as a whole, it is certainly the greatest one facing the American criminal justice system. When one surveys the momentous events that occur around the world every day, in the grand scheme of things the American death penalty is a relatively minor issue. But it is a big issue in both the practical and academic segments of criminal justice, and one of the most important issues of all for philosophers who have chosen ethics and morality as their specializations.

A 2015 Gallup Poll found that while 33% of the American public found capital punishment to be morally wrong, twice as many (62%) found it to be morally correct. The support or non-support of capital punishment differs greatly among segments of American society, but the only group among all political ideologies, political parties, races, and genders who oppose it more than support it are self-identified liberals. Liberals oppose it (50%) versus 47% who favor it. Those who oppose the death penalty accuse those who support it of being uninformed barbarians, and propose that the fact that most Americans support it marks American society as uncivilized, heartless, and Neanderthal. Proponents of capital punishment accuse those who oppose it of being arrogant bleeding-heart liberals living in a fantasy world, in which even violent killers will respond positively to acts of kindness and forgiveness. As we will see, the death penalty debate is everything but polite, which is to be expected with such an emotional issue.

Let us be upfront from the beginning: Both of your present authors are against the death penalty, but for quite different reasons. One of us would not support it under any circumstances, and the other would support it if certain conditions were different. We have both had personal experiences with capital cases, Professor Hatch as a mitigation specialist working for the Federal Defender's Office and as an Innocence Project investigator, and Professor Walsh as a police officer and probation officer. Acknowledging bias is the first step in controlling it. We have thus striven throughout this book to be as objective as possible. Too many books on the death penalty are so obviously biased in one direction or the other that they are off-putting to readers with contrary views. The authors of these kinds of books try to convince readers that their position is the morally right one, and hint that if the reader doesn't agree, then he or she is hopelessly ignorant. This is alienating and rarely changes students' minds. We have found in the classroom that students respond best when all aspects of an issue are explored as dispassionately as possible. This is what we have endeavored to do. However, most of the research literature we cite in this work was produced by opponents of capital punishment. This is unavoidable since it is usually left to those who oppose the status quo in any area to stir the pot; supporters rest content with things as they are, but there are some studies written by supporters of capital punishment that attempt to balance those who oppose it. Because scholarly research is supposed to be neutral, however, we rarely, if ever, find a research article in which the author(s) reveal their personal opinions.

Being presented with a balanced approach to an important policy issue like capital punishment may be refreshing to some, but it can be is disconcerting for those who want unambiguous answers and to those whose minds are already made up one way or the other. We are all eager to be informed by experts on important issues and may wonder why decades of research has not provided definitive answers to questions such as "Does the death penalty deter?," "Is it racist?," "Are there better alternatives?," and so forth. Charles Manski (2011) writes that our reluctance to consider views contrary to our own often results in us accepting claims of "incredible certitude" from those who produce scholarly work congenial to our point of view (p. 261). He further asserts that almost all arguments about social policies with moral content such as the death penalty involve "dueling certitudes" that conflate "science and advocacy," engage "wishful extrapolation," and result in "media overreach" in that the media over-interpret scholarly research as definitive. The American Society of Criminology was also guilty of "incredible certitude" when it called for the abolition of capital punishment in 1989 based on the "consensus" of death penalty scholars that it provides no deterrent effect. But as the eminent death penalty researcher Daniel Nagin (2012) points out "Consensus does not imply truth" (p. 4). Nagin further points out that "Certitude is easy to express. Expressing ambiguity but still maintaining clarity is very hard to do—it requires a lot of intellectual perspiration" (p. 4). We are big fans of Manski and Nagin's intellectual honesty and endeavor to expend our "intellectual perspiration" to provide clarity, while exposing the ambiguities inherent in both sides of the emotional debate over the issue of capital punishment in the United States.

The capital punishment debate is still largely centered on issues of morality, but has evolved into one of practicality as well. Moral issues discussed in this book range from philosophical dialogue on our need for punishment and social solidarity, to the execution of the innocent. Debates of practicality have become all too real in our country for a variety of economic, social, and political reasons. Some of the concerns include the exorbitant costs associated with implementation of capital punishment, to the difficulty of obtaining drugs needed to execute offenders from countries who disapprove of the death penalty and would like to pressure the United States to abolish its use. These are just a few of the dialogues that you will find in this book.

Each chapter is prefaced with a vignette related to the chapter topic and includes a feature we call "Perspectives from the Field." These perspectives are written by key players in our capital punishment system (judges, prosecutors, defense attorneys, executioners, expert witnesses, etc.). They offer the valuable viewpoints of practitioners themselves, detailing their roles in the capital punishment process and their thoughts about it. Each chapter concludes with thought-provoking discussion questions designed to challenge the reader's comprehension of the material.

We begin our book with a chapter that outlines the philosophical and theoretical explanations for punishment and its relevance in consideration of the death penalty debate. We explore the nature and origins of punishment from a number of different perspectives. The main concern of this chapter is to uncover the deep and ultimate reasons why the urge to punish is so strongly rooted in human nature, and how we can tame this impulse.

Chapter 2 explores the history of the death penalty in the United States, from colonial times to the present day. The pre-*Furman* era (an era prior to 1972 when the U.S. Supreme Court called a temporary halt to executions) represents a very different picture of the death penalty than what we see with modern-day practices. Included in this chapter is a Perspective feature from a former administrator of prisons who has worked in the prison system before and after lethal injection was adopted as a widely used method of execution. He discusses the death penalty in a historical context and compares the practices of old with the new.

A timeline presentation of the landmark U.S. Supreme Court cases during the modern period (*Furman* to the present) is the topic of Chapters 3 and 4. The landmark case of *Furman v. Georgia* (1972) marked a turning point in the way we view the death penalty. *Furman* and the foundational cases that have since followed shape the way in which the death penalty is implemented in the United States. Chapter 4 includes a Perspective from a prosecuting attorney who works on capital cases and recently argued a case before the U.S. Supreme Court.

Chapter 5 explains the history of public opinion and how it shapes the debate on capital punishment. A discussion of the role of public opinion and judicial decision-making provides the reader with an understanding of how opinion shapes the issue of capital punishment. This chapter features a Perspective offering the conflicted opinion on capital punishment of a woman who (unbeknownst to her) was married to a serial killer for a number of years.

In Chapter 6, we walk the reader through the history of U.S. execution methods, from the past to present day. Beginning with the early barbaric forms of punishment that marked colonial times and moving into a discussion of modern-day practices, the text provides the reader with a comprehensive understanding of the ways in which those on death row are executed. In the chapter's Perspective feature, a director of corrections explains how he prepares for an execution and the complexities that come with such a task.

Chapter 7 addresses the most commonly cited punishment justification for the death penalty—deterrence. An entire body of literature focuses on whether or not the death penalty deters crime. Utilizing both theory and empirical research, we attempt to answer this age-old question: *Does the death penalty deter?* The interesting aspect of this topic is that economists and criminologists often come to opposite conclusions. In this chapter's Perspective, an experienced chief justice of a state supreme court deliberates the value of deterrence and explains why it may never be an attainable goal as far as the death penalty is concerned.

We explore special populations in Chapter 8. One of the most contentious issues about the application of the death penalty is racial disparity, especially in terms of the racial makeup of the victim–offender dyad. We explore this issue by concentrating on studies using the same data conducted by different research teams arriving at opposite conclusions. We then examine the juvenile death penalty and the scientific evidence that led to its abolition. Next, we examine the huge gender disparity in death sentences and executions, and explore the reasons why this came to be. We then debate whether or not we should execute those with a diminished capacity to fully realize and appreciate the consequences of their actions. This chapter includes a Perspective from a neuropsychologist who has worked on nearly 100 capital cases. Specifically, he addresses the issue of intellectual disability and the death penalty.

Chapter 9 focuses on the techniques of modern science used in support of exoneration and mitigation. That is, how do CSI technicians turn bodily fluids into evidence of guilt or innocence, and how do neuroscientists determine what aspects of neurological functioning warrant some sort of mitigation? The chapter's Perspective feature, from a renowned neuroscientist considered the leading expert in death penalty mitigation and brain scan imagery, discusses the importance of understanding the inner workings of the brain when contemplating death as a punishment.

A thorough discussion of wrongful convictions as they pertain to the death penalty debate is presented in Chapter 10. There is reason to believe that the emergence of the Innocence Revolution has altered, and will continue to alter, the way Americans perceive capital punishment and whether its utilization is worth the risk of executing those who have been wrongfully convicted. This chapter includes a Perspective feature written by a former death row inmate who was accused and convicted of child rape and murder, but who had been wrongfully convicted and was later exonerated by DNA. He discusses his journey to freedom.

Chapter 11 outlines the costs associated with capital punishment. Numerous reasons explain why the death penalty has become such an expensive punishment. From special trials and expert witness fees, to the numerous appeals provided to capital offenders, the exorbitant costs are changing the way that we frame the death penalty debate. In this chapter's Perspective, an acting police chief weighs in on the costs of capital punishment and his general findings on the matter after serving on a special commission tasked with studying capital punishment.

The text's final chapter, Chapter 12, first examines the federal and military death penalties and then looks at the death penalty as it is applied internationally. We look at the often quite arbitrary use of the death penalty in Communist China and North Korea, and then its application in the Islamic countries of Saudi Arabia, Iran, and Iraq. The book concludes with an epilogue featuring a hypothetical dialogue between two fictional characters, Libby the Liberal and Conrad the Conservative. The dialogue between Libby and Conrad illustrates the differences between the opposing sides of the debate and is a distillation of many of the most important arguments presented by both sides throughout the text.

We believe this book provides the most thorough evaluation of capital punishment available today without getting bogged down in minutiae and without attempting to influence anyone's opinion on this important moral issue. The concluding debate between Libby and Conrad illustrates the futility of this, for as with all moral issues, this one is best left to each individual's private conscience after a thorough examination of the facts. Every aspect of capital punishment has been included that is traditionally covered in other books on the topic, and we have included chapters on two topics unique to this text. The first is an evaluation of why humans throughout history have found it necessary to punish others who have offended against the social order. The second is an emerging concern in the debate: that of the role of genetics and brain imaging in the matters of guilt or innocence and in the mitigation of punishment. We hope that students will go beyond the text to make use of the ancillary materials provided by Oxford University Press to further their knowledge of the ultimate criminal penalty.

Manski, C. (2011). Policy analysis with incredible certitude. *Economic Journal, 121,* 261–289.
Nagin, D. (2012). Scientific evidence and public policy. *The Criminologist, 37,* 1–6.

ACKNOWLEDGMENTS

We would first like to thank our editor, Steve Helba, for his faith in us and commitment to our project, and his assistant, Claire Benson. We are eternally grateful for Oxford's support. Also, thanks to Kelli Jauron and Patti Brecht for so diligently correcting the errors in our manuscript and improving the overall order and appearance. We are also most grateful for the help of Suzan Raney, who also reviewed each of our chapters and created our course companion materials. Thanks to Rachel Jones, whose expertise helped immensely with the creation of charts, graphs, and other illustrations that we could not have created without her technological expertise. Thanks also to our reviewers who took the time to provide thoughtful feedback that improved our final product considerably.

I (Hatch) would like to thank my husband, Jim, who is the most balanced and selfless person that I know. Thank you for your encouragement, advice, and patience for the past several years while this project nearly consumed me. Thanks to my son, Jackson, whose innocence and curiosity with the death penalty during the course of my writing this manuscript fueled my desire to thoroughly explore the human side of capital punishment. Your compassion and concern for humanity reminds me that there is much good in the world. Thanks to my mentor, friend, and colleague, Dr. Tony Walsh, who agreed to write this "bloody" book with me. You are truly one of a kind and it has been my honor and pleasure to work alongside you. Thanks to my parents, who have always supported me in everything that I do. Lastly, thanks to the people in our justice system who fight every day for those who do not have a voice or whose voices are silenced by the injustices all around us—you know who you are.

I (Walsh) would like to acknowledge the love and support of my most wonderful and drop-dead gorgeous wife, Grace Jean, aka "Grace the face." You are the nicest of persons, as all who know you will attest. Your love and support has sustained me for so long that I cannot imagine life without you; you are a real treasure and the center of my universe. Ti amo la mia bella donna!

CHAPTER 1

WHY DO WE PUNISH

The Origin and Purpose of Punishment

In February 1991, 25-year-old Stephen Mobley robbed a Domino's Pizza store in Atlanta, forced the store manager onto his knees, and then shot him execution style. Far from being remorseful, Mobley bragged to his friends about the murder and committed several other robberies. Mobley was apprehended by police and charged with aggravated murder, and he was sentenced to death. In an appeal to the Georgia Supreme Court to have his sentence commuted to life in prison, his primary defense boiled down to claiming that his "genes made me do it." Mobley's lawyers argued that four generations of Mobleys had histories of violent crimes, and they pointed to a Dutch family with a similar history of unprovoked violence. Scientists studying the Dutch family took DNA samples from 24 male members and found that those with violent records had a variation of a gene called MAOA that regulates certain brain chemicals. Mobley's lawyers requested the funds to retain a team of geneticists so they could test Mobley for the same genetic mutation.

The Georgia Supreme Court denied the request, saying in effect that even if Mobley had the gene, it doesn't mean that a direct link exists between the gene and his actions. The Court also reasoned that his possessing the gene should not mitigate his punishment either because it would not show he lacked the capacity to appreciate the wrongfulness of his acts or to conform to the requirements of the law. Although various courts have taken a wide variety of mitigating circumstances into consideration when determining a sentence, courts all the way up to the U.S. Supreme Court were unwilling to accept Mobley's genetic defense. After all his appeals were exhausted, Mobley received society's ultimate punishment—he was executed in 2005.

LEARNING OBJECTIVES

- Understand why we punish in terms of its function from both an evolutionary and sociological point of view.
- Explain the notion of forgiveness tit-for-tat in terms of correctional practice.
- Understand how the notion of free will and rationality is related to punishment justification.
- Understand the difference between consequentialist and non-consequentialist ethics as they relate to the effectiveness of punishment.
- Understand the major justifications for punishment.

THE EVOLUTIONARY ORIGINS OF PUNISHMENT

The Mobley case is a disturbing case of senseless violence. Such capital cases make us angry and serve as a great basis for discussion about the purpose and need for punishment. This chapter asks why we punish wrongdoers and why the impulse to punish is strong, and discusses typical justifications for doing so. The death penalty debate is first and foremost a moral debate, and as numerous brain imaging studies have shown, the foundation for morality is more emotional than rational (Haidt, 2012; Massey, 2002). The deep emotional underpinning of morality, and thus moral issues, is something not generally appreciated by people who cannot understand why equally reasonable people so often come to opposite conclusions regarding the issue of capital punishment. Two equally intelligent people can have access to exactly the same information on a deep moral issue, but differ radically as to its meaning based on the emotions it generates. As Philip Smith puts it in *Punishment and Culture*: "Punishment is a deeply meaningful activity that still needs to be interpreted if it is to be understood" (2008, p. 178). All too often we jump into discussions of punishment without understanding what it is we are really discussing beyond its surface manifestations. Thus, before we get into the various specific moral and practical issues surrounding capital punishment, it is necessary to gain some grounding in the concept, origins, and purpose of punishment in general.

Few others have gone to the heart of the matter as succinctly and as forcefully as Nathaniel Hawthorne in his opening words of *The Scarlet Letter*, first published in 1850. He writes: "The founders of a new colony, whatever Utopia of human virtue and happiness they might originally project, have invariably recognized it among their earliest practical necessities to allot a portion of the virgin soil as a cemetery, and another portion as the site of a prison" (2003/1850, p. 1).

Hawthorne is reminding us of two things we cannot avoid—death and human corruption, and that we must make provisions for both. Few of us ever give much serious thought to punishment and why we do it. The urge to punish wrongdoers is universal and strong. Consider the following questions: How did such an urge develop in us? What are the origins of punishment? What would society be like without it? How do we justify it? What do our justifications assume about human nature? These are some of the questions we explore in this chapter. We begin with the social function of punishment and the role of religion. We then examine the evolutionary reasons why the urge to punish became such a strong feature of human nature.

RELIGION, EMOTION, SOCIAL ORDER, AND PUNISHMENT

We cannot discuss capital punishment (or punishment in general) without discussing the role of religion. Garland tells us that "throughout the history of penal practice religion has been a major force in shaping the ways in which offenders are dealt with" (1990, p. 203). And Naas maintains that "every claim either for or against the death penalty borrows in some way from a theologico-political heritage informed by Christianity" (2012, p. 42). The holy books of the world's major religions consistently support the death penalty for those who violate the collective morality. For example, Exodus 21:12 of the Old Testament states: "He that smiteth a man so that he may die, shall he surely be put to death." The Old Testament demanded the death penalty for many other offenses, however, such as sodomy, adultery, cursing God, and many other acts. Religious scriptures can also be read as opposing capital punishment, as in the New Testament's Matthew 5:38–40 in which Jesus counseled to "turn the other cheek," because "Vengeance is mine, sayeth the Lord." The Bible provides us with a vast store of quotations from which we can cherry-pick those that serve our ends; after all, William Shakespeare wrote in *The Merchant of Venice* that even "the devil can cite Scripture for his purpose."

Émile Durkheim, one of the founding fathers of sociology, defined religion as "a unified system of beliefs and practices relative to sacred things, that is to say set apart and forbidden, beliefs and practices which unite into one single moral community, called a church, all those who adhere to them" (1965, p. 62). Durkheim believed that religion is necessary for moral constraint and that it was the emotional component of the collective conscience (or consciousness—since they mean the same thing in French). Religion is vital to reinforcing secular norms of behavior by investing them with an aura of the divine, and it is, of course, very useful to rulers if they can convince their subjects that the law comes from the divine, and that they rule by the divine right of kings

(Walsh & Hemmens, 2014). Religion adds emotional strength to cold, rational statutes, and as noted above, emotion trumps reason in moral discourse.

We should not draw sharp distinctions between emotion and rationality; they are two inseparable components of all that we think and do. Brain imaging has shown that emotion and cognition are fully *physically* integrated in areas of the brain that weigh rational and emotional information which travel from their respective regions of the brain to guide human actions (Pessoa, 2008).

Emotions are situated in a set of brain structures that predate the evolution of the structures where our reasoning power is housed by at least a million years (Suwa et al., 2009). Two highly respected contemporary scientists have explained the primacy of emotion. Douglas Massey notes: "Emotionality clearly preceded rationality in evolutionary sequence, and as rationality developed it did not replace emotionality as the basis for human interaction. Rather, rational abilities were gradually added to preexisting and simultaneously developing emotional capacities" (2002, p. 15). Jonathan Haidt puts it more strongly: "It [emotion] comes first in phylogeny [the developmental history of the species], it emerges first in ontogeny [the developmental history of the individual], it is triggered more quickly in real-time judgments, and it is more powerful and irrevocable [than rationality] when the two systems yield conflicting judgments" (2001, p. 819).

Paul Thagard (2005, p. 59) notes that many theologians and scientists have stressed the centrality of emotions in religion and the wealth of positive (love, joy, hope) and negative (fear, anguish, shame) emotions that it can generate. It is this emotional passion that is engaged when we contemplate the actions of criminals, especially actions that have resulted in the cruel deaths of others. There are plenty of opportunities in the modern world to engage such emotions. As Durkheim noted, crime is a universal feature of all societies (religion tells us this is the result of a deeply flawed human nature that must be controlled). He also noted that crime, although not welcome, serves a vital social function through the ritual of punishing criminals. It is by such punishment that the moral boundaries of society are clearly demarcated, and attachment to those boundaries is reinforced.

The real purpose of punishment for Durkheim is not to deter future crime or to rehabilitate the offender; rather, its true function is to strengthen social solidarity by the group expression of moral outrage, a moral outrage reinforced by the religious notion that crime (sin) is an affront to both God and man. This, says Durkheim, is an unappreciated function of punishment—maintaining social solidarity by reaffirming the justness of social norms. It strengthens social solidarity by reaffirming the moral commitment of law-abiding individuals who witness the punishment of the offender. This is the sort of indirect social control that Hawthorne emphasized in *The Scarlet Letter* by the public humiliation of Hester Prynne for committing adultery. Durkheim also recognized that the urge to punish is inherent in human nature, and that it serves to soothe, pacify, and even provide pleasant feelings for those witnessing it, vicariously or otherwise.

By punishing individuals for their crimes, we thereby allot moral responsibility to them, and the blame for their behavior is situated squarely in their flawed characters and cannot be ascribed to external circumstances. Religions have always stressed the notions of moral responsibility and free will, and the duty of all to behave according to their precepts. Thus, those who most strongly uphold the morality preached by their particular religion, those who see it as fundamental truth, are the most likely to support harsh punishments such as the death penalty. Grasmick and colleagues (1993, p. 289) believe that what they call the "increased punitiveness" of the criminal justice system in the 1980s was stimulated by public opinion, which coincided with the revival of Christian fundamentalism in the United States. Consistent with their hypothesis, they found that evangelical/fundamentalists were significantly more likely than Catholics or liberal Protestants to support strict punishment, including the death penalty.

However, the relationship between religion and capital punishment is far more complex than this in an age of the decreasing influence of religion. The majority of social science studies do not show a significant difference between church attenders and nonchurch attenders on support for the death penalty, although the majority of both groups support it (Douglas, 2000). Furthermore, religious Christians and Jews who support the death penalty in the United States are at odds with their religious leaders. We are told that the "Roman Catholic Church, both Reform and Conservative Jewish groups, and most mainstream Protestant denominations in the United States have taken a formally abolitionist stance in recent decades, indicating a significant difference of opinion between the 'pulpit and the pew'" (Brooks, 2013, p. 6). Even within each denomination, we find disagreement. A study by Unnever, Cullen, and Fisher (2005) found that Christians who believed in the wrathful and punitive God of the Old Testament were more likely to support capital punishment than those who considered themselves in a personal relationship with a loving God.

THE CO-EVOLUTION OF PUNISHMENT AND SOCIAL COOPERATION

The kind of punishment found in the ancient religious texts is of the eye-for-an-eye type. We refer to this kind of punishment as *retribution*, or punishment that is justly deserved for its own sake and need not be justified further. In his dissenting opinion in *Furman v. Georgia* in which the Supreme Court invalidated

Georgia's death penalty statute in 1972, Justice Potter Stewart wrote the following about retribution:

> I cannot agree that retribution is a constitutionally impermissible ingredient in the imposition of punishment. The instinct for retribution is part of the nature of man, and channeling that instinct in the administration of criminal justice serves an important purpose in promoting the stability of a society governed by law. When people begin to believe that organized society is unwilling or unable to impose upon criminal offenders the punishment they "deserve," then there are sown the seeds of anarchy—of self-help, vigilante justice, and lynch law.

What did Justice Stewart mean by locating the "instinct for retribution" in the "nature of man"? If retribution is indeed a part of human nature, how did it get there and why? We may start by noting that the evolutionary goals of all sexually reproducing animals, including human beings, are survival and reproduction. It is important for such animals to be motivated to take actions that are vital in the pursuit of these goals. To produce such motivation, nature has provided us with a built-in biological system that rewards us with pleasurable feelings when we do things that aid in achieving these goals. Such pleasurable feelings arise from a neurotransmitter (a brain chemical that transmits messages between brain cells) called dopamine that attaches itself to a part of the brain called the nucleus accumbens, the so-called pleasure center of the brain (Walsh, Johnson, & Bolen, 2012). Each surge of dopamine reinforces the behavior that makes us feel good and motivates us to repeat it. This is why we feel so good when we satisfy urges to eat, drink, and have sex, which are the most obvious requirements for survival and reproduction.

Given that the urge to punish wrongdoers is universal and strong (Penney, 2012), punishment must have played a role in helping our distant ancestors survive and pass on their genes. The survival and reproductive function of punishment is not at all as obvious as are the roles of food, drink, and sex, but there is little doubt that we find pleasure when wrongdoers are punished. Brain imaging studies have shown increased blood flow to the nucleus accumbens when subjects witness the punishment of those who have wronged them (de Quervain et al., 2004; Klein, 2012). Blood flow to reward centers has also been observed when people who have harmed others are punished, and the strength of the pleasure response is proportional both to the harm done and to the level of the offender's culpability (whether the act was purposeful, knowing, reckless, or negligent) (Buckholtz & Marois, 2012). These imaging studies provide us with some compelling evidence that the urge to punish must be an adaptive feature of human nature and a possible explanation for the old saying "vengeance is sweet."

Although imaging and other study methods tell us there must be good survival and reproductive reasons why our reward centers fire up when we punish or witness the punishment (vicariously via the news media) of wrongdoers, they do not reveal why punishment was so vital to our distant ancestors. We may approach the question by noting that *Homo sapiens* is an ultra-social species that alone among all animals live in groups consisting overwhelmingly of non-kin. We live under an implied social contract by which we surrender some of our freedoms to do as we please. A vital part of the contract is the agreement not to harm others, and if we do, the state then has the legitimate right to punish us. As Keally McBride explains, "Punishment is the midwife in the birth of the social contract" (2007, p. 122).

The vast majority of humans are never punished by the state because our species has evolved strong norms of cooperation without which our social groups would not survive. While the natural selection for **altruism** (an active concern for the well-being of another at some cost to the self) is adequate to understand cooperation among close kin for whom we have strong emotional feeling, it does not explain cooperation extended to non-kin. Cooperation among non-kin is explained by **reciprocal altruism**—the extending of a benefit to another with the unspoken expectation of obtaining a similar benefit from the recipient at some later date. Social animals cooperate because they can achieve more as a group than they can individually, and we feel good about ourselves when helping others. We are also rewarded by reciprocal behavior in the future, but even if the person we help is a stranger whom we are unlikely to encounter again, our brains still receive a shot of dopamine that makes us feel good (Brunero, 2002). Brain imaging studies consistently show that our pleasure centers "light up" when either giving or receiving something valued, but brain areas associated with the pleasures of social attachments only fire when giving (Moll et al., 2006), thus vindicating Jesus's claim that it is more blessed to give than to receive.

A population of cooperators provides a target-rich niche for people who cheat on the social contract and seek to gain resources at zero cost. Defectors or cheats (we call them criminals today) prosper in a population of unconditional cooperators (biologists call them "suckers") and would soon drive them to extinction. Most humans are not suckers; they are what evolutionary biologists call "grudgers" (conditional cooperators). Grudgers can be cheated because they abide by the norms of mutual trust and cooperation and expect the same from others. Unlike suckers, once cheated, grudgers will react differently to cheaters in the future by not offering them cooperation in obtaining resources (Wiebe, 2011).

People stealing resources and sexual mates in our species' evolutionary history constituted a severe threat to everyone in the group, and thus would have generated feelings of anger and outrage, and a desire to punish, just as they do today. As de Waal points out, "A taste of revenge is the other side of the coin of reciprocity" (1996, p. 160). Victims feel angry and hurt when treated unfairly, and confusion and frustration at losing the expectation of predictability ("I scratched your back, but you didn't scratch mine!"). The sum of these evolved emotions is moral outrage. Without moral outrage, there would be no motivation to react against those who violate the norms of reciprocal cooperation, cheats would have thrived without the threat of punishment in our ancestral environments, and we would have evolved as a quite different species of animal (Haidt, 2012; Nowak, 2006).

Natural selection does not pass judgment on emotions, or even on the behaviors they motivate if those behaviors do not result in enhanced reproductive success. Natural selection operates on the *consequences* of the behavior motivated by the emotion (Massey, 2002; Walsh, 2006). It is no use feeling angry and hurt when victimized if those feelings do not generate behavior designed to prevent it from occurring again. Negative feelings accompanying victimization are lessened by punishing violators because punishment signals the restoration of fairness and predictability (the perception that cheaters may be less likely to cheat in the future, and that potential cheaters may be deterred). The positive feelings accompanying the punishment of those who have wronged us, coupled with the reduction of negative feelings, provide powerful reinforcement for punitive responses and explain why we see increased blood flow to the brain's reward centers when wrongdoers are punished.

SECOND- AND THIRD-PARTY PUNISHMENT

It is not always possible to punish those who harm us and we must turn to others to carry the burden. Among primates, particularly among chimpanzees, our closest nonhuman genetic relatives, alpha males (the dominant males in the troop) take on the role of what is called *control behavior*, which includes the punishment of troop members who bully and exploit others (de Waal, 1996). This is a costly and risky role, but it confers a number of benefits on them. As arbiters, alpha males typically show a preference for the weaker party in most disputes. This not only develops support among the weaker rank and file, it also serves to level the hierarchy and thereby increases the gap between the alpha male and the more powerful members of the group who might seek to replace him (de Waal, 1996). Numerous computer simulation studies of human altruistic punishment (punishment on behalf of others) have conclusively shown that the punisher receives many benefits, including an increased likelihood of receiving future benefits, with enhanced status in the group being the most valuable (Ule et al., 2009). Dos Santos, Rankin, and Wedekind remark that "reputation is the key to the evolution of punishment, and that simple reputation games can explain the high preservation of punishment in humans" (2011, p. 376).

In human societies, punishment is meted out by third-party punishers who are individuals not directly harmed and who will not directly benefit (like second-party chimp alpha males) from meting out punishment. Third-party punishers in modern societies are the agents of the state operating in accordance with law. Numerous experiments have shown that third parties will punish cheats at a cost to themselves. A study involving 1,762 subjects from five continents found that, in all populations, people are willing to punish defectors who have harmed unknown others (Henrich et al., 2006). This study also found that "societies with high degrees of punishment will also exhibit more altruistic behavior" (p. 1770). This tends to suggest altruism and punishment co-evolved in the sense that "third-party punishment of norm violations ('I punish you because you harmed him') seems especially crucial for the evolutionary stability of cooperation and is the cornerstone of modern models of criminal justice" (Buckholtz & Marois, 2012, p. 655).

FROM PRIMITIVE VENGEANCE TO MODERN LAW

As with anything else that is useful in moderation, punishment can overstep its optimum and become dysfunctional (we can become alcoholics, morbidly obese, and sex addicts partaking too freely of what is good, or even vital, in the right proportions). In the imaging studies that show blood flow to the brain's pleasure center, when people witness the punishment of those who have harmed them, their reaction is proportional to the offender's level of culpability. In other words, brain images show that more pleasure is experienced by the person being imaged if the punished offender purposefully inflicted harm on him or her when compared to offenders who inadvertently inflicted harm. Only a callous sadist would take pleasure in seeing grossly disproportionate punishment imposed. Punishment that exceeds just and reasonable boundaries induces disgust and repugnance to all but the sadists among us, and many people believe that the death penalty is one such excessive punishment. Empathy and sympathy are also adaptive features of human nature that were necessary for survival and reproductive success (de Waal, 2008; Walsh, 2014). We have seen these emotions spreading beyond kin groups across the span of human history as punishment has evolved from retributive vengeance to modern notions of restitutive justice (justice driven by concerns about deterrence and rehabilitation).

Even given the well-founded evolutionary reasons for retributionist feelings, we must reflect on the moral propriety of acting on them. In other words, just because these feelings are natural, it does not mean that we should act on them and ignore rational considerations. If the primitive desire to "get even" is left untamed, it can tear apart a social group by generating a cycle of tit-for-tat blood feuds, many of which have smeared human history (Boehm, 2011). Even today, it has been estimated that approximately 30% of adult male deaths among the Yanomamo of South America are related to revenge feuds, which expand the very injustice that "righteous" revenge was supposed to assuage (Chagnon, 1988). As Susan Jacoby puts it:

> The struggle to contain revenge has been conducted at the highest level of moral and civic awareness at each stage in the development of civilization. The self-conscious nature of the effort is expectable in view of the persistent state of tension between uncontrolled vengeance as destroyer and controlled vengeance as an unavoidable component of justice. (1983, p. 13)

Culture may engage or neutralize the emotions that temper punishment with mercy or allow vengeance to run wild. The lasting influence of Cesare Beccaria (1963/1764), the father of modern criminal justice, rests on his recognition that the brutal acts of retribution which were common in his time (eighteenth century), and often based on the vengeance requirements of powerful aristocrats, resulted in general distrust and social alienation rather than altruistic cooperation. Many of Beccaria's recommended criminal justice reforms were implemented throughout much of Europe within his lifetime (Durant & Durant, 1967, p. 321). Such radical and rapid change suggests that Beccaria's ideas tapped into and broadened other evolved emotions such as sympathy and empathy among the European elite. We tend to feel empathy for those whom we view as being "like us," and empathy often leads to sympathy, which can transform the vicarious experience of the pain of others into an active concern for their welfare, even if they are wrongdoers. Vignette studies have shown that people tend to recommend more lenient punishment for criminals whom they perceive to be similar to themselves (reviewed in Miller & Vidmar, 1981), and the march of democracy has drawn more people into the circle of people we consider "us."

We have seen that Durkheim (1964) (see Figure 1.1) viewed crime and punishment as central to social life. Just as evolutionary scientists view cheating and punishment as vital to the evolution of cooperation, Durkheim saw it as necessary for maintaining social solidarity. Durkheim believed

FIGURE 1.1   Émile Durkheim

that punishing criminals maintains solidarity because it reaffirms the justness of the social norms. He recognized that the urge to punish is inherent in human nature and it serves an expiatory role, but he also recognized that we can temper the urge with sympathy. Durkheim noted that, over the course of human history, many societies have moved from retributive to restitutive justice. For Durkheim, retributive justice is driven by the natural passion for punitive revenge that "ceases only when exhausted . . . only after it has destroyed" (1964, p. 86). Restitutive justice, on the other hand, is driven by simple deterrence, and is more humanistic and tolerant, although it remains "at least in part, a work of vengeance" since it is still "an expiation" (1964, pp. 88–89). Although both forms satisfy the human urge for social regularity, repressive justice oversteps its adaptive usefulness and becomes socially destructive, whereas restitutive justice offers a rational balance between calming moral outrage on the one hand, and engaging empathy and sympathy on the other.

Contrast this with the barbaric treatment of criminals in many Arab Islamic states, often for "crimes" that do not exist in Western countries anymore (sodomy, adultery, sorcery, drinking alcohol, fornication, etc.). Some Islamic countries still operate on the basis of a strict equal harm "eye-for-an-eye" principle. For instance, in 2002, 14-year-old Ali Al-Khawahir got into a fight with a friend and stabbed him in the spine, leaving him paralyzed. After being imprisoned for ten years, he was sentenced to be surgically paralyzed in accordance with the *equal harm* concept. Crimes such as these can be forgiven by the victim or the victim's family upon the payment of *diyya* ("blood money"). Ali's mother desperately tried to raise blood money to compensate the victim's parents. Thankfully, in 2013, enough was raised to pay the *diyya* and Ali was released from prison (*The National*, 2013).

Other such punishments have involved gouging out the eye of a person who caused the loss of someone else's eye and the extraction of teeth. Such punishments are outrageously barbaric from a Western point of view, although equal harm justice is an aggressive commitment to a retributivist punishment philosophy. Putting aside Ali's age at the time of the offense, had an adult in the United States been convicted of aggravated assault in which the victim was paralyzed, a first-time offender would probably have received 10 to 15 years' imprisonment. Ten to fifteen years in a cage is quite different from turning the body itself into a cage from which there is no escape, something that would have happened to Ali had not the required blood money been raised.

There are some who may defend Saudi Arabia's harsh system by pointing out that a paralyzed man cannot commit further crimes, and that a quick snip of the spine is a lot cheaper than keeping someone in prison for 10 years. They may also point out that Saudi crime rates are remarkably low compared to those of Western societies. All this is true, but such cruel retributivist punishment brutalizes society and centers social order on fear.

THE ASSUMPTIONS ABOUT HUMAN NATURE AND PUNISHMENT JUSTIFICATIONS

Now that we have arrived at the modern system of third-party punishment by the state, a modern set of concerns regarding punishment must be addressed. The issue of free will and responsibility goes to the heart of many debates about punishment these days, particularly capital punishment. In the opening vignette of the chapter, a concern the various judges who heard Mobley's appeals probably had, and one that many others share, is that accepting defenses based on such factors as genetics and neuroscience would unduly sway jurors in ways that other defenses typically do not. It is disconcerting to some to see the prestige of science used to undermine the notion of free will and individual responsibility with such claims, although others welcome it as a major step forward in their goal of abolishing the death penalty. Most of us value the idea that we are masters and mistresses of our own lives; whether or not this is ultimately true, we have to live as if it were or succumb to fatalism. The notion that humans are free to choose their behavior has been so compelling historically that legal systems around the world accept it as a given. If we do not have free will, and if our behavior is fully determined by outside circumstances and/or inside genetic and neurological processes, then how can we be held accountable for our actions? How can we expect either praise or blame?

The notion of free will is central to the theoretical assumptions about human nature held by scholars associated with a school of criminology and criminal justice called the *classical school*. The other major assumptions are that human beings are hedonistic and rational. We briefly examine these assumptions before returning for a longer look at the concept of free will.

Hedonism's central idea is that happiness is the ultimate goal toward which all humans strive, and that all other goals are only a means to the end of achieving it. As eighteenth-century English philosopher Jeremy Bentham once explained: "Nature has placed mankind under the governance of two sovereign masters, pain and pleasure. It is for them alone to point out what we ought to do, as well as to determine what we shall do" (1948/1789, p. 125). Accordingly, hedonism is assumed to be the greatest single motivator of human action. Hedonism does not mean mad, helter-skelter lives consumed by sex, drugs, and rock and roll; rather, it is seeking out the kind of life that gives a person the most pleasure, tranquility, and peace of mind, which can be radically different for different people.

Rational behavior is behavior that has a logical "fit" between the goals people strive for and means they use to achieve them. The goal of human rationality is to serve hedonistic self-interest, and self-interest governs our behavior whether in conforming or deviant directions. Unwanted outcomes can be produced by rational behavior because rationality is both subjective and bounded.

We do not all make the same calculations or arrive at the same plan when pursuing the same goals because we pursue them with imperfect knowledge, and with different personalities and reasoning abilities. In other words, we may think we always behave in a way that best serves our self-interest, but our behavior may bring unwanted results because we are ignorant of some things and we misinterpret others. Rationality will be discussed in greater detail when we discuss capital punishment and deterrence in Chapter 7.

Hedonism and rationality are combined in the concept of the **hedonistic calculus.** The hedonistic calculus is a method by which individuals are assumed to logically weigh the anticipated benefits of a given course of action against its possible costs. If the balance of consequences of a contemplated action is thought to enhance pleasure and/or minimize pain, individuals will pursue it; if not, they will not. Rationality is thus pressed into service to reason ways by which we can maximally benefit ourselves.

Free will is the faculty that enables human beings to purposely and deliberately choose a calculated course of action. Whether or not you agree that we actually do enjoy such a faculty, it is central to the justifications we have for punishment, particularly those justifying the death penalty. It is therefore deemed imperative that we try to understand what is meant by free will and its limitations. The free will concept assumes that humans have the capacity to make choices and the responsibility to make moral ones. This is not a radical free will argument that denies any sort of constraints on the human will. The modern radical notion of free will often appeals to the supposed unpredictability found in subatomic physics (Schuster, 2009). It is doubtful, however, that anyone would want the kind of freedom in which their behavior could not be predicted with some degree of certainty. German sociologist Max Weber characterized this kind of freedom as the "privilege of the insane" (in Eliaeson, 2002, p. 35). The random, unpredictable firing of brain cells, which is essentially the free will argument from subatomic physics, is a defining characteristic of schizophrenia, and we assume that few would want to be saddled with that unfortunate illness.

FREE WILL, DETERMINISM, AND THE LAW

If free will means action without a definable cause, nothing would be predictable and chaos would reign. Most modern defenders of free will tend to be compatibilists who do not deny that behavior has causes. **Compatibilism** maintains that free will and determinism are compatible and that people are free to do what they want unless constrained by circumstances, either internal or external. When philosophers speak of agency, they are talking about the kind of constrained free will that compatibilists champion. That is, the concept of agency recognizes constraints on our ability to do what we please, but we still are morally obliged to act responsibly. This position was stated best by German philosopher Arthur Schopenhauer, who wrote: "You are free to do what you want, but you are not free to want what you want" (in Clark, 2007, p. 96). What this means is that we are free to wish only for things that are compatible with our natures, even though our natures have been shaped by our genes and developmental histories, neither of which were chosen by us. Schopenhauer is saying that we are not free to choose wishes or wants that run contrary to our natures. Even if we have to choose between two alternatives that are both agreeable to our nature, we will follow the strongest inclination.

This means that we are only free to follow our strongest inclination. Those who hold a radical free will position will deny that this is "really" free will since our actions are being determined by our nature and inclinations formed by genetic inheritance and developmental experiences. But we see no problem with it because your strongest inclination is *your* strongest inclination, and no one else's. Your nature is you and your will is yours, so if you follow the dictates of your nature, surely you are following your will. We cannot be free of the determining influences of our natures, so to ask for freedom beyond this is meaningless.

In many ways, we can see that compatibilist notions of free will and determinism are operating principles of modern law. The law recognizes that behavior is determined (caused) by many factors for which criminal defendants may not be responsible, such as the limitations of their natures (e.g., mental illness, low IQ) or their environments (e.g., childhood abuse that resulted in brain damage). This recognition is realized by the allowances the law makes for mitigating circumstances in determining punishment (see Chapters 3 and 4). But the law also maintains that most defendants are at least minimally rational, possess the necessary faculties to know the difference between right and wrong, and have the ability to resist acting on aspects of their natures that are contrary to civilized society. This is all that the law asks of free will. Defendants who did not meet these minimal legal requirements are, in theory, not supposed to be culpable in the eyes of the law.

A number of influential thinkers deny even a compatibilist version of free will and take a hard determinist position on criminal behavior. The great criminal lawyer Clarence Darrow is reputed to have said that criminals act when committing crimes only in the same sense as they do "when cut by bleeding" (in Walsh, 1981, p. 70). In other words, Darrow believed (or at least he urged juries to believe) that they could no more command the direction of their behavior than they could command their wounds to stop bleeding. Likewise, psychiatrist Karl Menninger (1968) believed that criminals are not purposefully bad individuals who deserve punishment. He further argued that the practice of punishment itself is a crime against humanity because society is harming those it calls criminal when they are sick and require treatment. Along similar lines, philosopher Michael Zimmerman (2011) maintains that people should be held responsible and punished only for behavior they can control. Zimmerman seems to consider most criminal behavior to be beyond the control of the criminal (completely determined by outside forces).

There are thus individuals who seriously question the philosophical assumptions that underlie the legal system. However, we should note that none of these hard determinists are saying that we should ignore criminal behavior; they are only calling *retributive* punishment (punishment for its own sake) immoral, and have no quarrels with placing serious criminals in prison for treatment to prevent them from committing further crimes, which they do not see as punitive. Going beyond treatment and incapacitation to inflict pain or death is what they object to most. We now briefly discuss the various philosophical justifications for punishment that have been argued.

PUNISHMENT JUSTIFICATIONS

Even though we assume most people agree that society has a right and a duty to punish those who harm it through harming others, because punishment involves the state depriving individuals of life or liberty in the name of the people, it is in need of ethical justification. A philosophy of punishment involves defining the concept of punishment and the values, attitudes, and beliefs contained in that definition, as well as justifying the imposition of a painful burden on someone. Punishment justifications—deterrence, incapacitation, rehabilitation–reintegration, and retribution—come and go in popularity depending on the ideology of the times. When we speak of justifying something, we typically mean that we provide reasons for doing it both in terms of morality ("It's the right thing to do") and in terms of the goals we wish to achieve ("Do this, and we'll get that"). In other words, we expect that punishment will have favorable consequences that justify its application. The first four justifications are such "consequentialist" or "utilitarian" justifications. **Utilitarianism** is an ethical philosophy that claims an action is morally right if it produces the most utility (defined as benefits, happiness, and pleasure) for the greatest number of people in society. In terms of punishment, it means that the beneficial consequences (hence the term **consequentialism**) assumed to result from it justify its application; punishment is a means to an end. Retribution, on the other hand, is non-consequentialist in that it justifies punishment by its intrinsic moral worth regardless of any benefits that may derive from it (Wood, 2010). Let us examine these justifications.

Deterrence

Deterrence has long been considered the primary function of punishment. It essentially means that because humans are rational actors who chose their behaviors in accordance with the hedonistic calculus, the punishment they may receive for committing a crime is weighed against the benefits they might obtain by committing it. In other words, the assumption is that many more individuals would engage in criminal and antisocial behavior than is now the case if they did not fear the possibility of punishment. Because deterrence as applied to the death penalty is explored at great length in Chapter 7, we will defer further discussion of it until then.

Incapacitation

Incapacitation refers to the inability of criminals to victimize people outside prison walls while they are imprisoned. The justification for incapacitation is aptly summarized by James Q. Wilson: "Wicked people exist. Nothing avails except to set them apart from innocent people" (1975, p. 391). It is obvious that incapacitation "works" while criminals are incarcerated. For instance, criminologist Elliot Currie (1989) tells us that in 1995 there were 135,000 inmates in prison whose most serious crime was robbery, and that each robber, on average, committed five robberies per year. Had these robbers not been imprisoned, they might have been responsible for an additional 135,000 × 5 or 675,000 robberies on top of the 580,000 actual robberies reported to the police that year. Of course, there are many limitations with predicting phenomena, especially when they involve predicting the behavior of people. We can never really know what someone *might* have done if not for an intervention (arrest and incarceration); such predictions would never have the ability to account for the many reasons that people refrain from committing a future crime (e.g., aging, a change in life circumstances, etc.).

The argument about the incapacitation effect of the death penalty is that the execution of convicted murderers prevents them from further killing. The fact that the offender has been incapacitated is, of course, uncontested and incontrovertible, and thus the most defensible of all pro-capital punishment arguments. A sentence of life without the possibility of parole would serve the same incapacitation purpose as execution, although the possibility exists (and has happened) that someone with such a sentence may kill a correctional officer or another inmate.

Researchers had an opportunity to examine the incapacitation effect when, in 1972, the U.S. Supreme Court ruled that the death penalty was unconstitutional in a famous case we will discuss at length later on, *Furman v. Georgia*. This case resulted in the death sentences of hundreds of death row inmates being commuted to life sentences or to a set period of incarceration (a few got new trials). This gave researchers the opportunity to assess the post-commutation behavior of former death row inmates both in prison and on parole, with the big question being, "Did their non-execution result in them committing additional murders?"

Comparing the *Furman*-commuted offenders with other murderers, Marquart and Sorensen write: "Of 11,532 [non-*Furman*-commuted] murderers released between 1971 and 1975, twenty-six committed new homicides in the first year after release from prison. However, our data reveal that after five years on parole, only one [Furman-commuted] murderer committed a second murder while in the larger society" (1989, p. 24). In other words, apparently the 322 *Furman*-commuted inmates who were paroled behaved less violently than other paroled murders. In their conclusion, Marquart and Sorensen further offered: "We cannot conclude from these data that their execution would have protected or benefited society" (1989, p. 28). The 11,532 non-*Furman*-commuted murderers serve as a better example of the incapacity effect.

The most recent study of the *Furman*-commuted 322 offenders who were paroled found that "only" six of them were known to have murdered again (Cheever, 2006). What the adverb "only" fails to impart is the number of victims and manner of death. For instance, *Furman*-commuted inmate Kenneth McDuff was sentenced to death in 1966 for the kidnapping, rape, torture, and murder of two teenage boys and a teenage girl. As a result of the *Furman* decision, McDuff was released in 1989 and proceeded to rape, torture, and murder at least nine women (Cassell, 2008). McDuff was executed in Texas for these horrific acts in 1998. Cassell (2008) documents a number of other brutal murders committed by former death row inmates who were released from the incapacitation effect of death row by the *Furman* decision and by an earlier ruling establishing the unconstitutionality of the death penalty in California.

Incapacitation obviously "works," but death penalty opponents argue that life without parole would provide the same effect as execution. Proponents of the death penalty, however, worry about the possibility of escape and the possibility that at some future date the courts will invalidate sentences of life without the possibility of parole statutes, as the European Court of Human Rights has done in the European Union (Tutro, 2014). Society has to decide on the ethics of the trade-off between not incapacitating (either by execution or life in prison) offenders and lives lost or ruined by paroled murderers, even if "only" a small portion of them murder again.

Rehabilitation

Rehabilitation means to restore or return to constructive or healthy activity. It is more forward-looking to offenders' future behavior than backward-looking to what they have done. The notion of rehabilitation plays almost no role in the capital punishment debate, but is becoming a part of the life without possibility of parole debate: "A life without parole sentence removes any emphasis on rehabilitation" (Tutro, 2014, p. 22). Tutro cites this as one of the reasons the European Court of Human Rights invalidated such sentences. The rehabilitative goal is based on a model championed by people who view criminal behavior as a sickness requiring treatment. Today's treatment model views criminality more in terms of "faulty thinking" rather than "sickness," and criminals as being in need of "programming" rather than "treatment." The goal of rehabilitation is to change offenders' attitudes so that they come to accept that their behavior was wrong, not to deter them by the threat of further punishment. The rehabilitation model is criticized by conservatives as "mollycoddling" and lacking in truth in sentencing. Liberals criticize it as contributing to sentencing disparity. It contributes to disparity because it requires indeterminate sentencing (a range of years in prison rather than a fixed number of years) since some people are "cured" faster than others. Libertarians also criticize it as forcing offenders into treatment programs against their will.

Reintegration

Reintegration has the forward-looking goal of using the time criminals are under correctional supervision to prepare them to reenter free society better equipped to remain there than they previously were. Reintegration is not much different from rehabilitation, but it is more pragmatic, focusing on concrete programs such as job training rather than a change in attitude. If the United States ever abolishes the death penalty *and* life without the possibility of parole sentences, this will have to be the preeminent goal of punishment.

Retribution

Retribution, like incapacitation, is backward-looking, focusing on what offenders have done. It differs from the other punishment justifications because it is non-consequentialist and believes that punishment for its own sake is morally justified. As opposed to the utilitarian or consequentialist position, non-consequentialism avers that any policy, practice, or behavior is to be judged by the motives behind it, not by the consequences that come from it. Thus, punishment is to be justified on its own intrinsic merits. Most criminologists abhor retribution as little more than state-sanctioned revenge (Rosebury, 2009), although it appears to be quite popular in the criminal justice system. For instance, California is among the states that have explicitly embraced retribution in their criminal codes (California Penal Code Sec. 1170a): "The Legislature finds and declares that the purpose of imprisonment for a crime is punishment" (in Barker, 2006, p. 12).

KANTIAN RETRIBUTION: THE MAJOR JUSTIFICATION OF CAPITAL PUNISHMENT

Capital punishment is justified by its modern proponents mostly in terms of deterrence (it prevents other murders) and retribution (it is simply deserved). Deterrence is a more complicated and contested area than retribution and will be discussed in Chapter 7. Among supporters of the death penalty, retribution is most often given as a rationale for supporting it (Bohm, 2012). This being so, we outline the main retributionist argument here in terms of the philosophy of its most famous adherent: the eighteenth-century German philosopher Immanuel Kant (see Figure 1.2).

Retribution is morally justified by its proponents in terms of the value, dignity, and agency of human beings. To understand Kant's retributionism, we must refer to his ideas of duty and strong beliefs in human reason and autonomy. Human beings, says Kant, are different from other animals because they are guided by reason, and it is from reason that we derive all duties and obligations. Humans have a duty to act out of reverence for moral law, which Kant conceived of as a set of categorical imperatives. A **categorical imperative** is a principle stating that an act should be done "in itself" regardless of any further end. In other words, a categorical imperative says "Do this," not "Do this *if*." Any action consistent with this is good (moral), says Kant, regardless of its consequences. Kant saw categorical imperatives as universal laws that guide humans toward their duties in the following way: "Act as if the maxim of your action were to become through your will a universal law of nature" (1785, p. 89).

FIGURE 1.2 Immanuel Kant

In his *Groundwork of the Metaphysics of Morals,* originally published in 1785, Kant says that a categorical imperative should be grounded in something that should be an *"end in itself, and an absolute value."* He finds this grounding in "man," who "exists as an end in himself, not merely as a means for arbitrary use for this or that will" (1785, p. 95). "Man," in all his actions, must always be regarded as an end in himself regardless of whether his actions are directed at himself or at others. Based on this, Kant arrives at a final definition of a categorical imperative: "Act in such a way that you always treat humanity, whether in your own person or in the person of any other, never simply as a means, but always at the same time as an end" (1785, p. 96).

Respecting humans as ends in themselves, and not as means to some other end, led Kant to a retributionist justification of punishment. From this viewpoint, punishing criminals for instrumental reasons such as for deterrence, or subjecting them to rehabilitative treatment, is morally wrong because it treats them as *means* to an end, not as *ends in themselves*. According to Kant, criminals are ruled by reason just as everyone else and thus live in accordance with maxims—universal moral standards ("Act as if the maxim of your action were to become through your will a universal law of nature"). If criminals harm others, they are violating the autonomy of others, and by doing so are endorsing criminal acts as universal laws, and thus in effect they are saying that others should act similarly. By punishing criminals, the state is treating them in accordance with their own maxims; that is, how they think others should be treated. The state is thus allowing criminals to decide how they will be treated, and by doing so it is respecting their judgment and autonomy. Thus, Kant says of the criminal: "His own evil deed draws the punishment upon himself" (Rachels, 1986, p. 123). Retribution is for Kant a "just deserts" model demanding that criminals be punished in proportion to the harm they have inflicted on their victims; therefore, death would be a proportional punishment for someone who has taken the life of another. Logan and Gaes (1993) claim that this is the most honestly stated justification for punishment because it taps into our punitive urges and posits no secondary purpose for it, and they mirror Kant in writing that only retributive punishment "is an affirmation of the autonomy, responsibility, and dignity of the individual" (p. 252).

Retribution and Emotion

We have seen how cheating on the social contract by others evokes deep emotional responses of hurt, anger, disgust, and a desire to punish. When we do so, our rational faculties dictate that we should provide reasoned justifications for doing so other than simply saying that the miscreant has upset us. Thus, our finely reasoned justifications for punishment may be nothing more than rationalizations of the deeply felt moral intuitions of those advancing them. Philosopher David Hume once famously wrote: "Reason is, and ought only to be the slave of the passions, and can never pretend to any other office than to serve and obey them" (1987/1738, p. 415). Modern science has experimentally shown that when we confront a moral issue (such as capital punishment), our emotions rule the day. That is, we encounter an issue, experience emotions, pass judgment on the issue based on the emotion it evokes, and then provide reasons for that judgment (Canton, 2015; Haidt, 2012; Kahan, 2010; Walsh, 2014).

Noting that retribution is the most frequently cited justification for punishment (capital or otherwise), Rob Canton (2015) takes Haidt's work on the emotional foundations of morality (2012) and applies it to the emotions underlying the desire for retributive punishment. Writing first of care and compassion, Canton remarks that "retributive emotions reflect a decent compassion for a victim's distress and a virtuous expression of solidarity with members of our community" (p. 62). He next focuses on the deep instinct of fairness, and asserts that retribution "restores a balance: the offender's unjust profit or gain from the crime must be redressed or annulled. . . . The retributivist does not hit, but *hits back*" (p. 63). The urge to punish, he says (echoing Durkheim), can be seen as loyalty to the group and an expression of commitment to it. Offenders are subconsciously viewed as traitors and enemies of the group—"not one of us"—which serves to neutralize our feelings of care and compassion for them (p. 64). By their crimes, offenders have demonstrated a lack of respect for authority, which represents the possibility of the breakdown of the social order. This possibility generates anxiety among those who have a deep respect for authority and the social order (p. 65). Finally, most death-eligible crimes evoke a deep sense of disgust, especially when multiple victims, children, and/or torture are involved. We often hear metaphors for such criminals as "filth" or "scum" and seeing them punished as "cleansing" (p. 66).

Reconciliation and Reintegration

If we engage a variety of emotions in the service of punishment, are there also emotions that militate against overly harsh, disproportionate, and discriminatory punishment? Canton asserts that the human instinct for fairness and distrust of bullies generates opprobrium against unjust punishment, and insisting on reasonable limits to punishment is a prominent feature of liberal democratic societies (p. 67). Let us see what possible benefits could be derived from strategies of reconciliation and reintegration with minor criminal offenders.

We have seen that a simple strategy of like-for-like reciprocity is highly effective for generating cooperative behavior in small groups. However, game theorists (people who model conflict and cooperation between decision-makers playing computer games) have repeatedly shown that if two strict tit-for-tat strategists play and one cheats, it tends to launch a long series of tit-for-tat punitive responses that result in mutual loss. Game theorists find that a measure of forgiveness works better to maintain social cooperation rather than always paying back cheats in kind (Rand, Ohtsuki, & Nowak, 2009). If people always punish noncooperation, they risk losing a valuable relationship if the cheating incident was uncharacteristic of the cheater or was accidental (Machalek & Cohen, 1991). A large number of game theory studies have found that strict

TABLE 1.1 Summary of Key Elements of Different Justifications for Punishment

	Retribution	Deterrence	Incapacitation	Rehabilitation	Reintegration
Justification	Moral	Prevention of further crime	Risk control Community protection	Offenders have correctable deficiencies	Offenders have correctable deficiencies
Strategy	Offenders simply deserve to be punished	Punishment should be certain, swift, and severe	Offenders cannot offend while in prison	Treatment to change offenders' attitudes	Concrete programs for reintegration into society
Focus	The offense and just deserts	Actual and potential offenders	Actual offenders	Needs of offenders	Needs of offenders
Image of criminals	Free agents—we affirm their humanity by holding them accountable	Rational beings who engage in cost–benefit calculations	Not to be trusted, but to be set apart from society	Good people whose circumstances led them astray	Rational folk who will respond to concrete help

tit-for-tat can be too costly because all parties tend to suffer to some extent, and the forgiving strategy invariably prevails (Rand, Ohtsuki, & Nowak, 2009).

The forgiveness strategy responds to a one-shot betrayal with cooperation rather than retaliation in the next round of the game, and in most circumstances it will return players to mutual cooperation. If it does not, victims will revert to punishment. Although these are experiments conducted in laboratory conditions, predictions based on game theoretical models have been remarkably consistent with real-world findings on numerous occasions (Levitt & List, 2007). Inviting cooperation in the face of defection is not a "sucker" strategy because it is not one that tolerates continued cheating. A forgiveness strategy is like sentencing first-time offenders to probation rather than prison, thus giving them an opportunity to redeem themselves and leaving the door open to future mutually advantageous cooperation between offenders and their communities. The probation sanction is still a response to criminal behavior, but the retaliation is conciliatory rather than punitive. Both offender and their communities benefit from methods that express disapproval but that also conform to the reintegrative ideal. On the other hand, if we always respond to defectors with strong punishment, the community risks losing a potentially future cooperator and offenders risk losing their connections to the community. None of this, of course, applies to capital murderers. It is only offered to show that emotions can lead to merciful responses as well as punitive ones.

Table 1.1 is a summary of the key elements (justification, strategy, etc.) of the five punishment philosophies or perspectives discussed. The commonality that they all share to various extents is the prevention of crime.

SUMMARY

This chapter provides insight into why human beings find it necessary to respond with painful sanctions against other human beings who have harmed them or the community. The question has occupied philosophers for centuries because they have stated punishment is something that should be morally justified.

We looked at the ultimate evolutionary reasons why the urge to punish is universal, noting that brain imaging studies show that our brain's reward centers "light up" when wrongdoers are punished. Since natural selections only build into animals the mechanisms that reward them when they perform actions necessary for their survival and reproductive success, punishing norm violators must be adaptive. Norm violation and punishment seemed to have been essential to the evolution of cooperation because it gave rise to the co-evolutionary arms race that strengthened the social emotions which demand justice. By helping to extinguish the negative emotions (anger, frustration, feelings of helplessness) associated with victimization of self or others, and generating satisfaction upon witnessing the imposition of sanctions against the miscreant, punishment reinforces our sense of the justness of moral norms. Thus, as Durkheim asserted, punishment is vital to the maintenance of a just society.

Although many thinkers agree that some sort of response to the predatory act of others is necessary, they differ in their justifications of such responses. Most philosophers and social scientists who have written about punishment have justified it on utilitarian or consequentialist grounds; that is, in terms of its positive consequences for society as a whole. Others such as Kant have taken a non-consequentialist position that justifies punishment as an intrinsic good and avers that criminals should be punished simply because they deserve to be. To punish them as a means to an end is to treat them as less than autonomous human beings. This position is a radical free will position maintaining that no matter the circumstances, people can always choose to do the right thing; if they don't, they are willfully disregarding the rights of others and deserve society's wrath. Others take a hard-line determinist position that maintains many of our actions are beyond our control. The law takes a compatibilist position that recognizes mitigating circumstances and does not hold individuals completely blameworthy while still responding appropriately to their wrongdoing.

Science tells us that emotions are more important than reason in generating human responses to events and issues, and thus if we are to understand the punishment response, we must understand the emotions evoked by criminal behavior. These emotions typically run the gamut of negative emotions that generate the demand for retribution. However, it was also argued that strict tit-for-tat strategies can be harmful, and that forgiveness is useful for the purposes of reconciliation and reintegration into the community.

DISCUSSION QUESTIONS

1. Explain what you think society would be like without punishment.
2. Why is reconciliation a better strategy than strict tit-for-tat? Is it always so?
3. Which of the justifications for punishment are appropriate for: (a) a burglar; (b) a child molester; (c) a rapist; (d) a man who killed his wife in a fit of rage; (e) a serial killer; (f) a woman who kills her abusive husband?
4. Discuss how Durkheim's ideas on punishment are similar to modern evolutionary thinking.
5. Kant believed that if we (individuals and/or governments) do something with good intentions, such an action is morally good regardless of the consequences. Do you believe this; or do you believe that the "path to hell is paved with good intentions"?
6. Defend the justification for punishment that most appeals to you.

GLOSSARY

Altruism: An active concern for the well-being of another at some cost to the self.

Categorical imperative: A moral principle associated with Immanuel Kant stating that an act should be done "in itself" regardless of any further end. In other words, a categorical imperative says "Do this," not "Do this if."

Compatibilism: A philosophical position maintaining that free will and determinism are compatible. People are free to do what they want unless constrained by circumstances, either internal or external.

Consequentialism: A philosophical position that justifies a practice in terms of the consequences assumed to result from it.

Free will: The faculty that enables human beings to purposely and deliberately choose a calculated course of action.

Hedonism: The idea that happiness is the ultimate goal toward which all humans strive, and that all other goals are only a means to the end of achieving it.

Hedonistic calculus: A method combining hedonism and rationality by which individuals are assumed to logically weigh the anticipated benefits of a given course of action against its possible costs.

Incapacitation: A justification for punishment referring to the inability of criminals to victimize people outside prison walls while they are imprisoned.

Rational behavior: A behavior that has a logical "fit" between the goals people strive for and the means they use to achieve them.

Reciprocal altruism: The act of extending a benefit to another person with the unspoken expectation of obtaining a similar benefit from the recipient at some later date.

Rehabilitation: A justification for punishment that is forward-looking to offenders' future behavior, with the aim of changing it in prosocial directions via treatment programs.

Reintegration: A justification for punishment that seeks to use the time criminals are under correctional supervision to prepare them to reenter free society better equipped to remain there than they previously were.

Retribution: A non-consequentialist position on punishment that believes punishment for its own sake is morally justified because criminals deserve it.

Utilitarianism: An ethical philosophy that claims an action is morally right if it produces the most utility (defined as benefits, happiness, and pleasure) for the greatest number of people in society.

REFERENCES

Barker, V. (2006). The politics of punishing: Building a state governance theory of American imprisonment variation. *Punishment & Society, 8,* 5–32.

Beccaria, C. (1963/1764). *On crimes and punishment.* Trans. H. Paulucci. Indianapolis, IN: Bobbs-Merrill.

Bentham, J. (1948/1789). *A fragment on government and an introduction to the principles of morals and legislation.* Ed. W. Harrison. Oxford: Blackwell.

Boehm, C. (2011). Retaliatory violence in human prehistory. *British Journal of Criminology, 51,* 518–534.

Bohm, R. (2012). *Deathquest: An introduction to the theory and practice of capital punishment in the United States.* Waltham, MA: Anderson.

Brooks, J. (2013, Spring). Strange bedfellows: Religious fundamentalism and the death penalty in the U.S. and Saudi Arabia. *Al Nakhlah: Online Journal on Southwest Asia and Islamic Civilization,* 1–11.

Brunero, J. (2002). Evolution, altruism and internal reward explanations. *Philosophical Forum, 33,* 413–424.

Buckholtz, J., and R. Marois. (2012). The roots of modern justice: Cognitive and neural foundations of social norms and their enforcement. *Nature Neuroscience, 13,* 655–661.

Canton, R. (2015). Crime, punishment and the moral emotions: Righteous minds and their attitudes towards punishment. *Punishment & Society, 17,* 54–72.

Cassell, P. (2008, Summer). In defense of the death penalty. *LACJ Journal,* 14–28.

Chagnon, N. (1988). Life histories, blood revenge, and warfare in a tribal population. *Science, 239,* 985–992.

Cheever, J. (2006). *Back from the dead: One woman's search for the men who walked off death row.* New York: Wiley.

Clark, T. (2007). *Encountering naturalism: A worldview and its uses.* Somerville, MA: Center for Naturalism.

Currie, E. (1989). Confronting crime: Looking toward the twenty-first century. *Justice Quarterly, 6,* 5–25.

De Quervain, D., U. Fischbacher, T. Valerie, M. Schellhammer, U. Schnyder, A. Buch, et al. (2004). The neural basis of altruistic punishment. *Science, 305,* 1254–1259.

de Waal, F. (1996). *Good natured: The origins of right and wrong in humans and other animals.* Cambridge, MA: Harvard University Press.

de Waal, F. (2008). Putting the altruism back into altruism: The evolution of empathy. *Annual Review of Psychology,* 59:279–300.

dos Santos, M., D. Rankin, and C. Wedekind. (2011). The evolution of punishment through reputation. *Proceedings of the Royal Society: Biology, 278,* 371–377.

Douglas, D. (2000). God and the executioner: The influence of Western religion on the use of the death penalty. *William & Mary Bill of Rights, 9,* 137–170.

Durant, W., and A. Durant. (1967). *Rousseau and revolution.* New York: Simon & Schuster.

Durkheim, É. (1964). *The division of labor in society.* New York: Free Press.

Durkheim, É. (1965). *The elementary forms of the religious life.* New York: Free Press.

Eliaeson, S. (2002). *Max Weber's methodologies: Interpretation and critique.* Malden, MA: Blackwell Press.

Garland, D. (1990). *Punishment in modern society.* Chicago: University of Chicago Press.

Grasmick, H., J. Cochran, R. Bursik Jr., and M. Kimpel (1993). Religion, punitive justice, and support for the death penalty. *Justice Quarterly, 10,* 289–314.

Haidt, J. (2001). The emotional dog and its rational tail: A social intuitionalist approach to moral judgment. *Psychological Review, 108,* 814–834.

Haidt, J. (2012). *The righteous mind: Why good people are divided by politics and religion.* New York: Pantheon.

Hawthorne, N. (2003/1850). *The scarlet letter.* New York: Barnes & Noble Classics.

Henrich, J., R. McElreath, A. Barr, J. Ensminger, C. Barrett, A. Bolyanatz, et al. (2006). Costly punishment across human societies. *Science, 312,* 1767–1770.

Hume, D. (1987/1738). *A treatise of human nature.* Ed. L. Selby-Bigge. Oxford: P.H. Nidditch.

Jacoby, S. (1983). *Wild justice: The evolution of revenge.* New York: Harper & Row.

Kahan, D. (2010). Fixing the communications failure. *Nature, 463,* 296–297.

Kant, I. (1785). *Groundwork of the metaphysics of morals.* Trans. H. Paton. New York: Harper & Row.

Klein, R. (2012). The neurobiology of altruistic punishment: A moral assessment of its social utility. In Eds. K. Plaisance and T. Reydon, *Philosophy of behavioral biology,* pp. 297–313. Boston: Springer Science.

Levitt, S., and J. List. (2007). What do laboratory experiments measuring social preferences reveal about the real world? *Journal of Economic Perspectives, 21,* 153–174.

Logan, C., and G. Gaes. (1993). Meta-analysis and the rehabilitation of punishment. *Justice Quarterly, 10,* 245–263.

Machalek, R., and L. Cohen. (1991). The nature of crime: Is cheating necessary for cooperation? *Human Nature, 2,* 215–233.

Marquart, J., and J. Sorensen. (1989). National study of the *Furman*-commuted inmates: Assessing the threat to society from capital offenders. *Loyola of Los Angeles Law Review., 23,* 5–28.

Massey, D. (2002). A brief history of human society: The origin and role of emotion in social life. *American Sociological Review, 67,* 1–29.

McBride, K. (2007). *Punishment and the political order.* Ann Arbor: University of Michigan Press.

Menninger, K. (1968). *The crime of punishment.* New York: Penguin Books.

Miller, D., and N. Vidmar. (1981). The social psychology of punishment reactions. In Eds. M. Lerner and S. Lerner, *The justice motive in social behavior,* pp. 145–172. New York: Plenum Press.

Moll, J., F. Krueger, R. Zahn, M. Pardini, R. de Oliveira-Souza, and J. Grafman. (2006). Human fronto-mesolimbic networks guide decisions about charitable donation. *Proceedings of the National Academy of Sciences of the United States of America, 103,* 15623–15628.

Naas, M. (2012). The philosophy and literature of the death penalty: Two sides of the same sovereign. *Southern Journal of Philosophy, 50,* 39–55.

The National. (2013). Saudi man spared paralysis sentence. http://www.thenational.ae/news/world/middle-east/saudi-man-spared-paralysis-sentence.

Nowak, M. (2006). Five rules for the evolution of cooperation. *Science, 314,* 1560–1563.

Penney, S. (2012). Impulse control and criminal responsibility. *International Journal of Law and Psychiatry, 35,* 99–103.

Pessoa, L. (2008). On the relationship between emotion and cognition. *Nature Neuroscience, 9,* 148–158.

Rachels, J. (1986). *The elements of moral philosophy.* New York: Random House.

Rand, D., H. Ohtsuki, and M. Nowak. (2009). Direct reciprocity with costly punishment: Generous tit-for-tat prevails. *Journal of Theoretical Biology, 256,* 45–57.

Rosebury, B. (2009). Private revenge and its relation to punishment. *Utilitas, 21,* 1–21.

Schuster, P. (2009). Free will, information, quantum mechanics, and biology: It pays to distinguish different forms of free choice and information. *Complexity, 15,* 8–11.

Smith, P. (2008). *Punishment and culture.* Chicago: University of Chicago Press.

Suwa, G., B. Asfaw, R. Kono, D. Kubo, C. Lovejoy, and T. White. (2009). The *Ardipithecus ramidus* skull and its implications for hominid origins. *Science, 326,* 68e1–68e8.

Thagard, P. (2005). The emotional coherence of religion. *Journal of Cognition and Culture, 5,* 58–74.

Tutro, J. (2014). Eliminating the effective death sentence of life without parole. *The Forum: A Tennessee Student Legal Journal, 1,* 11–28.

Ule, A., A. Schram, A. Rieddl, and T. Cason. (2009). Indirect punishment and generosity toward strangers. *Science, 326,* 1701–1704.

Unnever, J., F. Cullen, and B. Fisher. (2005). Empathy and support for capital punishment. *Journal of Crime and Justice, 28,* 1–34.

Walsh, A. (1981). *Human nature and love: Biological, intrapsychic, and socio-behavioral perspectives.* Lanham, MD: University Press of America.

Walsh, A. (2006). Evolutionary psychology and criminal behavior. In Ed. J. Barkow, *Missing the Revolution: Darwinism for social scientists,* pp. 225–268. Oxford: Oxford University Press.

Walsh, A. (2014). *Criminological theory: Assessing philosophical assumptions.* Waltham, MA: Anderson/Elsevier.

Walsh, A. & C. Hemmens. (2014). *Law, justice, and society: A sociolegal introduction,* 3rd edition. New York: Oxford University Press.

Walsh, A., H. Johnson, and J. Bolen. (2012). Drugs, crime, and the epigenetics of hedonic allostasis. *Journal of Contemporary Criminal Justice, 28,* 314–328.

Wiebe, R. (2011). The nature and utility of low self-control. In Eds. K. Beaver and A. Walsh, *The Ashgate research companion to biosocial theories of crime,* pp. 369–395. Farnham, UK: Ashgate.

Wilson, J. (1975). *Thinking about crime.* New York: Vintage.

Wood, D. (2010). Punishment: Consequentialism. *Philosophy Compass, 5,* 455–469.

Zimmerman, M. (2011). *The immorality of punishment.* Buffalo, NY: Broadview Press.

CHAPTER 2

HISTORY OF THE DEATH PENALTY IN THE UNITED STATES

Past and Present

Mary Latham was an 18-year-old girl living in Puritan Massachusetts in 1641. After suffering a broken heart from a failed relationship, Mary vowed to quickly get over her ex-lover by marrying the next man who came into her life. Indeed, she met and married a man much older than herself shortly thereafter. She soon regretted her decision and began having extramarital relationships with other men—a crime punishable by death according to Massachusetts law at the time. Officials learned of this crime because one of Mary's lovers, James Britton, felt remorse for his actions and confessed that he and Mary had carried on an affair. Both Mary and her lover were executed for committing adultery.

John Winthrop, then governor of the Massachusetts Colony, wrote:

> James Britton . . . and one Mary Latham, a proper young woman about 18 years of age, whose father was a godly man and had brought her up well, were condemned to die for adultery. The woman proved very penitent, and had deep apprehension of the foulness of her sin, and at length attained to hope of pardon by the blood of Christ, and was willing to die in satisfaction to justice. . . . They both died very penitently, especially the woman, who . . . gave good exhortation to all young maids to be obedient to their parents, and to take heed of evil company.

LEARNING OBJECTIVES

- Understand the role of religion and punishment in colonial America.
- Identify the differences between the Puritans and Quakers in terms of penology.
- Understand the concept of collective guilt and how it played a role in the determination of punishment.
- Understand the importance of "saving souls" and how this idea often directed the practice of the death penalty for the early settlers in America.
- Identify the differences in types of death-eligible crimes as the population shifts in America.
- Understand the importance of deterrence as it pertains to public versus private executions.
- Compare and contrast capital punishment practices from the pre-modern and modern eras.

Mary Latham's case illustrates the stark contrast between the capital punishment practices of the past and present. Even a staunch supporter of the death penalty would surely oppose executing a person for committing an act of adultery. And if Latham had been just one year younger at the time of her crime, she would not even be eligible for execution by today's standards.

CAPITAL PUNISHMENT IN ANTIQUITY

The killing of someone by the common assent of his or her fellow group members for one reason or another is doubtless as old as species themselves. Today, we call such killings executions or capital punishment. According to Michael Reggio (1997), the first death sentence in recorded history occurred in Egypt during the sixteenth century. It was probably recorded because the condemned was a member of the nobility who was accused of magic. He was ordered to take his own life, which he likely did as quickly and as painlessly as possible. This do-it-yourself execution saved the nobleman from the extreme forms of execution practiced throughout history designed to prolong the suffering as long as possible and to maximize the pain felt by the condemned.

We have seen that punishment is a necessary function of any organized group if the rules of reciprocal cooperation are to be maintained, but we also observed that punishment can overstep its optimum and perhaps result in fear and distrust of authority rather than respect for it. Worse yet, executions for trivial affronts that are not even considered misdemeanors in most Western societies today often became occasions for public spectacles of brutality. Public executions were meant to strike terror into those witnessing them, but many apparently enjoyed the inhumane acts of cruelty. Written accounts of public executions mention onlookers shrieking with laughter with each scream emitted by the poor tortured soul. Even if not actually enjoying the spectacle, most showed a chilling indifference to others' suffering. This is evidenced by Samuel Pepys, a member of Parliament and father of the British Navy, who entered the following in his diary in 1660:

> Out to Charing Cross, to see Major-general Harrison hanged, drawn, and quartered; which was done there, he looking as cheerful as any man could do in that condition. He was presently cut down and his head and heart shown to the people, at which there was great shouts of joy . . . from hence to my Lord's, and took Captain Cuttance and Mr. Sheply to the Sun Tavern and did give them some oysters. (in Pinker, 2011, p. 145)

Pepys wrote this as offhandedly as any of us might remark that we went off to the ballgame and then to the bar for a beer and sandwich. The callous "wit" with which he wrote about Harrison "looking as cheerful as any man could do in that condition," and the revulsion with which I assume the reader has reacted to it, speaks volumes about how far we have advanced in our concerns for our fellow human beings since Pepys's time. We noted in Chapter 1 that humans have a built-in concern for the well-being of close kin, and that history shows a slow but steady widening of the circle of humanity included in our compassion. We also noted how Beccaria's plea for a more just system of punishment was met favorably by the powers in Europe, and how Durkheim documented the move from retributive to restitutive justice throughout much of the world. The point is, if we witness the suffering of others without having sympathy for them, we are in danger of losing the emotion altogether. This is why the death penalty has been considered the moral field on which the battle for the better angels of our nature has been fought. Let us see how this battle has progressed in the United States from colonial times to the present.

THE HISTORY OF THE DEATH PENALTY IN AMERICA

The death penalty is perhaps the quintessential debate taking place in our nation's moral landscape. Some think it a necessary evil, but wish to make it relatively painless; many think it a justly deserved penalty for an egregious evil done; and others despise it as a barbaric holdover from our uncivilized past that ought to be eliminated. In short, as a nation, we are deeply ambivalent about capital punishment. As Banner (2002) phrased this ambivalence:

> The death penalty is intended in part to deter others from committing crimes, but we inflict it in private. It is often justified in retributive terms, and yet we take great care to make it as painless as possible. We can resolve these apparent paradoxes only by looking back at how they came to exist. (p. 3)

Looking back at Banner's (2002) "apparent paradoxes" is the substance of this chapter. Indeed, Americans have juggled with the goals of punishment and how to implement the death penalty in accordance with modern-day standards of "decency." For example, we can see that the Latham case illustrates the significance of the church and its enormous influence on the form and function of punishment in the pre-modern era, something that is of little significance when considering the present-day separation of church and state in the American criminal justice system.

The death penalty was considered a "necessity" in colonial America because there were no prisons in the colonies and few holding facilities for those accused of crimes. Punishments were limited to banishment, fines, corporal punishment, and death. If offenders persisted in their ways or were deemed too dangerous to be allowed back into the community, there was no viable punishment alternative other than sentencing them to the gallows (Acker, 2003). On the other hand, the death penalty was not as regularly practiced as one might imagine given the lack of prisons. It simply did not make sense for colonists to utilize the death penalty with any kind of regularity, because labor was a sparse commodity and prisoners were needed to develop the colonies (Filler, 1952).

The first documented execution on American soil took place in 1608 when British officials executed a Virginian, George Kendall, after learning he was a spy for the Spanish (Acker, 2003). More than four centuries later, the death penalty is still utilized in over half of the states in our country.

This chapter outlines the evolution of the death penalty during the pre-modern and modern eras (eras defined in the context of capital punishment). *Furman v. Georgia* (1972) is arguably the most significant death penalty case to be decided by the U.S. Supreme Court, and it was decided during a time that serves as a logical divide between the eras. From this point forward, we will refer to it as *Furman*. The Court declared the administration of the death penalty unconstitutional, effectively reversing more than 600 active death sentences (Banner, 2002). The *Furman* case is discussed at length in Chapter 3.

PRE-MODERN ERA/PRE-*FURMAN*

Seventeenth and Eighteenth Centuries

The Puritans brought the death penalty to America from England during the seventeenth century. They sought refuge on American soil to exercise their religion freely, though they did not extend this freedom to others who followed in their footsteps. When the Quakers (aka "Friends") arrived from Europe, they were met with fierce resistance by the Puritans. An excerpt from a Quaker minister in 1742 explains that the Puritans "came to America and settled in New England, expecting there to enjoy that reasonable right, the liberty of their consciences; and forgetting the golden rule of doing to others as they would be done unto. . ." (Pestana, 1993, p. 466).

The Quakers arrived first in the Massachusetts Bay Colony in 1656, with hopes of spreading their own religious beliefs. At least four of their missionaries were executed by the Puritans shortly thereafter for refusing to leave. The Puritans demanded that the Quakers obey their codes and failure to do so was considered a direct violation of God's command (requiring Christians to "obey magistrates" as outlined in biblical scripture); hence, the highest order of punishment was thought to be justified. The Puritans soon learned, however, that the executions did little to deter the Quakers who considered themselves prophets and martyrs driven to spread their message of "truth" at any cost (Pestana, 1993).

Capital punishment garnered widespread support in seventeenth- and eighteenth-century colonial America because the colonists came from England where the death penalty was common practice. Colonies varied on the crimes for which the death penalty could be imposed. The average colony listed the punishment of death for approximately a dozen crimes, whereas the English included more than 200 death-eligible offenses in their statutes, commonly referred to as the "Bloody Code" (Filler, 1952). Often, death-eligible crimes were those that were serious, such as murder, treason, robbery, rape, and arson, but capital punishment was also used to punish theft, counterfeiting, burglary, and other less serious offenses (Banner, 2002). There is no question the English were harsh punishers and utilized the death penalty much more than the colonists did, but there were some capital offenses that were unique to American colonies. For example, adultery was a crime punishable by death, as we learned with the Latham case. To be an unruly male child was also a capital crime in the seventeenth century. The Laws and Liberties of Massachusetts (1648) declared that stubborn boys who "will not obey the voice of his father, or the voice of his mother" shall be put to death (Trumbull & Hammond, 1821, p. 70).

Religion

Religion played a key role in the day-to-day life of colonial Americans. Citizens attended mandatory church services and were required to pay taxes for the salaries of ministers (Latzer & McCord, 2011). Accordingly, many of the crimes for which a person could be executed were those that threatened the religious order. For example, the seventeenth-century Massachusetts colonists condemned to death those who committed crimes such as witchcraft, idolatry (worshipping of idols), blasphemy, murder, and adultery. Each one of these crimes was listed in the respective statutes of each colony, with corresponding biblical scripture serving as the justification for punishment (Bedau, 1982).

It made sense to colonists that punishments should reflect the religious sentiment which played such an integral role in their lives because punishment was inextricably linked to religious concepts of penitence, forgiveness, and redemption. Repentance for one's sins was key to salvation and, therefore, it was paramount for authorities to "save the souls" of those condemned to die. And there was no better time for people to get their religious affairs in order than when confronted with death. In fact, officials planned for this. The condemned were given a couple of weeks, and sometimes months, after being convicted of a crime to get ready for the afterlife. It was critical to aid offenders in the process of getting their minds "right" before the execution. The repentance process was guided by ministers' regular visits to the offenders in jail (Banner, 2002).

The actual execution day was carefully planned, beginning with a ceremonial procession whereby the offender would be escorted to the gallows by his or her ministers and other officials wishing to partake in the ceremony. The route to the gallows would have been public knowledge, allowing anyone to witness the entire ceremony beginning with the offender walking out of jail. In some cases, the prisoner would wear a special robe for the solemn event. Once he or she arrived at the execution spot, it was common for the sheriff to read the death warrant, followed by the preaching of a sermon and singing of religious hymns. Lastly, the prisoner would be given the opportunity to utter final words before having a cloth draped over his or her face and then hanged (Banner, 2002). Executions, therefore, were viewed as religious occasions for all and very much served to reinforce community solidarity—purging "evil" from the community and celebrating the salvation of those soon to be condemned.

Few executions have drawn as much attention as those taking place during the **Salem Witch Trials** in 1692 (see Figure 2.1). These trials are most commonly known for the tragic executions of innocent people accused of witchcraft, the "devil's magic," in Salem, Massachusetts.

Salem was a community with strong Puritan religious doctrine (King, 2010). Its members believed that the devil could make deals with witches allowing them to harm people if they would remain loyal to him. Colonial law clearly prohibited "witchcraft, and dealing with evil and wicked spirits," under the penalty of death (Hill, as cited in Blumberg, 2007, p. 1). The trials lasted for about a year and began when a few young girls made false claims that witches had cursed them. Their accusations resulted in mass hysteria, creating fear and paranoia in Salem, and leading many to believe that behaviors out of the ordinary must be a sign of witchcraft. Ministers in Salem used the hysteria to encourage people to seek salvation and return to their religious roots that were

FIGURE 2.1 Salem Witch Trials

being threatened by the growth of secularization. Ultimately, 20 people were accused, convicted, and executed; most died by hanging (Blumberg, 2007).

Deterrence

The goal of deterrence was another key justification for the death penalty practice in colonial America. Executions were intended as warnings to those who might be tempted to commit crimes like that of the accused. There are two types of deterrence: specific and general. **Specific deterrence** is a form of deterrence that assumes the effect of imposed punishment on the future behavior of the person being punished. This type of deterrence has little relevance to discussions concerning the deterrence of individuals who are executed considering that they will not be alive to commit future crimes. **General deterrence**, on the other hand, has greater application to death penalty debates. The general type of deterrence assumes the effect of punishment on those who have witnessed it, but not personally experienced it. Although we devote an entire chapter to deterrence (see Chapter 7), we discuss general deterrence here as it pertains specifically to public executions.

In order for an execution to have the desired deterrent effect, it must be both visible and well-advertised. The *Virginian Gazette* newspaper in 1751 characterized the death penalty as "counterbalancing Temptation by Terror, and alarming the Vicious by the Prospect of Misery." Therefore, the condemned man served as "an Example and Warning, to prevent others from those Courses that lead to so fatal and ignominious a Conclusion . . . and thus those Men whose Lives are no longer of any Use in the World, are made of some Service to it by their Deaths" (cited in Banner, 2002, p. 10).

Visibility was achieved by holding executions in public view, usually in a town square or some other public space. Not only did executions need to be visible, they also had to be followed with "circumstances of solemnity," because this would instill a sense of unforgettable fear among all types of citizens (Banner, 2002, p. 11). Given the meticulous planning of the execution from start to finish, there is little doubt that this was achieved. Indeed, executions drew healthy crowds—in some cases, up to 50,000 spectators (Banner, 2002)! Warnings by the state were reinforced even after the execution by leaving the body of the deceased on display, often with a sign around his or her neck warning others of the executed person's crimes. The bodies of the executed were usually set close to roadways or in crime-prone areas where authorities desired to reinforce the power of the law the most. If two people were executed, the bodies were often displayed in different places in an effort to maximize the deterrent value of the punishment (Banner, 2002). In some cases, authorities went to great lengths to preserve the bodies of the executed from the elements, so they could be displayed longer. Gibbet irons were used to encase the body for display. This cage-like contraption consisted of iron bands linked together to form the shape of a human body and had a bolt on the top from which the gibbet hung (see Figure 2.2). Sometimes the body was dipped in tar prior to being gibbetted (Sellin, 1955).

FIGURE 2.2
Gibbet Irons
This material is copyright by, and used with permission of, the Independence Hall Association, on the web at ushistory.org.

Executions were celebrated by the local townsmen and advertised extensively, attracting people from neighboring towns as well. Though intended to be solemn events, the crowds attending executions and gibbetting displays "created an atmosphere of festivity, drawn to the sight of the corpses of the condemned as grisly entertainments" (Fearnow, 1996, p. 17). The weeks preceding an execution, meant to prepare the offender's salvation, provided authorities time to publicize the event, though the deterrent value became somewhat diminished as the time between penitence and executions grew longer. Offenders learned that they could "buy" more time in order to plan an escape by simply expressing their desire to have more time for penitence. After all, the condemned had nothing to lose for trying. Indeed, numerous accounts exist of capital inmate escapees during these times, largely due to the loose security in jails (Banner, 2002). Despite these obvious logistical problems, penitence rituals remained in effect for centuries.

Retribution

Retribution is the final justification for punishment cited in colonial American literature. Retribution refers to the innate desire to get even or to pay back the blameworthy for their actions (see Chapter 1). In the most basic terms, retribution is punishment for the sake of punishment or revenge. The **Code of Hammurabi** (one of the first legal codes, written in 1750 B.C.) is known for the phrase "an eye for an eye, and a tooth for a tooth," which was equated with the legal concept of *lex talionis* and translates into the "the law of retaliation" (as cited in Welch, 2011). For colonial Americans, retribution was more than a legitimate justification for punishment—it was morally necessary. The death penalty was used not only to rid society of the evildoer, but also to free the community of the guilt that would be shared by all if they did not execute the offender. "Guilt belonged to the land as well as the criminal. Execution was the only way to expiate that collective guilt" (Banner, 2002, p. 14). The concept of retribution has strong religious and biblical underpinnings that were often recited by authorities at executions: "Blood it defileth the land . . . and the land cannot be cleansed of the blood that is shed therein, but by the blood of him that shed it" is a passage from the Old Testament (cited in Banner, 2002, p. 14). Printed poetry sold at the 1757 execution of John Harrington read:

> *Go Murd'rous Wretch, deep-drench'd in Gore;*
> *With human Blood prophan'd;*
> *Thy Life we must admit no more,*
> *A Burthen to the Land.* (cited in Banner, 2002, p. 15)

It was largely accepted that if offenders were not punished, their guilt would spread to the entire community, thus contaminating it.

Despite widespread support of the death penalty in the colonies, there were attempts by some to limit its usage and thereby the number of death-eligible crimes. William Penn, the founder of the Pennsylvania Colony (hence the name), was an influential *Friend* and political figure who was wealthy, educated, and an avid supporter of Quaker ideals (Graves, 2007). Penn sought to reform the harsh punishments that had dominated colonial penology by drafting a legal code in 1682 called the **Great Law**. The Law set forth numerous recommendations that were rather progressive for the time. The Great Law restricted the use of capital punishment to the crimes of intentional murder and treason (Bedau, 1982). Other recommendations included the following:

1. All prisoners were to be eligible for bail.
2. Those wrongfully imprisoned could recover double damages.
3. Prisons were to provide free food and lodgings.
4. All counties were to provide houses of detention to replace the pillory, stocks, and the like (cited in Welch, 2011, p. 54).

The Great Law's application was limited to the Quaker colonies that Penn had influence over and stayed in effect until his death in 1718. The day after his death, however, the English code was restored, replacing the Great Law and returning to the harsh punishment and execution practices that preceded the Pennsylvania colony (Welch, 2011).

Reform efforts intensified at the end of the eighteenth century. **Cesare Beccaria** (1963), an Italian economist, wrote *On Crimes and Punishment*s in 1764, which had a significant impact on prominent Americans, such as Thomas Jefferson, Benjamin Rush, Benjamin Franklin, and others, who sought capital punishment reform. Like Penn, Beccaria was a progressive thinker who proposed major changes in the criminal justice system, which included abolishment of the death penalty. He believed that the death penalty was excessive and there were other forms of punishment, such as banishment, that would function to protect society without having to resort to the extinguishment of human life. Beccaria took issue with the state for imposing capital punishment, calling it tyrannical (Welch, 2011). He states, "It seems to me absurd that the laws, which are an expression of public will, which detest and punish homicide, should themselves commit it, and that to deter citizens from murder they order a public one" (Beccaria, 1764, p. 50). Beccaria added that in order for punishment to deter future criminal actions, it must be *certain*, *swift*, and *severe*, though not out of proportion with the crime (Welch, 2011). Jefferson was an avid supporter of Beccaria's work and effectuated change in his state of Virginia by limiting the death penalty to the crimes of murder and treason. Rush was also a supporter of Beccaria and shared his belief that the state should not execute people, because doing so violates the social contract between the people and the government (Banner, 2012).

Nineteenth Century/Abolitionist Movement

The nineteenth century marked the first legitimate movement toward abolition. By this time, it was widely accepted that the death penalty ought to be either severely restricted or outlawed. New Hampshire and Ohio, for example, only had two death-eligible crimes by 1815. Reformers successfully lobbied most states to ban mandatory capital punishments, arguing that the death penalty should only be used under the most "compelling circumstances" (Acker, Bohm, & Lanier, 2003). Maryland was one of the first states to give juries the discretion, in 1809, to punish offenders with death for crimes other than murder, such as treason, rape, and arson (Bedau, 1982). In an effort to adopt a middle ground between abolitionists and supporters, Maine crafted legislation that required every capital offender to spend one full year in a prison before being considered for execution. At the end of that year, the governor would then exercise discretion in deciding whether to order an execution. This compromise became widely known as the "Maine law" (Davis, 1957).

Jurors also played a key role in eliminating mandatory death sentences. **Jury nullification** refers to the inherent power of a jury to acquit a defendant by ignoring the law, even in cases with strong evidence to support a conviction. Jurors cannot be punished for their verdict decisions and, therefore, are able to veto the government's power in a sense (Conrad, 1999). This practice became relatively common in the nineteenth century as growing discontent with capital punishment continued. By refusing to find guilty verdicts for mandatory-death crimes, juries became a powerful ally in capital reform efforts (Acker, Bohm, & Lanier, 2003). One Missourian commented in 1872 that "it is now difficult to find 12 men who have not conscientious scruples in pronouncing the sentence of death even if they find the party guilty as charged" (Banner, 2002, p. 214). Abolitionists consistently argued that the "conscience of mankind revolted against the death penalty, and that therefore, it could not be enforced. . . . [The] death penalty assured the complete freedom of most murderers" (Filler, 1952, p. 132). In 1894, for example, there were 9,800 recorded murders in the United States, but only 132 legal executions resulted from jury verdicts (Filler, 1952).

Many states sought to remedy the nullification problem by assigning various degrees to crimes, namely murder, so that juries could convict a defendant for the same crime at a lesser degree in order to avoid imposing a death sentence. And Tennessee, Alabama, and Louisiana even went as far as allowing juries complete discretion to utilize the death penalty for all crimes of murder (with life imprisonment as an alternative) (Banner, 2002). By 1900, twenty states and the federal government made life in prison an alternative to the death penalty for crimes that previously carried mandatory death sentences (Bedau, 1982).

Another problem for death penalty advocates was executive clemency. Essentially, whoever held the "executive" power for a state (the modern-day equivalent to a governor) had absolute discretion to commute death sentences. This practice was common and inevitably led to corruption in favor of those who were well "connected," had money, or were friends of powerful constituents. Slaves were sometimes pardoned, but only because wealthy slave-owners wanted their "property" returned to them (Margulies, 2004).

Legislatures were forced to respond to concerns by their constituents about capital punishment because jury nullification and executive clemency were already being practiced and undermined the power of the state. The emergence of anti-gallows groups, such as the American Society for the Abolition of Capital Punishment, founded in 1845, became influential advocates for abolition. Michigan, in 1846, became the first territory to abolish the death penalty for all crimes except treason and was soon followed by Rhode Island and Wisconsin, which completely abolished it. Iowa and Maine were next to follow suit in the 1870s (Bedau, 1982).

Retentionists had not completely lost the battle, however, as illustrated by the numerous unsanctioned public executions that took place toward the end of the nineteenth century and into the twentieth century. Without the government "taking care of" criminals who committed crimes believed to be worthy of death, a form of vigilante justice emerged—lynchings. This form of punishment might be described as a form of unofficial capital punishment used primarily in the South on blacks and carried out by whites for a variety of crimes, including rape, murder, and various acts of disobedience (Banner, 2002). The statistics on blacks lynched in the South reveal that 3,959 lynchings occurred between 1877 and 1950, with most cases in Georgia, Mississippi, and Louisiana (Equal Justice Initiative [EJI], 2015).

Lynchings also occurred in our western United States, most commonly during the "Wild West." Indeed, there are numerous documented cases of horse thieves, bank robbers, and the like brought to justice by mobs of citizens who exercised swift justice. Consider the power of vigilantism in the case of L. H. Musgrove. Musgrove was the leader of a notorious horse thief gang in Wyoming and Colorado who targeted government horses, mules, and cattle (blaming the thefts on the Indians). A friend of Musgrove's in Colorado turned him in to Denver authorities, who promptly apprehended and then held him in jail; he faced the death penalty. Musgrove was quite confident and convinced of his ability to escape from jail and even bragged to the locals that he would soon escape when his friends arrived to break him out. Hundreds of locals decided to respond by gathering around the jail and demanding that the jailers release Musgrove to them. He was released by authorities without conflict or question and taken by the mob. They marched him to a bridge where a wagon was waiting underneath. His arms and legs were bound and a noose was placed around his neck; he was then hanged to death. There are many accounts of similar types of executions, with horse thievery, in particular, considered as bad as murder, if not worse (Cook, 1958). Proponents of capital punishment argued that lynching frequency necessitated the use of the death penalty as a formal sanction (Banner, 2002).

A historical change in capital punishment emerged with the removal of public executions. These events were becoming nuisances, marked by drunks and unruly spectators, far from the solemn ritual that they were originally intended to be. Most states decided to take control by centralizing executions at the state level, rather than local, and allowing only a few guests to witness executions (Latzer & McCord, 2011). The first attempts to remove executions from public view began in New York during the 1830s. County sheriffs were encouraged to hold executions out of public view, though they were given the discretion to comply. Pennsylvania and New Jersey banned public executions, requiring them to be administered within jail walls. Previously, the gallows were constructed in front of the jails that housed the condemned prisoners. Critics argued that given the loose security characterizing jails during this time, those who really wanted to see an execution could easily position themselves nearby to catch a glimpse of it (Bedau, 1982). In 1834, Pennsylvania became the first state to move executions indoors (Davis, 1957). It was more than one hundred years later when the last public execution took place in Galena, Missouri, in 1937. Roscoe Jackson was hung in front of 500 spectators who paid to witness the event, many of whom went home with pieces of the rope used to hang Jackson as souvenirs (Bedau, 1982).

As public executions became less popular toward the end of the nineteenth century, the widespread use of electricity captured the interest of state authorities. Thomas Edison's electrical company invented electricity using direct current (DC) and began staging demonstrations to illustrate the danger involved with his competitor's (George Westinghouse's) use of alternating current (AC). Edison's intent was to show that electricity produced with AC was so dangerous that it could kill animals and, therefore, would be too risky for residential and commercial use (Bedau, 1997). He demonstrated this by electrocuting animals with AC current during highly publicized events. Most famously, he executed an elephant named Topsy.

Edison escalated the battle with Westinghouse by using his influence as a successful inventor to convince the state of New York to use Westinghouse AC generators to execute capital offenders. The first man to be executed by electric chair was William Kemmler in 1890. Westinghouse hired a group of New York attorneys to represent Kemmler in an effort to stop his execution, fearing that AC would be labeled the "executioner's current" (Moran, 2003, p. xix). Edison testified that death by electrocution would be quick and painless if used with AC (Moran, 2003). Kemmler was executed, but the event was far from quick or painless, as we will learn in Chapter 6. Much to Edison's satisfaction, local newspaper headlines stated that Kemmler had been "Westinghoused."

Ironically, death by electrocution was soon considered the *humane* method of execution when compared to hanging and other methods thought to be too brutal, even though, electrocution is arguably one of the least humane death experiments society has attempted thus far. Bedau opines that executions must be "quick, painless and reliable" for societies that intend to remain civilized

(Bedau, 1997, p. 10). He goes on to explain that both abolitionists and retentionists agree societies are less willing to support capital punishment when the process is barbaric (Bedau, 1997).

Changing the method of execution had major implications on the deterrent effect assumed with public hangings. Recall the tenets of general deterrence require would-be offenders to witness the punishment in order to dissuade them from breaking the law. Given the weight and importance of community solidarity and deterrence as capital punishment goals, it is curious that supporters turned to methods that completely obscure the process.

Twentieth Century/Pre-*Furman*

The abolishment movement gained more success at the turn of the twentieth century (aka the Progressive era), with nine more states adopting abolition practices: Kansas, Minnesota, Washington, Oregon, South Dakota, North Dakota, Tennessee, Arizona, and Missouri (Bedau, 1982, p. 21). Nevertheless, as Pohlman (2005) points out, these abolishment advancements were short-lived once the Roaring Twenties and Great Depression (1929–1940) hit. World War I renewed public support for the death penalty as the growing discontent with foreigners combined with fears of an impending "crime wave" resulting from the Great Depression emerged. By 1920, six states that had previously abolished the death penalty reinstated it, and execution numbers reached all-time highs in the 1930s and 1940s—with a total of 2,951 executed (see Table 2.1).

The 1950s, however, brought about yet another wave of discontent with the death penalty. The annual average number of executions in the 1950s was 72, a significant reduction (by approximately half) compared to the numbers in the 1930s and 1940s. There is no agreed-upon explanation for the drop in executions. Increasing concern for capital case review by the federal courts may be partially responsible for the decline (Bedau, 1997).

The abolishment movement regained its strength in 1960, but not with the same fervor that characterized the nineteenth century. At this time, America was experiencing declining crime rates and the civil rights movement, among other related issues, that weakened support for the death penalty. Indeed, 1966 marked the only time in Gallup Poll history that public opposition outweighed support (see Chapter 5). At the close of the 1960s, 14 states had either abolished or nearly abolished the death penalty (Acker, 2003).

The issue of race and the death penalty has always been a point of concern, but was highlighted in the pre-*Furman* days. One study that gained attention during this period was conducted by Zimrig, Eigen, and O'Malley (1976). Their study utilized data from 204 Philadelphia homicide cases in 1970 and focused on how the 245 defendants in those cases were punished. They found that 65% of the defendants whose victims were white were sentenced to either a life

TABLE 2.1 Executions in the United States (1930–1949)

Year	Number of Executions
1930	155
1931	153
1932	140
1933	160
1934	168
1935	199
1936	195
1937	147
1938	190
1939	160
1940	124
1941	123
1942	147
1943	131
1944	120
1945	117
1946	131
1947	153
1948	119
1949	119

Source: Adapted from Bedau (1997).

sentence or the death penalty (only three death sentences resulted, however), while those defendants who killed black victims received similar sentences in only 25% of the cases (Zimrig, Eigen, & O'Malley, 1976). With so few death sentences accounted for in their study, Zimrig and colleagues (1976) learned more about racial discrimination in the sentencing of life imprisonment than death penalty cases, though any of those cases *could* have been death cases. Their findings are nevertheless instructive.

The death penalty debate moved into the courtroom in the 1960s when the National Association for the Advancement of Colored People (NAACP) challenged its legality (Acker, 2003). The basis for legal recourse had to do with the issue of race. The NAACP Legal Defense Fund began by representing African Americans who were charged with rape in the South and shortly thereafter expanded to a multitude of other issues centering on race to include the death penalty (Pohlman, 2005). A victory was soon realized when the U.S. Supreme Court agreed to hear a group of three cases (collectively known as *Furman v. Georgia*), whereby each of the defendants asserted Eighth Amendment violations of *cruel and unusual punishment* (with one of the cases involving murder and the other two rape).

Furman v. Georgia (1972)

On June 29, 1972, the U.S. Supreme Court consolidated the three capital cases before them that asserted Eighth and Fourteenth Amendment violations and issued its landmark decision in *Furman v. Georgia*, arguably the most significant capital decision case to date. Not only did *Furman* mark the first time in history that death penalty practice was found to violate the Eighth Amendment's "cruel and unusual" protection clause, but it dramatically changed the way death cases are handled and plunged the nation into the modern era of capital punishment (Acker, Bohm, & Lanier, 2003).

A commonly held misconception about *Furman* is that the constitutionality of the death penalty itself was at issue, though this is not the case. The Court ruled that the heart of the problem was the *imposition* of the death penalty at sentencing, citing the process as arbitrary and capricious. Justice Potter Stewart wrote:

> These death sentences are cruel and unusual in the same way that being struck by lightning is cruel and unusual . . . petitioners are among a capriciously selected random handful upon whom the sentence of death has in fact been imposed . . . the Eighth and Fourteenth Amendments cannot tolerate the infliction of a sentence of death under legal systems that permit this unique penalty to be so wantonly and so freakishly imposed. (*Furman v. Georgia*, 1972, p. 310)

The Court also explained that death sentences disproportionately impact minorities and the poor (*Furman v. Georgia*, 1972). The Court placed a moratorium (legal stop or delay in practice) on capital punishment, effectively halting all executions in the 39 states with death penalty statutes. There were more than 600 inmates on death row at the time, each ultimately receiving a sentence commutation to life imprisonment (Bedau, 1997). The details of how the Court came to its conclusion and the "remedies" implemented to restore capital punishment are discussed at length in Chapter 3.

The *Furman* decision changed the face of capital punishment forever. The Court effectively set the stage for what we now call "super due process," a term used to describe the many resources that capital defendants must have when the state/government seeks a sentence of death (see Chapter 3). This form of due process includes extra protections and resources at each level in the criminal justice system, from the pretrial phase to the execution itself and all the legal proceedings in between (Acker, Bohm, & Lanier, 2003). But why would the Court allow so many resources for a person who, by today's standards, is presumed to be the "worst of the worst," having committed a crime (or crimes) so heinous that he or she would be sentenced to die? Why waste such precious resources on this type of offender? The Court answered this question in a roundabout way when explaining that death is different because of its finality and irreversible nature, thereby requiring states to develop higher standards when imposing the "ultimate" sanction (Bedau, 1997).

PERSPECTIVE FROM AN ADMINISTRATOR OF PRISONS: DAVE PASKETT

Dave Paskett has worked in prisons for approximately 30 years. He has played an important role in the progression of the Idaho prison system during some of its most pivotal changes—the introduction of prisoner classification, offender programming, and notably, the advancement of execution practices in Idaho. Mr. Paskett's intimate knowledge of the inner workings of capital punishment and vast experience working in the corrections field enable him to compare and contrast the executions of the past with those of modern day.

FIGURE 2.3 Dave Paskett

I began my first day of work at the Old Idaho State Penitentiary in 1973 as a prison guard and worked there until an inmate riot burned down much of the facility, forcing its closure. The Old Pen was built in 1870 and is now a landmark with historical significance, especially when considering the evolution of capital punishment. It is the site of 10 executions, all of which took place during the pre-*Furman* era and prior to the practice of lethal injection. Ten men were executed by hanging at this prison—nine outside in public view and one inside the facility.

My first day of work began after only a week of training—I had no idea what to expect. I was assigned to work the graveyard shift in tower four and was given a bucket to use for the bathroom and access to a shotgun, rifle, and pistol with no firearms training; luckily, I had experience with firearms and could handle them if needed. My tower overlooked the rose garden, which was the site of all but one of the executions that had taken place at the Old Pen. Back then, hanging was the method used to execute prisoners on death row. I used to look down from my post and wonder what went through the minds of the condemned when they walked between the chow hall and the rose garden, knowing that their necks were about to be broken. I knew that some of the roses were over 100 years old and had been around during these executions.

The gallows would have been constructed and assembled for each execution and placed in the center of the rose garden for public viewing. You could imagine what it would have looked like when the horse-drawn carriages with people gathered in the foothills to witness the event. The prisoners would have been shackled with leg irons and belly chains and had a black sac over their heads. They likely would have needed help walking up the steps to the gallows. It had to be terrifying.

In the 1950s, there was a movement to separate the more serious offenders from the general population. There was a maximum security facility constructed at the Old Pen which housed inmates on death row (house five). With the new facility came a new death chamber. Now executions would take place indoors and out of public view, though the method was the same—death by hanging.

The new execution chamber was considered state-of-the-art for its time. Indeed, if the hanging method were to be brought back today, I believe that this facility would still meet the standards necessary to proceed with such an execution. The death row inmates were kept in a hall adjacent to the execution chamber. The chamber was fitted with windows, allowing a viewing platform for the witnesses. A circular metal frame hung from the ceiling to secure the rope and there was a trap door which opened and dropped the body to the prison hospital below. A man by the name of Raymond Snowden was the only one hanged in this chamber and was the last to be executed by hanging in Idaho. I heard his execution did not go well.

When the death warrant was signed for the next Idaho execution in 1994, it was nearly 40 years after Snowden's execution and times had changed. Idaho, like much of the country, adopted the lethal injection method. This was the first execution that I helped to prepare and witness. Preparations for executions now are quite different than those that took place at the Old Penitentiary. Today, the protocol is well rehearsed, meticulously planned, and guided by the courts in many respects with little room for error. Lethal injection is a much more humane way to execute a person because he feels no pain, whereas death by hanging can result in a lengthy and agonizing death. The lethal injection process is also much easier on those who have to carry out the execution. The execution that I witnessed seemed to go smoothly; the man never even moved, he just blinked and took his last breath. He was pronounced dead in just twelve minutes.

When the execution was over and I was driving home, an eerie feeling came over me that is hard to explain. I had just been part of executing a man and was so focused on getting the job done properly that I didn't consider the magnitude of the event that I witnessed until it was over. This was the first time that I had time to really think about the execution with all of the pressure gone. I imagine it would have been similar to the feelings of those who participated in the executions of the past as well as those who will participate in future executions.

MODERN ERA/POST-*FURMAN*

The Court reinstated the death penalty in 1976, just four years after issuing the *Furman* opinion. One might predict that the *Furman* decision would have strengthened the abolitionist agenda, but it had the opposite effect. Thirty-five states reinstituted capital punishment and public support was remarkably high given the legal climate surrounding the debate. Gallup Poll data indicate that 57% of Americans supported the death penalty in the months following *Furman* (Gallup, 2015). Of those states that reinstated their capital punishment statutes, approximately one-third also went on to reinstate mandatory sentencing practices for death-eligible offenses in an effort to meet the standards set forth in *Furman* (requiring states to adopt methods that would eliminate arbitrary sentencing practices). Although mandatory sentencing would no doubt eliminate jury discretion and thus aid in limiting arbitrary sentencing in capital cases, the U.S. Supreme Court referred to historical lessons learned from past experiments with this practice—the power of jury nullification and executive clemency review. Not only did the Court wish to avoid the concerns of the past, it reiterated that the Eighth Amendment requires individual considerations of both the offense and offender when making determinations about the death penalty. Consequently, in the same year that the death penalty was reinstated, the Court ruled that mandatory death sentences for specified crimes are unconstitutional (Acker, Bohm, & Lanier, 2003).

The question that remained after *Furman* was whether or not there was still arbitrary and discriminatory decision-making in capital cases. In 1990, the General Accounting Office (GAO) sought to answer this question in a report to the U.S. Senate. It conducted an extensive evaluation of empirical studies on capital punishment from the 1970s and 1980s (taking care to exclude studies with primarily pre-*Furman* data) to determine if race for both the victim and defendant influenced capital sentencing decisions. Twenty-eight empirical studies with 23 data sets were analyzed after it was determined that they were methodologically sound and included analyses of race as a factor contributing to death penalty decisions.

The GAO (1990) found that in 82% of cases, the race of the victim influenced whether a defendant was charged with capital murder or received the death penalty. More specifically, the studies consistently found that defendants whose victims were white were much more likely to receive death sentences than defendants whose crime involved black victims (GAO, 1990). With regard to the race of the defendant as a contributing variable to capital punishment decisions, however, the studies' findings varied with no real consensus among them. For example, one of the studies determined that the race of the defendant and likelihood of receiving a death sentence were dependent on whether the case was from a rural or urban area. Some studies found that black defendants with white victims were more likely to be sentenced to death, but it was unclear whether the effect was more closely related to the race of the victim or defendant. When examining the studies that did find a race effect tied to the defendant, three-fourths determined that black defendants were more likely to receive death sentences than white defendants, while the remaining studies found the exact opposite to be true (GAO, 1990). The GAO ultimately concluded: "Our synthesis of the 28 studies shows a pattern of evidence indicating racial disparities in the charging, sentencing, and imposition of the death penalty after the *Furman* decision" (1990, p. 5). These findings mirror those of Zimrig and colleagues (1976) from the pre-*Furman* era. We revisit the complex issue of race in much more detail in Chapter 8.

The current state of capital punishment is that more than 3,000 offenders sit on death row in the United States. Thirty-one states have death penalty statutes and 19 do not (Death Penalty Information Center, 2015). Capital crimes must be those that involve murder or the death of a victim (as applied to state, not federal, statutes). The modern state of capital punishment is explored further in Chapters 3 and 4 in the context of U.S. Supreme Court rulings as well as in the methods of execution chapter.

SUMMARY

This chapter provides an overview of capital punishment in America in the premodern and modern eras within the context of *Furman v. Georgia* (1972). We began by exploring the reasons and justifications cited by colonists for utilizing the death penalty. We learned that they adopted many of the same capital statutes as the English, but not all of them. Among the most important justifications for capital punishment included religion or efforts to "save souls," retribution, and deterrence. We then explored the abolitionist movement. Those who sought to abolish the death penalty cited issues of morality, brutality in punishment, the power of jury nullification, and executive clemency as public support waned. The abolishment movement lost momentum in the 1920s and 1930s with World War I and the Great Depression.

Furman v. Georgia (1972) marked significant changes in death penalty practice. The U.S. Supreme Court placed a moratorium on all executions in the United States, ruling that the death penalty was being applied arbitrarily and disproportionately affected minorities and the poor. The Court required states to develop methods of sentencing to eliminate these disparities. Essentially, *Furman* transformed capital punishment by creating super due process. Today, the effects of *Furman* remain evident (see Chapter 3).

DISCUSSION QUESTIONS

1. Why was religion so important to colonial Americans and how did executions during that period reflect religious symbolism?
2. Do you believe that religion should play a significant role in capital punishment? If an offender has "found God," should that be considered grounds for clemency or life commutation?
3. Are religion and deterrence legitimate punishment justifications for capital punishment? Why or why not? Explain.
4. Explain the importance and significance of jury nullification and why public opinion drives the legitimacy of the death penalty.

GLOSSARY

Cesare Beccaria: Becarria was an Italian economist who wrote *On Crimes and Punishment* in 1764. This book had a significant influence on American prison reformers and the efforts to abolish capital punishment.

Code of Hammurabi: One of the first legal codes, written in 1750 B.C. The code is known for the phrase "an eye for an eye, and a tooth for a tooth," which was equated with the legal concept of *lex talionis* and translates into the "the law of retaliation."

Jury nullification: The inherent power of a jury to acquit a defendant by ignoring the law, even in cases with strong evidence to support a conviction.

General deterrence: The effect of punishment on those who have witnessed but not personally experienced it.

Great Law: A law written by Quaker reformer William Penn in 1682 that restricted the death penalty to the crimes of homicide and treason.

Salem Witch Trials: Trials in the town of Salem, Massachusetts, in 1692 that resulted in the death of numerous innocent people thought to be engaged in witchcraft. The trials and executions lasted for approximately one year and ended with the accusers admitting that they falsely accused the condemned.

Specific deterrence: A form of deterrence defined as the assumed effect of the imposed punishment on the future behavior of the person being punished.

REFERENCES

Acker, J. (2003). The death penalty: An American history. *Contemporary Justice Review, 6*(2), 169–186.

Acker, J., R. Bohm, and C. Lanier. (2003). *America's experiment with capital punishment: Reflections on the past, present, and future of the ultimate penal sanction.* Durham, NC: Carolina Academic Press.

Banner, S. (2002). *The death penalty: An American history.* Cambridge, MA: Harvard University Press.

Beccaria, C. (1963/1764). *On crimes and punishment.* Trans. Henry Paolucci. Englewood Cliffs, NJ: Prentice Hall.

Bedau, H. (1982). *The death penalty in America.* New York: Oxford University Press.

Bedau, H. (1997). *The death penalty in America: Current controversies.* New York: Oxford University Press.

Blumberg, J. (2007). "A Brief History of the Salem Witch Trials: One Town's Strange Journey from Paranoia to Pardon." http://www.smithsonianmag.com/history-archaeology/brief-salem.html#.

Conrad, C. (1999). Jury nullification: Jurors flex their muscles. *USA Today, 128*(2654), 30.

Cook, D. (1958). *Hands up; or, twenty years of detective life in the mountains and on the Plains.* Norman, OK: University of Oklahoma.

Davis, D. (1957). The movement to abolish capital punishment in America, 1787–1861. *American Historical Review, 63*(1), 23–46.

Death Penalty Information Center. (2015). "States With and Without the Death Penalty." http://www.deathpenaltyinfo.org/states-and-without-death-penalty

Equal Justice Initiative. (2015). "Lynching in America: Confronting the Legacy of Racial Terror." http://www.eji.org/lynchinginamerica

Fearnow, M. (1996). Theatre for an angry God: Public burnings and hangings in colonial New York. *Drama Review, 40*(2), 15–36.

Filler, L. (1952). Movements to abolish the death penalty in the United States. *Annals of the American Academy of Political and Social Science, 284*, 124–136.

Furman v. Georgia, 408 U.S. 238 (1972).

Gallup. (2015). "U.S. Death Penalty Support Lowest in More Than 40 Years." http://www.gallup.com/poll/165626/death-penalty-support-lowest-years.aspx

General Accounting Office. (1990). "Death Penalty Sentencing: Research Indicates Pattern of Racial Disparities." http://www.gao.gov/assets/220/212180.pdf.

Graves, M. (2007). Travelers here in this vale of tears: William Penn preaches a funeral sermon. *Quaker Studies, 12*(1), 7–25.

King, E. (2010). Religiosity and the political economy of the Salem witch trials. *Social Science Journal, 47*(3), 678–688.

Latzer, B., and D. McCord (2011). *Death penalty cases: Leading U.S. Supreme Court cases on capital punishment.* Burlington, MA: Elsevier.

Margulies, J. (2004). Tinkering through time: A history of America's experiment with the death penalty. *Georgetown Law Journal, 92*(2), 369–404.

Moran, R. (2003). *Executioner's current: Thomas Edison, George Westinghouse, and the invention of the electric chair.* New York: Knopf Doubleday.

Pestana, C. (1993). The Quaker executions as myth and history. *Journal of American History, 80*(2), 441–469.

Pinker, S. (2011). *The better angels of our nature.* London: Penguin.

Pohlman, H. (2005). *Constitutional debate in action: Criminal justice.* Lanham, MD: Rowman & Littlefield.

Reggio, M. (1997). "History of the Death Penalty." http://www.pbs.org/wgbh/pages/frontline/shows/execution/readings/history.html.

Sellin, T. (1955). Philadelphia gibbet iron. *Journal of Criminal Law and Criminology, 46*(1), 11–25.

Trumbull, J., and J. Hammond. (1821). *The True-Blue Laws of Connecticut and New Haven and the False Blue-Laws invented by the Rev. Samuel Peters.* Hartford, CT: American Publishing Co.

Welch, M. (2011). *Corrections: A critical approach.* New York: Routledge.

Zimrig, F., J. Eigen, and S. O'Malley (1976). Punishing homicide in Philadelphia: Perspectives on the death penalty. *University of Chicago Law Review, 43*(2), 227–252.

CHAPTER 3

THE FOUNDATIONAL CASES: *FURMAN* TO *STANFORD*

Daniel McNaughton was a 29-year-old woodworker from Glasgow, Scotland, who moved to London in 1841. Those who knew McNaughton described him as an awkward man who seemed very serious, shy, and not fond of socializing with others. He also suffered from frequent and severe headaches. McNaughton spent his days in London worrying that the prime minister, Sir Robert Peel, and members of his "crew" were harassing him. McNaughton's paranoia led him purchase two pistols that he carried on the inside of his coat pockets. He frequented government buildings and Parliament so much that police officers believed McNaughton was a plainclothes, off-duty officer. On a January day in 1843, McNaughton walked up behind a man whom he believed was Prime Minister Peel and shot him in his back. The victim was actually the prime minister's secretary, Edward Drummond. Drummond died from his wound several days later.

McNaughton was surprised to learn that he had shot someone else. He was tried for murder, a crime punishable by death. When asked how he would plead, McNaughton replied: "I was driven to desperation by persecution." For years McNaughton struggled with delusions and paranoia, beginning from the days he lived in Scotland. He believed there were "spies" following him when no one else was watching, explaining: "They follow me and persecute me wherever I go, and have entirely destroyed my peace of mind. . . . I can get no rest from them night or day . . . in fact, they wish to murder me." Mental health experts testified at McNaughton's trial that his delusions were so strong he could not have stopped himself from committing the crime. The jury agreed that McNaughton could not distinguish between right and wrong and returned a not guilty, by reason of insanity, verdict. After the trial, he was moved to the Bethlehem Asylum for the Criminally Insane and died of heart failure at 52-years-old.

The Queen of England was not satisfied with the public perception that McNaughton had "got off easy." Following the verdict, she called the House of Lords to meet with the judges of the Queen's Bench to clarify the boundaries of an insanity defense. The "McNaughton test" resulted, the first test of its kind. The test has four prongs and has since been modified, though its roots are still evident in criminal courts today.

LEARNING OBJECTIVES

- Understand how the U.S. Supreme Court has guided the death penalty in both policy and practice.
- Discover the various death penalty-related issues that the U.S. Supreme Court has agreed to review.
- Learn how the Court has responded to claims that the death penalty violates the Eighth and Fourteenth Amendments.
- Know all of the landmark death penalty cases entailed in this chapter and the effects that they have had on capital punishment.
- Consider the issues that are likely to be reviewed by the U.S. Supreme Court in the near future based on the rulings discussed in this chapter.

The McNaughton case represents a significant departure from the standard court dealings in England because Parliament established specific guidelines for the "criminally insane" based on the Court's decision. McNaughton would likely be labeled a paranoid schizophrenic today. U.S. courts actually utilized the McNaughton test for many years before developing other insanity tests. Recall that we inherited the English common law tradition and that our constitutional amendments are modeled after the British Bill of Rights. The U.S. Supreme Court has issued multiple rulings with regard to the constitutionality of executing those with mental deficiencies along with a range of other capital issues addressed in this chapter.

As we learned in Chapter 2, capital punishment fundamentally changed in 1972 when the Court issued its ruling in *Furman v. Georgia*. The *Furman* case, therefore, serves as a logical divide between what capital punishment once was (pre-modern era) and has now become (modern era). *Furman* was the catalyst for the numerous death penalty challenges for which the Court would grant review. This chapter will guide you through the foundational U.S. Supreme Court cases that have shaped capital punishment in the modern era. Though some of the landmark cases are related and are often discussed together, we present them to you in timeline order to provide historical context. A timeline understanding is necessary for one to fully appreciate and consider the evolution of the Court's stance on capital punishment and how it has (or has not) evolved with society. You will notice that for each case, an accompanying illustration shows which justices voted in the majority (top line) and which dissented (bottom line). The image of the presiding chief justice of the Court is highlighted. Additionally, the illustration indicates which president appointed each of the justices, so we have the context of their political ideologies.

FURMAN V. GEORGIA (1972)

In the summer of 1972, William Henry Furman, a 24-year-old African American, broke into the home of William and Lanell Micki in Savannah, Georgia. The couple was asleep when they were awakened by a noise coming from their hallway. William Micki assumed it was one of his children and got up to check; he saw a man in the hallway. Furman let himself into the home by breaking into a screened-in porch and then unlocking the back door of the house by reaching through an open kitchen window. When Furman saw Micki, he went running down the hall and back through the door that he had broken into. Micki chased Furman and ran into the door, forcing it to slam shut and separating the two men from one another. It was then that Micki was hit by a bullet shot through the door by Furman as he ran away from the home. Furman fired a round from his .22 caliber pistol, apparently unaware that he had just shot William Micki. Micki died while lying in a pool of his own blood. Police caught up with Furman shortly after the incident. Furman initially admitted to shooting back at the door as he fled, but later changed

FIGURE 3.1 *Furman v. Georgia* (1972)

his story claiming that he tripped, which accidentally caused his gun to discharge. In any event, William Micki was dead and Furman was charged with capital murder (Stevens, 1978).

Furman's court-appointed attorney was given a total of $150 to represent Furman at trial. At the time, attorneys in private practice made $40–50 per hour. The $150 allowance was expected to cover any and all expenses related to his case (expert witnesses, investigation, etc.). The state of Georgia, however, argued its case with virtually no monetary restrictions (Stevens, 1978). With no guidelines to follow, the jury found Furman guilty of murder and sentenced him to death. It took them an hour and a half to reach their verdict (*Furman v. Georgia*, 1972).

Like most cases before it, the U.S. Supreme Court granted review of the *Furman* case via a **writ of certiorari**. This is an order issued to a lower court to send its record of a case to the Supreme Court for review. The Court's review of *Furman* involved a simultaneous review of two other cases: *Jackson v. Georgia* (1972) and *Branch v. Texas* (1972), both having African American defendants convicted of capital rape, not murder. The Court specifically agreed to address the issue of whether or not it was a violation of the Eighth and Fourteenth Amendments to impose and carry out the penalty of death in all three of these cases (*Furman v. Georgia*, 1972).

In the summer of 1972, the U.S. Supreme Court reached a decision on *Furman* in a 5-4 vote (see Figure 3.1). The Court shocked the world when it declared the death penalty, as it was currently administered, unconstitutional. The ruling was delivered in a rare **per curiam decision**, an unsigned opinion from the Court. Per curiam decisions are meant to signify a decision by the Court as an institution, rather than belonging to individual justices. The Latin translation for *per curiam* is "by the court" (Robbins, 2012, p. 1). In most cases, the Court releases an opinion that is signed by one justice who wrote it on behalf of the majority. The Court issues per curiam decisions when they are deeply divided about a case or individual justices wish to protect themselves from public scrutiny; each of the nine justices in *Furman* issued separate opinions, indicating division among them. The per curiam opinion was less than one page in length, but the entire decision was 231 pages! Each justice articulated, in detail, his position in either concurring (finding the death penalty unconstitutional) or dissenting (upholding the constitutionality of the death penalty) (Robbins, 2012).

Concurring Opinions

The majority, while divided in their reasoning, agreed on one issue—capital punishment was not fairly applied in the cases before the Court and was thereby unconstitutional. The problem lay with the unbounded discretion by juries (or judges for that matter) to make decisions about who should get the death penalty.

At the time *Furman* was before the Court, there were no standards or guidelines for juries to utilize when making their decisions, so they just used what they had before them, which were the details of the crime, sometimes horrific and sometimes not. As Justice William Brennan explained, all that the jury knew about Furman himself was his age, where he worked, and that he was black.

Justice Potter Stewart's opinion came as somewhat of a surprise and echoed Brennan's sentiment, describing the death penalty as "cruel and unusual in the same way that being struck by lightning is cruel and unusual" (*Furman v. Georgia*, 1972). In the past, Stewart had ruled against legislation that challenged capital punishment, so few expected him to join the concurring opinion (Banner, 2002). Stewart was concerned that the defendants in the *Furman* trio were "among a capriciously selected random handful upon whom the sentence of death has in fact been imposed" (*Furman v. Georgia*, 1972). He believed that the "Eighth and Fourteenth Amendments cannot tolerate the infliction of a sentence of death under legal systems that permit this unique penalty to be so wantonly and freakishly imposed" (*Furman v. Georgia*, 1972). Stewart clearly indicated, however, that while he joined the majority in this case, he still supported capital punishment. He believed that retribution is both part of human nature and critical for social stability, thus a valid punishment philosophy and practice. Stewart warned of the effects of abolishing a punishment practice that people want or believe defendants "deserve"—anarchy and vigilante justice.

Like Stewart, Justice Byron White's concurrence also came as a surprise. Historically, White had shown little sympathy for criminal offenders, but agreed that the death penalty was arbitrarily administered simply because when given the same sets of facts, one jury will choose death while another will not (Banner, 2002).

Each member of the majority expanded on his reasoning a little differently. Justice William Douglas used *Furman* to bolster his belief that the death penalty is discriminatory toward disadvantaged classes of people. He argued that issues of race and class have always played a role in determining who is sentenced to death and, therefore, capital punishment is "unusual" and thus cruel. Although the issue of race was not an official consideration in *Furman*, three of the majority justices discussed it in their individual opinions and two of the dissenting justices acknowledged the long history of differential treatment of blacks. Race was also insinuated as being correlated to the "randomness" of death penalty application (Banner, 2002). Brennan and Thurgood Marshall were the only two justices to set forth arguments that categorically called into question the constitutionality of capital punishment; the others argued that it is the process of assigning the death penalty or the administration of it that is unconstitutional (Douglas, White, and Stewart). Brennan's argument rested on the sporadic use of the death penalty. He believed that if the number of executions were declining, then it must be the result of growing dissatisfaction with its use (Banner, 2002). Banner (2002) opines that Brennan's position is easily challenged because states could abolish the death penalty if they did not desire to keep it. Further, public opinion polls had consistently indicated either a fair division or majority of people favoring the death penalty. Marshall took the position that the death penalty failed to serve a legitimate punishment purpose. Specifically, he asserted that it fails to deter others from capital crimes and that retribution is not a valid penological goal (Banner, 2002). As we learn in Chapter 5, Marshall hypothesized that the more knowledgeable people become on the issue of capital punishment, the less likely they will be to support it (the so-called Marshall hypothesis). Consequently, his claims have been studied profusely by social scientists and legal scholars.

Dissenting Opinions

The four dissenters were the most recent Supreme Court members at the time, all appointees of President Richard Nixon: Chief Justice Warren Burger, Justice Harry Blackmun, Justice Lewis Powell, and Justice Willliam Rehnquist. It came as no surprise that these four upheld the constitutionality of capital punishment, given that Nixon's presidential campaign centered largely on "getting tough on crime" and limiting the rights of criminals (Banner, 2002). Burger reiterated that the Court's decision did not declare the punishment of death itself unconstitutional and that legislators should create laws which will provide "standards for juries and judges to follow in determining the sentence in capital cases or by more narrowly defining the crimes for which the penalty is to be imposed" (*Furman v. Georgia*, 1972). Burger, Blackmun, and Powell also addressed the issue of public opinion in their dissent, explaining that public opinion polls largely indicate support for the death penalty.

The *Furman* decision resulted in the reversal of over 600 death sentences in 39 states (Banner, 2002). But what were the long-term implications of *Furman*? We know that capital punishment is still in existence, so what happened? If states hoped to persuade the Court to allow the use of the death penalty again, they would have to make some changes. They were essentially left with two options if they hoped to comply with the Court's ruling in *Furman*. One option was for states to attach mandatory death penalty sentences to certain crimes, which would prevent randomness in application (Bedau, 1982). Although such an option may have intuitive appeal, it is not new, and as we already learned in Chapter 2, this practice is not always effective because it can lead to negative implications in society (jury nullification, etc.). The other option would be to set standards for juries and judges that would guide their decision-making processes, thus addressing concerns of arbitrary application (Bedau, 1982). It would not be long until the Court revisited these issues.

GREGG V. GEORGIA (1976)

Just four years after *Furman*, the U.S. Supreme Court granted writ of certiorari in *Gregg v. Georgia* (1976) to revisit the issue of capital punishment. Troy Gregg was a white man charged with armed robbery and murder in Georgia. In November 1973, Gregg and his friend Floyd Allen were hitchhiking in Florida when Fred Simmons and Bob Moore gave them a ride. The four eventually stopped at a highway rest stop. Allen told police that while Simmons and Moore were out of the car, Gregg pulled out a .25 caliber pistol and waited for the two men to return. When they returned, Gregg fired three shots, knocking both men down. Then Gregg fired two more shots at close range into each man's head, killing them both. He subsequently stole items from the pair. Gregg told a different story (that he killed the men in self-defense), but the jury did not buy it and found him guilty. He was subsequently sentenced to death.

The U.S. Supreme Court decided to rule on the issue of whether or not the death penalty for murder was constitutional (Eighth and Fourteenth Amendments). Following Justice Burger's lead in *Furman*, Georgia created new death penalty provisions in accordance with the Court's ruling, hoping they would pass constitutional muster. Gregg argued that Georgia's new provisions still failed to prevent the random application of the death penalty (*Gregg v. Georgia*, 1976).

Georgia, like other states, adopted a variation of the bifurcated system set forth in the **Model Penal Code**. The Model Penal Code is a quasi-criminal code adopted by the American Legal Institute (ALI), a highly regarded non-profit organization in the legal community. The ALI was created by a prominent group of attorneys, judges, and legal academics who sought to provide legal

FIGURE 3.2 *Gregg v. Georgia* (1976)

professionals and legislators with a written guide and recommendations for applying criminal law. The code outlined the way that capital punishment *ought* to be administered according to ALI members. Specifically, it recommended the use of a two-phase provision for capital cases requiring both a guilt and penalty phase. The first phase is the traditional trial phase in which guilt must be proven in order to move on to the second phase. The second phase occurs when the actual sentence is determined (death, life without parole, etc.) (Steiker & Steiker, 2010). The Model Penal Code specified that the death penalty would only be appropriate for the crime of murder. Furthermore, juries (or judges) must consider both aggravating and mitigating factors when determining whether a death sentence is appropriate.

Aggravating factors are those that increase an offender's level of culpability or the severity of the crime. For example, if a person intentionally tortures and kills another person, then the act of torture may be considered an aggravating factor to the murder. **Mitigating factors** then decrease offender culpability or the severity of the crime. If a person with intellectual impairments commits murder, for instance, then the offender's mental capacity may be considered a mitigating factor in his or her case. The Model Penal Code lists eight of each aggravating and mitigating factors and requires that at least one aggravating factor be present with no mitigating factors substantial enough to negate a death sentence in order for the death penalty to be a sentencing option (Steiker & Steiker, 2010). Though adopted by the ALI in 1962, it was not until the Court ruled in *Furman*, and then *Gregg*, that the Model Penal Code provisions were recognized. In *Gregg*, Georgia's new capital punishment statute allowed jurors to consider aggravating and mitigating circumstances, but required the finding of at least one of Georgia's ten statutorily defined aggravating factors (*Gregg v. Georgia*, 1976).

Though the ALI had always been careful not to take a formal position on capital punishment (for or against), in 2009, it announced that the Model Penal Code would no longer contain capital punishment provisions. The ALI grew tired of America's experiment with capital punishment and declared the practice incapable of meeting even minimal standards of adequacy; thus, reformation attempts were deemed futile and the portion of the Model Penal Code that addressed the death penalty was removed (Steiker & Steiker, 2010). The ALI opted to send a clear message—it is time to abolish capital punishment in the United States.

In July 1976, the U.S. Supreme Court upheld Gregg's death sentence in a 7-2 decision, effectively reinstating the death penalty (see Figure 3.2). The Court found Georgia's newly adopted process for capital cases constitutional, rejecting Gregg's claims to the contrary. His death sentence was affirmed. The night before his execution, however, Gregg escaped from prison (making him the first Georgia prisoner to ever escape from death row). Ironically, he was killed the following evening in a bar fight.

Concurring Opinions

Seven justices affirmed Gregg's death sentence, but their decisions were broken into three separate concurring opinions. Justice Stewart wrote for the majority and was joined by Justices Powell and Stevens. The justices reached three conclusions in their joint opinion. First, they declared that the death penalty for crimes of murder, in some cases, is constitutional, acknowledging that both retribution and deterrence are valid punishment justifications. Capital punishment, the justices explained, has been a widely accepted practice since the birth of our Constitution and still is, as evidenced by the federal government and the 35 states that redrafted their capital punishment statutes since the *Furman* ruling in hopes of reinstituting the practice. Second, they addressed the revisions made by Georgia to improve the issue of arbitrary application. The justices applauded the promise of a bifurcated system because it allows for careful consideration of capital cases. Third, the justices remarked on the individual consideration each case is given under Georgia's new system with regard to careful review of the specific circumstances in each case and the defendant's character. They noted that this new process allows several outlets for mercy or less severe punishments (plea bargaining, juror discretion, and pardoning authority by the governor to commute death sentences). The Court also pointed to the built-in safeguard by Georgia's Supreme Court; the court automatically reviews each death sentence and compares it to other cases and defendants with similar backgrounds to ensure fair application.

Justice White, Chief Justice Burger, and Justice Rehnquist issued an opinion together that essentially echoed the same sentiments of Justices Stewart, Powell, and Stevens. Justice Blackmun also concurred, but did not issue an opinion.

Dissenting Opinions

In line with their opinions in *Furman*, Justices Brennan and Marshall split from the rest of the Court and, again, reiterated their reason(s) for dissenting. Both justices maintained that capital punishment is categorically unconstitutional and serves no penal purpose that cannot otherwise be addressed with the lesser sentence of lifetime imprisonment (*Gregg v. Georgia*, 1976).

The message by the Court in *Gregg* was that states could once again proceed with executing capital defendants as long as they implement a system, like Georgia's, that would limit the discretion of the sentencing authority. The *Furman* and *Gregg* decisions resulted in more than just stirring up the death penalty debate; due process was dramatically expanded in capital cases to what has been aptly labeled **super due process** (Radin, 1980). Now that capital defendants are provided with two separate judicial proceedings, they have more rights which, in turn, translates into the need for more resources. Consider how many resources are utilized in the traditional trial phase of our system (to prove guilt or innocence); now think about the amount of resources needed for the penalty phase where the matter in question is quite literally one of life or death. Super due process is expensive, as you will learn in Chapter 11.

Now that the U.S. Supreme Court had ruled the death penalty per se did not violate the Eighth and Fourteenth Amendments, the Court would move on to clarify the many other questions surrounding capital punishment.

Additional Case of Interest

Woodson v. North Carolina (1976): The Court declared mandatory death sentences unconstitutional. Recall that the only other solution for eliminating the issue of discriminatory application would be for states to create mandatory death penalty statutes for certain crimes. Indeed, some states tried just that and on the same day that *Gregg* was decided, the Court issued its ruling in *Woodson*. The Court took issue with mandatory death sentences because they fail to take into consideration the individual characteristics and history of the defendant.

COKER V. GEORGIA (1977)

The U.S. Supreme Court granted a writ of certiorari in the case of *Coker v. Georgia* (1977) one year after *Gregg*. The issue before the Court was whether or not it is constitutional, according to the Eighth and Fourteenth Amendments, to sentence a

FIGURE 3.3   *Coker v. Georgia,* 1977

person to death for the crime of rape. In September 1974, Ehrlich Anthony Coker, a white male, escaped from a state prison in Georgia where he was serving several life sentences for rape, murder, and kidnapping. His first victim had been a 16-year-old female whom he raped and stabbed to death in 1971. Eight months later, Coker victimized another 16-year-old female. He raped and brutally beat her with a club and then dragged her body to a wooded area, where she was left to die (*Coker v. Georgia*, 1977). Coker had been incarcerated for approximately 18 months when he managed to escape from the prison.

Coker entered the home of Allen and Elnita Carver in the small town of Waycross, Georgia. The Carvers were a young couple that just had a baby and were sitting at their kitchen table when Coker forcibly entered their home brandishing a large piece of wood as a weapon. He tied up Mr. Carver and proceeded to rape Mrs. Carver at knifepoint. Mr. Carver was forced to listen to his wife being assaulted as he remained helplessly bound in the other room. Coker then kidnapped Mrs. Carver, taking the couple's vehicle and threatening to kill Mrs. Carver if her husband called the police (*Bangor Daily News*, 1977; Karp, 1978).

Soon after terrorizing the Carvers, Coker was apprehended by authorities. He was tried and convicted of rape, kidnapping, armed robbery, prison escape, and motor vehicle theft. This time Coker was sentenced to die (by electric chair) for the rape of Mrs. Carver. Georgia was the only state to authorize capital punishment for adult rape at the time; North Carolina and Louisiana's mandatory capital rape statutes had recently been invalidated by *Woodson v. North Carolina* (1976) (Bedau, 1982).

In a 7-2 vote (see Figure 3.3), the Court agreed with Coker that a death sentence would be a "grossly disproportionate and excessive punishment" for rape (*Coker v. Georgia*, 1977). Coker's death sentence was reversed and he is currently serving multiple life sentences for his crimes.

Concurring Opinions

Justice White announced the judgment for the Court with Justices Stewart, Blackmun, and Stevens joining. They explained that the Eighth Amendment protects us from more than just punishments that are *cruel*; it also protects us from those that are excessive or out of proportion to the crime committed. The justices additionally reminded us that the Eighth Amendment should carry a fluid interpretation that changes as we grow and evolve as a society. Indeed, the Court utilizes the **evolving standards of decency** standard of review for analyzing controversial topics such as the death penalty (see also Chapter 5). This type of review allows the Court to consider how the framers of the Constitution might have acted today when determining whether or not a certain current punishment is in violation of the Eighth Amendment.

As with many controversial cases, the Court weighs heavily on the practices used by states at the time a case is decided. In *Coker*, it considered what most states had in the way of capital rape statutes. Given that Georgia was the only state with valid capital rape statutes, and that juries in Georgia rarely imposed the death penalty for rape, the Court determined that the practice was generally rejected by modern society. The Court reasoned that if Georgia law did not authorize death sentences for murderers unless there were aggravating circumstances, it would certainly not make sense to execute a person for the lesser crime of rape. Nonetheless, the justices were careful to acknowledge the serious nature of rape and ultimately concluded:

> Rape is without doubt deserving of serious punishment; but in terms of moral depravity and of the injury to the person and to the public, it does not compare with murder, which does involve the unjustified taking of human life. . . . The murderer kills; the rapist, if no more than that, does not. Life is over for the victim of the murderer; for the rape victim, life may not be nearly so happy as it was, but it is not over and normally is not beyond repair. (*Coker v. Georgia*, 1977)

Justices Brennan and Marshall issued separate concurring opinions, but once again asserted absolute opposition to the death penalty under all circumstances. Justice Powell joined with the majority, but issued a partial dissent. Powell believed that the death penalty in Coker's case was unconstitutional because the defendant's actions did not amount to "excessive brutality" (*Coker v. Georgia*, 1977). He did not agree, however, that the Court should have issued a sweeping opinion that would effectively prevent states from creating capital rape statutes entirely. Powell felt that the Court's decision unnecessarily restricts states from creating more appropriate death statutes for rape.

Dissenting Opinions

Chief Justice Burger wrote a dissent joined by Justice Rehnquist. Like Powell, they believed that the Court should have limited its decision to the specific issues in Coker's case, rather than deciding on the broader ruling of whether the death penalty is constitutional for rape. They reasoned that because Coker was a serial rapist who had escaped from prison and then committed another rape almost immediately, it cannot be presumed that a prison term would sufficiently prevent him from victimizing others. According to this logic, the death penalty might be a useful mechanism to protect society from offenders who cannot be deterred by prison.

Burger and Rehnquist also took issue with claims by the majority that the death penalty for rape is not proportionate to the severity of the crime.

They argued that rape is much more serious than characterized by the majority:

> A rapist not only violates a victim's privacy and personal integrity, but inevitably causes serious psychological as well as physical harm in the process. The long-range effect upon the victim's life and health is likely to be irreparable; it is impossible to measure the harm which results. . . . Rape is not a mere physical attack—it is destructive of the human personality. . . . Victims may recover from the physical damage of knife or bullet wounds, or a beating with fists or a club, but recovery from such a gross assault on the human personality is not healed by medicine or surgery. (*Coker v. Georgia*, 1977)

Despite the Court's ruling in *Coker*, some states would go on to create statutes authorizing capital punishment for the rape of a child. Recall one of the arguments made by the majority of justices in *Coker* to justify their ruling—rape does not amount to loss of life—so it seemed that the same constitutional challenges would attach to the crime of child rape as well. The Court eventually clarified its position on the matter in *Kennedy v. Louisiana* (2008).

Additional Case of Interest

Kennedy v. Louisiana (2008): Louisiana authorized the death penalty for child rape and the Court ruled that the statute violated the Eighth Amendment for the same reasons outlined in *Coker*. The crime of child rape cannot be punishable by death.

LOCKETT V. OHIO (1978)

The Court granted a writ of certiorari in a pair of cases, *Lockett v. Ohio* (1978) and *Bell v. Ohio* (1978), to decide whether or not Ohio's capital murder statutes were too restrictive because they did not allow individual considerations of the defendant and the crime committed. Specifically, the statute in question limited the number of mitigating circumstances that jurors were allowed to consider.

Sandra Lockett was a 21-year-old black woman from Ohio convicted of aggravated robbery and aggravated murder. Lockett befriended Al Parker and Nathan Dew while she was away from her home and living in New Jersey. Parker and Dew traveled back to Ohio with Lockett. When it was time for them to return to New Jersey, they did not have the funds to make the trip. Lockett allegedly suggested that they rob a nearby grocery store where she knew the clerk. By the time the group devised their plan, however, the store was closed so they decided to rob a nearby pawnshop instead. The plan was

FIGURE 3.4   *Lockett v. Ohio* (1978)

for Lockett's brother and Dew to enter the pawnshop and browse for merchandise. Parker would then enter and pretend to be interested in buying a gun. Parker would arrange to have the bullets for the gun prior to entering the shop so that he could then load the gun and rob the clerk. Lockett would be the getaway driver because she did not want to be recognized. The plan was carried out, but went awry when Parker loaded the gun. The clerk tried to grab the loaded gun and Parker pulled the trigger, shooting and killing the clerk instantly (O'Shea, 1999).

Parker was charged with aggravated robbery and murder, which made him a candidate for the death penalty in Ohio. He took a deal and agreed to testify against his co-defendants in exchange for provisions that would remove the possibility of him receiving the death penalty, despite the fact that he was directly responsible for the death of the pawnshop clerk. Lockett, Lockett's brother, and Dew were convicted of aggravated robbery and murder as well. At the time, an Ohio statute allowed juries to circumvent the requirement of intent by assigning equal blame to offenders who aid and abet in capital crimes as if they were the principal offenders themselves (commonly known as the felony-murder rule); therefore, Lockett was eligible to receive a death sentence because of her involvement as the getaway driver. Dew did not receive the death penalty because he met one of Ohio's three mitigating circumstances that preclude offenders from being sentenced to death—his actions were "primarily the product of mental deficiency" (*Lockett v. Ohio*, 1978). Lockett wanted a trial and the jury found her guilty; the trial judge sentenced her to death.

At the heart of the *Lockett* case was the Ohio statute that required the imposition of the death penalty if at least one of the three following mitigating circumstances were not present: (1) "the victim induced or facilitated the offense";

(2) the offense would not likely have been committed but for the fact that the defendant was "under duress, coercion, or strong provocation"; or (3) the criminal act was "primarily the product of psychosis or mental deficiency" (*Lockett v. Ohio*, 1978). A pre-sentence report and several psychological reports indicated that Lockett had a low IQ and a minor criminal history, and was likely to rehabilitate, but did not find her to have "psychosis" or "mental deficiency" as specified by the third element in the statute. The other two elements were not formally addressed at sentencing because they were clearly not issues in Lockett's case. The trial judge, therefore, explained he had no choice but to sentence Lockett to death.

The U.S. Supreme Court issued a 7-1 vote (with Justice Brennan abstaining), siding with Lockett's claims that her Eighth and Fourteenth Amendment rights had been violated (see Figure 3.4). Ohio's death statute was declared unconstitutional. Lockett's death sentence was reversed and she is currently serving a life sentence.

Concurring Opinions

Chief Justice Burger and Justices Stewart, Powell, and Stevens issued a joint opinion. The justices asserted that the Eighth and Fourteenth Amendments require all aspects of a defendant (character, age, intent, etc.), his or her criminal history, and circumstances wherein a defendant asserts a lesser role in the offense, be considered as mitigating factors in capital cases (*Lockett v. Ohio*, 1978). Further, they explained that capital cases are unique in that there needs to be a stronger emphasis placed on the unique characteristics of the defendant. The justices concluded that any attempt made by legislators to prevent a sentencing authority from weighing the above mitigating factors and mandating a death sentence absent the findings of a few statutorily set mitigating factors is "incompatible with the commands of the Eighth and Fourteenth Amendments" (*Lockett v. Ohio*, 1978).

Justices Blackmun, Marshall, and White each issued their own opinions. Justice Blackmun agreed with most of the majority's opinion, but addressed additional issues. First, he asserted that there should have been more of an emphasis placed on the lack of the *mens rea* (intent) element. Clearly, Lockett had no intention of causing the death of the clerk as the getaway driver. Second, he addressed Ohio's statutory provision that allowed full sentencing discretion by the judge for imposing the death penalty only if the defendant pleads guilty or no contest, not if he or she goes to trial. This issue was actually raised by Lockett but not considered by the majority (at least in writing). Justice Marshall responded as he always has in each of the previous capital cases heard by the Court—the death penalty is unconstitutional in all circumstances. Justice White, like Blackmun, was particularly concerned with the fact that Lockett did not intend for the victim to die and chastised the majority for largely ignoring the felony-murder rule issue.

Dissenting Opinion

Justice Rehnquist was the sole dissenter in *Lockett*. He did not agree that the Court should force states to consider essentially unbounded mitigation in capital cases. Rehnquist reasoned that in doing so, the Court would be reverting back to the initial problems that were raised in *Furman*—too much discretion results in the arbitrary use of capital punishment.

Additional Cases of Interest

Eddings v. Oklahoma (1982): The U.S. Supreme Court clarified the language from *Lockett* that required courts to consider mitigating circumstances in a defendant's case. The Court ruled that trial courts must consider all mitigation offered by the defense in capital cases.

Enmund v. Florida (1982): The Court held that it is unconstitutional to impose a death sentence on a defendant who did not kill, attempt to kill, or intend for a killing to happen. This ruling essentially invalidated the felony-murder rule for capital cases when the above circumstances are applicable.

Lockhart v. McCree (1986): The removal of prospective jurors who state that they oppose capital punishment and cannot impose the death penalty, under any circumstances, does not violate a defendant's Sixth Amendment rights.

Payne v. Tennessee (1990): The Court ruled that the Eighth Amendment does not prohibit the jury in a capital case from considering the impact that a victim's death has had on the surviving members of the family. The pain and suffering of family members is relevant information for prosecutors to present to capital sentencing juries.

MCCLESKEY V. KEMP (1987)

In 1987, the U.S. Supreme Court decided to issue yet another landmark ruling in a Georgia death penalty case, that of Warren McCleskey. McCleskey's argument centered on the issue of racial discrimination in capital sentencing, echoing Justice Douglas's concerns in *Furman*. Warren McCleskey, a black man from Georgia, robbed a furniture store with three accomplices. All four of the men were armed. McCleskey went through the front entrance and forced customers to lie on the ground, while the other three made their way into the store through the back entrance to secure its employees. They bound the employees with rope

Chapter 3 THE FOUNDATIONAL CASES: *FURMAN* TO *STANFORD*

FIGURE 3.5 *McCleskey v. Kemp* (1987)

and duct tape. At some point, a silent alarm was triggered and Frank Schlatt, a white police officer, responded to it. Schlatt entered the front of the building and was shot two times. The fatal bullet hit him in the face. McCleskey admitted to taking part in the robbery, but denied shooting Schlatt. The bullets, however, matched McCleskey's gun and he was convicted of armed robbery and murder. During the sentencing phase, jurors found two aggravating circumstances to justify a death sentence: (1) The murder happened during an armed robbery and (2) the victim was an on-duty police officer. There were no mitigating factors presented on McCleskey's behalf (*McCleskey v. Kemp*, 1987).

McCleskey's attorneys argued that America's experiment with capital sentencing in the years after *Furman* failed to "fix" the problems with discriminatory application, especially with regard to race. They supported this position with a statistical study conducted by Baldus and colleagues (1983). The **Baldus study** examined over 2,000 capital cases in Georgia during the 1970s (also see Chapter 8). Researchers studied the effects of race on sentencing decisions by examining 230 variables. They examined key variables such as the race of both the victims and the defendants. The study revealed that race did indeed play a role in Georgia death penalty decisions. When controlling for nonracial variables (aggravating circumstances, etc.), Baldus and his colleagues found that the odds of receiving death sentences for defendants (regardless of race) who murdered white victims were 4.3 times the odds of receiving death sentences for those who killed black victims. More specifically, black defendants whose victims were white had the greatest chance of receiving a death sentence (*McCleskey v. Kemp*, 1987).

The U.S. Supreme Court accepted the validity of the study, but focused its attention on whether such a study should be grounds for declaring the death penalty unconstitutional. The Court issued its ruling in a 5-4 vote (see Figure 3.5) upholding McCleskey's death sentence and, in effect, the constitutionality of capital punishment once again. Warren McCleskey was executed in Georgia's electric chair in 1991.

Concurring Opinions

Justice Powell delivered the opinion of the Court and was joined by Chief Justice Rehnquist and Justices White, O'Connor, and Scalia. Their opinion rested on several key issues. McCleskey alleged that his Fourteenth Amendment equal protection rights were being violated. He based this allegation entirely on the Baldus study findings. The majority explained that in order to successfully argue a violation of this magnitude, McCleskey would have to show purposeful discrimination. McCleskey, however, did not provide any specific information in his case to support the claims that his particular death sentence resulted from racially discriminatory decisions. Under McCleskey's reasoning and application of the Baldus study, in Georgia, all black capital defendants whose victims were white would have the same argument. His claims essentially attacked discretionary decision-making as the culprit for racial discrimination across the board.

While upholding the validity of the study, the justices argued that McCleskey would need to do more; he would have to proffer evidence to show he was specifically discriminated against. A mere study that concludes a reality of racial discrimination in some cases does not *prove* that discriminatory practices were specifically at issue in McCleskey's case. In other words, the Court wanted to ensure that Fourteenth Amendment claims like those of McCleskey would depend on the individual defendants and facts of their cases, rather than generalizing Baldus's study (or any study for that matter) to all cases. As it opined in *Gregg*, the Court once again recognized the importance of discretion in our justice system:

> Discretion in the criminal justice system offers substantial benefits to the criminal defendant. Not only can a jury decline to impose the death sentence, it can decline to convict or choose to convict of a lesser offense. Whereas decisions against a defendant's interest may be reversed by the trial judge or on appeal, these discretionary exercises of leniency are final and unreviewable. . . . [T]he power to be lenient [also] is the power to discriminate. (*McCleskey v. Kemp*, 1987)

The justices further explained that arguments like that of McCleskey are best addressed by legislative bodies. They reasoned that legislatures are able to view studies like that of Baldus and colleagues (1983) in the context of their "own local conditions and with a flexibility of approach that is not available to the courts" (*McCleskey v. Kemp*, 1987). Another concern by the majority was that if McCleskey's claims were to prevail, then the floodgates would be open for certain groups (other minority groups, females, etc.) to claim that they, too, suffer from discriminatory application of the death penalty. This type of reasoning adheres to the slippery slope theory—if one event occurs, a chain of worse events will inevitably follow.

Dissenting Opinions

Justices Brennan, Marshall, Blackmun, and Stevens joined together in the majority of their dissent(s) (some wrote portions apart from the others). As expected, Brennan and Marshall reiterated their longstanding belief that the death penalty always amounts to cruel and unusual punishment. The dissenters addressed each of the major justifications cited by the majority for upholding McCleskey's death sentence.

With regard to discretion, they argued that the Baldus study did indicate the greater likelihood of black defendants receiving a death sentence and, therefore, the general devaluing of their lives. They reasoned: "When confronted with evidence that race more likely than not plays such a role in a capital sentencing system, it is plainly insufficient to say that the importance of discretion demands that the risk be higher before we will act—for in such a case the very end that discretion is designed to serve is being undermined" (*McCleskey v. Kemp*, 1987). The minority (dissenters) thus took issue with the majority's acceptance of the Baldus study's validity, but refusal to count the "probability of prejudice insufficient to create constitutional concern" (*McCleskey v. Kemp*, 1987). If racial discrimination is a reality of capital punishment, as identified in the Baldus study, then the practice ought to be eliminated according to the minority opinion, even if McCleskey could not prove prejudice specific to his own case.

The justices also disagreed with the majority that the issues raised by McCleskey are best addressed by state legislatures, arguing that it is precisely the role of the U.S. Supreme Court to interject themselves in such matters when the decision-makers in our system may not be able to see beyond the strong desire to punish: "Those whom we would banish from society or from the human community itself often speak in too faint a voice to be heard above society's demand for punishment. It is the particular role of courts to hear these voices, for the Constitution declares that the majoritarian chorus may not alone dictate the conditions of social life" (*McCleskey v. Kemp*, 1987).

The minority criticized the majority for applying the slippery slope theory to McCleskey's case by citing concerns of future floodgates of constitutional challenges. They likened the majority's position to an absurd fear of "too much justice" (*McCleskey v. Kemp*, 1987).

McCleskey was particularly significant because it was the last case before the Court to challenge the constitutionality of the death penalty (in general) and, in effect, ended the avenue for courts to rely on statistical studies to challenge the same. With a 5-4 vote, we know that the decision could have very well followed the path of *Furman* if only one justice had come to a different conclusion. Indeed, Justice Powell (the writer for the majority) publicly acknowledged that he had reservations about the *McCleskey* decision and even admitted that he would have changed his vote if given the opportunity. Although much too late for Warren McCleskey, Powell reached the conclusion that the death penalty was not a workable punishment under any circumstances (*The New York Times*, 1994).

Additional Cases of Interest

Turner v. Murray (1986): Capital defendants, in cases involving interracial crime, may inform potential jurors of the victim's race and question them about racial prejudice in an effort to obtain an unbiased jury.

Miller-El v. Dretke (2005): The Court ruled that it is unconstitutional for prosecutors to use peremptory challenges to exclude jurors based on race; the Court had already made this rule in an earlier case—*Batson v. Kentucky* (1986). Prosecutors in Miller-El's case excluded 10 out of 11 black jurors that were eligible to serve on his jury; the Court would not accept that the exclusions were based on happenstance and found that Miller-El's Fourteenth Amendment equal protection rights had been violated.

Snyder v. Louisiana (2008): The Court ruled, once again, on the issue of prosecutors using peremptory challenges to exclude jurors based on race. It essentially upheld the ruling in *Miller-El v. Dretke* (2005), also finding that Snyder's Fourteenth Amendment rights were violated.

STANFORD V. KENTUCKY (1989)

The *Stanford* ruling was a decision by the Court involving a pair of juvenile death penalty cases. The question before the Court was whether imposing the death penalty on juveniles who are 16 or 17 years of age is constitutional. The primary case was that of Kevin Stanford. Stanford was 17 years old when he and a friend decided to rob a convenience store in Kentucky. They

Chapter 3 THE FOUNDATIONAL CASES: *FURMAN* TO *STANFORD*

FIGURE 3.6 *Stanford v. Kentucky* (1989)

stole 300 cartons of cigarettes, a couple gallons of gasoline, and cash. Their crimes did not end there, however. The pair also kidnapped, raped, and killed the 20-year-old gas station attendant, Barbel Poore. After they repeatedly raped and sodomized Poore, they drove her to a nearby secluded area, where Stanford proceeded to shoot Poore, at pointblank range, in her face and then again in her head. Later, Stanford recounted the crime to a correctional officer, explaining: "I had to shoot her, [she] lived next door to me and she would recognize me. . . . I guess we could have tied her up or something or beat [her up] . . . and tell her if she tells, we would kill her . . ." (*Stanford v. Kentucky*, 1989). Stanford reportedly laughed while explaining the details of the crime to the officer.

Stanford's case was waived to adult court because he was charged with a capital offense and had a lengthy juvenile record. He was convicted of murder, sodomy, and robbery (among other crimes). Stanford was sentenced to death. On appeal to the Supreme Court, he asserted that capital punishment for juveniles violates the Eighth Amendment. He argued that prosecutors seldom seek the death penalty for juveniles, and even when they do, juries are reluctant to impose it. He further argued that state laws have long recognized the need for differential treatment of juveniles due to age and limited decision-making capabilities (e.g., laws that restrict driving privileges, purchasing and consuming alcohol, and voting). In a marginal 5-4 vote (see Figure 3.6), the Court disagreed with Stanford and affirmed the judgments of the lower courts. Stanford's death sentence was not in violation of the Eighth Amendment's cruel and unusual punishment protection; thus, the execution of 16- or 17-year-olds by states that wish to do so is permitted (*Stanford v. Kentucky*, 1989).

Concurring Opinions

Justice Scalia wrote the majority opinion and was joined by Chief Justice Rehnquist and Justices White and Kennedy in various parts of the decision. Justice O'Connor wrote a separate concurrence. The majority arrived at its decision by utilizing *evolving standards of decency*. A review of the statutes in the 37 death penalty states revealed that 15 states did not permit death sentences for juveniles 16 and under; 12 states banned it for juveniles 17 and under. The majority's conclusion was that the various state restrictions did not constitute a national consensus on banning capital punishment for juvenile offenders (*Stanford v. Kentucky*, 1989).

The Court countered Stanford's claims that prosecutors and juries rarely utilize the death penalty by explaining that such behaviors do not "establish constitutional standards" (*Stanford v. Kentucky*, 1989). The Court also clarified the difference between state laws governing legal ages for certain activities and imposing the death penalty on juveniles:

> There is no relevance to the state laws cited by petitioners which set 18 or more as the legal age for engaging in various activities, ranging from driving to drinking alcoholic beverages to voting. Those laws operate in gross, and do not conduct individualized maturity tests for each driver, drinker, or voter; an age appropriate in the vast majority of cases must therefore be selected. In the realm of capital punishment, however, individualized consideration is a constitutional requirement. Twenty-nine States, including Kentucky and Missouri, have codified this requirement in laws specifically designating age as a mitigating factor that capital sentencers must be permitted to consider. (*Stanford v. Kentucky*, 1989)

Justice O'Connor agreed with the majority that no national consensus had been reached on the issue of capital punishment for juveniles, but believed that the Court had a constitutional obligation to consider "proportionality analyses and should consider age-based statutory classifications that are relevant to that analysis" (*Stanford v. Kentucky*, 1989).

Dissenting Opinions

Justice Brennan wrote the dissent and was joined by Justices Marshall, Blackmun, and Stevens. The justices addressed the question of national consensus, disagreeing with the majority that no national consensus on capital punishment for juveniles had been reached. Indeed, they countered with the argument that a majority of states do not allow the death penalty to be imposed on juveniles. Their rationale was that when one adds the number of states which have the death penalty, but not for juveniles (12), with the number of states that do not permit the death penalty for any offenders (15), a total of 27 states do not execute juveniles—thus, a majority of states do not permit the practice and a national consensus actually exists in favor of abolishing the punishment entirely for juveniles.

The justices agreed with Stanford that the rare use of the death penalty for juveniles by prosecutors and juries is in itself an argument that the punishment is "unusual," thus violating the cruel and unusual punishment clause of the Eighth Amendment. At the time, juveniles on death row constituted approximately 1.37% of the total death row population (30 out of 2,186 inmates) (*Stanford v. Kentucky*, 1989). The dissenting opinion also addressed the issue of differential treatment of juveniles by states in other legislative matters (drinking, driving, voting, etc.). It rejected the arguments made by the majority and sided with Stanford that the implementation of such laws reflects a general acknowledgment that juveniles are not as responsible and, therefore, not as blameworthy. Accordingly, subjecting juveniles to the death penalty is unconstitutional. The dissenters decided to go ahead and entertain the majority's argument, however, that each case ought to be considered individually, rather than by gross analysis. In refuting the majority, the dissenters pointed to the findings by experts who evaluated Kevin Stanford. The juvenile division of the Kentucky district court found that Stanford:

> . . . has a low internalization of the values and morals of society and lacks social skills. That he does possess an institutionalized personality and has, in effect, because of his chaotic family life and lack of treatment, become socialized in delinquent behavior. That he is emotionally immature and could be amenable to treatment if properly done on a long term basis of psychotherap[eu]tic intervention and reality based therapy for socialization and drug therapy in a residential facility. (*Stanford v. Kentucky*, 1989)

If the majority wanted each case to be considered individually according to an offender's maturity level among other considerations used to determine culpability, then how did Stanford receive a death sentence? Stanford's trial court findings reveal that he was emotionally immature and would even be a good candidate for treatment.

Finally, the justices argued that neither retribution nor deterrence is served by executing juvenile offenders. Because juveniles lack absolute culpability for their crimes, retribution is not a valid punishment consideration. And the

TABLE 3.1   Foundational Cases Summary

Name	Issue	Ruling
Furman v. Georgia 408 U.S. 238 (1972)	Capital punishment process	The capital punishment process is unconstitutional as administered at the time.
Gregg v. Georgia 428 U.S. 153 (1976)	Capital punishment process	The death penalty is constitutional for extreme cases, as long as the sentencing process is carefully employed.
Coker v. Georgia 433 U.S. 584 (1977)	Rape	The death penalty is an unconstitutional punishment for rape.
Lockett v. Ohio 438 U.S. 586 (1978)	Sentencing authority discretion/mitigation	The sentencing authority must consider a variety of mitigating factors in capital cases.
McCleskey v. Kemp 481 U.S. 279 (1987)	Race	A defendant must show purposeful discrimination in order for a capital case to be unconstitutional. This may not be done by generalizing academic studies to individual cases.
Stanford v. Kentucky 492 U.S. 361 (1989)	Executing juveniles	It is constitutional to sentence juveniles (ages 16 and 17) to death.

deterrence argument operates on "the assumption that we are rational beings who always think before we act, and then base our actions on a careful calculation of the gains and losses involved" (*Stanford v. Kentucky*, 1989). Clearly, juveniles are not always capable of engaging in this type of thoughtful consideration before acting; thus, deterrence considerations are not applicable. Essentially, the justices were making the point that when considering that retribution and deterrence are the only valid punishment purposes served by capital punishment, when both fail to apply to a certain group of offenders, then the punishment is no longer valid.

Additional Cases of Interest

Thompson v. Oklahoma (1988): In this case, decided just one year before *Stanford*, the Court ruled that it is unconstitutional to execute juveniles who committed crimes at the age of 15.

Roper v. Simmons (2005): Like *Stanford*, this case is another foundational case involving the constitutionality of executing juveniles (discussed at length in the next chapter). The Court essentially overturned the *Stanford* decision, thereby declaring it unconstitutional to execute juveniles of any age under 18.

SUMMARY

This chapter provides an overview of the foundational U.S. Supreme Court case rulings on capital punishment in the modern era (Table 3.1). We began our timeline with the *Furman* and *Gregg* cases and explored the significance of the overturning and then reestablishment of the death penalty. We then moved on to the *Coker* case that resulted in the Court banning the practice of executing offenders for rape. Then we explored the Court's stance on the importance of mitigation as part of determining who should get the death penalty. The *McCleskey* case was a controversial ruling with regard to racial biases in our system and the use of statistical research to illustrate the same. We wrapped up the chapter with a discussion of the *Stanford* decision, the case where the Court found the execution of juveniles constitutional. Each of these cases has greatly impacted the policy and practice of capital punishment in America. The next chapter picks up where we left off in this timeline—beginning with cases decided at the turn of the twenty-first century.

DISCUSSION QUESTIONS

1. How did the *Furman* decision impact capital punishment? Do you think *super due process* is necessary?
2. Why did the Court reinstate the death penalty in *Gregg v. Georgia* (1976)? How did Georgia restructure its capital punishment system and how did the Court respond to these changes?
3. What were the primary arguments made by the majority of justices in the *Coker* case and how did the dissenters respond?
4. Explain what the Baldus study is and its significance to capital punishment.
5. How did both the majority and dissenting justices arrive at different conclusions on the issue of national consensus in the *Stanford* case?

GLOSSARY

Aggravating factors: Factors that increase offender culpability or the severity of the crime.

Baldus Study: A study conducted by a university professor that found racially discriminatory application in capital cases in Georgia. This study's findings were at the center of debate in the *McCleskey* case.

Evolving standards of decency: A type of review that allows the Court to consider how the framers of the Constitution might have acted today when determining whether or not a certain current punishment is in violation of the Eighth Amendment.

Mitigating factors: Factors that diminish offender culpability or the severity of the crime.

Model Penal Code: A quasi-criminal code adopted by the American Legal Institute (ALI), a highly regarded non-profit organization in the legal community.

Super due process: The dramatic expansion of due process and the rights of capital defendants.

Per curiam decision: An unsigned opinion from the Court that is meant to represent the decision of the Court as an institution, rather than belonging to individual justices.

Writ of certiorari: An order issued to a lower court to send its record of a case to the Supreme Court for review.

REFERENCES

Baldus, D., C. Pulaski, and G. Woodworth. (1983). Comparative review of death sentences: An empirical study of the Georgia experience. *Journal of Criminal Law and Criminology, 74*(3), 661–753.

Bangor Daily News. (March 28, 1977). "Court to Decide if Death Is Just Penalty for Rape." http://news.google.com/newspapers?nid=2457&dat=19770328&id=_uIzAAAAIBAJ&sjid=YzgHAAAAIBAJ&pg=2498,3900517.

Banner, S. (2002). *The death penalty: An American history.* Cambridge, MA: Harvard University Press.

Bedau, H. (1982). *The death penalty in America.* New York: Oxford University Press.

Bell v. Ohio. (1978). 438 U.S. 637.

Coker v. Georgia. (1977). 433 U.S. 584.

Eddings v. Oklahoma. (1982). 455 U.S. 104.

Enmund v. Florida. (1982). 458 U.S. 782.

Furman v. Georgia. (1972). 408 U.S. 238.

Gregg v. Georgia. (1976). 428 U.S. 153.

Karp, D. (1978). *Coker v. Georgia*: Disproportionate punishment and the death penalty for rape. *Columbia Law Review, 78*(8), 1714–1730.

Lockett v. Ohio. (1978). 438 U.S. 586.

McCleskey v. Kemp. (1987). 481 U.S. 279.

The New York Times. (1994, June 11). "Justice Powell's New Wisdom." http://www.nytimes.com/1994/06/11/opinion/justice-powell-s-new-wisdom.html.

O'Shea, K. (1999). *Women and the death penalty in the United States, 1900–1998.* Westport, CT: Praeger.

Radin, M. (1980). Cruel punishment and respect for persons: Super due process for death. *Southern California Law Review, 53,* 1143–1185.

Robbins, I. (2012). Hiding behind the cloak of invisibility: The Supreme Court and per curiam opinions. *Tulane Law Review, 86,* 1197.

Stanford v. Kentucky. (1989). 492 U.S. 361.

Steiker, C., and J. Steiker. (2010). No more tinkering: The American Law Institute and death penalty provisions of the model penal code. *Texas Law Review, 89*(2), 353–365.

Stevens, L. (1978). *Death penalty: The case of life vs. death in the United States.* New York: Coward, McCann & Geoghegan.

CHAPTER 4

THE FOUNDATIONAL CASES: *ATKINS* TO *BAZE*

Scott Hain lived in Tulsa, Oklahoma, and was just 17 years old when he was arrested for the murders of Michael Haughton and Laura Sanders in 1987. Hain and his friend, Robert Lambert, had been drinking on the night that they encountered Haughton and Sanders in a bar parking lot as the couple walked to Haughton's car. Hain and Lambert approached the two and forced them into Haughton's car at knifepoint. After driving to a different location, Hain and Lambert robbed the couple and then forced them to get into the trunk of their own car. Lambert cut the gas line and set fire to the car before he and Hain left the scene, leaving Haughton and Sanders to burn to death in the trunk. The men could hear the screams of their victims as they walked away. Both Hain and Lambert were sentenced to death for their crimes.

Hain was a teenager when he committed these heinous acts. Hain's attorneys argued that he should not be executed because of his age, the circumstances of his childhood, and his drug addiction, and because he had no prior record of violent behavior. Hain experienced a tumultuous childhood—both parents were alcoholics who spent most of their nights at the local bar while their children had to fend for themselves at home, often having to make their own meals and get themselves ready for school in the morning. Hain was held back in the first and fifth grades, a possible indicator of developmental problems. His father was physically abusive and beat Hain with a wooden paddle. His father also introduced Hain to drugs. When he was around 13 years of age, Hain left home to live with a friend; he was doing hard drugs daily by 17. While on the streets, he met Lambert, who was four years older than him.

Should Hain have been sentenced to death despite his young age and the mitigating circumstances of his childhood? His lawyers asserted that he should have received life imprisonment. The courts disagreed, however, and he was sentenced to death. Hain was executed by lethal injection in 2003, nearly 16 years after the murders.

LEARNING OBJECTIVES

- Understand how the U.S. Supreme Court has guided the death penalty in both policy and practice.
- Discover the various death penalty-related issues that the U.S. Supreme Court has agreed to review.
- Learn how the Court has responded to claims that the death penalty violates the Eighth and Fourteenth Amendments.
- Know all of the landmark death penalty cases entailed in this chapter and the effects that they have had on capital punishment.
- Consider the issues that are likely to be reviewed by the U.S. Supreme Court in the near future based on the rulings discussed in this chapter.

As we will learn in this chapter, states are no longer permitted to sentence juveniles to death. Indeed, the U.S. Supreme Court declared the practice unconstitutional just two years after Hain was executed. This was a controversial practice even in 1987 when Hain was sentenced. Recall the Court's ruling in the 1989 *Stanford* case that upheld the death penalty for juveniles by a 5-4 marginal vote (Chapter 3). The justices in *Stanford* were deeply divided on the issue, as were the states, and it was only a matter of time before the Court would reconsider. There are many significant differences between adults and juveniles that impact culpability, thereby calling into question whether the *ultimate* penalty is appropriate for juveniles. The Court has addressed this and a number of other issues (executing offenders with mental disabilities, who can issue death sentences, appropriate methods of execution, etc.) pertaining to capital punishment that are discussed in this chapter.

This chapter picks up where Chapter 3 ended on the timeline of foundational U.S. Supreme Court cases. We will now review and discuss the cases of the twenty-first century to date. The rulings from *Atkins* to *Baze* represent the most recent Court decisions on capital punishment. As explained in the previous chapter, you will notice that for each case, an accompanying illustration shows which justices voted in the majority (on the top line) and which dissented (bottom line). The image of the presiding chief justice of the Court is highlighted. Additionally, the illustration indicates which president appointed each of the justices, so we have the context of their political ideologies.

ATKINS V. VIRGINIA (2002)

Like the *Stanford* case before it (see Chapter 3), the issue in *Atkins* centers on the question of *who* or *which types* of defendants can be executed. The specific question in *Atkins* relates to individuals with an intellectual disability (IIDs).

Chapter 4 THE FOUNDATIONAL CASES: *ATKINS* TO *BAZE*

FIGURE 4.1   *Atkins v. Virginia* (2002)

With the publication of the fifth edition of the **Diagnostic and Statistical Manual of Mental Disorders (DSM-V)** in 2013, this new terminology replaced the term "mental retardation." The DSM-V is a manual published by the American Psychiatric Association (APA) that outlines criteria for diagnosing mental disorders. Mental health professionals utilize the DSM-V for identifying a particular mental disorder. When an offender has been diagnosed with a mental disorder or disability, this bears significance in our criminal justice system because such a finding often mitigates criminal culpability. This, in turn, may very well determine the scope of that defendant's punishment.

Daryl Renard Atkins, an 18-year-old black man, was convicted of kidnapping, robbery, and murder in the summer of 1996. Atkins and a friend, William Jones, had been drinking and smoking marijuana for the better part of a day when they decided to go to a convenience store in Virginia to purchase more alcohol. At the store, they encountered Eric Nesbitt, a 21-year-old Air Force mechanic stationed nearby at Langley Air Force Base. They followed Nesbitt to his car and demanded that he give them the money from his wallet. The pair next drove Nesbitt to an ATM machine, where they forced him to withdraw more money ($200). Atkins and Jones then drove Nesbitt to a deserted field and shot him eight times with a semiautomatic handgun, despite Nesbitt's repeated pleas to spare his life. Nesbitt died and both men were charged with murder. Atkins and Jones each claimed that the other actually shot Nesbitt. The jury believed that Atkins shot the victim and he was sentenced to death (*Atkins v. Virginia*, 2002).

Atkins's defense attorneys argued that he should not be subjected to the death penalty because he suffered from an intellectual disability. After evaluating

Atkins, a forensic psychologist reported that he had an IQ of 59, which placed him in the IID category. The prosecutors put their own expert on the stand, who testified that Atkins was not an IID. As we will learn in Chapter 8, the average IQ score is 100 and scores within the 70–75 range are indicative of an IID; Atkins's IQ score thus placed him in the bottom (one) percentile. The evaluator based his conclusion on interviews of those who had known Atkins his entire life, Atkins's school records, and of course the results of his IQ test (*Atkins v. Virginia*, 2002).

The question before the U.S. Supreme Court was whether executing IIDs violates the Eighth Amendment. In a 6-3 vote (see Figure 4.1), the Court ruled that executing the "mentally retarded" is *excessive*, amounts to cruel and unusual punishment, and is not permitted by the U.S. Constitution. Atkins's death sentence was reversed and remanded for resentencing (*Atkins v. Virginia*, 2002).

Concurring Opinions

Justice Stevens delivered the Court's opinion and was joined by Justices O'Connor, Kennedy, Souter, Ginsburg, and Breyer. Of great importance to the Court's decision in this case was the *evolving standards of decency*. The justices utilized this standard when reaching a determination that a national consensus existed against executing IIDs. They began their consensus analysis by considering the number of states that had created legislation banning the execution of IIDs—18 states in total. After the Court's ruling in *Penry v. Lynaugh* in 1989 (upholding the practice of executing IIDs; see additional cases of interest below), 16 states had adopted laws to exempt IIDs from the death penalty, with six of them doing so in the two years prior to *Atkins*. The Court explained that more important than the numbers was the "consistency of the direction of change" (*Atkins v. Virginia*, 2002). Following this logic, the Court also remarked:

> Given the well-known fact that anticrime legislation is far more popular than legislation providing protections for persons guilty of violent crime, the large number of States prohibiting the execution of mentally retarded persons (and the complete absence of States passing legislation reinstating the power to conduct such executions) provides powerful evidence that today our society views mentally retarded offenders as categorically less culpable than the average criminal. . . . And it appears that even among those States that regularly execute offenders and that have no prohibition with regard to the mentally retarded, only five have executed offenders possessing a known IQ less than 70 since we decided *Penry*. The practice, therefore, has become truly unusual, and it is fair to say that a national consensus has developed against it. (*Atkins v. Virginia*, 2002)

The Court also took note of the opposing stances by various professional and social/religious organizations. The justices further considered that international opinion was largely against the practice (*Atkins v. Virginia*, 2002).

The Court then addressed the goals of capital punishment—retribution and deterrence—and whether utilizing the death penalty for IIDs is consistent with those goals. The analysis began with a discussion of retribution, explaining that the severity of a punishment necessarily rests on the culpability of the offender. In other words, the concept of retribution lacks effective application on someone who is not completely blameworthy for his or her actions. The justices reasoned that if states do not find the culpability of an "average murderer" sufficient for capital punishment (because we typically reserve the death penalty for the worst of the worst), then the "lesser culpability of the mentally retarded offender surely does not merit that form of retribution" (*Atkins v. Virginia*, 2002).

The Court then moved to the deterrence debate. Deterrence theory is built on the idea that the threat of punishment, if severe enough, will prevent an offender from choosing to commit criminal acts. IIDs however, are not able to adequately process information, control their impulses, and logically consider the consequences of their actions; therefore, these individuals are not likely to alter their conduct based on the threat of punishment. It is highly unlikely that an individual with these limitations would fully appreciate and consider that killing might result in a death sentence. Further, the justices explained that prohibiting the death penalty for IIDs will not impact the deterrent value for other capital offenders (if such a relationship exists) because they will remain "unprotected by the exemption and will continue to face the threat of execution. Thus, executing the mentally retarded will not measurably further the goal of deterrence" (*Atkins v. Virginia*, 2002).

Dissenting Opinion

Chief Justice Rehnquist and Justices Scalia and Thomas dissented, quite strongly, to the Court's ruling. The justices attacked the majority's conclusion that a national consensus had emerged on the topic of executing IIDs. They explained that the concurring justices' count of 18 states did not constitute a majority consensus, because there were 19 remaining death states which had not banned the practice of executing IIDs, leaving it up to judges and juries to decide. Indeed, Atkins's mental disabilities were a key issue considered at sentencing and nevertheless the jury sentenced him to death. The dissenters supported the power of juries to decide:

> The jury concluded, however, that his alleged retardation was not a compelling reason to exempt him from the death penalty in light of the brutality of his crime and his long demonstrated propensity for

violence. "In upsetting this particularized judgment on the basis of a constitutional absolute," the Court concludes that no one who is even slightly mentally retarded can have sufficient "moral responsibility to be subjected to capital punishment for any crime. As a sociological and moral conclusion that is implausible; and it is doubly implausible as an interpretation of the United States Constitution." (*Atkins v. Virginia*, 2002, as cited in *Thompson v. Oklahoma*)

The justices lambasted the majority for relying, even in part, on the opinions of professional social and religious organizations in its opinion. They found it even more absurd that the consideration of international opinion would impact the Court's decision:

> . . . The views of professional and religious organizations and the results of opinion polls are irrelevant. Equally irrelevant are the practices of the "world community," whose notions of justice are (thankfully) not always those of our people. We must never forget that it is a Constitution for the United States of America that we are expounding. . . . Where there is not first a settled consensus among our own people, the views of other nations, however enlightened the Justices of this Court may think them to be, cannot be imposed upon Americans through the Constitution. (*Atkins v. Virginia*, 2002)

The dissenters also rejected the arguments regarding retribution and deterrence as they pertain to executing IIDs. They accused the majority of misapplying the goals to fit their personal beliefs about the topic at hand.

Interestingly, Daryl Atkins's sentence was not commuted to a life sentence after the Court's ruling. Recall that his case was reversed and remanded for resentencing. This means that the Virginia trial court was required to conduct another sentencing hearing to consider the evidence of Atkins's mental abilities (or lack thereof). If it was determined that Atkins was indeed an IID, then the state of Virginia would not be allowed to impose a death sentence, consistent with the *Atkins* ruling. After considering the conflicting expert testimony from both sides in Atkins's case, the jury concluded that he was not an IID and, once again, sentenced Atkins to death. Yet another twist developed in Atkins's case in 2008—a defense attorney for Atkins's co-defendant came forward with information that prosecutors coached his former client (William Jones) on what to say when implicating Atkins as the actual shooter. Virginia law permits only the triggerman to receive a death sentence. In fact, 15 minutes of Jones's recorded debriefing were missing because prosecutors turned off the recording when Jones's account of events did not match the physical evidence in the case. A state judge overturned Atkins's death sentence as the result of prosecutorial misconduct (Liptak, 2008).

Atkins is a significant case because it categorically exempts a certain class of people from receiving the death penalty—IIDs. Though seemingly a straightforward ruling, the matter was far from settled. There are many questions that went unanswered by the Court. For example, it did not define the concept of "mental retardation" or what we now refer to as IID. The justices also did not provide guidelines for states to follow when determining what defendants fall into this category. Instead, the Court left these questions entirely up to the states to answer. The vagueness in the *Atkins* decision has therefore resulted in a wide range of application among states. The first real clarification that we have gotten on this issue since *Atkins* appeared in the Court's recent decision in *Hall v. United States* (2014) (see additional cases of interest and the Perspective feature in this chapter). *Atkins* also set the stage for another landmark case discussed in this chapter—*Roper v. Simmons* (2005). The Court relied heavily on the logic applied in *Atkins* when revisiting the issue of executing juveniles in the *Roper* case.

Additional Cases of Interest

Ford v. Wainwright (1986): It is a constitutional violation of the Eighth Amendment to execute a defendant who is insane at the time of execution, even if he or she was sane during the trial and sentencing phase(s).

Penry v. Lynaugh (1989): The Court upheld the practice of executing "mentally retarded" persons (IIDs) who have the ability to reason. This opinion was issued on the same day as *Stanford v. Kentucky* (1989).

Tennard v. Dretke (2004): The Court strengthened its position in *Atkins* by ruling that it is unconstitutional to execute a person with "mental retardation" even if the crime is not directly attributed to his or her "retardation."

Panetti v. Quarterman (2007): The Court ruled that a defendant's *awareness* of a state's reasoning for executing him or her is not the same as *understanding* the same reasoning. Thus, in order for a court to impose the death penalty, a defendant must clearly understand the legal reasons for the imminent execution.

Hall v. Florida (2014): In response to the *Atkins* decision, Florida developed a rule that prevented capital defendants with an IQ over 70 from presenting any other evidence of an intellectual disability. The Court ruled that Florida's rule was too rigid and violated the Eighth and Fourteenth Amendments. The majority concluded this rule created an "unacceptable risk that persons with intellectual disability will be executed." (You will learn in Chapter 8 that IQ scores are not infallible and have a five-point margin of error. Florida law did not take into account such a margin of error.)

RING V. ARIZONA (2002)

The Court issued an opinion in *Ring v. Arizona* just a few days after the *Atkins* ruling. At issue in *Ring* is the Sixth Amendment's guarantee of a defendant's right to a jury trial. This is somewhat unusual given that most of the landmark capital cases have addressed Eighth Amendment questions. The Court granted writ of certiorari in *Ring* to decide whether or not judges may determine findings of fact or aggravating circumstances, separate from the jury, that serve to increase an offender's punishment to death. In Ring's case, the judge made a finding of fact (an aggravating circumstance) that the jury did not, which resulted in Ring being eligible for the death penalty.

In November 1994, Timothy Ring and James Greenham robbed an armored Wells Fargo van outside of the Arrowhead Mall in Glendale, Arizona (though the extent of Ring's involvement is disputed). One of the guards went into a department store to make a cash pickup, leaving the other guard in the van. Ring and Greenham approached the van when the driver, John Magoch, opened the door to smoke a cigarette. Either Ring or Greenham shot Magoch in the head with a rifle, killing him (who fired the fatal shot is disputed). The two men took $562,000, along with some checks, from the van and drove to a church parking lot where Ring's truck was waiting. They transferred the stolen monies to it. Deputies from Maricopa County Sheriff's Department found the van with its motor running and Magoch's body still inside (*Ring v. Arizona*, 2002).

Ring, Greenham, and a third accomplice were caught and charged with armed robbery and murder. The jury in Ring's trial did not return a guilty

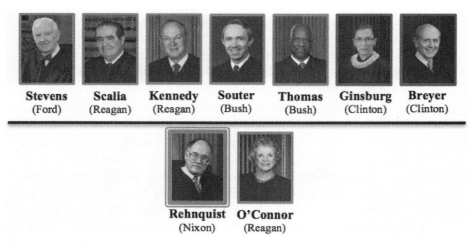

FIGURE 4.2   *Ring v. Arizona* (2002)

verdict on the premeditated murder charge, instead finding him guilty of felony murder in the course of committing armed robbery. Recall from Chapter 3 that under the felony-murder rule, a defendant can be guilty of murder even if that defendant was not the actual killer or did not intend for death to occur; mere participation in the felony that led to the murder (armed robbery) is sufficient. The law in Arizona allows a defendant to receive the death penalty in cases like Ring's only if a judge finds the presence of statutory aggravating factors, not outweighed by mitigating circumstances, in a separate sentencing hearing. In other words, if the judge can find a compelling reason to sentence a defendant to death that is listed in the statute (so-called aggravating circumstances), then the judge is permitted to issue a death sentence as long as there are no mitigating factors strong enough to necessitate leniency. The rationale for this law, according to Arizona, is that leaving these decisions to a judge is more likely to result in a fair and unbiased process for imposing the death penalty.

The judge in Ring's case determined that the co-defendant's testimony at Ring's trial was credible; Greenham said Ring was the shooter. Furthermore, the judge found that the crime was committed for monetary gain, which is listed as an aggravating circumstance in Arizona's statute. The judge also found one mitigating factor, Ring's limited criminal history, but did not believe it should justify leniency. The judge entered a "special verdict" sentencing Ring to death, thereby trumping the jury's original sentence (*Ring v. Arizona*, 2002).

In a 7-2 vote (see Figure 4.2), the Supreme Court sided with Ring, ruling that only juries can decide whether to sentence a defendant to death. According to the majority, Arizona's statute allowing judges to decide aggravating factors that serve to increase a defendant's punishment to death violates the Sixth Amendment. Ring's death sentence was reversed and his case was remanded for resentencing (*Ring v. Arizona*, 2002).

Concurring Opinions

Justice Ginsburg delivered the majority opinion and was joined by Justices Stevens, Scalia, Kennedy, Souter, and Thomas. Breyer concurred with the judgment of the Court, but wrote a completely separate opinion. Justices Scalia and Kennedy both joined the majority opinion and filed separate concurring opinions of their own as well. The justices explained that all facts in a case which are used to subject the defendant to a punishment must be those found by a jury. The majority acknowledged the state's argument that leaving the power to determine aggravating factors to the judge was an effort to limit arbitrary decision-making, but countered the claim:

> The Sixth Amendment jury trial right, however, does not turn on the relative rationality, fairness, or efficiency of potential factfinders.

> Entrusting to a judge the finding of facts necessary to support a death sentence might be "an admirably fair and efficient scheme of criminal justice designed for a society that is prepared to leave criminal justice to the State. . . . The founders of the American Republic were not prepared to leave it to the State, which is why the jury-trial guarantee was one of the least controversial provisions of the Bill of Rights. It has never been efficient; but it has always been free." (*Ring v. Arizona*, 2002, as cited in *Apprendi v. New Jersey*)

Essentially, the justices were making the point that it would be a mistake to take this power away from juries because doing so would fundamentally alter the process—keeping the power with the "people" or juries is important. The justices also explained that the great majority of states leave the finding of fact and aggravating circumstances to juries and that Arizona's law was somewhat of an anomaly.

Although Justice Breyer agreed with the Court's ruling, he issued a separate concurrence to illustrate a fundamental difference between his thinking and that of the other justices. Breyer believed jury sentencing in capital cases is a protection offered by the Eighth Amendment, rather than the Sixth (as the other justices concluded). His logic was that the Court (in *Gregg*) required states to switch to a bifurcated system in order to place special emphasis on the sentencing phase to limit arbitrary decision-making, which the justices found to be an Eighth Amendment requirement (see Chapter 3). He reasoned that because of that decision, the issues in *Ring* necessitate Eighth Amendment consideration and application. Breyer also discussed retribution as a justification for the death penalty and asserted that juries are in the best position to ensure this end. He defended his position by explaining that jurors are

> . . . more attuned to the community's moral sensibility because they reflect more accurately the composition and experiences of the community as a whole. Hence they are more likely to express the conscience of the community on the ultimate question of life or death and better able to determine in the particular case the need for retribution, namely, an expression of the community's belief that certain crimes are themselves so grievous an affront to humanity that the only adequate response may be the penalty of death. (*Ring v. Arizona*, 2002)

Dissenting Opinion

Justice O'Connor filed a dissenting opinion joined by Chief Justice Rehnquist. The dissenting justices believed that judicial discretion should be given more respect. They opined that the Court should not treat the facts or aggravating circumstances that increase sentencing penalties as "element[s] of the crime" because doing so is "not required by the Constitution, by history, or by our prior cases." They further argued that such rules ignore the history of "discretionary sentencing by judges" (*Ring v. Arizona*, 2002).

The *Ring* decision was significant because it invalidated statutes in states that permitted judges to make the ultimate death penalty decisions, thus diminishing the power of judicial discretion in capital cases. The Court did not immediately make clear whether or not the decision would be retroactive, but later clarified that the ruling did not apply to cases prior to *Ring*.

Additional Cases of Interest

Walton v. Arizona (1990): The Court ruled that trial judges have complete sentencing authority in capital cases.

Apprendi v. New Jersey (2000): The Court ruled that only juries can make determinations of facts that lead to an increase in the severity of a defendant's sentence. This case was reaffirmed in the *Ring* decision for capital defendants.

PERSPECTIVE FROM A PROSECUTOR: ALLEN WINSOR

Solicitor General Allen Winsor has been practicing law for 12 years. He received his law degree from the Fredric G. Levin College of Law, where he was editor in chief of the Florida Law Review. *After graduating from law school, Winsor clerked for Justice Ed Carnes of the Eleventh U.S. Circuit Court of Appeals. Winsor practiced law privately for approximately 10 years, specializing in constitutional litigation and appeals. He was recently appointed by Florida's attorney general to serve as the solicitor general for the state of Florida. In 2014, he argued a capital case,* Hall v. Florida, *before the U.S. Supreme Court. The* Hall *decision attempts to clarify how states may define IIDs when determining if a death sentence is appropriate.*

FIGURE 4.3   Allen Winsor

The Eighth Amendment to the United States Constitution prohibits "cruel and unusual punishments." How does this provision limit application of the death penalty? The answer has changed over the years. The United States Supreme Court, which has the final word on this and all other questions of federal constitutional law, has said the Amendment "draw[s] its meaning from the evolving standards of decency that mark the progress of a maturing society." Therefore, "as the basic mores of society change," the Court has held, so too must the Eighth Amendment's applicability.

For several years, the United States Supreme Court has established certain death penalty exemptions; it has determined that some types of crimes (or criminals) never deserve the ultimate punishment. The Court has held, for example, that states cannot execute defendants for crimes committed before they turned eighteen. And it has held that crimes against individuals cannot justify the death penalty unless the victim dies. In either case, it does not matter how horrific the crime: if the perpetrator is under eighteen or there is no death, capital punishment is off the table.

It is usually not difficult to determine when a particular crime fits into one of these exemptions. Either the victim died, or he did not. Either the perpetrator was over eighteen, or he was not. But what happens when the line dividing those eligible for the death penalty from those not eligible is less clear? That was at issue in this year's decision in *Hall v. Florida*, the United States Supreme Court's most recent decision regarding who is eligible for the death penalty.

Ten years before *Hall*, in *Atkins v. Virginia*, the Supreme Court held for the first time that the Eighth Amendment precludes states from executing the intellectually disabled. (Until recently, the term "mentally retarded" prevailed, but "intellectually disabled" has now replaced it. Starting with *Hall*, the Supreme Court switched to the new term.) The Court concluded that because of their impairments, the intellectually disabled "do not act with the level of moral culpability that characterizes the most serious adult criminal conduct." But the Court also recognized that there would be disagreement "in determining which offenders are in fact" intellectually disabled. It recognized that "[n]ot all people who claim to be [intellectually disabled] will be so impaired as to fall within the range of [intellectually disabled] offenders about whom there is a national consensus [against execution]." The Court therefore left "to the State[s] the task of developing appropriate ways to enforce the constitutional restriction."

The question became how states do that. Unlike age, which is easily measured, intellectual disability turns on subjective assessments. The intellectual disability dividing line is not only subject to frequent expert disagreement, but it is also a moving target. Experts once put the IQ dividing line at 85, making some sixteen percent of all people eligible for an intellectual disability diagnosis. At some point, the experts who draw those lines decided that this was too many people. They adjusted the line, moving it down to 70. This change was not because science discovered the earlier cutoff was invalid; it was because policy determinations changed—some wanted intellectual disability diagnoses to be rarer.

The American Association on Intellectual and Developmental Disabilities (AAIDD), which openly opposes the death penalty, also publishes one of the leading guides on how to diagnose intellectual disability. Since the Supreme Court's 2002 *Atkins* decision prohibiting executions of the intellectually disabled, the diagnostic criteria the AAIDD and others promote have become murkier, making it easier to achieve a diagnosis. Over the years, the various editions of various guides have changed the clinical definitions, and today's definitions differ from those the Supreme Court relied on in *Atkins*. Along the way, Florida did not change its statutory definition; it used the same three-part test it had for years. In *Hall*, the Supreme Court ultimately held that Florida's definition was too rigid, relying too heavily on IQ test scores and too little on current views in the medical community. It therefore held that Florida's approach was unconstitutional.

Should the Court look to the professional community (or professional organizations that oppose the death penalty) to help establish the line between those who are constitutionally ineligible for execution and those who are not? The four dissenting Justices in *Hall* expressed concern with the problems that approach might bring. They noted that because professional associations' opinions often change, tying Eighth Amendment determinations to those opinions would lead to greater uncertainty and more litigation. And more litigation and uncertainty leads to more delay. In Hall's case, decades have passed since the crime, and the litigation regarding his punishment continues.

Only time will tell the extent to which still further changes of opinion in the medical community might lead to still further capital litigation. In the meantime, States will have to continue working through the issue that led to the *Hall* case in the first place: How to go about determining who is, and who is not, exempt from the death penalty based on intellectual disability?

ROPER V. SIMMONS (2005)

The Court granted review of *Roper* to revisit the issue of executing juveniles. Recall from its ruling in *Stanford* that sentencing juveniles (ages 16 and 17) to death did not violate the constitution at the time. Christopher Simmons was 17 years old and a junior in high school when he decided that he wanted to know what it felt like to kill someone. He discussed his plans to carry out a murder with two of his high school friends, explaining that they could get away with it because they were juveniles. Simmons wanted to break into a home and steal items of value, tie up the victim, and then throw that person over a bridge.

The three boys decided to implement their plan to kill someone on a September night in 1993. One of the boys changed his mind, leaving Simmons and Charles Benjamin to carry out the crime on their own. Simmons and Benjamin broke into a Missouri home belonging to a woman named Shirley Crook. They entered the home by reaching in through an open window and unlocking the door. Startled by the opening door, Crook yelled out to ask who was there. Simmons entered her bedroom and bound her with duct tape. Simmons realized that he actually knew Crook from a previous car accident that both had been party to. The boys taped her eyes and mouth shut and then put their victim into her vehicle; they proceeded to drive her to a state park. Once there, they placed a towel over her head and bound her hands and legs once more with electrical wire. Simmons and Benjamin then threw Crook over the side of a bridge and into the water, where she drowned to

FIGURE 4.4 *Roper v. Simmons* (2005)

death. Fishermen recovered her body in the river later that afternoon (*Roper v. Simmons*, 2005).

Simmons was arrested and charged with burglary, kidnapping, and murder after bragging about the crime to his friends and subsequently confessing to police. Simmons explained that he killed Crook "because the bitch seen my face" (*Roper v. Simmons*, 2005). The jury found Simmons guilty and sentenced him to death after considering a number of aggravating factors. Some of the aggravating factors were as follows: the crime had been committed, in part, for monetary gain; the victim had been killed to avoid the defendant's arrest (the victim recognized him from a prior car accident); and the crime "involved depravity of mind and was outrageously and wantonly vile, horrible, and inhuman" (*Roper v. Simmons*, 2005). Simmons's defense attorneys presented limited mitigation to the jury during the sentencing phase. They discussed his lack of criminal history (no prior convictions) and members of Simmons's family and friends testified that he was a good person. Only during closing arguments did Simmons's defense team address his age as a mitigating circumstance, reminding the jury of the laws that states use to regulate juvenile behavior because juveniles are not as "responsible" as adults (e.g., laws that bar underage drinking, serving on juries, or attending certain movies in a public theater).

On appeal, Simmons maintained that he received poor representation by his defense attorneys at trial, in part because they did not present expert testimony from clinical psychologists who evaluated him. The experts found that Simmons was extremely immature, impulsive, and particularly susceptible to the influence of others. He also abused drugs and alcohol, had a troubled childhood, and performed poorly in school. His new defense counsel argued that each of these circumstances (and much more) should have been presented to the jury at sentencing (*Roper v. Simmons*, 2005).

Simmons was unsuccessful in his appeals until the U.S. Supreme Court issued its ruling in *Atkins v. Virginia* (2002). Though the *Atkins* case declared the practice of executing IIDs unconstitutional, not juveniles, Simmons argued that the Court's reasoning (on questions of culpability, national consensus against the practice, etc.) should also apply to executing juveniles. The Missouri Supreme Court agreed with Simmons and overturned his death sentence, commuting it to life without the possibility of parole (*Roper v. Simmons*, 2005). The state of Missouri appealed to the U.S. Supreme Court. The Court agreed with the lower courts, finding that the Eighth and Fourteenth Amendments do not permit the execution of juveniles. Simmons's life sentence was affirmed. The marginal 5-4 ruling (see Figure 4.4) forbids states to impose the death penalty on offenders younger than 18 years of age, as required by the Eighth and Fourteenth Amendments.

Concurring Opinions

Justice Kennedy delivered the Court's opinion and was joined by Justices Stevens, Souter, Ginsburg, and Breyer. Stevens filed an additional concurring opinion joined by Ginsburg. As might be expected, the Court began its Eighth Amendment analysis by considering the evolving standards of decency to determine if a national consensus had been reached by states on the matter of executing juveniles. The Court found that the majority of states reject the juvenile death penalty, there is consistency and a trend to abolish it, and of the states that do maintain the juvenile death penalty, they rarely use it (*Roper v. Simmons*, 2005). The Court explained that, like *Atkins* in referring to IIDs, juveniles are "categorically less culpable than the average criminal" (*Roper v. Simmons*, 2005). It is fitting that the Court would analyze *Roper* alongside *Atkins*. The last time the Court decided on the matter of juvenile execution was in *Stanford v. Kentucky* (1989), in which the practice was upheld. On the same day, the Court upheld the practice of executing the "mentally retarded" in *Penry v. Lynaugh* (1989). At the time of *Roper*, society seemed to have evolved to a point that the Court felt obligated to overturn its earlier decisions in both of those cases—no longer would it be constitutional to execute IIDs or juveniles.

The Court set forth three differences between juvenile and adult offenders. First, juveniles are immature and irresponsible, which means that their criminal conduct is not as "morally reprehensible" as that of adults. They noted studies that indicated the statistical overrepresentation of juveniles participating in reckless behavior in all categories. It is for these reasons, the Court opined, that states regulate the activities of juveniles (e.g., voting, serving on juries, getting married). Second, juveniles are vulnerable and have less control over their surroundings than adults, which means that they are not always able to remove themselves from criminogenic environments and are thus subject to negative influences; of particular concern is peer pressure. Third, juveniles are in a life stage where they are struggling to find their identity. Therefore, it is "less supportable to conclude that even a heinous crime committed by a juvenile is evidence of irretrievably depraved character" (*Roper v. Simmons*, 2005). Juvenile traits are "more transitory, less fixed" (*Roper v. Simmons*, 2005).

The majority also addressed the punishment goals of retribution and deterrence, explaining that neither justification is served by executing offenders with diminished culpability (refer to the same arguments made by the Court in *Atkins* and in the *Stanford* dissent). The petitioner (State of Missouri) argued that the Court has historically insisted on individual consideration of capital cases, and that by placing a categorical ban on executing juveniles, the Court was going against its own principles. In response to this criticism, the Court explained:

> An unacceptable likelihood exists that the brutality or cold-blooded nature of any particular crime would overpower mitigating ar-

guments based on youth as a matter of course, even where the juvenile offender's objective immaturity, vulnerability, and lack of true depravity should require a sentence less severe than death. (*Roper v. Simmons*, 2005)

The Court briefly discussed global opinion on the juvenile death penalty. Although it was careful to assert that international opinion had no control or influence on its opinion in this case, the Court cited lack of support in the international community as confirmation that its decision was the "right" one. The justices pointed to the unfortunate reality that the United States was the only country in the entire world to officially sanction the execution of juveniles.

Justice Stevens's additional concurrence served only to reiterate the importance of respecting the fluidity of the Eighth Amendment. Stevens reminded us that as we (society) evolve, so should the Constitution in accordance with the intent of its original writers.

Dissenting Opinions

Justice O'Connor filed a dissenting opinion. Justice Scalia also filed a dissenting opinion and was joined by Chief Justice Rehnquist and Justice Thomas. Justice O'Connor disagreed with the majority on all points. She did not believe that a mere majority of states banning the juvenile death penalty constitutes national consensus on the matter. She felt strongly that the decision to execute juveniles should rest in the hands of jurors who are able to consider the individual circumstances of cases before them, as well as the circumstances surrounding the defendant's actions. While she recognized that adolescents, as a class, are less mature and thus less culpable for their behavior than adults, O'Connor explained that there may very well be 17-year-olds who are mature enough to deserve a punishment of death. Consequently, she opposed a categorical ban on the juvenile death penalty. Justice O'Connor also criticized the majority for so closely relating the issue of culpability to both "mentally retarded" and juvenile defendants. She expressed distinct differences between the two groups:

A mentally retarded person is, "by definition," one whose cognitive and behavioral capacities have been proven to fall below a certain minimum. . . . [A] mentally retarded offender is one whose demonstrated impairments make it so highly unlikely that he is culpable enough to deserve the death penalty or that he could have been deterred by the threat of death, that execution is not a defensible punishment. There is no such inherent or accurate fit between an offender's chronological age and the personal limitations which the Court believes make capital punishment excessive for 17-year-old murderers. Moreover, it defies common sense to suggest that 17-year-olds as a class are somehow equivalent to mentally retarded persons with regard to culpability or susceptibility to deterrence. Seventeen-year-olds may, on average, be less mature than adults, but that lesser maturity simply cannot be equated with the major, lifelong impairments suffered by the mentally retarded. (*Roper v. Simmons*, 2005)

Lastly, O'Connor asserted her view that international opinion should not alter the Court's determination on the juvenile death penalty. Justice Scalia's dissent echoed many of the same opinions expressed by O'Connor, though he added several additional criticisms. One of his problems with the majority ruling was that he believed the justices had relied more on their personal and subjective opinions than what was best for the American people. He also took issue with the majority's lack of concern over the prior decision made by the Missouri Supreme Court. The Missouri Court had completely ignored the precedent set by the U.S. Supreme Court in *Stanford*. Instead, it took matters into its own hands by overturning Simmons's death sentence, which disrespected the precedent established by the Supreme Court in *Stanford*—that juveniles may be executed. Scalia pointed out that only the U.S. Supreme Court could overturn its own decisions, not state supreme courts.

Additional Cases of Interest

Thompson v. Oklahoma (1988): The Court ruled that it is unconstitutional to execute juveniles who committed crimes at the age of 15. This case was decided just one year before *Stanford*.

Stanford v. Kentucky (1989): The death penalty is permissible for juveniles who are 16- or 17-year-olds.

BAZE AND BOWLING V. REEZ (2008)

The Court granted certiorari in two cases (collectively known as "*Baze*") to address the constitutionality of lethal injection. This method of execution had been under intense scrutiny for years in light of numerous botched executions (see Chapter 6). Specifically, the Court agreed to rule on whether the three-drug protocol used by Kentucky (and most of the death states) passed Eighth Amendment scrutiny.

Ralph Baze and Thomas Bowling, two men living in Kentucky, were convicted of murder and sentenced to death. The men challenged their executions, arguing that the three-drug protocol has the potential to result in "unnecessary pain and suffering" (*Baze and Bowling v. Reez*, 2008). Kentucky's protocol used the following three drugs: Sodium Thiopental, Pancuronium Bromide, and Potassium Chloride. The first drug is an anesthetic and is meant to induce unconsciousness so that the offender does not feel the painful effects of the second

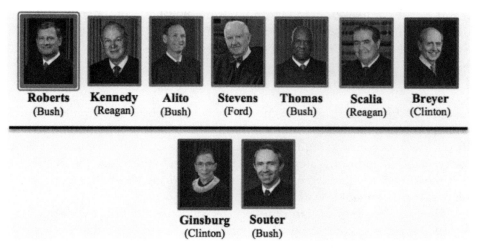

FIGURE 4.5   *Baze and Bowling v. Reez* (2008)

and third drugs. The second drug causes paralysis and the third drug induces cardiac arrest. As we will learn in Chapter 6, a variety of factors can impact whether or not a lethal injection execution is carried out as planned (does not result in unnecessary pain). Some of these factors include improper administration and inadequate dosage.

In a 7-2 vote (see Figure 4.5), the Court upheld the constitutionality of lethal injection, ruling that the administration of the three-drug protocol does not "create a substantial risk of wanton and unnecessary infliction of pain, torture, or lingering death" (*Baze and Bowling v. Reez*, 2008). The Court thus affirmed the decision of the lower court, allowing states to continue using lethal injection.

Concurring Opinions

Chief Justice Roberts wrote the opinion of the Court and was joined by Justices Kennedy and Alito. Justices Stevens, Thomas, Scalia, and Breyer each concurred, but wrote their own opinions. The *Baze* decision is a rather complex and lengthy ruling primarily focused on the errors that can result from lethal injection. Because we address most of the issues pertaining to the three-drug protocol and its vulnerabilities in Chapter 6, we limit the discussion here to the Court's main holdings in the interest of avoiding redundancy.

The Court held that an execution method amounts to cruel and unusual punishment if it presents "a 'substantial' or 'objectively intolerable' risk of serious harm" (*Baze and Bowling v. Reez*, 2008). The Court reasoned that the risk of pain always exists with all execution methods, not just lethal injection. The Court further explained that the Constitution does not require methods to entirely eliminate the risk of pain: "Simply because an execution method may result in pain, either by accident or as an inescapable consequence of death, does not establish the sort of 'objectively intolerable risk of harm' that qualifies as cruel and unusual" (*Baze and Bowling v. Reez*, 2008).

Dissenting Opinion

Justice Ginsburg wrote the dissent and was joined by Justice Souter. Justice Souter's concerns about Kentucky's lethal injection protocol centered largely on the lack of procedural safeguards in place. More specifically, the justices were concerned that additional steps needed to be taken to minimize the likelihood that the offender would experience pain (e.g., ensuring the first drug properly renders the defendant unconscious).

The *Baze* decision was significant because not only did it clarify the question of lethal injection's constitutionality, but it also created a reaction from states similar to a moratorium—states essentially stopped all executions while waiting for the Court to issue its ruling. In doing so, many of them began preparing back-up methods in the event that the Court determined lethal injection was unconstitutional. The Court was clear that it did not want its ruling to be interpreted as a debate on the constitutionality of the death penalty in general terms, just the method in question. However, Justice Stevens did challenge the constitutionality of capital punishment in his concurrence and other justices hinted at the notion that they might consider such a debate in the future. Only time will tell.

Additional Cases of Interest

> *Wilkerson v. Utah* (1879): The Court ruled that a firing squad is a constitutionally permissible method of execution. In *In re Kemmler* (1890), death by electrocution was deemed a constitutional method of execution.
>
> *Louisiana ex rel. Francis v. Resweber* (1947): It is not unconstitutional to attempt to execute a person a second time if the first time is a failure. The Fifth Amendment's double jeopardy protection does not protect a person from this occurrence. It also does not constitute cruel and unusual punishment (Eighth Amendment) to attempt to execute a person twice.
>
> *Glossip v. Gross* (2015): The use of midazolam (the first drug used in the execution process) for lethal injection does not amount to cruel and unusual punishment (Eighth Amendment) and is, therefore, constitutional.

SUMMARY

This chapter completes our timeline overview of the foundational U.S. Supreme Court case rulings on capital punishment in the modern era (Table 4.1).

TABLE 4.1   Foundational Cases Summary

Case	Issue	Ruling
Atkins v. Virginia 536 U.S. 304 (2002)	Executing individuals with intellectual disabilities (IIDs)	It is unconstitutional to execute IIDs (individuals formerly termed "mentally retarded").
Ring v. Arizona 536 U.S. 584 (2002)	Capital sentencing authority	Juries, not judges, weigh aggravating factors and decide the death penalty.
Roper v. Simmons 543 U.S. 551 (2005)	Executing juveniles	It is unconstitutional to sentence juveniles (under the age of 18) to death.
Baze and Bowling v. Reez 553 U.S. 35 (2008)	Lethal injection/execution method	The three-drug protocol used in the lethal injection of capital defendants does not violate the Constitution.

We began our timeline with the *Furman* case in Chapter 3 and ended with the *Baze* case here. *Atkins* was the first landmark capital case in the twenty-first century and resulted in a ban on the practice of executing defendants with intellectual disabilities. We then discussed the *Ring* decision, which gave juries the ultimate power in determining whether defendants should receive the death penalty. The Court revisited the issue of executing juveniles in *Roper* and ultimately ruled that the practice is unconstitutional, effectively overturning its ruling in *Stanford*. Finally, we discussed the *Baze* case, in which the Court upheld the practice of lethal injection.

DISCUSSION QUESTIONS

1. How did the Court's decision in *Atkins v. Virginia* (2002) impact capital punishment? What were the implications for future cases (not just those related to individuals with intellectual disabilities)?
2. Explain the fallout from the Court's lack of guidance and ambiguity in defining "individuals with intellectual disabilities" in *Atkins v. Virginia* (2002).
3. In arriving at its *Ring v. Arizona* (2002) ruling, there was disagreement among the Court's justices about which constitutional amendments were applicable to the issue of juries deciding death sentences. Explain.
4. Why did the Court change its position on executing juveniles in *Roper v. Simmons* (2005)? How has society evolved since it first ruled on the issue in 1989?
5. According to the U.S. Supreme Court in *Roper v. Simmons* (2005), what are the three main differences between juveniles and adults?
6. How did the Court justify the acceptance of the risk of pain in executions in its *Baze* decision?

GLOSSARY

Diagnostic and Statistical Manual of Mental Disorders (DSM-V): A manual published by the American Psychiatric Association that outlines criteria for diagnosing mental disorders.

REFERENCES

Apprendi v. New Jersey. (2000). 530 U.S. 466.
Atkins v. Virginia. (2002). 536 U.S. 304.
Baze v. Rees. (2008). 553 U.S. 35.
Hall v. Florida. (2014). 572 U.S. ___.
In re Kemmler. (1890). 136 U.S. 436, 447.
Liptak, A. (2008, January 19). "Lawyer Reveals Secret, Toppling Death Sentence." *The New York Times.* http://www.nytimes.com/2008/01/19/us/19death.html?pagewanted=all&_r=0.
Panetti v. Quarterman. (2007). 551 U.S. 930.
Penry v. Lynaugh. (1989). 492 U.S. 302.
Ring v. Arizona. (2002). 536 U.S. 584.
Roper v. Simmons (2005). 543 U.S. 551.
Stanford v. Kentucky. (1989). 492 U.S. 361.
Walton v. Arizona. (1990). 497 U.S. 639.
Wilkerson v. Utah. (1878). 99 U.S. 130.

CHAPTER 5

THE DEATH PENALTY AND PUBLIC OPINION

Salem Village in the Massachusetts Colony was the center of some bizarre occurrences in the winter of 1692. Two young girls, ages 9 and 11, began to have fits described as "beyond the power of epileptic fits or natural disease." The girls uttered strange words, screamed grotesquely, and severely contorted their bodies. A few days later, other young girls began acting similarly, and church services were interrupted a number of times by afflicted children's outbursts. Three women of "irreligious reputation" were arrested for allegedly causing the afflictions by filling the girls' heads with stories about sexual encounters with demons from the notorious book Malleus Maleficarum *on the prosecution of witches. A physician called to examine the girls suggested that their problems might have a supernatural origin in witchcraft.*

The widespread belief in witchcraft and the hardships being suffered by the colony (it was then at war with Native Americans and experiencing harsh economic times) served as fertile ground for moral outrage and for wanting to blame and punish someone for the colony's misfortunes. Who better to blame than the devil in the guise of powerless individuals who had already demonstrated their devilish ways by not attending church, swearing, and being suspected of illicit sexuality? Public opinion was thus very much in favor of "doing something" to end the evil in the colony's midst by trying and executing witches. A special court was convened in Salem to hear witchcraft cases as the hysteria spread throughout Massachusetts. The first person convicted (Bridget Bishop) was hanged, followed by 18 others, and some 150 more men, women, and children were accused and jailed. Of course, witches do not exist (at least, not the broom-riding and spell-casting witches of folklore), and so everyone accused of, and executed for, witchcraft was innocent.

LEARNING OBJECTIVES

- Understand the role of public opinion in the death penalty debate.
- Understand the attitudinal and political adjustment models and how they allegedly affect judicial decisions.
- Understand how the crime rate influences opinion about the death penalty.
- Explain the Marshall hypothesis and its importance in the death penalty debate.
- Be knowledgeable about public opinion on the death penalty in other countries.

The hysteria that precipitated the Salem Witch Trial executions did not develop overnight; rather, it resulted from public opinion of the time that strongly supported draconian religious principles. The collective belief that the rules of "the church" were to remain unquestioned resulted in the people of Salem ignoring all other evidence to seek convictions. We learn from the witch trials that if people (the public at large) define something as "real," it is real in its consequences. It is in this way that public opinion exerts its power. Indeed, as more and more people were accused of witchcraft for obviously vindictive reasons, the hysteria in the colony abated and public opinion turned against the trials. It is thought by many that the trials left such a bad taste in the mouths of colonists that they signaled the beginning of the end of theocratic rule there. The point is that unusual events of an unwelcome nature generate feelings in the public that "something must be done," and that politicians are sensitive to such an outcry and suggest and pass legislation that they believe will make the public happy and keep its members voting for them.

Juvenile executions are a modern-day example of how the power of public opinion can influence policy. Much of the Western world finds it inconceivable that the United States executed juveniles until 2005 (see *Roper v. Simmons* in Chapter 4). Despite a plethora of available research on the underdevelopment of the adolescent brain (available long before 2005), we continued to uphold the practice of executing juveniles. There can be no doubt of the immense power that public opinion has on our decision-making and policy-making in the criminal justice system.

THE UPS AND DOWNS OF PUBLIC OPINION

The death penalty has always been an intensely debated and emotionally charged issue for the American public. It evokes such an emotional response because we are quite literally considering the matter of life and death. Capital punishment tends to be a particularly divisive issue for Americans because opponents and proponents alike are strongly committed to their respective positions. U.S. Supreme Court Chief Justice Thurgood Marshall remarked that there is no point in trying to dissuade people of their beliefs in the death penalty if they cite religion or retribution as the primary reasons for supporting capital punishment. He believed that it is unlikely for people to objectively consider capital punishment or overcome such belief systems if subscribing to them from an emotional standpoint (*Furman v. Georgia*, 1972).

Perhaps there is no greater player in the capital punishment debate than the court of public opinion. Indeed, the U.S. Supreme Court case of *Trop v. Dulles* (1958), having to do with the revocation of citizenship, not the death penalty, referenced the need for justices to consider the *"evolving standards of decency"* (see Chapter 3). Essentially, this means that judges must consider what the states (the people) deem "decent" while recognizing that societal standards change as society evolves. Since *Trop*, the Court has utilized this standard when attempting to settle a variety of controversial cases and issues, such as making determinations about what constitutes *cruel and unusual punishment* (Eighth Amendment).

Though the very nature of today's U.S. Supreme Court is designed to eliminate fears of public reprisal arising from judicial decision-making (as evidenced in the justices' lifetime appointment), there is no escaping the power of public opinion and influences of personal belief systems. U.S. Supreme Court Justice Benjamin Cardozo (1921) acknowledged the human element of judicial decision-making when he remarked: "[The] great tides and current which engulf the rest of men do not turn aside in their course and pass the judges by. . ." (Dodd, 1922, pp. 710–711). U.S. Supreme Court Chief Justice Rehnquist also commented on the same:

> Judges, so long as they are relatively normal human beings, can no more escape being influenced by public opinion in the long run than can people working at other jobs. . . . Judges need not "tremble before public opinion" in the same way that elected officials may, but it would be remarkable indeed if they were not influenced by [public opinion]. . . . (Steel Seizure case of 1954, as cited in Yates, 2002, p. 10)

Capital punishment exists because it is largely supported by the American public (Gallup, 2015). (See Table 5.1.) It would make little sense to permit the death penalty as a punishment option if it were rejected by greater society. Let us revisit Émile Durkheim's position that societies need punishment. **Social solidarity** is characterized by the degree of cohesiveness in a society. Essentially, it is the common ground shared by individuals that binds them together in our social institutions (Durkheim, 1933). The death penalty is arguably a

TABLE 5.1   Demographics of Public Opinion on the Death Penalty

Ideology	Favor	Oppose	Party	Favor	Oppose	Race	Favor	Oppose	Sex	Favor	Oppose
Conservative	75%	18%	Republican	80%	15%	White	68%	28%	Male	67%	28%
Moderate	60%	34%	Independent	65%	32%	Black	49%	45%	Female	59%	35%
Liberal	47%	50%	Democrat	51%	42%						

mechanism of social solidarity when it is perceived as justly administered. When a high level of public support for the death penalty exists, sentencing a person to death for heinous acts may be considered a necessary link in the chain of social solidarity. As we saw in Chapter 3, U.S. Supreme Court Justice Stewart expressed the importance of recognizing the instinctual nature of man and his desire for retribution in our system of justice (*Furman v. Georgia*, 1972). He feared that without a mechanism of ridding society of perceived *evil* (the worst criminals), like the death penalty, the emergence of anarchy and vigilante justice would be an inevitable consequence.

THE WAYS THAT PUBLIC SUPPORT MAINTAINS THE DEATH PENALTY

Robert Bohm (2012) lists numerous ways that public opinion contributes to the continued use of the death penalty in the United States. Perhaps most obvious is the influence of public support for the death penalty. This influences lawmakers to support capital punishment statutes because they are not likely to ignore the will of their constituents. And support for capital punishment demonstrates a politician's willingness to "get tough" on crime, which is an unfortunate necessity for many politicians hoping to secure legislative seats.

Prosecutors and judges also play a critical role in the administration of capital punishment. A prosecutor might seek the death penalty in lieu of other alternatives (e.g., life without the possibility of parole) for political reasons. Judges must similarly consider their election platforms. In states with partisan election/appointment of district judges, a district judge might feel pressure by the public to sentence a defendant to death in order to conform with public sentiment so that he or she can retain his or her elected position. The same can be said for appellate judges who feel pressure to affirm a lower court's decision to impose the death penalty. Indeed, there are numerous examples of judges/justices who have been unable to retain their seats in office for making death penalty decisions contrary to public opinion (Bohm, 2012). For example, former California

Supreme Court Chief Justices Rose Bird, Cruz Reynoso, and Joseph Grodin received considerable public scrutiny for their perceived opposition to the death penalty. Bird claimed that she would affirm or uphold a death sentence if it were free of legal errors, but during her nine years on the bench, she voted to reverse every death penalty case that came before her; the Bird Court as a whole reversed decisions in over 90% of capital cases (Traut & Emmert, 1998). Public support for capital punishment in California was notably strong in 1986 (83% favored) when the three justices were up for retention election.[1] Consequently, the justices were not retained on California's Supreme Court after political leaders led a powerful campaign against them, claiming that the justices were antideath penalty (Traut & Emmert, 1998). Few judges thus wish to be labeled as being "soft" on crime.

Governors are also key players in capital punishment. Bohm (2012) opines that some governors may not veto antideath penalty legislation in a climate where the public is strongly supportive of capital punishment. Quite simply, governors are less willing to grant clemency in a political climate rife with death penalty support. Indeed, prior to 1970 (*Furman* era; see Chapter 3), the governors of death penalty states commuted death sentences in approximately one-third of all cases that were brought to them for consideration. This was a time marked by low public support for capital punishment. In contrast, today's governors rarely commute death sentences because the post-*Furman* era marks a time when public support has increased for the death penalty; therefore, a governor granting clemency is an extremely rare event (Bohm, 2012). Such an unusual event did occur, however, in 2003; Governor George Ryan of Illinois commuted the sentences of the 167 inmates on death row (Illinois' entire death row population). He justified his actions by explaining that his state's system was discriminatory and the chance of error (convicting the wrong person) was too great. While it seems that Governor Ryan acted for humanitarian reasons, he was careful to time the mass commutation strategically—just two days before leaving office. Of course, we cannot blame him for this course of action, as he would likely have not been an effective governor (or popular for that matter) after making such a controversial decision. In today's political climate, governors wishing to grant clemency or pardons tend to do the same thing as Ryan—wait until it is time to leave office.

Courts may use public support as a measure of evolving standards of decency. *Evolving standards of decency* is a phrase first used in the U.S. Supreme Court case of *Trop v. Dulles* (1958) in which the justices attempted to infer what the framers of the Constitution might consider to be a proper standard for

---

[1] In California, appellate judges are initially appointed for a term and then have the opportunity to be retained in general elections. Retention elections do not involve other judicial candidates; rather, voters choose to either retain a sitting justice or replace him or her.

determining whether the death penalty is a violation of the Eighth Amendment in modern-day America. More specifically, evolving standards of decency is a measure of what the people want. This concept, as it applies to U.S. Supreme Court cases, is discussed at length in Chapter 3.

ATTITUDINAL MODEL AND POLITICAL ADJUSTMENT HYPOTHESIS

There is great debate about the extent to which judges base their decisions on public opinion and whether they are directly or indirectly affected by the same. One can deduce that U.S. Supreme Court justices are, at a minimum, indirectly influenced by public opinion because they are nominated by our democratically elected president and then confirmed by our democratically elected Senate. Considering the immensely powerful positions that U.S. Supreme Court justices hold, there are few tasks more important to the president of the United States than that of appointing the "right" justice when given the opportunity (Dahl, 1957).

With the exception of Jimmy Carter, every president in recent history has nominated at least one Supreme Court justice during his term in office. Barack Obama nominated two justices in his first two years as president (Justice Sonia Sotomayor and Justice Elena Kagan). This provides an obvious opportunity for a president to tip the balance in his or her party's favor by selecting a judicial candidate who would presumably decide issues with the ideological framework most in line with the current administration.

We will never know to what extent judges are responsive to public opinion, but it is helpful to consider two theoretical constructs often cited to explain judicial decision-making among U.S. Supreme Court justices: the **attitudinal model** and the **political adjustment hypothesis**. The attitudinal model has two primary assumptions. First, judges' behaviors (decisions) are the primary result of their individual ideological attitudes. For example, a judge with liberal values may support procedural law aimed at strengthening due process with regard to search and seizure protocols, whereas a judge with conservative ideological values might be in favor of loosening the constraints of procedural law by providing police with more discretion in regard to Fourth Amendment searches. Second, those attitudes are fundamental and long-lasting (Segal & Spaeth, 1993). The attitudinal model assumes that little can be done to change the individual attitudes of judges.

The political adjustment hypothesis offers the alternative view: that justices are likely to be strategic when deciding cases strongly linked to public views and are willing to step outside of their individual belief systems in order for the Court to maintain a positive public image. This view assumes that justices must consider how their decisions will be perceived by elected officials and the public because the Court needs to have its judgments respected and instituted in order to be efficacious (Mishler & Sheehan, 1996).

EXPRESSION OF PUBLIC OPINION

Before polls were used to gauge public opinion for capital punishment, one would look to the obvious signs of societal approval or disapproval—cheering by onlookers during an execution suggested support for the death penalty, while public demonstrations provided avenues for opponents to voice their position. Another less visible form of opposition to the death penalty was jury nullification. **Jury nullification** is a practice that serves as an indirect expression of public opposition for capital punishment. It refers to the inherent power of a jury to acquit a defendant and ignore the law with no consequences, even in cases with strong evidence to support a conviction (Haney, 2005). In other words, the practice of jury nullification allows jurors to decide a case based on what they believe ought to be the law, rather than what the law is (Hreno, 2008). This practice was so powerful that it was often cited by abolitionists who argued that jurors would use their power to nullify death sentences regardless of whether the law permitted them to do so (Haney, 2005).

Historically, the level of public support for capital punishment has been characterized by the movements to abolish it. The **Enlightenment**, or *Age of Reason*, marked a period in mid-eighteenth-century Europe when people turned away from the rule of the church and began to look to science for answers, with a strong emphasis on reason to understand greater society and the world around it. The well-known jurist, philosopher, and politician **Cesare Becarria** proposed major changes to the criminal justice system, including the abolishment of the death penalty for most crimes (Beccaria, 1981/1764). Becarria believed that the death penalty was excessive and that there were other punishments which would protect the public from offenders, such as banishment (prolonged exile from one's country by official decree). Prominent Americans such as Benjamin Franklin, Thomas Jefferson, and James Madison were influenced by the Enlightenment thinkers and therefore adopted many of the same ideas (Welch, 2011).

Another similar public movement to abolish the death penalty was the *anti-gallows movement* in the first half of the nineteenth century. This movement was facilitated by religious leaders, social reformers, legislatures, and of course the general public. Organizers focused on spreading the word about the atrocities of executions, particularly hangings, via newspapers and by other means of public communication. Though unsuccessful at accomplishing its goal to abolish hangings throughout America, the movement had a lasting impact. Public executions were eliminated, the number of capital crimes was reduced, and three states formally abolished the death penalty altogether. The anti-gallows movement was eventually disrupted by the Civil War (Jones, 2011).

Systematic polling dramatically changed the way that we measure public opinion with regard to capital punishment in the United States. The most prominent and widely accepted public opinion poll is the **Gallup Poll**, produced by the American Institute of Public Opinion. The Gallup organization surveys respondents by utilizing statistically representative samples to measure public opinion on a variety of issues (Gallup, 2015).

The first nationwide death penalty Gallup Poll was conducted in 1936 and revealed that 59% of Americans supported capital punishment when asked: *Are you in favor of the death penalty for a person convicted of murder*? The lowest level of public support for the death penalty was recorded in the 1960s at the height of the abolition movement. Between 1953 and 1966, Gallup data revealed a 38% decrease in public support—the largest decline since Gallup began polling on this issue in 1936. The 1966 Gallup Poll marked the only time in Gallup history that public opposition surpassed support (47% vs. 42%). Times were changing (or so it seemed), and in 1968 the Supreme Court referenced the supporters of capital punishment as "a distinct and dwindling minority" (*Witherspoon v. Illinois*, 1968). Politicians also began voicing opposition to capital punishment during this time. History was made when President Lyndon Johnson's administration became the first to ask Congress to abolish the death penalty. The Department of Justice and the National Crime Commission also announced their opposition to the death penalty, a sentiment that would be echoed in the case of *Furman v. Georgia* (1972) just a few short years later (see Chapter 3) (Lain, 2007).

In the landmark U.S. Supreme Court case of *Furman v. Georgia* (1972), the Court ruled (in a 5-4 vote) that capital punishment laws were unconstitutional in their application (see Chapter 3). The Court referenced the will of the people when they stated that the death penalty "violates the Eighth Amendment because it is morally unacceptable to the people of the United States at this time in their history" (*Furman v. Georgia*, 1972). The *Furman* decision resulted in the High Court placing a de facto moratorium on capital punishment, an act of historical significance.

Gallup Poll data were collected on two occasions in 1972. Three months prior to *Furman*, public support for the death penalty was at 50%, and five months later, there was a seven-point increase (57%) in public support for the death penalty (Gallup, 2015). Despite relatively low capital punishment support during the *Furman* era, the law-and-order movement was gaining momentum and the political winds were beginning to shift.

By modern standards, public support for capital punishment is positively correlated with support for "get tough" crime initiatives (Lain, 2007). Death

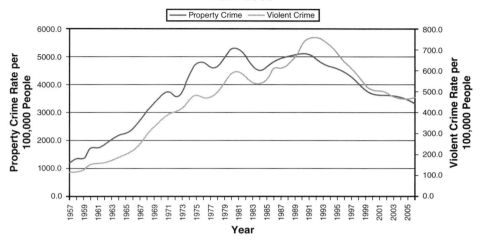

FIGURE 5.1   Trends in Violent and Property Crime Rates: 1957–2006

penalty support was the greatest in the 1980s and 1990s, with 1994 marking the highest level of support (80%) in the Gallup Poll's history. It is instructive to note that 1994 marked a time when crime was at an all-time high (Gallup, 2015). Accordingly, numerous law and order initiatives were formed to combat the "crime problem," such as the Crime Control Act of 1990 and the Violent Crime Control and Law Enforcement Act of 1994.

The **crime rate** (a statistic calculated by taking the total number of crimes in a given population divided by the population number and then multiplied by 100,000) appears to be a predictor of public support for the death penalty. According to **Uniform Crime Report (UCR)** data, the violent crime rate in 1994 was 713.6 per 100,000 when public opinion strongly favored capital punishment, and in 1966 the violent crime rate was significantly lower (220 per 100,000) when public opinion opposed it (U.S. Department of Justice, 2012). See Figures 5.1 and 5.2 (parts A and B) for crime rate and Gallup Poll comparisons.

The most recent Gallup Poll data (2015) reveal that approximately 63% of respondents are in favor of the death penalty and 33% are against it when asked the traditional "either/or" question. However, the levels of support for the death penalty are altered significantly when respondents were provided with an alternative to the death penalty—life without the possibility of parole (LWOP)—during the same interview. The new question asked of respondents

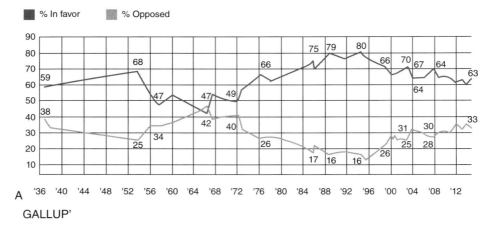

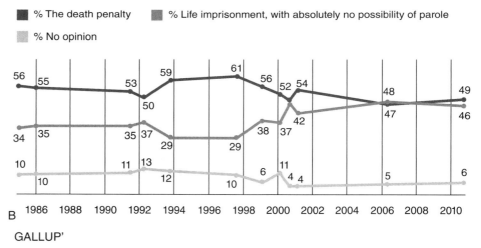

FIGURE 5.2 A: Trend in Favoring or Opposing Death Penalty. B: Opinions Given the LWOP Option

became: *If you could choose between the following two approaches, which do you think is the better penalty for murder: the death penalty or life imprisonment, with absolutely no possibility of parole?* Asking the question in this way appears to be a game changer for public opinion. The most recent Gallup Poll revealed that half of respondents (50%) still supported the death penalty, but the gap is closing, with approximately 45% of respondents opting for the alternative punishment of LWOP (with the remaining 5% having no opinion) (Gallup, 2015). Similar results were found in 2010 when the death penalty support was 49% compared to 46% of those choosing the alternative punishment.[2]

PERSPECTIVE FROM THE FORMER WIFE OF A SERIAL KILLER: HEATHER ASBURY

Heather Asbury led a seemingly normal life in Lake Havasu, South Carolina. She married Dallen Bounds, a 28-year-old man who worked as a butcher at a local grocery store. Heather was married to Bounds for three years and they had a child together. They divorced but were in the midst of reconciliation when Heather discovered a terrible secret—Bounds was a serial killer. Heather got a call from police informing her that Bounds had killed himself after murdering two people in 1999. Heather soon learned that six months prior, Bounds murdered Jonathan Lara, a Radio Shack employee, who was found dead and tied to a chair in the store after being stabbed in the neck with a screwdriver. After murdering Lara, Bounds turned off the lights and put a "closed" sign in the window. The night before taking his own life, Bounds had killed again. In a similar attack, Bounds walked into a floral shop and murdered Karen Hayden, a young wife and mother, whose body was found in a pool of blood after being nearly decapitated by a knife wound to her throat. Again, Bounds turned off the lights in the shop and placed the "sorry, we're closed" sign in the window. The following day, Bounds killed Sandra and Timothy Ott before barricading himself in a room with hostages and taking his own life. Prosecutors told Heather that if Bounds had not committed suicide, they would have sought the death penalty in his case. He is also believed to have been responsible for numerous other murders for which he was never charged.

FIGURE 5.3 Heather Asbury

---

[2]The Gallup Poll is not administered every year. The alternative LWOP question was asked in both 2014 and 2010, but not in between.

> I didn't know what was going on when Dallen was doing the crimes, so when I found out what he had done, I was in shock. Though, at the same time, I wasn't totally surprised because he was abusive to me. In one instance, he strangled me and I blacked out. When I awoke, he said, "You are still alive because I didn't know where I would put your body, so I stopped." I still struggle between love and hate for this man who gave me the world and held my life in his hands.
>
> Just as sure as I was in knowing he would always embrace me, I also knew he would take my life with that same passion. I know what it is like to see light turn into blackness, then see that "bright light" with his hands wrapped around my throat. The fear of seeing that flickering light bouncing off the blade of his knife, closing my eyes wishing for peace and the light of God as he held that knife to my throat.
>
> I thought I knew all of his secrets, yet there was one that he never shared. His desire to kill. I will never forget the exact words the detective said to me: "he (Dallen) is a sadistic serial killer, it's one thing to shoot someone, it's another to hold them close to you and slice their throat." The detective went through the accounts of each crime they were able to pin him to, yet he needed more information. He asked me for anything I thought could help them solve dozens of unsolved cases that happened to occur in every town we passed through and lived in.
>
> I support the death penalty because I feel like if someone is willing to take someone's life then I think they lose their right to live in our society. I don't think that there is the possibility of rehabilitation and I don't think that we should waste our resources on them. I believe in the retributive element of the death penalty, "an eye for an eye." If you kill someone, you should be killed. After being married to Dallen, I am a stronger supporter of the death penalty because I have firsthand knowledge of the damage that these killers can cause. On the side of the victims left behind, I put myself in their shoes and if someone I loved was murdered, I believe I would want the closure of seeing them given the death penalty. Although, I would not have supported a sentence of death in Dallen's case because I loved him and for the sake of our daughter.

Heather's story represents an all-too-familiar issue in the capital punishment debate. The experience of people who contemplate the death penalty as an abstract notion, in deciding whether they support or oppose it, is very different from that of someone intimately connected to a death penalty case. For these individuals, the issue becomes much more complex. Like the families of victims in capital cases, Heather is emotionally connected to her ex-husband's case, thereby making it difficult for her to objectively decide whether the death penalty ought to be utilized as a matter of public policy. We do not mean to imply that the idea of retribution is not a valid punishment consideration, however. Indeed, we have already explored the concept and importance of retribution as a punishment philosophy at length in Chapter 1. When considering the concepts of retribution and just deserts, the death penalty may very well be justifiable, but what about the practical considerations associated with the death penalty (the possibility of executing an innocent person, its costs, discriminatory practices in its application, etc.)? Should these matters be set aside in the name of retribution?

THE MARSHALL HYPOTHESIS

U.S. Supreme Court Chief Justice Thurgood Marshall highlighted the significance of public opinion when considering the constitutionality of capital punishment in *Furman v. Georgia* (1972). He explained that even when punishment is not excessive and has a legitimate legal purpose, "it still may be invalid if popular sentiment abhors it" (*Furman v. Georgia*, 1972, sec. 332). Marshall furthered his opinion by adding the element of knowledge requirement: "It is imperative for constitutional purposes to attempt to discern the probable opinion of an informed electorate" (*Furman v. Georgia*, 1972). He stressed the need for the public to be adequately informed about capital punishment before making determinations about one's stance.

Marshall is commonly cited for his hypothesis, subsequently deemed the **Marshall hypothesis**, which first posits that when Americans are properly informed about the death penalty, "the great mass of citizens would conclude . . . that the death penalty is immoral therefore unconstitutional" (*Furman v. Georgia*, 1972). Essentially, he proposed that the American public supports the death penalty because it is largely uninformed on the subject. Marshall opined:

> It has often been noted that American citizens know almost nothing about capital punishment. . . . [T]he death penalty is no more effective a deterrent than life imprisonment, that convicted murderers are rarely executed, but are usually sentenced to a term in prison; that convicted murderers usually are model prisoners, and that they almost always become law-abiding citizens upon their release from prison; that the costs of executing a capital offender exceed the costs of imprisoning him for life; that while in prison, a convict under the

sentence of death performs none of the useful functions that life prisoners perform; that no attempt is made in the sentencing process to ferret out likely recidivists for execution; and that the death penalty may actually stimulate criminal activity. . . . I cannot believe that at this state in our history, the American people would ever knowingly support purposeless vengeance. . . . [C]apital punishment is imposed discriminatorily against certain identifiable classes of people; there is evidence that innocent people have been executed before their innocence can be proved; and the death penalty wreaks havoc with our entire criminal justice system. (*Furman v. Georgia*, 1972)

Essentially, Marshall believed that an "informed citizen" would choose not to support capital punishment. His second proposal/hypothesis was that if a person's underlying belief in the death penalty is retributive in nature, then proper education would do little to change his or her position (*Furman v. Georgia*, 1972).

There have been numerous empirical studies conducted by social science researchers attempting to test the Marshall hypothesis, but operationalizing the concept of what constitutes an "informed citizenry" is problematic because Marshall never defined what precisely he meant by this. He simply stated that American citizens would need to consider capital punishment "in the light of all information presently available" (*Furman v. Georgia*, 1972, sec. 362). The lack of explanation makes comparing the studies somewhat challenging because different studies have operationalized the concept differently. In any event, several early studies were conducted that attempted to test the Marshall hypothesis.

One such study was that of Sarat and Vidmar (1976), who surveyed 181 subjects from Amherst, Massachusetts. The subjects were provided with essays on death penalty topics that served to "educate" them on the issue. The study ultimately found a significant reduction in death penalty support after participants became "informed" about the death penalty. A follow-up study by Vidmar and Dittenhoffer (1981) targeted 39 college undergraduates in Canada, where the death penalty was abolished in 1976. Like the previous study, the participants were required to read essays on death penalty issues. The pretest data revealed that approximately half of the participants were in support of the death penalty in both the experimental and control groups. There was a significant decline in the death penalty support in the posttest findings—71% opposed capital punishment in the experimental group, with only 24% continuing to support it (Vidmar & Dittenhoffer, 1981). These studies suggest that Marshall's hypothesis may have merit, though there is at least one study that found the opposite—increased knowledge of death penalty issues results in greater support for capital punishment (Lambert & Clarke, 2001). As Bohm (2012) points out, however, many of the early Marshall hypothesis studies are inapplicable and invalid today due to issues related to social conditions during the data collection and methodological shortcomings.

Perhaps Marshall should have required an "informed citizen" in today's world to consider the numerous death row DNA exonerations that have come to light in a post-*Furman* era. Since *Furman*, the advent of DNA testing has spawned the so-called Innocence Movement or Revolution (see Chapter 10). While Marshall warned about innocents on death row, he lived in a time when innocence was a mere abstraction with no real means to prove its existence (short of a guilty person confessing to a crime that another has been falsely accused, and found guilty, of committing). A study by Lambert and Clarke (2001) sought to bridge the gap between the older body of research conducted on the Marshall hypothesis with new research. The new research captures the opinions of participants who live in today's world and acknowledge that wrongful convictions have become an indisputable reality. Among other research questions, Lambert and Clarke (2001) sought to discover if educating 730 college students about the realities of sentencing innocent people to death (likelihood of, frequency, etc.) would impact their opinion of capital punishment. They predicted it would and they were correct. There was a statistically significant decline in death penalty support after students became "informed" about the realities of innocents on death row, though the change was not as dramatic as Marshall postulated. Few of the students who strongly favored capital punishment prior to the study actually changed their view to strongly oppose the penalty; rather, they would only partially support it (Lambert & Clarke, 2001).

Hatch, one of the authors of this book, has taught a university-level capital punishment course (admittedly, a small-sized class, with approximately 30 students) for several years and has put the Marshall hypothesis to the test in each of her classes. Hatch asks her students to fill out a questionnaire designed to gauge their support before the course begins and after it concludes. Her findings continually mirror those of Lambert and Clarke (2001)—education and support for the death penalty seem to have an inverse relationship (as education goes up, support goes down).

Perhaps a current test of the Marshall hypothesis would reveal a more dramatic decrease in public support if study applicants were to learn that there have been more than 330 DNA exonerations of the wrongfully accused, 20 of whom served time on death row (Innocence Project, 2015). The Marshall hypothesis may also be considered when looking at the Gallup Poll question that allows participants to choose the alternative option for the death penalty—LWOP. We already know that asking the question including the LWOP alternative creates a near 50/50 divide in public support/opposition. When we provide participants with this additional option to choose from, are we effectively *increasing* their information? If so, then we might surmise that such a decline in support is due, in part, to participants' utilization of more information when selecting their choice on the survey.

GLOBAL PERSPECTIVES ON THE DEATH PENALTY

There is a global trend to abolish the capital punishment. Since 2003, an average of two countries each year have abolished the death penalty (Amnesty International, 2013). The European Union requires countries to abolish the death penalty as a requirement for membership. Amnesty International, a global organization that campaigns for human rights, tracks capital punishment practices around the world and reports a growing trend of abolishment. As of 2010, 96 countries have abolished the death penalty (two-thirds of countries) compared to only 16 countries in 1977.[3] The five countries leading in the number of executions are China, Iran, Saudi Arabia, Iraq, and the United States (Amnesty International, 2013). The United States is the only developed Western country in which the death penalty is still imposed, though some individual states have abolished it. Currently, 31 U.S. states continue to apply the death penalty (see Figure 5.4; Death Penalty Information Center, 2015).

Why should we take into account the opinions and penal sanctions of other countries when considering the use of the death penalty in the United States? After all, we are a nation that takes pride in our unique values and belief systems, even when they stand in opposition to those of other countries. Babcock (2007) opines that the death penalty debate is no longer one of "domestic penal policy," but one of human rights, thereby making the matter of global concern (p. 2).

We know that the U.S. Supreme Court takes into consideration public opinion, especially when ruling on controversial and hotly debated issues. In some of these cases, they allow the international community to "weigh in." Let's not forget *Trop v. Dulles* (1958), in which the Court first references the concept of *evolving standards of decency*. The *Trop* Court was specific in referring to global opinion when characterizing the practice of banishment as "universally deplored in the international community of democracies" (*Trop v. Dulles*, 1958). Similarly, the Court often references the global move toward abolition when deciding whether the practice of the death penalty is constitutional.

In *Wilkerson v. Utah* (1879), a U.S. Supreme Court case concerning the constitutionality of the firing squad (see Chapter 6), the Court upheld the practice and supported its opinion by pointing to the use of firing squads by other countries. In *Atkins v. Virginia* (2002), the Court determined that executing the

---

[3]If one takes into account countries that have not abolished the death penalty by law, but have not exercised the practice in the past 10 years, de facto abolitionists, the number of abolitionist countries is approximately 140 (Amnesty International, 2013).

Chapter 5 THE DEATH PENALTY AND PUBLIC OPINION   119

FIGURE 5.4   States with and without the death penalty as of 2015

mentally retarded was an Eighth Amendment violation (see Chapter 4). It did so by referencing a brief by the European Union that outlined the vast disapproval of such a sentencing practice within the global community (Babcock, 2007). The case of *Roper v. Simmons* (2005) is another landmark case in which the Court held that executing juveniles was unconstitutional, violating the Eighth Amendment protection against cruel and unusual punishment (see Chapter 4). Although the Court made note that international law did not control its decision, the justices did cite international opinion as being both "instructive" and "significant" when reviewing the issues of capital punishment. Indeed, the Court cited that since 1990, very few countries (seven) had implemented the execution of juveniles and even those countries have since "disavowed the practice in recent years" (Babcock, 2007, p. 2). The Justices went on to say that the United States is "the only country in the world that continues to give official sanction to the juvenile death penalty" when justifying their ruling to abolish the practice (*Roper v. Simmons*, 2005).

Though public opinion is clearly a factor in determining courts' decisions to rule in a particular way, abolishment sometimes happens despite strong public support for capital punishment. Zimrig and Hawkins (1986) assert that, historically, abolishment of the death penalty has not been the result of popular demand and that most countries which have abolished it did so against the will of the people, though the authors' research was conducted in 1986 and much has changed in abolishment trends since then. Indeed, the move to abolish capital punishment gained momentum in the 1990s (Neumayer, 2008). In any event, one might conclude that despite public support, abolishment is certainly possible in non-democratic countries (isolated from public opinion). It is very unlikely, however, that abolishment in the United States would take place without the support of the public (Bohm, 2012).

Once a country abolishes the death penalty, it is highly improbable that nation will ever restore the punishment. Italy, however, is one such exception. The death penalty was abolished in 1889 under the influence of Beccaria (see Chapter 2) and then reinstated in 1926 under the Fascist rule of Mussolini, but was once again abolished in 1948 (Neumayer, 2008). Canada also attempted to bring back the death penalty in 1987, albeit unsuccessfully (Correctional Service Canada, 2013). Two-thirds of Britons wish to see the death penalty restored as a punishment option in the United Kingdom (Angus Reid Public Opinion Poll, 2012). That nation abolished the death penalty in 1965 for most crimes, except treason and piracy, and completely abolished it for all crimes in 1998.

Eric Neumayer (2008) posits that political factors play a central role in the abolition trend. The global movement toward establishing democratic governments is key when considering abolition. Neumayer concludes that the global trend to abolish the death penalty will continue if "democracy continues to spread around the world" (p. 241). This is especially true if we frame the death penalty debate in the context of violating human rights—an issue that will no doubt place political pressure on countries which choose not to conform to the will of the international community.

SUMMARY

This chapter explains the role of public opinion as it pertains to capital punishment. There are many ways that the will of the people shapes our policy decisions and the death penalty is an issue that many have strong opinions about. While we attempt to balance best practice approaches with public sentiment, there is often a disconnect between what is practical and what feels morally right (or wrong).

We learned that strong public support exists for the death penalty in the United States; otherwise, it would cease to exist. It is the U.S. Supreme Court, however, that is the ultimate decision-maker when it comes to determining the constitutionality of the death penalty. The Court refers to the Eighth Amendment when considering if capital punishment violates the right to be free from cruel and unusual punishment. In numerous landmark cases, we see how critically the Court weighs public opinion or *evolving standards of decency* when reaching its decisions. The Court additionally takes into account the concerns of the international community. We also learned that public opinion affects not only judicial decision-making; it is a key factor for governors when determining clemency and for prosecutors when deciding whether to seek the death penalty.

We reviewed the history of the Gallup Poll and how it has shaped the death penalty debate, especially when asking the "right" questions. Exploring the trends of public opinion with regard to the death penalty is important when trying to determine the future of capital punishment in the United States. We must also keep in mind the social context of the times. There is little doubt that in the wake of the Innocence Revolution (see Chapter 10), public sentiment will be impacted. Few are likely to accept the execution of an innocent person and when more hard evidence of this result emerges, it could become a game changer in terms of public opinion.

DISCUSSION QUESTIONS

1. Do you believe that public opinion should influence judicial decision-making? Why? Explain your answer.
2. Can you think of another highly debated criminal justice topic in which jury nullification has been (or might be) an issue?
3. Do you believe that the family of victims should have a role in determining whether an offender receives the death penalty? Explain your answer.
4. Do you believe that we should consider the penal practices utilized by other countries when considering what is appropriate in our own?
5. If the majority of the public wants the death penalty retained or reinstated (as in the United Kingdom), should the government be responsive to its wishes, or do you believe that the opinions and rulings of the elites in government should be the deciding factor?

GLOSSARY

Attitudinal model: A model with two assumptions: Judges' decisions are the result of their individual attitudes/ideologies and those attitudes are fundamental and long-lasting.

Cesare Becarria: An Italian jurist and philosopher who proposed major changes to the criminal justice system, including the abolishment of the death penalty.

Crime rate: A statistic calculated by taking the total number of crimes in a given population divided by the population number and then multiplied by 100,000.

Enlightenment: Also known as the Age of Reason, a period in mid-eighteenth-century Europe when people turned away from the rule of the church and began to look to science for answers, with a strong emphasis on reason to understand greater society and the world around it.

Gallup Poll: A poll produced by the American Institute of Public Opinion that surveys respondents by utilizing statistically representative samples to measure public opinion on a variety of issues.

Jury nullification: A practice that serves as an indirect expression of public disdain for the death penalty. It refers to the inherent power of a jury to acquit a defendant and ignore the law, even in cases with strong evidence to support a conviction.

Marshall hypothesis: U.S. Supreme Court Chief Justice Thurgood Marshall hypothesized that if Americans were adequately informed about the death penalty, they would not be in favor of it. He further posited that if a person's underlying belief in the death penalty is retributive in nature, then proper education would do little to change his or her position.

Political adjustment hypothesis: A model suggesting that justices are likely to be strategic when deciding cases strongly linked to public views and may be more willing to step outside of their individual belief systems in order for the Court to maintain a positive public image.

Social solidarity: Durkheim's concept referring to the common moral ground shared by individuals that binds them together in social institutions.

Uniform Crime Report (UCR): A national program administered by the Federal Bureau of Investigation. Official arrest data are collected, statistically analyzed, and reported.

REFERENCES

Amnesty International. (2013). "Death Penalty." https://www.amnesty.org/en/what-we-do/death-penalty.

Angus Reid Public Opinion Poll. (2012). "Two Thirds of Britons Would Bring Back Capital Punishment." http://angusreid.org/two-thirds-of-britons-would-bring-back-capital-punishment/.

Atkins v. Virginia. (2002). 536 U.S. 304.

Babcock, S. (2007). The global debate on the death penalty. *Human Rights, 34*(2), 1–8.

Beccaria, C. (1981/1764). *On crimes and punishments.* Trans. Henry Paolucci. Indianapolis, IN: Bobbs-Merrill.

Bohm, R. (2012). *Deathquest: An introduction to the theory and practice of capital punishment in the United States.* Boston: Anderson.

Cardozo, B. (1921). *The nature of the judicial process.* New Haven, CT: Yale University Press.

Correctional Service Canada. (2013). "Abolition of the Death Penalty 1976." http://www.csc-scc.gc.ca/text/pblct/rht-drt/08-eng.shtml.

Dahl, R. (1957). Decision-making in a democracy: The Supreme Court as a national policy-maker. *Journal of Public Law, 6,* 279–295.

Death Penalty Information Center. (2015). "States with and without the Death Penalty." http://www.innocenceproject.org/free-innocent/improve-the-law/fact-sheets/dna-exonerations-nationwide

Dodd, W. F. (1922). The nature of the judicial process by Benjamin N. Cardozo. *The American Political Science Review, 16*(4), 710–711.

Durkheim. (1933). *The division of labor in society.* New York: Macmillan.

Furman v. Georgia. (1972). 408 U.S. 153.

Gallup. (2015). "Death Penalty Poll." http://www.gallup.com/poll/1606/death-penalty.aspx.

Gallup Poll. (2015). George H. Gallup, Founder: 1901–1984. http://www.gallup.com/corporate/178136/george-gallup.aspx

Gregg v. Georgia. (1976). 428 U.S. 153.

Haney, C. (2005). *Death by design: Capital punishment as a social psychological system.* New York: Oxford University Press.

Hreno, T. (2008). The rule of law and jury nullification. *Commonwealth Law Bulletin, 34*(2), 297–312.

Innocence Project. (2015). "DNA Exonerations Nationwide." http://www.innocenceproject.org/free-innocent/improve-the-law/fact-sheets/dna-exonerations-nationwide

Jones, P. (2011). *Against the gallows: Antebellum American writers and the movement to abolish capital punishment.* Iowa City: University of Iowa Press.

Lain, C. (2007). *Furman* fundamentals. *Washington Law Review, 82*(1), 1–74.

Lambert, E., and A. Clarke. (2001). The impact of information on an individual's support of the death penalty: A partial test of the Marshall hypothesis among college students. *Criminal Justice Policy Review, 12*(3), 215–234.

Mishler, W., and R. Sheehan. (1996). Public opinion, the attitudinal model, and Supreme Court decision making: A micro-analytic perspective. *Journal of Politics, 58*(1), 169–200.

Neumayer, E. (2008). Death penalty: The political foundations of the global trend towards abolition. *Human Rights Review, 9,* 241–268.

Roper v. Simmons. (2005). 543 U.S. 551.

Sarat, A., and N. Vidmar. (1976). Public opinion, the death penalty, and the Eighth Amendment: Testing the Marshall hypothesis. *Wisconsin Law Review, 17,* 71–206.

Segal, J., and H. Spaeth. (1993). *The Supreme Court and the attitudinal model.* New York: Cambridge University Press.

Traut, C., and C. Emmert. (1998). Expanding the integrated model of judicial decision making: The California justices and capital punishment. *Journal of Politics, 60*(4), 1166–1180.

Trop v. Dulles. (1958). 356 U.S. 86.

U.S. Department of Justice. (2012). "Uniform Crime Reporting Statistics." http://www.ucrdatatool.gov.

Vidmar, N., and T. Dittenhoffer. (1981). Informed public opinion and death penalty attitudes. *Canadian Journal of Criminology, 23,* 43–56.

Welch, M. (2011). *Corrections: A critical approach.* New York: Routledge.

Wilkerson v. Utah. (1879). 99 U.S. 130.

Witherspoon v. Illinois. (1968). 391 U.S. 510.

Yates, J. (2002). *Popular justice: Presidential prestige and executive success in the Supreme Court.* Albany: State University of New York.

Zimrig, F., and G. Hawkins. (1986). *Capital punishment and the American agenda.* Cambridge, UK: Cambridge University Press.

CHAPTER 6

METHODS OF EXECUTION

Ronnie Lee Gardner was executed in 2010 by a Utah firing squad. He is the last man in the United States to be executed by this method. Gardner was arrested in 1984 for robbing and murdering a Salt Lake City bartender, Melvyn Otterstrom, who died of a gunshot wound to the face. Gardner was convicted and sentenced to life without the possibility of parole. While making a court appearance a year later in the same case, he orchestrated an escape plan that involved an accomplice supplying him with a gun to use for securing a hostage. The plan failed when Gardner was shot in the chest by a security officer, but not before he was able to shoot and wound a bailiff and then run into another room, where he shot and killed attorney Michael Burdell in the face while Burdell hid behind a door. Burdell was doing pro bono legal work for his church at the courthouse that day.

After serving 25 years on death row, Gardner met his execution date. When asked why he chose to die by firing squad, he replied: "I lived by the gun, I murdered with a gun, I will die by the gun." Gardner entered a cinderblock room located in the Utah state prison and was strapped to a metal chair. His chair was surrounded with sandbags in order to prevent ricochets from the bullets. Five police officers volunteered to shoot Gardner. Each of them was equipped with a .30 caliber Winchester rifle, one of which was loaded with a blank so that the executioners would not know exactly who fired the fatal bullet. A small black target was situated over Gardner's heart on his chest to serve as the executioners' target. He was asked if he had any last words just before his head was covered with a black hood. He replied, "I do not, no." After a brief countdown, family members of the victim, correctional administrators, and nine journalists watched as officers opened fire. Gardner was pronounced dead two minutes later.

LEARNING OBJECTIVES

- Understand the shift in execution protocols as they have evolved over time.
- Identify the steps states have taken to lessen the impact of pain experienced by the offender during the execution process.
- Identify the strengths and weaknesses of the various methods of execution as characterized by the experts.
- Understand the domestic and international challenges associated with lethal injection drugs.
- Identify the ethical dilemmas that prevent medical doctors and nurses from participating in executions.

Gardner's execution was unique in that he became one of only three people to be executed by firing squad since the death penalty was reinstated in 1976 (*Gregg v. Georgia*). All three of these executions took place in Utah (see picture of Utah's firing squad execution chamber on p. 142). Although Utah replaced the firing squad option with lethal injection in 2004, Gardner was sentenced prior to the change and was therefore allowed to choose this form of execution. For both the states and the federal government, the primary execution method used today is lethal injection (Death Penalty Information Center, 2014a).

THE EVOLUTION OF EXECUTION METHODS

More than 1,200 executions have occurred since 1976 (post-*Furman* era), when we began reliably tracking the number of executions (Amnesty International, 2014). There is no doubt that we have a long history of utilizing a wide range of execution methods in this country, with many of them being quite brutal (burning alive, beheading, quartering, etc.). We can thank our English roots for many of the "creative" ways in which states have sought to extinguish human life. Indeed, when thinking of the evolution of execution methods in our country, one might conjure the grisly images of early executions. We might picture groups of spectators who have gathered to watch the executioner march the condemned to a gruesome death. Fortunately, times have changed. No longer do executioners lie out their bags of torture devices before the condemned and seek pain in the execution process.

Execution protocols now require methods that inflict as little pain as possible. Execution practices are frequently debated in context of the Eighth Amendment that protects us from *cruel and unusual punishment*. Such cases challenging the constitutionality of the death penalty have gradually changed

Chapter 6 METHODS OF EXECUTION   **127**

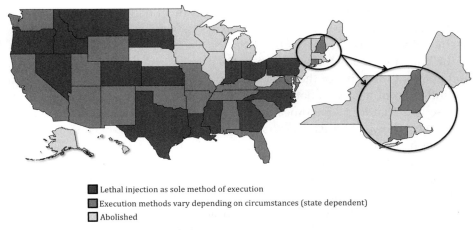

■ Lethal injection as sole method of execution
■ Execution methods vary depending on circumstances (state dependent)
□ Abolished

FIGURE 6.1   Execution Method(s) by State

the administration of capital punishment (see Chapters 3 and 4). When this happens, states often respond by adopting new methods out of fear that the old will be declared unconstitutional. Indeed, many death penalty states have multiple methods of execution that serve as back-ups should the method of the time be eliminated (see Figure 6.1) (Death Penalty Information Center, 2014b).

The evolution of execution methods is a topic that needs to be understood in the context of how we have evolved as a society because what we want or deem acceptable has changed over time. Recall from Chapter 2 that early executions were meant to be terrifying experiences for both the executionee and the witnesses in order to meet standards of deterrence and retribution. In a gradual turn of events, we now seek to eliminate pain and the visibility of executions. The most common and widely adopted methods of execution in recent history include hanging, electrocution, the gas chamber, the firing squad, lethal injection. Each of these methods is described at length in this chapter.

HANGING

Hanging first became popularized by colonial Americans and was the predominant method of execution until the 1890s. It was a widely used method because of its convenience, simplicity, and low cost to implement. After all, one only needs a rope, tree, and a person who knows how to tie a noose in order to commence a hanging execution. (And there is minimal damage to the body when compared to other methods of execution.) Ideally, a hanging death is supposed to be quick and painless, resulting from instant severing of the spinal cord after the condemned is dropped from the rope. While seemingly foolproof, few hangings were carried out as planned (Banner, 2002).

Banner (2002) explains that the variable nature of hangings complicates efforts to ensure ideal results. A fine line exists between a painful and painless death, to include the "height of the drop, the elasticity of the rope, the position of the knot, the weather, the tension in the condemned person's neck muscles, and not least the skills of the hangman" (Banner, 2002, pp. 170–171). Although the infliction of pain was not a desirable outcome of hanging, the general response was that it is sometimes an unavoidable and necessary consequence. There were, however, great lengths taken by executioners experimenting with the design of gallows to make them more efficient. For instance, the first departure from traditional hanging practices consisted of the "upright jerker" method. This method was designed to create more force to break the condemned man's neck than could be exerted in the traditional "drop" (Banner, 2002, p. 171). It was believed that using a system of pulleys to suspend the body on one side and securing the opposite side of the rope with sandbags, which considerably exceeded the body's weight, would sever the spinal cord with more efficiency. This system would theoretically allow better control of the rope's weights at both ends.

Unfortunately, the upright jerker method proved to be a failure because the rope and pulleys were not always set correctly by the executioner, resulting in a long period of suffering for the condemned. With both the traditional and upright jerker methods, the lack of experience by the executioner proved to be a key factor in determining success or failure. As we learned in Chapter 2, there was really no training for executioners because executions during this time occurred in the county where the crime had occurred and, therefore, were relatively rare events. Gallows were typically constructed on short notice when an execution was ordered, requiring officials to scramble for volunteer executioners.

Another attempt at improvement included adjusting the length of the rope used for hangings. Experimenters theorized that by extending the length of the rope, the body would drop further and faster, thereby increasing the likelihood of instant breakage of the neck. Although this theory proved to be true in some cases, a new side effect was realized—decapitation. Decapitation resulted from the high velocity and force of the body weight reaching the end of the rope (Banner, 2002). A series of gruesome decapitations necessitated the termination of this practice. Other attempts consisted of using water for weighting and experimenting with various trapdoor constructions. Some officials even allowed prisoners themselves to construct their own methods of hanging. Ultimately, executioners and onlookers alike expressed their discontent with hanging and so the quest to seek better methods continued (see Figure 6.2) (Banner, 2002).

When the state of Delaware sought to execute convicted murderer Billy Bailey by hanging (his choice) in 1996, they had to learn how to do it because

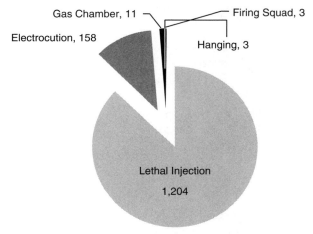

FIGURE 6.2 Number of Executions by Method Since 1976
Adapted from Death Penalty Information Center data

there had not been a hanging in Delaware for more than 50 years. Correctional officials turned to the Washington Department of Corrections for help because they had executed a man by hanging three years prior (Westley Allan Dodd, who was the first convict to be hanged after *Furman*). Officials also consulted the U.S. Army hanging manual from 1969, though the military had already terminated hanging as a method of execution. The manual outlined specifications for rope diameter and length (too long results in decapitation and too short results in lengthy strangulation), directions for boiling the rope to prevent coiling, and even methods of lubricating the rope to achieve a smooth sliding action (Hillman, 1993; *The Corrections Professional*, 1996). Delaware corrections officials constructed a gallows located on the grounds of the Delaware Correctional Center. Their execution plan worked—Bailey was marched up the steps to the platform of the two-story gallows and hanged until death (*The Baltimore Sun*, 2003). Bailey became the last death row inmate to be hanged in the United States.

Ultimately, hanging as a method of execution has been largely discontinued due to the inability of states to ensure efficiency and/or protect the condemned from suffering. The growing distaste for hangings resulted in regular citizen complaints and an enormous amount of pressure on government officials to discontinue the practice, though it is still an authorized method in three states: Delaware, New Hampshire, and Washington (Death Penalty Information Center, 2014a). The time for introducing a new method of execution was ripe and those concerned with finding the solution turned to science for answers. Experiments with electricity piqued the interest of officials and fueled the demand for a new method.

ELECTROCUTION

The idea of utilizing science to guide execution protocols made sense, given the disastrous results with previous methods. If there is one thing learned from hangings, it would be the need to standardize the process. Just too many variables had to be taken into account in order to achieve a "successful" hanging. By *successful*, we mean a hanging that does not result in unnecessary pain and suffering by the condemned, as required by the Eighth Amendment.

Using electricity to kill humans emerged from a couple of sources, namely the bitter battle between two of America's renowned inventors—Thomas Edison and George Westinghouse. As we learned in Chapter 2, the fierce competition over the use of DC and AC forms of electricity ignited the creation of a new method of execution—death by electrocution. Recall that the public demonstrations, used by Edison to prove the danger of Westinghouse's AC form of electricity, involved Edison killing animals to prove that AC electricity was too dangerous for residential and commercial use.

Edison and Westinghouse both advocated for use of the other's type of electrical current for the death penalty. Neither wanted the distinction of distributing the form of electricity that would be used to kill people. Interestingly, "electrocution" was not the first term considered for this form of execution. Experiments with catchy phrases such as "having an offender Westinghoused" were advocated by Edison's camp, while other labels considered were "electromort," "electricide," "electrodited," and "judicial lightning" (Moran, 2003, p. xxii).

Eventually, the idea to secure offenders to a chair while administering the electricity was decided to be the most efficient and practical method—hence, the term "electric chair." This idea was first discussed in an editorial for the *Scientific American*. The article suggested that offenders be strapped into a chair with a bulb fixed to their head that would also be attached to a live electrical wire connected to a streetlight. The chair would then be fitted with a "clock-like apparatus," allowing executioners to set the time for death. The use of the timer would be particularly useful because it relieved the executioner of the burden associated with directly causing death (Moran, 2003, p. 94). The authors of the editorial opined that the use of an electric chair would be successful on two fronts—it would provide offenders with a quick and painless death and circumvent the need for an executioner.

Dr. Alfred Southwick, a New York dentist, also played a pivotal role in the emergence of the electric chair. He witnessed the accidental electrocution of a man who touched electrical wires, which prompted him to consider utilizing electricity for executions (Denver, Best, & Haas, 2008). Southwick experimented with electrocution by electrocuting dogs. Determining that this practice was humane, he consulted with his friend and New York senator who, in turn, convinced the New York State Legislature to appoint a committee to search for a new execution method. In 1886, the New York Death Penalty Commission was formed. The committee acknowledged the need to depart from traditional hanging methods and called for a less barbaric manner for executing offenders. The commission's goal was to find the most humane method of execution and report its findings to the legislature. It considered 34 various methods of execution, but focused on electrocution as its primary consideration. Two of the three committee members immediately voted in favor of electrocution and the third member voted the same after Southwick prompted Edison to write the commission a letter explaining that electrocution was the most humane method. The committee's findings prompted the New York Legislature to make electrocution its sole method of execution (Denver, Best, & Haas, 2008). Other states quickly followed suit.

Death by electrocution involves the offender being placed in a wooden chair and secured by straps on the arms, waist, and legs. Moran (2003) describes in detail the construction of the chair (see Figure 6.3):

> The electrode, which passed through a wooden figure four, fastened to the back of the chair and adjustable to any height, was suspended from a horizontal arm attached to the back of the chair, above the headrest. A rubber cup containing a natural sea sponge hung above the head of the chair, and another cup and sponge were attached to its lower back. From these cups two wires ran out the window and across the roof to the dynamo in the northwest corner of the prison, about one thousand feet away. (Moran, 2003, p. 37)

Straps were used not only to prevent the escape of the offender, but also to ensure that the body would remain in place while the electricity was discharged. Without being secured, the body could very well be launched across the execution room (Moran, 2003).

William Kemmler was the first man to be executed by electrocution. He was executed in the Auburn State Prison on August 6, 1890. On the morning of his execution, Kemmler ate breakfast; his head was then shaved so that the skullcap containing the sponge would have direct contact with his skin. Eleven straps were used to hold Kemmler to the chair; Kemmler repeatedly asked the warden to tighten them, concerned that the process would not go as planned. Next, a leather muzzle was placed across his head, forehead, and chin. The process was somewhat impromptu, as the warden and doctor (charged with declaring Kemmler's death) exchanged comments about how long the electric current should be on, just minutes before the execution was carried out. They settled on a 10-second time period after concurring that 15 seconds would be too long. The switch was pulled and the execution lasted approximately 17 seconds, concluding when the doctor signaled that the electrical current should be discontinued because Kemmler appeared to be dead. After officials declared the execution successful, spectators watched in horror as Kemmler's body began twitching. He was still breathing and had a heartbeat (Moran, 2003). The current was switched back on and the execution proceeded as follows:

> Froth oozed out of Kemmler's strapped mouth. The small blood vessels under his skin began to rupture. Blood trickled down his face and arms. Twice Kemmler's body twitched as the current was switched on and off. The awful smell of burning flesh filled the death chamber. Kemmler's body first smoldered and then caught fire. (Moran, 2003, pp. 39–40)

This time the electrocution ended after eight minutes. One of the execution doctors commented: "All this goes to show that the new method will not take from capital punishment the barbarous features of an execution" (Moran, 2003, p. 44). Southwick then released a statement proclaiming the execution to be an absolute success (one has to wonder if he was paying attention).

Although the first execution in New York was considered a failure by prison staff and witnesses, the method became the next "big thing" and garnered widespread support in states across the country. Proponents maintained the perception that death by electrocution was quick, painless, and akin to natural death. And scientists continued to team up with politicians who promised the public that continuing improvements would increase the efficiency of electrocution (Denver, Best, & Haas, 2008). Despite the efforts of those who desired to retain the electric chair as standard practice, however, the mounting evidence of botched executions began to raise suspicions that it was really not the most humane method.

Another case associated with electric chair malfunction was that of convicted murderer Willie Francis in 1946. Francis suffered an extremely powerful electrical shock at his initial execution and, like Kemmler, managed to survive. He was then returned to his cell until authorities could determine what the appropriate next step would be. The U.S. Supreme Court ruled that the malfunction was an

FIGURE 6.3 "Old Sparky," the electric chair used in New York's Sing Sing prison

unforeseeable accident and that the executioners were acting with care; therefore, Francis would be sent back to the electric chair for another attempt at executing him (see Chapter 4). The Court explained that a "second attempt would not force Francis to suffer unnecessary pain" (Denver, Best, & Haas, 2008, p. 238). The second attempt proved successful.

Botched electrocution executions continued well into the 1990s. Consider the case of Jesse Tafero. His execution in 1990 did not go as planned either. Tafero was a Florida death row inmate who required three jolts of electricity to die. The executioners used a synthetic sponge on his head, rather than a natural sponge, which they believe was the reason for the "six-inch flames" that ignited on his head (Death Penalty Information Center, 2014c, p. 2). Another execution mishap occurred in the 1999 Florida case of Allen Lee Davis (see Figure 6.4). Davis was not yet pronounced dead, after receiving an electrical shock, when blood came pouring out of his mouth. Florida Supreme Court Justice Leander Shaw remarked that the execution amounted to brutal torture. He also referenced the botched executions of offenders before Davis, calling them "barbaric spectacles . . . acts more befitting a violent murderer than a civilized state" (Death Penalty Information Center, 2014c, p. 3).

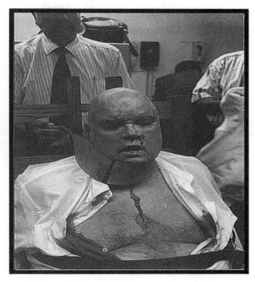

FIGURE 6.4   Allen Lee Davis

Death by electrocution was the most popular execution method until the 1960s, though it is still used today. The most recent electric chair execution took place in Virginia in 2013 (Death Penalty Information Center, 2014b). Eight states currently include electrocution as an authorized method: Alabama, Arkansas, Florida, Kentucky, Oklahoma, South Carolina, Tennessee, and Virginia (Death Penalty Information Center, 2014a). In 2014, Tennessee legislators passed a law that would effectively replace lethal injection with electrocution in the event that the drugs used for lethal injection become unavailable (*USA Today*, 2014). (We will learn more about drug availability in the lethal injection section of this chapter.) Tennessee became the first state to reinstate the use of the electric chair without giving offenders the option to choose other methods (*USA Today*, 2014).

As with hangings before it, electrocution became a less popular method as reports of botched executions continued to surface. People began to think of more humane methods and one such attempt was made by the state of Nevada with the introduction of the gas chamber.

GAS CHAMBER

The gas chamber technique was introduced in the late nineteenth century, after electrocution and in response to the botched executions associated with the electric chair method. The conclusion that death by gas was more humane than the electric chair was made by the Medical Society of Allegheny County, Pennsylvania, and received a great deal of attention. The method was first popularized by its initial concept that offenders could be humanely executed while they slept soundly in their cells. Part of this plan was to not allow the condemned to know the exact date of his or her execution so any anxiety associated with such knowledge might be avoided. As Banner (2002) points out, some questioned the ability of the state to alleviate this prisoner anticipation: "Was the suspense of knowing that any night's sleep could be one's last any easier to bear than the certainty that one would die at an appointed hour? In such circumstances, would a condemned person be able to sleep at all?" (p. 197). One might surmise that a scheduled execution would produce less anxiety because it allowed the condemned the opportunity to prepare him- or herself for the "final" day (see Figure 6.5).

FIGURE 6.5 Wyoming Gas Chamber
Source: Glenn Nagel Photography

Use of the gas chamber method did not require much convincing, as the practice of gassing unwanted pets had already become commonplace in some communities. It was only a matter of time before this technique was extended to end human life as well. There was some consternation, though, over the amount of time that it would take to "gas" a person in comparison to electrocution, which was thought to be more immediate (Banner, 2002).

In 1921, the Humane Death Bill was introduced by Nevada's legislature as an effort to, once again, ensure that executions were "humane" (Bedau, 1982). Nevada lawmakers did not specifically address how to carry out executions; they left the task up to prison officials, with the understanding that the prisoner would be sleeping in his cell with only a small number of witnesses watching. Gee Jon, a convicted murderer, became the first man to die by this method in 1924. Prison officials quickly realized that their original plan to execute Jon while he lay asleep in his cell would not be practical, largely because prison cells were not constructed to be airtight. They decided that it would be much easier to construct a special chamber to administer the gas efficiently. Prison officials created a small chamber large enough to hold a wooden chair. The chamber had a window for viewing purposes. Spectators could see the prisoner's head during the execution (Banner, 2002).

The lethal gas was obtained by officials who had to drive to California to purchase hydrocyanic acid, a chemical gas used by farmers in California to protect orange trees from parasites, because the manufacturer refused to ship it due to safety concerns. When exposed to humans, the gas would prevent cells from receiving oxygen, thereby suffocating the condemned to death (Banner, 2002). Before using the lethal gas to execute Jon, it was successfully tested on bedbugs and kittens. A pump was used to spray four pounds of the chemical into the chamber for Jon's execution. Despite a heater malfunction, which prevented the acid from quickly gasifying, Jon appeared to have died without pain. It took a total of six minutes for him to die (Banner, 2002).

The physical structure of gas chambers varies by state. California, for example, has an octagon-shaped chamber with windows on all sides. The chamber was constructed to execute two prisoners by lethal gas at the same time (it allows the placement of two chairs). Clinton Duffy, a former warden of California's San Quentin death row, participated in 90 executions. According to Duffy (1962), lethal gas executions take approximately 15 minutes and are achieved by mixing cyanide poison with sulfuric acid and water. He explains:

> On the morning of an execution the executioner got two pounds of cyanide from the prison armory and took it to a mix room off the gas chamber. Regardless of whether there was to be one execution or two, he carefully measured out into little gauze bags one pound

of cyanide for each chair. These bags were placed on hooks directly under the chairs, hanging down toward the wells a few inches below. . . . When a door was sealed with the prisoner inside, the executioner pulled a lever controlling a suction fan that drew some of the air out of the chamber. He then signaled an assistant in the mix room, who opened the valves releasing the sulphuric acid from the jars into the wells beneath the chairs. After the valves were closed, the executioner informed the warden, standing beside him outside a window to the left of the condemned man, that everything was in readiness. At the warden's nod, the executioner pulled another lever which lowered the cyanide into the sulphuric acid, causing gas fumes to rise. The whole operation took less than two minutes. . . . In order to make death as quick and painless as possible, the condemned man was instructed to take deep breaths at the warden's signal. This would be a few seconds after the cyanide and sulphuric acid came together. Without the inhalations, loss of consciousness would take longer and choking might result. (Duffy, 1962, pp. 101–103)

In order to ensure that the prisoners were indeed dead, their bodies were left in the chamber for an extra half hour after the physician confirmed that their hearts had stopped (Duffy, 1962).

Death by lethal gas has several features that make it more complex than hanging and electrocution. This method is very costly to implement. Consider that the chambers must be built indoors, are stationary, and must be airtight in order to ensure that the lethal gas is entirely contained in the chamber. Consequently, lethal gas administration requires expertise on the part of the executioner. This method is also the only one that actually poses a potential risk to witnesses of the execution. It is critical that the lethal gas be dispersed only in the chamber and remain contained there to ensure proper gas concentration so that the offender dies quickly and onlookers are not exposed to the gas. In Arizona, witnesses complained of tasting a metallic-like substance in their mouths while awaiting an execution, prompting prison officials to evacuate the premises. It was later discovered that the metallic smell and taste did not derive from lethal gas; they came from the ammonia that prison officials had on hand to neutralize any lethal gas that may have remained on the bodies of the executed upon their removal. Another operational mishap in North Carolina made prison officials nervous. During an execution in that state, cyanide pellets became stuck in the apparatus designed to drop them in the gas chamber. The executioner had to then throw the pellets in the chamber by hand and quickly run out with the warden, slamming the door shut behind them (what a sight that must have been). In spite of such close calls, though, no unintended deaths resulted during gas executions (Banner, 2002). But as Banner (2002) asserts, "It is likely that a single mishap would have ended the use of lethal gas in the United States" (p. 201). For all the above reasons, it did not make sense to continue constructing gas chambers in the various counties throughout participating states; a more prudent course was to build one chamber at a centralized location, usually in a state prison, that could be operated by those who specialized in such executions (Banner, 2002).

Though lethal gas executions were popular for a short time in the mid-twentieth century, the majority of states never implemented the practice (Denver, Best, & Haas, 2008). Nevada was the only state to utilize lethal gas for nearly a decade. A total of ten other states eventually followed. Most of them were Western and Southern states that had yet to adopt electrocution as a method of execution and wanted to find something to replace hangings. At first, few doubted that lethal gas was more humane than hanging. However, as Banner (2002) explains, there were mixed reactions to the use of gas chambers. Some believed the use of a chamber that separated the offender from everyone, leaving him alone to die, had an eerie and barbaric feel to it. No other method involved leaving the offender entirely by himself to die. The fact that gas is not visible to the human eye, which does not allow the offender or spectators to know when it takes effect, was also an unsettling idea. The gas did, however, make a jarring hissing sound when entering the chamber. On a final note, many Americans were reluctant to support gas executions because of the horrors associated with the use of poisonous gas during World Wars I and II (Banner, 2002).

Although many gas executions were considered successful, there were numerous other examples of cases that called into question whether death by lethal gas was indeed humane. Arizona's first gas chamber execution resulted in the offender gasping for air, making obscene gestures, and twitching for more than 10 minutes. The state transitioned to execution by lethal injection soon thereafter (Denver, Best, & Haas, 2008). One of the last gas executions was that of Jimmy Gray in 1983. After gas was released into the death chamber, Gray continued gasping for air eight minutes later. Prison officials led the witnesses out of the room because they were so appalled by what they saw. One defense attorney noted that he "died banging his head against a steel pole in the gas chamber while the reporters counted his moans" (Death Penalty Information Center, 2014c).

Currently, there are four states that allow lethal gas as an execution option: Arizona, California, Missouri, and Wyoming. Each of these states utilizes lethal injection as its primary method of execution, but allows lethal gas as either an offender option or to be used in the event that lethal injection is declared unconstitutional (Death Penalty Information Center, 2014a). Walter LaGrand, in 1999, was the last person to be executed by this method.

PERSPECTIVE FROM A DIRECTOR OF CORRECTIONS: BRENT D. REINKE

FIGURE 6.6   Brent D. Reinke

Director Reinke has over 40 years of experience in corrections. Prior to becoming the director of the Idaho Department of Corrections, Reinke served as the director of the Idaho Department of Juvenile Correction. He oversees eight state prisons, three privately owned prisons, four community work centers, and seven district probation and parole offices.

In 2010, when we started planning Idaho's first execution in 18 years, Governor C. L. "Butch" Otter told me he expected the solemn duty to be performed with professionalism, respect, and dignity.

I will remember that moment forever. The Governor spoke with such conviction that I felt the full weight of his office bearing down on me as if he were giving me a direct order. From that day on, *professionalism*, *respect*, and *dignity* were the watchwords for the Idaho Department of Correction.

The most important decision that is made in preparation for an execution is the selection of the men and women who will be directly involved in the process. Typically, when staffing an important assignment, you look for people who have great enthusiasm for it. That's not the case for an execution.

Volunteers who displayed a "hang 'em high attitude" were immediately disqualified. Instead, we quietly recruited dedicated professionals who, over the course of their careers, had demonstrated a strong sense of duty to their families, their colleagues, and their nation.

I was well aware of the irony. One late night, as a group of us sat around the boardroom table and hashed out a plan to comply with an unexpected court order, it occurred to me that seldom in Idaho's history had so many people—hundreds of people including correctional officers, planners, and attorneys—worked so hard to accomplish a goal for which they had no real passion.

Over the course of dozens of seemingly endless practice sessions, the escort team and medical team honed their movements to assure absolute precision. The teams tried to imagine everything that could go wrong, and they sought to make their rehearsals as realistic as possible. Once they perfected their procedures on mannequins, they switched to staff volunteers. The volunteers were subjected to every procedure with just one variation. Instead of injecting lethal doses of chemicals into the volunteers' arms, the medical team used a saline solution.

It wasn't just big things that were rehearsed. Little things were considered, too. The warden, who directed the procedure from a podium in the execution chamber, practiced how he would hold his pen and look at the clock. There was not a movement, nor a facial expression that was left unrefined.

We found that military veterans, especially those who had seen combat, were well suited for this assignment. Such people appreciate the value of rigorous training, and they have already confronted the emotions that result from witnessing death in the course of duty.

Among all of our veterans, the warden's résumé was the most notable. In addition to having served on the escort team for Idaho's last execution in 1994, he is a decorated Marine who has witnessed death many times and in many forms.

His skills were invaluable. With one hand, he directed his staff and with the other he reached out to the inmate. I mean that literally. As the last minutes ticked down, the warden reached out to the inmate with his hand to express respect and dignity.

But the warden's effort in this regard actually began well before the day of the execution. When it appeared certain a judge finally would be issuing a death warrant after 23 years of appeals and delays, the warden met with the inmate face to face in one of the rooms at the prison where attorneys consult with their clients.

Carefully and with great sensitivity, the warden described the entire process. He asked the inmate whom he wished to have witness his execution on his behalf and what he wanted done with his remains. It was a difficult but necessary conversation.

There were more meetings between the warden and the inmate—about three or four times a week in the month that followed. For each meeting, the warden would dismiss the officers whom he had assigned to monitor the inmate, and the two men—the chief executioner and the condemned—would have a private conversation. As the day of the execution neared, the inmate grew more anxious, but he seemed to take comfort from these visits with the warden.

During this time, there was another conversation going on—a conversation between the Department of Correction and the public. This conversation took many forms, but to them we applied the same watchwords.

We sought to be as transparent as possible. We posted our complete execution protocol on the department's website, and our public information officer issued regular updates on new developments. He made himself available to the news media around the clock and followed through on his promise to return every phone call within one hour.

We also reached out to other government agencies for assistance. I suspect most citizens have no idea what a huge job it is to carry out an execution, and the fact is my department could not have done it on its own.

In many places across the country, government agencies wage bitter turf battles. That is not so in Idaho. I know how lucky the Department of Correction is to have such reliable partners, and I shall be forever grateful to my colleagues for helping us through this difficult day.

Perhaps the most important conversation we had during this time was with the victims' family members. On many occasions over the years, I've been disappointed to see convicted killers become virtual celebrities while their victims are forgotten. As a consequence, making sure our staff treated these families with professionalism, respect, and dignity was my top priority.

Shortly after the death warrant was issued, the chief of the department's Operations Division gave the families his personal cell phone number and offered them regular updates on what was happening. On the day of the execution, we took special measures to meet the needs of the family members who chose to witness the process. The Operations chief and other senior department administrators met these family members at a location several miles from the prison. We gave them a private briefing and transported them into the prison complex in state vehicles. We wanted to be absolutely sure they would encounter no difficulties.

When the execution was over, we invited the family members, in fact all of the witnesses, to make use of the department's Critical Incident Stress Management team. The team is comprised of veteran correctional professionals who are available around the clock to help people cope with the powerful emotions that sometimes result from exposure to traumatic events.

On his last morning, the inmate's level anxiety was intense. Despite the impossible odds, he still hoped for a stay. He was moved to the execution chamber and the meticulously planned sequence of events began to unfold.

Then, a phone rang. Everything stopped. An attorney, who had no connection to the inmate or to any aspect of the case, had faxed a motion of stay to a judge. It took about 30 minutes for the judge to determine the motion was groundless, but for the inmate the delay was agonizing. He broke down; he began shaking and weeping.

Emotion flowed from the inmate's eyes and nose, but he could not move. He was fully restrained. So the warden, who had seen many men suffer as death drew near, calmly set aside his script and approached the execution table. He removed the inmate's glasses, wiped away his tears, and squeezed his hand.

The moment seemed suspended in time. Finally, the phone rang again and the process resumed. Within seconds of the first chemical entering the inmate's bloodstream, he lost consciousness. Twenty-two minutes later, after all three chemicals had been administered, the coroner declared the inmate dead.

I know there will be critics who will be angry that the inmate was treated so humanely. They want killers to suffer just as their victims suffered. But I suspect few of those critics have seen as much death as the warden.

If you ask the warden why he did what he did, his answer will be quick and direct: "Because the inmate was a human being." But if you ask more questions, you will discover there was another reason: because the men and women around that table were human beings, too.

They were covered from head to toe in surgical garb to conceal their identities. But the warden did not need to see their faces to know what they were feeling. He was, after all, the one who had personally vetted them and chosen them for this duty. Of course, their guts were wrenching. So he reached out, wiped away the inmate's tears, and by doing so, helped comfort everyone.

Let there be no doubt, the warden supports capital punishment. I do, too. In fact, after witnessing two executions alongside three murder victims' families, I support the death penalty more strongly than ever. These people still ache for the loss of their loved ones, but they feel justice was finally served.

What's more, like the warden, I am well aware of the inmate's crimes. We, too, felt flashes of rage as we read the unspeakable details of his crimes in his file. But as director of a state correctional department, it is my firm conviction there is no place for rage in an execution chamber. When members of an escort or medical team start deriving pleasure from death, they become no different than the killer they have strapped to the table.

That's why professionalism, respect, and dignity must be the standing orders for every execution. Without those watchwords we lose our sense of humanity. And without compassion we lose the strength to go on.

FIRING SQUAD

The firing squad is the only other method besides hanging, the electric chair, and the gas chamber adopted by states to execute offenders prior to the late 1900s when lethal injection was introduced. The only two states to utilize the firing squad were Utah and Nevada; Nevada abolished the practice when it adopted the gas chamber in 1921 (Banner, 2002). The firing squad is rarely used, as only three people have been executed by this method since the death penalty was reinstated in 1976. And as we learned at the beginning of the chapter, Ronnie Lee Gardner was the last of these executions in 2010. (See the chamber constructed for his execution in Figure 6.7.) Currently, death by firing squad is an option for offenders in only Utah and Oklahoma. In both states, however, the squad is a backup method only employed in the event that lethal injection and/or electrocution are deemed unconstitutional; there is an exception for Utah inmates who were sentenced to die prior to 2004 (when the statute changed to lethal injection). These inmates are considered "grandfathered in" and are given the option to choose between a firing squad and lethal injection. There are still a couple of upcoming executions by firing squad to come in Utah.

FIGURE 6.7 Utah's Firing Squad Execution Chamber
Source: Image provided by Utah Department of Corrections

The firing squad was originally adopted in Utah by Mormon lawmakers. Early capital punishment legislation was strongly connected to the religious doctrine of **blood atonement**. This principle requires an offender who commits murder to sacrifice his or her own life in a manner that sheds blood, so the offender can partially atone for the sin committed (Gardner, 1979). This would not be possible with forms of execution that do not shed blood, such as hanging, electrocution, and gassing. Utah territory death penalty statutes also allowed for beheading as a method that offenders could choose to ensure blood atonement (Banner, 2002). Elder Charles Penrose (1916) discussed this principle in his book *Blood Atonement as Taught by Leading Elders of the Church of Jesus Christ of Latter-day Saints*:

> The man who commits murder, who imbrues his hands in the blood of innocence, cannot receive eternal life, because he cannot get forgiveness of that sin. What can he do? The only way to atone is to shed his blood. Hanging is not the proper method. . . . That is the law of God as laid down in the beginning; that if a man shall shed blood,

by man shall his blood be shed. . . . A murderer, by the shedding of his blood, may make some atonement for his sin; but he cannot come forth and inherit an exaltation in eternal life, he must be content with a less degree of glory. (p. 21)

Some argue that the firing squad is the most humane method of execution because an accurate shot will kill an offender quickly and "painlessly," though states are hesitant to adopt the practice because shooting people is considered messy and barbaric.

Utah has been the only state to carry out post-*Gregg* firing squad executions. Corrections officials for Gardner's execution provided basic information to the public about the protocol they used:

> The room is approximately 20 feet by 24 feet and is fitted with curtains to cover the windows into the adjacent witness rooms. The windows are fitted with bullet-proof, reflective glass to protect the witnesses from unintended ricochet, and to separate and protect the identities of the witnesses.
>
> Executioners, pre-selected by the Department of Corrections, must be law-enforcement certified in the state of Utah. The five law enforcers remain anonymous, and will be stationed behind a gun ported brick wall in the execution chamber. The executioners will be armed with .30 caliber rifles, four of which will be loaded with live rounds. The weapon carrying the blank round will be unknown to the law enforcers.
>
> The condemned will be secured to a chair, and a target will be placed over his heart and a hood over his head. At the conclusion of the condemned's last words, the execution team will commence fire. A physician will be on site to certify that death has occurred. (Utah Department of Corrections, internal document, 2010)

LETHAL INJECTION

Lethal injection is the most widely used method of execution today. As of 2015, all of the 31 death penalty states and the federal government use lethal injection as their primary execution method (Death Penalty Information Center, 2014a). The process of an execution by lethal injection is described by Harrison and Melville (2007) as follows:

> The prisoner is usually escorted into the execution chamber and strapped to a gurney. A member of the execution team then connects the inmate to a cardiac monitor by placing several heart monitors

onto the skin. Two intravenous tubes are inserted into usable veins, usually one in each arm, in case a backup is needed, and these are then threaded through an opening in the wall and attached to several intravenous drips. Once the tubes are properly inserted a harmless saline solution is passed through them to ensure that the lines are working efficiently. A curtain may then be drawn away from the window or one-way mirror exposing the prisoner to the witnesses in an adjoining room. At this moment the inmate may make a verbal or written statement and if left unrestrained the inmate may turn his head to view the witnesses. Unless a call is received from state officials staying the execution the inmate is injected. . . . (p. 174)

The process seems fairly straightforward, but as you will see, a lot can go wrong. (See Figure 6.8 for a picture of San Quentin's execution chamber.)

The first lethal injection statute was enacted in Oklahoma in 1977, shortly after capital punishment was reinstated in *Gregg v. Georgia* (1976) (see Chapter 3). It was introduced by Oklahoma politicians Bill Wiseman and Bill Dawson. Oklahoma's electric chair needed to be repaired at an estimated cost to the state of $62,000; building a gas chamber would have cost approximately $300,000 (Denno, 2002). Wiseman proposed a new method that would consist of administering a lethal drug intravenously. He asked the Oklahoma Medical Association to develop a drug cocktail that would result in a quick and painless death. The association refused to help, citing ethical dilemmas with medical practitioners assisting the state to kill (we will learn more about this issue soon). Wiseman then turned to Dr. Jay Chapman, Oklahoma's medical examiner, for help. Chapman agreed to develop the lethal injection drug protocol, though he admitted that he was "an expert in dead bodies but not an expert in getting them that way" (Denno, 2014, p. 1340). Chapman told Wiseman how lethal injection could be achieved, suggesting two types of drugs to get the job done: "An intravenous saline drip shall be started in the prisoner's arm, into which shall be introduced a lethal injection consisting of an ultra-short-acting barbiturate in combination with a chemical paralytic" (Human Rights Watch, 2006, p. 14). This information was essentially all that Wiseman and Dawson needed to write the legislation. When asked why he chose this combination, Chapman responded: "I didn't do any research. I just knew from having been placed under anesthesia myself, what we needed. I wanted to have at least two drugs in doses that would each kill the prisoner, to make sure if one didn't kill him, the other would" (Human Rights Watch, 2006, p.14). Chapman later added a third drug—potassium chloride. When interviewed about his reasoning for the additional drug, he stated: "Why not? . . . You just wanted to make sure the prisoner was dead at the end, so why not just add a third lethal drug? . . . Why does it matter why I chose it?" (Human Rights Watch, 2006, p. 14). Chapman did, however, warn of the risks with improper administration, explaining that offenders could potentially experience extreme pain (Denno, 2014). It seems that Chapman's warning was not taken seriously.

Three- vs. One-Drug Injection

Most states utilize a three-drug lethal injection to execute offenders, but some have switched to a one-drug method. With the three-drug method, the offender is supposed to be properly anesthetized prior to the administration of the second and third drugs, so he or she is spared excruciating pain, including "asphyxiation, a severe burning sensation, massive muscle cramping, and finally cardiac arrest" (Koniaris et al., 2005, p. 1412). A barbiturate is the first of the three drugs in the lethal cocktail. Barbiturates suppress the central nervous system and function as a general anesthetic in surgical procedures. For executions, they are used to sedate the offender or induce unconsciousness (Denno, 2002). There have been a few different types of barbiturates used in lethal injection executions, as drug availability concerns have forced states to find new drugs (see below). The second drug is a paralytic that paralyzes the lungs and diaphragm, ultimately stopping the offender from breathing. The most common paralytic used for executions is pancuronium bromide. The third drug is potassium chloride, which stops the heart. This drug is typically used by medical practitioners to induce a heart attack for bypass surgeries and in large enough doses results in death.

If the anesthesia is improperly administered or the offender is given an improper dose (not enough), he or she may appear unconscious, but actually be conscious. Under these circumstances, the offender would feel the painful effects of the paralytic and then the subsequent burning sensation from the potassium chloride (Koniaris et al., 2005). Of course, it would then be difficult to ascertain if an execution is going awry and the offender is experiencing pain because, physically, he or she will appear unconscious from the first and second drugs. Dr. Mark Heath, a practicing anesthesiologist and professor of clinical anesthesiology at Columbia University, is a medical expert in lethal injection who has warned about the harmful effects of offenders not receiving an adequate dosage of the first drug:

> Infiltration and/or leakage could cause an insufficient amount of thiopental or pentobarbital to reach the prisoner's brain to sufficiently anesthetize him for the next two steps of the execution, paralysis and cardiac arrest. In this scenario, if partial or complete doses of the pancuronium bromide and potassium chloride are subsequently delivered into the inmate's bloodstream, the inmate would experience the extreme pain and suffering of conscious paralysis and cardiac arrest. Moreover, an insufficiently anesthetized person would experience burning in his or her veins upon administration of concentrated

potassium chloride, and any amount of potassium chloride delivered to the surrounding tissue or to the bloodstream would cause extreme pain absent sufficient anesthetic. . . . A person can be unconscious but easily aroused, for example by touching their shoulder or saying their name. Alternatively, a person can be unconscious but unarousable, such that no stimulus, no matter how noxious or intense, can bring them to consciousness or elicit any response at all. . . . A person who is unconscious but not aroused by lighter forms of stimulation may still be arousable by an intense or highly noxious stimulus. The levels of stimulation produced by pancuronium injection (which causes suffocation by inability to draw breath) or by potassium injection (which causes excruciating pain) are the types of highly noxious stimuli that could easily arouse an unconscious person and revert them to a state of consciousness in which they would experience the agonizing effects of pancuronium and potassium. [Affidavit of Dr. Heath in *Rhoades v. Reinke et al.*, CV11-445 (2011)]

It should come as no surprise that the haphazard construction of Dr. Chapman's three-drug protocol has resulted in significant complications and a floodgate of Eighth Amendment litigation. A variety of problems exist in the application of the drugs, including the effects of improper dosage and unskilled administration. Most states do not individualize the drug dosage according to the offender's size and weight and prescribe a set dosage for all offenders. This is an issue that has been pointed out by physicians like Dr. Heath since the lethal injection protocol first came into existence. The most obvious concern is that an offender does not receive the amount needed to be fully anesthetized. When barbiturates are used for surgeries, anesthesiologists use sophisticated technology while monitoring their patients to ensure that they are properly anesthetized. If there are problems with the dosage or injection administration, then the offender may not receive the entire prescribed dose. An additional concern lies with offenders who suffer from anxiety or substance abuse issues, and may require higher doses to experience unconsciousness (Koniaris et al., 2005).

A study published in the esteemed British medical journal *The Lancet* found that post-mortem levels of sodium thiopental in executed individuals were not always sufficient for achieving adequate levels of sedation. Toxicology reports from 49 offenders from four states were examined. Forty-three (88%) subjects had concentrations lower than what would be required for a surgical procedure and 21 (43%) had levels indicating levels of awareness (Koniaris et al., 2005). Critics of the *Lancet* study argue that levels of sodium thiopental in the bloodstream would naturally be lower after an offender is deceased because the drug loses its concentration shortly after death.

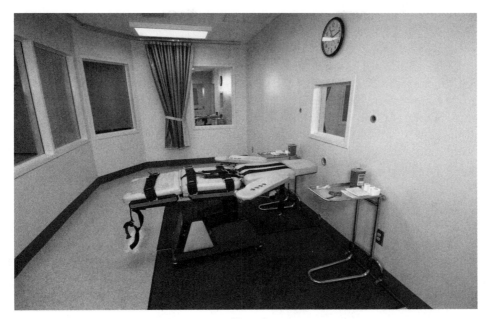

FIGURE 6.8   San Quentin Execution Chamber

There have been numerous botched executions documented by the media who have witnessed them. Consider the case of Angel Diaz in Florida. After receiving the first drug, Diaz was still moving around and trying to mouth words. It took Diaz nearly 34 minutes to die. A prison official initially claimed that Diaz's execution did not go as planned because he had a diseased liver, although a later autopsy revealed that his liver was healthy. The medical examiner found that the needle used during the execution had been pushed through his vein, thereby releasing the chemicals into his soft tissue. Consequently, Diaz suffered from extreme pain during his execution. Autopsy photos also revealed that Diaz's skin displayed obvious signs of severe chemical burns (Death Penalty Information Center, 2014c). The more recent case of Clayton Lockett in Oklahoma has additionally received a great deal of attention. Problems began when Lockett's executioner (a phlebotomist) had trouble locating a vein in his arm. A "good" vein was eventually located in the condemned man's groin area. After Lockett was deemed "unconscious" from the first drug, the second and third drugs were administered in accordance with the protocol. Within a few minutes of the final injection, Lockett "began breathing heavily, writhing on the gurney, clenching his teeth and straining to lift his head off the pillow" (Williams, 2014, p. 1). In response to the clear indicators of Mr. Lockett's suffering, prison officials abruptly halted the execution and evacuated the witnesses. Officials decided to stay the execution for two weeks, but it was too late because Lockett died of a heart attack while still in the execution room (Williams, 2014).

Cases like those of Diaz and Lockett have raised the question of why the second and third drugs are used at all in executions. If the barbiturate can be administered in a lethal dosage, then why take the unnecessary risks of pain from the paralytic drug and potassium chloride? By using only the first drug, the risk for pain would be virtually eliminated and the offender would die while appearing to fall asleep. Ohio was the first state to adopt a one-drug protocol consisting of only the continual flow of a barbiturate until the offender is pronounced dead (Denno, 2014). Other states soon followed Ohio's one-drug protocol, some for humanitarian reasons and others in response to a massive new challenge that would change the face of lethal injection—drug availability.

Drug Availability

The challenges with drug availability primarily concern the first drug in the execution, the barbiturate or sedative. Sodium thiopental was the first barbiturate used by all states in the lethal injection trio until it was no longer available. In 2009, the U.S. manufacturer of sodium thiopental, Hospira, ceased production after it became difficult to obtain a key ingredient from another manufacturer. Hospira considered producing the drug again at one of the company's plants in Italy, but the Italian government required them to ensure that it would not reach the hands of corrections officials in U.S. prisons. The following year, the British government, who adamantly opposes the death penalty, decided to ban all exportation of sodium thiopental to the United States after discovering that it was being heavily sought out for executions (Denno, 2014). Corrections officials panicked as sodium thiopental supplies diminished and began purchasing the drug from other countries. In 2011, however, the U.S. Drug Enforcement Agency (DEA) confiscated supplies of sodium thiopental from states that purchased it from international sources because they failed to meet U.S. standards of importation.

The inability to obtain sodium thiopental resulted in death states needing to find a substitute for the first drug. They quickly replaced sodium thiopental with another barbiturate called pentobarbital, though it was not long before there were problems with this drug as well. Unlike sodium thiopental, pentobarbital is not commonly used on humans; it has long been used by veterinarians to anesthetize or euthanize animals. The same concerns exist with pentobarbital as with sodium thiopental in terms of both efficacy and availability. More recently, Missouri has tried to obtain propofol (the drug that killed Michael Jackson) for executions, but most European manufacturers refuse to sell it to corrections departments. Consequently, corrections officials, once again, are scrambling to locate other venues for a substitute drug to prevent future execution delays. Some states have even turned to compounding pharmacies to obtain these drugs and their variants in order to circumvent Food and Drug Administration (FDA) regulations (Denno, 2014). The problem with using compounding pharmacies is that the lack of regulation prevents the purchaser from knowing exactly what the drug's ingredients are. In South Dakota, a batch of pentobarbital obtained from a compounding pharmacy was found to have a fungus contamination after it had already been used in an execution; the offender was snoring after it was administered and his eyes never shut, calling into question the drug source and its efficacy.

Several states have created laws to protect their drug sources in an effort to prevent external pressures that might impede future production. For example, Georgia enacted the Lethal Injection Secrecy Act in 2013 to protect drug suppliers, calling this information a "state secret" (Denno, 2014, p. 1377). Most states also protect the identity of their executioners.

EXECUTIONERS

The Hippocratic oath strictly prohibits physicians from participating in executions. The following major organizations that develop professional and ethical guidelines for medical professionals also clearly forbid their assistance in executions: American Medical Association, American College of Physicians, American Society of Anesthesiologists, and the American Nurses Association (Harrison & Melville, 2007, p. 174). If a member of one of these organizations opts to participate in an execution, he or she will likely lose membership status, which may have some social consequences, but will not likely have much of an impact on that person's career beyond the loss of membership. However, other types of organizations or specialty boards such as the American Board of Anesthesiology (ABA) have sanctions that are much more severe and carry potentially devastating consequences for physicians who violate their rules. As of 2010, the ABA announced that if anesthesiologists participate in executions, they will lose their board certification. If physicians lose their certification, they may have to forfeit their ability to practice medicine (Nelson & Ashby, 2011). The obvious objection here is that the medical profession is in existence to *help* people and killing is not in line with this goal. Alternatively, some have made the argument that doctors actually do more harm by not participating and ensuring that an execution is painless (Denver, Best, & Haas, 2008). Consider physician-assisted suicide for terminally ill patients (euthanasia). Are both execution and euthanasia scenarios the same as far as ethics are concerned? Or, is there a fundamental difference between patients who wish to die and those who are being executed against their will? There is no simple answer or solution, but one could argue that enlisting a doctor to assist in effecting death for a person who is terminally ill is very different than asking a physician to participate in an execution because the doctor is acting out of compassion and, arguably, not violating the Hippocratic oath.

In any event, most states cannot find doctors or registered nurses to assist in executions. In the absence of these professionals, corrections officials appoint execution teams with phlebotomists, medical assistants, EMTs, and military medics instead. As we have already learned, without a physician to monitor the offender's level of consciousness or advise what to do when needle infiltration occurs and adequate doses are not delivered to the condemned, there will be elevated and continual risks of botched executions.

LAST WORDS AND LAST MEALS

When a date for an execution is finally set and then arrives, there are two more rituals afforded the condemned by the state before it carries out the sentence of the courts. The first is a last meal request, and the second is the opportunity to speak their final words. The last actions and words of the condemned are unique expressions. Unlike those of us for whom judgment day is unknown, these individuals have had years to think about what their last message to the world will be. Most people probably consider these provisions as gestures of kindness by restoring to the condemned a small measure of control over what remains of their lives. This control is signified by giving them the opportunity to indulge in whatever culinary peculiarities they may have, and then to broadcast any message they want the world to hear, knowing that it is one time they will be listened to by the thousands who will read about their execution.

There are others, however, who see these rituals as retributive and serving state functions. The rituals signify to the public that the state is committed to humane due process, but they also incite public animosity by contrasting the perceived offender's relatively painless "luxury-filled death with his victim's cruel, unadorned death" (LaChance, 2007, p. 717). This may be an unintended consequence, but it rings true nonetheless (see Judge Schroeder's perspective in Chapter 7 in which he remarked that he received a lot of criticism for allowing a condemned man a final meal of his own choosing). Daniel LaChance (2007) supports his position by quoting a newspaper letter commenting on capital offenders' deaths: "They have nice last meals and in six minutes are put to sleep—on a nice clean cot, no blood, no gore—with protesters outside praying for them. That is definitely not an 'eye for an eye'" (p. 717).

The state of Texas banned last meal requests after Lawrence Russell Brewer, who was convicted of a 1998 racially motivated murder, ordered a feast consisting of pizza, fajitas, a pound of barbecued meat, half a loaf of bread, a bowl of okra, a triple-bacon cheeseburger, a beef omelet, two chicken-fried steaks with gravy and onions, a pint of ice cream, a slab of peanut butter fudge with crushed peanuts, and three root beers, and then basically told the warden to "stuff it." Because of Brewer's actions, death row inmates in Texas will now receive the same meal served to other offenders in the prison and many other death states have since followed suit.

SUMMARY

This chapter reviewed the various methods of executions that have been used in the United States before and after *Furman*. We learned that our system of justice requires methods that will limit and/or prevent offenders from feeling pain during execution. The evolution of execution practices toward more "humane" methods is a function of the people, not just their government. As society evolves, so do our mechanisms for punishment, and we demand better techniques to keep up. Failure to respond to this demand feeds abolitionist movements. And when execution methods are on the brink of being declared unconstitutional, new methods are quickly devised in order to protect the death penalty, a trend that has been noted time and time again. Denver, Best, and Haas (2008) refer to these trends as "institutional fads" (p. 227). Despite all of their efforts, promises made by politicians to find new and "improved" methods of execution continually fail to deliver.

There are numerous challenges with lethal injection, some of which were covered in this chapter; the rest are addressed in the chapters discussing the death penalty's foundational cases (Chapters 3 and 4). Although lethal injection may be one of the more intuitively appealing methods as an abstract principle, there are many variables that can prevent a "successful execution." The greatest challenge right now is drug availability, an issue that will ultimately have to be decided by the U.S. Supreme Court before a definitive solution (if any) develops. Additionally, our nation's High Court will have to decide whether the recent trend of corrections departments hiding the key details of their execution practices violates our constitutional rights. As history dictates, lack of transparency in government is a slippery slope that often results in constitutional violations.

GLOSSARY

Blood atonement: The religious principle that requires an offender who commits murder to sacrifice his or her own life in a manner that sheds blood, so the offender can partially atone for the sin committed.

DISCUSSION QUESTIONS

1. Identify some of the trends that have existed throughout the use of capital punishment in the United States.
2. Which method of execution do you think is the most humane? Do you believe that executions, by their nature, can be humane? Explain.
3. Do you believe that the identity of executioners ought to be concealed by the state/government?
4. Given the existence and history of botched executions, do you believe that the death penalty should be abolished? Explain why or why not.
5. Should lethal injection remain constitutional? Do you believe that states should be allowed to keep information on the lethal drugs they use for executions secret from the public? Explain your position.
6. How do you feel about offenders being able to choose their last meal before execution? Are you for or against this practice?

REFERENCES

Amnesty International. (2014). "Death Penalty Facts." http://www.amnestyusa.org/pdfs/DeathPenaltyFactsMay2012.pdf.

The Baltimore Sun. (2003, July 9). "Delaware Brings Down Relic of Death Penalty." http://articles.baltimoresun.com/2003-07-09/news/0307090032_1_gallows-lethal-injection-death-penalty.

Banner, S. (2002). *The death penalty: An American history*. Cambridge, MA: Harvard University Press.

Bedau, H. (1982). *The death penalty in America*. New York: Oxford University Press.

The Corrections Professional. (1996). Executions—preparing staff for the hard task ahead. *The Corrections Professional, 1*(11), 1–30.

Death Penalty Information Center. (2014a). "Authorized Methods." http://www.deathpenaltyinfo.org/methodsexecution?scid=8&did=245#state.

Death Penalty Information Center. (2014b). "Searchable Execution Database." http://www.deathpenaltyinfo.org/views-executions.

Death Penalty Information Center. (2014c). "Post-*Furman* Botched Executions." http://www.deathpenaltyinfo.org/some-examples-post-furman-botched-executions?scid=8&did=478.

Denno, D. (2002). When legislatures delegate death: The troubling paradox behind state uses of electrocution and lethal injection and what it says about us. *Ohio State Law Journal, 63*, 1–155.

Denno, D. (2014). Lethal injection chaos post-*Baze*. *Georgetown Law Journal, 205*(5), 1331–1382. http://papers.ssrn.com/sol3/papers.cfm?abstract_id=2328407.

Denver, M., J. Best, and K. Haas. (2008). Methods of execution as institutional fads. *Punishment and Society, 10*(3), 227–252.

Duffy, C. (1962). *88 men and 2 women*. New York: Doubleday.

Gardner, M. (1979). Mormonism and capital punishment: A doctrinal perspective, past and present. *Dialogue, 12*(1), 9–26.

Harrison, K., and C. Melville. (2007). The death penalty by lethal injection and *Hill v. McDonough*: Is the USA starting to see sense? *Journal of Criminal Law, 71*(2), 167–180.

Hillman, H. (1993). The possible pain experienced during executions by different methods. *Perception, 22*(6), 745–753.

Human Rights Watch. (2006, April 23). "So Long as They Die: Lethal Injections in the United States." http://www.hrw.org/reports/2006/04/23/so-long-they-die.

Koniaris, L., T. Zimmers, D. Lubarsky, and J. Sheldon. (2005). Inadequate anaesthesia in lethal injection for execution. *Lancet, 365*, 1412–1414.

LaChance, D. (2007). Last words, last meals, and last stands: Agency and individuality in the modern execution process. *Law and Social Inquiry, 32*(3), 701–724.

Moran, R. (2003). *Executioner's current: Thomas Edison, George Westinghouse, and the invention of the electric chair*. New York: Knopf Doubleday.

Nelson, L., and B. Ashby. (2011). Rethinking the ethics of physician participation in lethal injection execution. *Hastings Center Report, 41*(3), 28–37.

Penrose, C. (1916). *Atonement as taught by leading elders of the Church of Jesus Christ of Latter-day Saints*. Salt Lake City: The Deseret News.

Rhoades v. Reinke et al., CV11-445 (2011).

USA Today. (2014, May 23). "Tennessee Ready to Bring Back Electric Chair: Execution Methods Vary by State." http://www.usatoday.com/story/news/nation/2014/05/22/tennessee-electric-chair/9474435/.

Williams, P. (2014, April 30). "Witnesses to a Botched Execution." http://www.newyorker.com/online/blogs/newsdesk/2014/04/witnesses-to-a-botched-execution.html.

CHAPTER 7

DETERRENCE AND THE DEATH PENALTY

In 1996, a twice-convicted murderer from Iowa named Christopher Langley being transported to New Mexico was passing through Texas along with a group of other prisoners. An opportunity arose for these prisoners to escape by overpowering their guards. Langley protected the prison guards from the harmful intentions of the other prisoners, including one female guard from being raped. Upon his subsequent capture, he related that his actions had been motivated by fear of the death penalty because the escape took place in Texas, which, unlike Iowa, is a death penalty state. Langley also stated that he protected the female guard because he was under the (false) impression that in Texas rape was punishable by the death penalty. Law professor Alan Dershowitz has said, "Of course the death penalty deters some crimes. That's why you have to pay more for a hitman in a death penalty state than in a non-death penalty state."[1]

On the other hand, we occasionally encounter stories of people who commit murder so that they can be executed, just as we sometimes hear of people confronting the police in order to secure "suicide by cop." Daniel Colwell was afraid to commit suicide, so he shot two innocent strangers in Georgia with the expectation that the state would kill him for the crime. Likewise, John Blackwelder, who was doing life without parole in Florida, killed a fellow inmate so that he would be executed because he couldn't stand the thought of spending the rest of his life in prison. If you desperately wanted someone dead, would the possibility of receiving the death penalty deter you, or if you were incarcerated for life, would execution be preferable to you?

Although the above is anecdotal evidence for one side or the other on the question of the deterrent effect of capital punishment, the so-called scientific approach to ascertaining this (using statistical models) is not much more definitive. Death penalty scholars have battled among themselves to the point of exhaustion over the deterrent effect of capital punishment, with the only

---

[1]Debate among Paul Cassell, Alan Dershowitz, and Wendy Kamenar on the death penalty (Harvard Law School, March 22, 1995).

honest conclusion being "The jury is still out." The issue involves determining whether the threat of capital punishment prevents someone from murdering a potential victim. But, how can we possibly prove why something didn't happen without knowing if it would have under different circumstances? Proving a negative is an awfully difficult task, as we shall see.

LEARNING OBJECTIVES

- Understand the assumptions of deterrence theory, and differentiate between specific and general deterrence.
- Identify the three elements of deterrence as defined by Cesare Beccaria.
- Know how the deterrence argument has been used in the Supreme Court's landmark death penalty cases.
- Know and understand why economists, sociologists, and criminologists come to different conclusions regarding the death penalty.
- Understand the brutalization effect.
- Understand Pascal's wager as applied to the death penalty and why it may be irrelevant to some.

THE ASSUMPTIONS OF DETERRENCE THEORY

As noted in Chapter 1, because punishment involves the state depriving individuals of life or liberty in the name of the people, it is in need of ethical justification. This is especially true in the case of the ultimate punishment—death. Deterrence has long been considered the primary function of punishment because the threat of punishment is assumed to prevent people from committing acts that they may otherwise commit. For some engaged in the death penalty debate, capital punishment is ethically justified only if it can be conclusively shown that taking the life of convicted killers saves the lives of innocent victims by preventing others who are aware of the death penalty from committing murder. These individuals are consequentialists who want to see some kind of positive outcome from the death penalty. For others who follow Immanuel Kant's non-consequentialist ethics, the deterrence issue is irrelevant because the death penalty is morally demanded in the name of justice, and for yet others for whom the taking of a life by the state is morally wrong under any circumstances, the deterrence debate is also irrelevant.

The scholars who put the most faith in deterrence to govern behavior are economists and criminologists who favor a theory called *rational choice theory*. The assumption of these scholars is the same as that of behavioral psychologists; that is, the assumption that behavior is governed by its consequences. If the net effect of that behavior is rewarding, the behavior is said to be reinforced and will be repeated; if the net effect is negative, the behavior is said to have been punished and will be extinguished. Punishment (pain) will deter crime only if it exceeds the gain (pleasure) crime offers. These pleasures may be material (money, property, sex, drugs); psychological (self-esteem, feelings of power and control, excitement, reputation, revenge); or a combination of both. Of course in order for a person to weigh options in this manner, the ability of the individual to rationalize and calculate his or her options must exist. Deterrence theorists assume that offenders are both rational and free-willed, which is both a strength and weakness of such theories. The notion that people carefully consider their options and then *choose* to commit a crime is intuitively appealing, but not all offenders are rational. Consider drug offenders who are high or "out of their minds" when they commit their crimes (violent or nonviolent)—are they able to rationally consider the consequences of their crimes? Perhaps *some* do, but we can logically conclude that not all are able to do so. Or, consider offenders with a serious mental illness—many are unable to process information the same as those without such limitations. Lack of rational thinking or calculation does not mean that all offenders in this category should not be held accountable; we just point out that deterrence theories have limited application with nonrational actors.

Deterrence theorists assert that offenders must fully understand and appreciate the long-term consequences of their behavior as well as its short-term consequences. Short-term rewards are easier to appreciate than long-term consequences, and there is a tendency to abandon consideration of the latter when confronted with temptation unless a person has a well-developed conscience and is future-oriented. The weak of conscience and the present-oriented tend to discount long-term consequences in favor of short-term rewards.

Economists and rational choice criminologists posit that a person's choice to engage in crime (even murder), like any other choice, is made to benefit the chooser. For them, criminal acts are just another example of the general principle that human behavior reflects the rational pursuit of maximizing pleasure and minimizing pain. They believe that people are conscious actors who are free to choose crime, and they will do so if they perceive that its pleasures exceed the possible pains in the form of punishment that the actor may suffer.

Deterrence scholars do not assume that all people are equally at risk to commit crimes—certainly not the kinds of heinous murders that can result in the death penalty. These scholars recognize that personal factors such as temperament, intelligence, cognitive style, and strength of conscience, as well as background factors such as family structure, class, and neighborhood, impact everyone's choices. However, they largely ignore these factors in favor of exploring how factors in the environment, such as the probability of apprehension and the severity of the punishment attached to a particular crime, impact criminal decision-making (Clarke & Cornish, 1985).

Economists and rational choice theorists also acknowledge that rationality is both subjective and bounded, and that unwanted outcomes can be produced by rational strategies (Boudon, 2003). We do not all make the same calculations or arrive at the same game plan when pursuing the same goals because we contemplate our actions with imperfect knowledge, with different mindsets, different values, and different reasoning abilities. We do the best we can to order our decisions relating to our self-interest with the knowledge and understanding we have about the possible outcomes of an anticipated course of action, and this knowledge and understanding can be seriously flawed. All sane people have mental models of the world and behave rationally *from their point of view*, even if others might consider their behavior to be highly irrational. Criminals also behave rationally from their private models of reality, but their rationality is constrained, as is everyone's, by ability, knowledge, emotional input, and time (Cornish & Clarke, 1986). If people miscalculate, as they frequently do, it is because they are ignorant of the full range of consequences of a given course of action, or because they discount them, not necessarily because they are irrational. As noted in Chapter 1, rationality is always bounded by many factors, especially the rationality of criminal offenders.

SPECIFIC AND GENERAL DETERRENCE

As briefly discussed earlier, criminologists divide deterrence into specific and general deterrence. In more detail, *specific deterrence* is the dissuasive effect of the imposed punishment on the future behavior of the person punished. Specific deterrence does not seem to work very well when we consider parolee recidivism rates of about 67% by the third year after release from prison (Stohr & Walsh, 2015). Why do we see more than two-thirds of released criminals going back to prison? Like the rest of us, criminals are not walking calculating machines who routinely take time to weigh the pros and cons of their every move. As van den Haag (2003) puts it: "Law-abiding people habitually ignore criminal opportunities. Law breakers habitually discount the risk of punishment. Neither calculates" (p. 47). Incentives and disincentives to law-abiding or criminal behavior are thus perceived differently because of ingrained habits, but this does not mean that criminals are impervious to realistic threats of punishment.

The effect of punishment on future behavior depends heavily on the **contrast effect**. The contrast effect is the distinction between the conditions of the threatened punishment and the conditions of the everyday lives of those being punished. For people who enjoy a loving family and a well-paid and valued career, the threat of arrest and punishment is a nightmarish contrast.

The prospect of the public disgrace that would threaten the loss of these things is a strong deterrent against criminal behavior. On the other hand, the threat of punishment has little effect on people with nothing to lose because the contrast between their everyday lives and prison life is not that dramatically different. The irony is that specific deterrence works best for those who need deterring the least, and works least for those who need it the most.

General deterrence is the effect of punishment on those who have witnessed (directly or indirectly) it but not personally experienced it. Few of us would dispute the value of general deterrence. Punishing criminals serves as an example to the rest of us of what may happen if we violate the law. Radzinowicz and King assert that "people are not sent to prison primarily for their own good, or even in the hope that they will be cured of crime. Confinement is used as a measure of retribution, a symbol of condemnation, a vindication of the law. It is used as a warning and deterrent to others. It is used, above all, to protect other people . . . from the offender's depredations" (1979, p. 296). Punishment is a practice, then, that provides the greatest utility or benefit for the greatest number of people by preventing an unknown number of people who may be inclined to harm others were it not for the threat of punishment.

THREE PRINCIPLES OF PUNISHMENT

In his influential book *On Crimes and Punishment* (1963) first published in 1764, Cesare Beccaria, the father of the classical school of criminal justice, made three important observations regarding the deterrent effect of punishment that we sometimes fail to consider when debating the death penalty. Beccaria maintained that punishment must be applied with certainty, it must be swiftly applied, and its severity must outweigh any benefits offenders get from crime if they are to be deterred from future crime. Though Beccaria adamantly opposed the death penalty, his logic for deterrence is useful for the debate. He made the following observations (1963) regarding certainty, swiftness, and severity of punishment:

Certainty: "The certainty of punishment, even if it be moderate, will always make a stronger impression than the fear of another which is more terrible but combined with the hope of impunity." (p. 58)
Swiftness: "The more promptly and the more closely punishment follows upon the commission of a crime, the more just and useful will it be." (p. 55)
Severity: "For a punishment to attain its end, the evil which it inflicts has only to exceed the advantage derivable from the crime; in this excess of evil one should include the . . . loss of the good which the crime might

have produced. All beyond this is superfluous and for that reason tyrannical." (p. 43)

In other words, there must be a relatively high degree of certainty that punishment will follow a criminal and that it will be administered as soon as possible after the act; and its severity must be calibrated to exceed the gains from the crime and the harm caused. These three conditions are extremely problematic in the United States, especially for the crime of murder. Murder remains the crime most likely to be solved, but the Federal Bureau of Investigation (2014) indicates that in 2013 only 64.8% of homicides were cleared by the police as opposed to 90% in 1960 (Keel, Jarvis, & Muirhead, 2009). To put it another way, about 1 out of 3 murderers gets away with his or her crimes in the United States today, versus 1 out of 10 in 1960. Unfortunately, the clearance rate is lowest in cities with the highest homicide rates. For instance, in 2008, the clearance rate in Chicago was 35%, in New Orleans was 22%, and in Detroit was 21% (Hargrove, 2010). Furthermore, only about 2% to 6% of murders (depending on jurisdiction) are tried as capital cases (Berk, Li, & Hickman, 2005), and only 15% of people sentenced to death since the death penalty was reinstated in 1976 have actually been executed (Nagin & Pepper, 2012). *So much for certainty.*

If a person is arrested for murder, the wheels of criminal justice grind excruciatingly slowly, with many months or even years passing between the act and the imposition of punishment, especially if the death penalty is involved. Just as the certainty of apprehension for murder has dropped dramatically, so has the swiftness of execution. In the early days of the United States, the time elapsing between conviction and execution was measured in days or weeks, but has risen steadily ever since. The time lapse between conviction and execution dropped from an average of 14.4 months in the 1950s to an average of 122 months in 2000 (Peterson & Bailey, 2003), and to 174 months (14.5 years) in 2010 (Snell, 2011). In California, the average waiting time is 25 years. As we learned earlier, federal judge Cormac Carney used this fact to vacate the death sentence of Ernest Jones and the entire California death row. In essence, the courts create the delays and then call the delays cruel and unusual punishment. *So much for swiftness.*

This leaves the justice system with the least effective aspect of punishment—severity. Unlike certainty and swiftness, severity can be manipulated almost at will for any number of crimes, but for death-eligible crimes the death penalty is already the most severe punishment we have, so we can't manipulate severity here either. *So much for severity.*

Studies using official data from the United States and the United Kingdom find substantial negative correlations between the likelihood of conviction (a measure of certainty) and crime rates for a variety of crimes, but a much weaker negative correlation for the severity of punishment (Langan & Farrington,

1998). A negative correlation means that as one variable goes up (in this case, the likelihood of conviction), the other one (crime rate) goes down. It has been claimed that increased incarceration rates have accounted for between 20% and 30% of the decline in violent crime over the past decade or so (Paternoster, 2010; Spelman, 2000; Rosenfeld, 2000). Unfortunately, we cannot determine from raw incarceration rates if this represents a *deterrent* effect (has violent crime declined because more people have perceived harsher punitiveness attached to criminal acts?) or an *incapacitation* effect (has violent crime declined because more violent people are behind bars and thus not at liberty to commit violent crimes on the outside?).

No one doubts that the threat of punishment influences the decisions of many offenders to act in certain ways. But as we have seen, there is wide variation in its power to do so among different people with different characteristics and in different situations. Nor would anyone disagree that the death penalty is the most severe penalty available to the criminal justice system. However, with the lessening of certainty of apprehension (particularly in our most crime-ridden cities) and the ever-slowing average pace at which the executioner approaches his task, one has to wonder how we can engage in a serious debate about something as final as the death penalty when the most important ingredients of deterrence are practically impotent in the United States today. As Justice Byron White declared in *Furman v. Georgia* (1972):

> I accept also the effectiveness of punishment generally, and need not reject the death penalty as a more effective deterrent than a lesser punishment. But common sense and experience tell us that seldom-enforced laws become ineffective measures for controlling human conduct, and that the death penalty, unless imposed with sufficient frequency, will make little contribution to deterring those crimes for which it may be exacted.

However, up until the advent of DNA testing and the attendant switch of abolitionist emphasis to innocence (see Chapter 9), the issue of whether or not the death penalty deters *as currently administered in the United States* was paramount. Of course, the deterrence debate is still very important, and scholars continue to butt heads over it. We will thus briefly explore what both sides of the debate have to say.

THE DEATH PENALTY/DETERRENCE DEBATE

The death penalty is unique in that it is the only punishment required to demonstrate its deterrent effect to validate its constitutionality. As Supreme Court Justice White put it, "Deterrence [is] the principal battleground on which the war over the constitutionality of the death penalty [is] to be fought" (in Peterson & Bailey, 2003, p. 275). We take it for granted that penalties applied to other crimes have a general deterrent effect, if not always the desired specific effect. We have seen that the major argument for punishing wrongdoers is to deter a specific wrongdoer from repeating the act and to prevent potential wrongdoers from committing a similar act. If murderers are executed, it is obvious that they will not be able to harm anyone else, so the issue is one of general, rather than specific, deterrence. The question thus becomes: "Will the presence of the death penalty deter some unknown number of individuals from committing murder?" The question does not apply to all murders; it applies only to the heinous kinds of murder for which the death penalty is an option. We will see that it is extraordinarily difficult (some say impossible) to arrive at a robust conclusion given that less than 1% of those who have received a death sentence since 1977 have actually been executed (Garland, 2014).

The deterrence argument generates an enormous amount of heat created by those who state "conclusively" that it deters and those who also state just as "conclusively" that it does not. This is an example of what Charles Manski calls "incredible certitude" (2011, p. 261). Manski warns us against taking such a stance and asks us to remember all arguments about emotional ideological issues such as the death penalty involve "dueling certitudes," each claiming truth and thus conflating "science and advocacy." Both sides of the death penalty debate bring mountains of data to the battleground, and both sides claim that the studies of the other side are based on "seriously flawed" data or methodology, or erroneous interpretation.

Peterson and Bailey's (2003) excellent article on the history of death penalty deterrence studies going back to 1925 tells us that early studies were extremely simplistic ones that tended to examine homicide rates in neighboring states with and without the death penalty, or homicide rates before and after abolition in states that abolished capital punishment. These studies almost always showed that the death penalty had no discernible effect on reducing homicides and that most abolitionist states had lower homicide rates than most death penalty states (Nagin & Pepper, 2012). This is illustrated in Figure 7.1. However, we should not interpret this in terms of cause and effect. That is, we cannot say that most non-death penalty states had lower homicide rates in 2009 (or any other year) than death penalty states *because* they did not have the death penalty. Some non-death penalty states had higher homicide rates than some death penalty states, and perhaps some death penalty states retain the death penalty *because* they have a high homicide rate. This graph's visual impact will be less persuasive today since two high-murder-rate states—Maryland and Illinois—have joined the ranks of non-death penalty states.

Chapter 7 DETERRENCE AND THE DEATH PENALTY 163

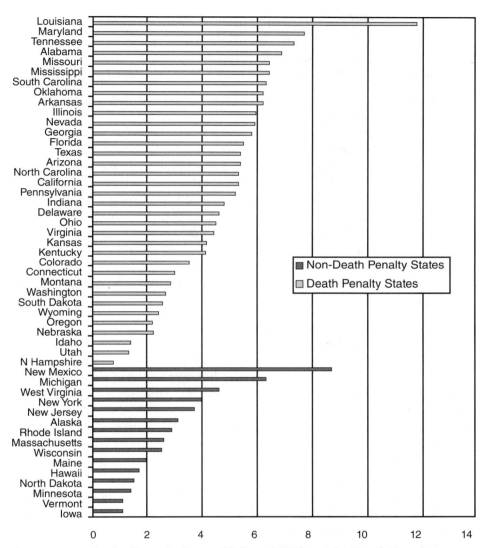

FIGURE 7.1 Murder Rates in States With and Without the Death Penalty in 2009

Primarily comparing homicide rates across states with and without the death penalty led sociologist Thorsten Sellin to conclude that "the presence of the death penalty in law and practice has no discernible effect as a deterrent to murder" (1967, p. 138). Many of these studies, however, did not control for the effects of any number of other factors (demographics, social and economic factors, certainty of death penalty, etc.) that may have influenced either or both the homicide rate and the presence or absence of the death penalty in the states examined. Regardless of any shortcomings, these studies—Sellin's in particular—had a great impact on the Supreme Court's decision to suspend the death penalty in *Furman v. Georgia*. As Justice Thurgood Marshall put it:

> Despite the fact that abolitionists have not proved non-deterrence beyond a reasonable doubt, they have succeeded in showing by clear and convincing evidence that capital punishment is not necessary as a deterrent to crime in our society. This is all that they must do. We would shirk our judicial responsibilities if we failed to accept the presently existing statistics and demanded more proof. It may be that we now possess all the proof that anyone could ever hope to assemble on the subject. But, even if further proof were to be forthcoming, I believe there is more than enough evidence presently available for a decision in this case. . . . In light of the massive amount of evidence before us, I see no alternative but to conclude that capital punishment cannot be justified on the basis of its deterrent effect.

Most of the remainder of the chapter is devoted to exploring Marshall's assertion that capital punishment abolitionists have provided "clear and convincing evidence" (again, Manski's "incredible certitude" argument) that capital punishment does not serve to prevent further murders. It is patently obvious that the threat of the death penalty fails every time a murder is committed, and we can easily document the number of these failures. On the other hand, it is just as obvious that we cannot number the times the death penalty threat succeeded since we cannot count non-events. That is, we cannot know how many (if any) people who might otherwise have committed murder did not do so for fear of forfeiting their own lives.

As we have seen, in a 5-4 decision, the U.S. Supreme Court declared a suspension of the death penalty in 1972 in *Furman*, with concurring justices citing statistical evidence of the nondeterrent effect of capital punishment. We have also seen that the Court ended the four-year moratorium on the death penalty in *Gregg v. Georgia* in 1976 in a 7-2 decision. The issue of deterrence came up as it did in *Furman*, but with the opposite conclusion reached by the majority of the justices. After acknowledging that the death penalty does not deter murders that occur in the heat of passion (such murders are rarely death-eligible anyway), Justice Potter Stewart went on to write in his opinion: "But for many others, the death penalty undoubtedly is a significant deterrent. There are carefully contemplated murders, such as murder for hire, where the possible penalty of death may well enter into the cold calculus that precedes the decision to act."

DETERRENCE: CRIMINOLOGISTS AND SOCIOLOGISTS VERSUS ECONOMISTS

One of the factors that reversed the thinking on deterrence among some justices in *Gregg* was a study by economist Isaac Ehrlich (1975), whom Justice Stewart cited. Ehrlich's study used more sophisticated statistical techniques than did previous studies and national data from 1933 to 1969. He also included a variable most previous studies omitted—the certainty of the death penalty. Ehrlich found that over this period a significant rise occurred in the murder rate paired with a significant decline in the execution rate. Based on these data, Ehrlich concluded that the death penalty was a significant deterrent to murder, and that each execution may have prevented seven or eight murders.

Ehrlich's study produced a long line of studies using the same as well as different data that led to the general dismissal of his conclusions. The main issue seemed to have been his logarithmic transformation of his data (logarithmic transformation is used to "pull" outlying data points of a variable in a skewed distribution closer to the bulk of the data in order to make the data conform to what statisticians call a "normal distribution"). Most of these contrary studies were conducted by sociologists or criminologists. For instance, sociologist William Bailey (1980) used equally sophisticated statistical tools, adding certainty and celerity (swiftness) of execution, and concluded that the data failed to support the deterrence argument. A consistent pattern soon emerged in these studies revealing that most studies that arrive at more or less the same conclusion (with different data sets and methodologies) as Ehrlich are made by economists, and those that arrive at the opposite conclusion are usually conducted by sociologists or criminologists. According to law professor and economist Joanna Shepherd, "all modern studies that use panel data [comprehensive data from all 50 states and/or across time periods] find a deterrent effect. . . . [In] contrast to economics studies, most of the sociological studies find no deterrence" (2005, pp. 214–218). Similarly, Bushway and Reuter tell us that "economists and criminologists have actively butted heads over the topic of deterrence almost since economists began studying the topic [and] have clashed heatedly over empirical research on the death penalty since the 1970s" (2008, pp. 390–391). Thus, the deterrence/no-deterrence split seems to involve economists versus criminologists or sociologists.

The different discipline ideologies, training, and theoretical assumptions probably play a large part in the contrary findings and the subsequent arguments. Economists, criminologists, and sociologists use the same rigorous statistical models, but no amount of mathematical sophistication can compensate for the problem of incomplete and ambiguous data. Another difference is the ideological and theoretical assumptions that go consciously or subconsciously into selecting the ways in which members of each discipline go about conceiving of and conducting their research. Economists assume a human nature that is rational and self-serving (the view of the classical scholars discussed in Chapter 1); that is, humans respond to incentives and disincentives to maximize their pleasure and to minimize their pain. The deterrent effect of punishment is thus taken for granted by economists (Kirchgässner, 2011). On the other hand, most criminologists are sociologically trained (Cooper, Walsh, & Ellis, 2010) and tend to either be agnostic about human nature or deny that such a thing exists.

The problems inherent in attempting to determine the effect of something (execution) that so rarely follows something else (murder), with potentially hundreds of factors between the time of the crime and execution, are legion. No matter how sophisticated the mathematics used, even small changes in the assumptions underlying a particular statistical model are many and can change the interpretation of the results. The inclusion or exclusion of a particular state that abolished capital punishment during the study period; the exclusion of why a particular prosecutor did not seek the death penalty for a particularly heinous crime, while another sought it for a less heinous crime; the failure to include the different probabilities of execution in different states for people sentenced to death; and many, many other factors may change the results. Then one must consider the issue of the statistical techniques involved. Understanding these techniques requires broad and deep statistical training. The modern deterrence literature contains such esoteric terms as "vector autoregression," "two-stage least squares regression," and "autoregressive integrated moving average," to name just a few, and we cannot engage issues relating to them or to the research methodologies to which they are applied in this book.

Nevertheless, the Supreme Court justices were still arguing statistics and the deterrent effect of the death penalty in *Baze v. Rees* (2008), the case having to do with the constitutionality of the drug mixture in the injection used in executions (see Chapter 4). While Justice John Paul Stevens upheld the constitutionality of the mixture, he took the opportunity to question the usefulness of the death penalty: "The legitimacy of deterrence as an acceptable justification for the death penalty is also questionable, at best. Despite 30 years of empirical research in the area, there remains no reliable statistical evidence that capital punishment in fact deters potential offenders." Justice Antonin Scalia responded to this by writing: "Justice Stevens' analysis barely acknowledges the 'significant body of recent evidence that capital punishment may well have a deterrent effect, possibly a quite powerful one.'" Scalia was quoting Sunstein and Vermeule (2006), two researchers who claimed that each execution saved up to 18 innocent lives, a claim that even most fellow economists find excessive.

DOES CAPITAL PUNISHMENT HAVE A BRUTALIZING EFFECT?

Some criminologists and sociologists argue that capital punishment has a **brutalizing effect** rather than a deterrent effect. That is, executions are perceived by some as saying that it is all right to kill people who have offended us, and that a segment of those who perceive the situation this way will act on that perception, with executions thus increasing the number of homicides. Executions may also be seen as legitimizing the notion that revenge is acceptable, and that the state is setting an example for others to follow—"The state can kill its enemies, so can I."

An opportunity to test the brutalization effect came with Oklahoma's resumption of the death penalty in 1990. According to two studies (Bailey, 1998; Cochran, Chamlin, & Seth, 1994), the resumption of capital punishment in the state was followed by an increase in "stranger" killings (murders committed by people unknown to their victims), with an increase of one stranger homicide per month in a year following an execution. Neither of these studies, of course, claimed that there was an actual *causal* connection between Oklahoma's reinstatement of capital punishment and the one additional stranger murder per month since any number of factors not included in the study might account for the increase, as could pure chance.

Once again, brutalization is an issue where economists and other social science scholars disagree: "The brutalization idea is not one that economists have given much credence" (Cameron, 1994, p. 206). Dudley Sharp (1997), the director of the pro–death penalty organization Death Penalty Resources, says the following about it:

> If the brutalization effect is real, it would be the only known legal sanction to cause an increase in wrongful behavior. Why would criminals become more likely to engage in illegal activities because the punishments for those activities become more severe? How absurd. Have dramatic increases in the rates of incarceration resulted in dramatic increases in kidnappings? Just the opposite.

Other scholars point to the brutal public punishments meted out in Saudi Arabia (see Chapter 12) and opine that if the brutalization effect were true, it would be most evident in that nation, but Saudi Arabia is noted for its low level of violent crime (van den Haag, 2003). Here again, we cannot draw any conclusion from this set of circumstances. Perhaps brutalization lies under the surface waiting to be unleashed if the strict social controls of Saudi Arabia were to be loosened. Perhaps most telling regarding the effect is that even most (81.2%) anti–death penalty criminologists surveyed by Radelet and Lacock (2009) either disagreed or strongly disagreed that the death penalty has a brutalizing effect.

The presence of capital punishment would incite others to kill if applied to crimes such as rape, robbery, or kidnapping. Under such circumstances, the criminal would have an increased incentive to kill his victims to reduce the probability of being caught because he is already facing the maximum penalty and can be executed only once. However, we can never discount the presence of individuals who actually might respond to executions in a way that proponents of the brutalization effect aver, even if they are not moved by other state examples such as increased arrests or increased welfare benefits to increase their own kidnappings or generosity. The cases of Daniel Colwell and John Blackwelder in this chapter's opening vignette illustrate this, although they did not demonstrate brutalizing effects as such effects are alleged to operate; that is, the criminals did not model their behavior on the state's. Rather, what they did is hatch complicated suicide plots.

Further complicating the issue, economist and law professor Joanna Shepherd (2005) found evidence for both the deterrent and brutalizing effects of capital punishment depending on the number of executions in a state. Shepherd's model is based on 3,054 counties in states with capital punishment and covered the years 1977 through 1996. She found a threshold effect whereby states with a deterrent effect (5 states) had an average of 32 executions over the time period; states with neither a deterrent or brutalizing effect (25 states) had an average of 6.7 executions, and states (6 states) with a brutalization effect had an average of 8.6 executions. These effects differed across time periods, but she found an overall deterrent effect of 4.5 fewer murders per execution. In other words, in states where executions are rare, they *may* have a brutalizing effect, and in states where they are relatively common, they *possibly* have a deterrent effect.

THE INCONCLUSIVE CONCLUSION OF THE COMMITTEE ON DETERRENCE AND THE DEATH PENALTY

Shepherd's study was nevertheless just another in a series of studies followed by others claiming the contrary. What then can we conclude about the deterrent (or brutalization) effect of capital punishment if the studies conducted on the issue come to contrary conclusions? The National Academy of Science convened a subcommittee to try to come to some sort of conclusion regarding this question. This Committee on Deterrence and the Death Penalty (CDDP) was composed of nine highly respected death penalty scholars from sociology, criminology, economics, and statistics, who examined the entire empirical literature on the deterrent (and brutalizing) effect of the death penalty available up to 2011. Their analysis of the data is by far the most extensive to date.

It examines every possible facet of death penalty studies, both their strengths and inevitable weaknesses, and provides sound mathematical and logical reasons why the existing deterrence and brutalization literature is deficient in enabling us to reach firm conclusions one way or the other. The committee's conclusion and recommendation was that deterrence studies should not be used to influence judicial deliberations. The committee's conclusion reads:

> The committee concludes that research to date on the effect of capital punishment on homicide is not informative about whether capital punishment decreases, increases, or has no effect on homicide rates. Therefore, the committee recommends that these studies not be used to inform deliberations requiring judgments about the effect of the death penalty on homicide. Consequently, claims that research demonstrates that capital punishment decreases or increases the homicide rate by a specified amount or has no effect on the homicide rate should not influence policy judgments about capital punishment. (Nagin & Pepper, 2012, p. 102)

Two Dutch statisticians came to similar conclusions using data from 102 U.S. deterrence studies from 1975 through 2011. They also went a few steps further to demonstrate how opposite findings can be derived from the same data set with only slight changes in assumptions. In their own words: "Using a panel data set of U.S. states, we show how easy it is to derive contradictory results by employing alternative specifications. Thus, our results reinforce the claim that the empirical evidence presented to date is by far too fragile in order to base political decisions on it" (Gerritzen & Kirchgässner, 2013, p. 1). They further concluded that ideology (pro– or anti–death penalty bias) may account for most contradictory findings: "Our results also reinforce the considerations of W. S. McManus that selective perceptions might be the cause for divergent findings. If rather different results can be obtained under reasonable assumptions, researchers will consider those outcomes as being reliable which correspond to their preconceptions" (p. 24).

WHAT IS NEEDED TO DEMONSTRATE IF THE DEATH PENALTY IS A DETERRENT?

If statistical studies are not up to the task of demonstrating what we as a society need to know in order to make a decision regarding the abolition or retention of the death penalty, is there anything else that could? Only randomized experiments can provide acceptably definitive answers to tough questions. A randomized experiment is one in which a large group of individuals—say, migraine sufferers—are randomly assigned to one of two groups. The first group is called the *experimental* (or *treatment*) *group*; they will receive a new drug thought to be effective in treating migraines. The second group, made identical on average in every way to the experimental group by random assignment, is called the *control group*. The control group receives an identical-looking pill, but a placebo sugar pill rather than the real thing. Neither the researchers nor the experimental and control group members will know which group received the real medicine and which received the placebo until the end of the experiment. If the drug is effective, members of the experimental group will have significantly greater symptom relief than members of the control group. Researchers can be confident that the medicinal effect of the drug was real because the only systematic difference between members of the two groups was the treatment they received; that is, the drug they took.

Let us see what would have to be done to reach a similar level of certainty about the effects of the death penalty in the United States. First, we would have to randomly assign the 50 states to the experimental (death penalty) and control (non-death penalty) groups. Then we would have to take every man, woman, and child in the United States and randomly assign them to live in one of the states. When this is done, we would have to make sure that everyone convicted of death-eligible murder (all states would be consistent with their definitions of this) would be executed within, say, two years—no exceptions. Everyone convicted of a similar murder in a non-death penalty states would receive life without the possibility of parole—no exceptions. Run this experiment for 10 years and then look at the murder rates in the treatment and control states to see if a significant difference exists. If there is a significant difference such that the death penalty states have lower homicide rates, then the death penalty saves innocent lives; if no difference is found, then it serves no useful purpose, and its retention can only be justified on retributive grounds.

Such an experiment, of course, is ridiculously impossible, but it is what is required to make "beyond a reasonable doubt" claims about the death penalty one way or the other. This is not to say that we should cease empirical studies of the death penalty using statistical methods. More sophisticated statistical techniques and models will emerge, and it would certainly be useful if economists and criminologists/sociologists would work together on the issue, thus averaging out their biases. On the issue of future deterrence studies, the CDDP wrote: "The committee recommends further investigation of capital punishment using assumptions that are weaker and more credible than those that have traditionally been invoked by empirical researchers" (Nagin & Pepper, 2012, p. 121).

The following Perspective feature was written by a state Supreme Court justice who has personally sentenced felons to death and has heard death penalty appeals. Note what he has to say regarding the deterrent effect of capital punishment and the assumptions of certainty, swiftness, and severity. Also, note his stance on retribution.

PERSPECTIVE FROM A STATE SUPREME COURT CHIEF JUSTICE: GERALD SCHROEDER

Idaho Supreme Court Chief Justice Gerald Schroeder served on the bench for nearly 39 years and became Idaho's longest-serving state judge. He is a Harvard Law School graduate who was appointed to the Idaho Supreme Court in 1995. Justice Schroeder has vast experience working on a variety of cases, which includes presiding over death penalty cases as the sentencing judge and as an appellate judge.

I have sentenced two men to death for horrific crimes. One of these men has been executed and I attended his execution. I believe that if you are going to sentence a man to die, you better be willing to look the person in the eye at the time they are executed. Oddly enough, the most criticism that I received as a judge was for allowing this man the choice of his last meal. I think he ordered $80 of seafood. I grew up watching 1930s movies and in them the condemned men always got their last meals. It seemed like the decent thing to do, but I got dozens of angry phone calls and letters from the public about that.

FIGURE 7.2 Idaho Supreme Court Justice Gerald Schroeder

The longstanding problem with trying to figure out if the death penalty deters potential offenders suffers from the obvious—we don't have any way to measure this. Though, I would suspect that the death penalty does not deter when considering the way that it is implemented today. Consider the three tenets of deterrence: *certainty*, *swiftness*, and *severity*. The *certainty* that punishment will result from illegal behavior is an important element of deterrence when we are talking about most crimes, but it has less application when we talk about a small number of crimes. Capital crimes are few in number and we know that people commit these crimes for a variety of reasons (hatred, money, enjoyment of seeing people suffer, etc.). All of these factors play a role in determining if someone gets a death sentence and they are weighed differently depending on who is evaluating these factors. Consequently, it is unlikely that we will ever apply the element of certainty to the death penalty. Even if we were to use the death penalty on a regular basis, it would be unlikely to deter anyone because it is out of view. Executions are an abstract construct to most people because they don't see it and it does not affect them. I don't have a problem with executions in public view. Witnessing an execution is a powerful event. When you show it in a movie or television, it has a very profound effect on the viewer, as would a public execution.

The *swiftness* requirement of deterrence is also far from being met when we consider the legal process that takes place prior to an execution. In the past, we could say that the punishment of death was somewhat swift. For example, in the 1950s we had three executions in Idaho and all of them took place after only about a year following the crime. There were no federal appeals. We have taken such a sorry turn in our system of justice that the concept of swift punishment in the post-*Furman* era is almost nonexistent. Some delays, however, are necessary. For example, recent DNA technology is a wonderful thing that should be used to prove guilt or innocence, but it should not be used as an excuse to delay the process for an unreasonable amount of time.

Lastly, *severity* of the punishment is a necessary element of deterrence because you want someone to fear the punishment. And the death penalty is the most severe sanction that can be given, even though we seek to implement execution practices that are painless for the condemned. As a human being, I would like to see some of these capital offenders tortured like their victims, but as a judge I know that it would be dangerous and impossible to institutionalize such a practice. You need an objective protocol and torture would be much too subjective.

In my third year as a law student, I wrote a paper on the philosophies and justifications for punishment. I looked at the works of Kant and Bentham, which have played a part in shaping my views of punishment and the death penalty. What I realized is that the death penalty does not have to have a deterrent value to be a valid punishment. There are just some people who do things that are so terrible that you must consider what punishment will be *just* under the circumstances and will bring some semblance of closure to the families of the victims and the community. And that is the biggest factor that I weigh in death penalty cases—closure for those most closely impacted by the crime. That is very important. If I had a member of my family savagely murdered and knew that the offender was sitting in the penitentiary, I would be angry all the time. Bentham referred to the utilitarian principle to shape decision-making. There are times as a judge that you must consider what the greatest good for the greatest number of people is and sometimes sentencing a man to die meets that burden. Some crimes are so heinous that the people in the community where the crime took place live in fear, and restoring that sense of order may require a death sentence for a man or woman who is to blame for disrupting the solidarity. Consider the Boston Marathon bombing. If the accused is guilty, then he should get the death penalty because of the devastation and fear he created in that community. There are good philosophical underpinnings for retribution or "an eye for an eye."

The only kind of capital crimes that might result in a deterrent effect would be that of organized crime killings. Maybe we could use the death penalty to deter the mafia types who rationally decide to kill for economic reasons or to protect their turf because they are making calculated decisions that stem from greed. For example, if a member of an organized crime organization decides to kill a shopkeeper in a neighborhood because he won't pay the money for protection, knowing that he (offender) might get the death penalty for committing such a crime may deter him. Perhaps the same could be true for contract killings with these types of groups.

In any event, deterrence and retribution are both valid punishment considerations, though achieving deterrence is a much more complicated goal in our criminal justice system when considering the death penalty.

THE OPINIONS OF CRIMINOLOGISTS AND POLICE CHIEFS ON THE DEATH PENALTY

In 1989, the American Society of Criminology (ASC) issued a resolution with respect to the death penalty that made it very clear what its position is. Note the "incredible certitude" of their resolution:

> Be it resolved that because social science research has demonstrated the death penalty to be racist in application and social science research has found no consistent evidence of crime deterrence through

execution, The American Society of Criminology publicly condemns this form of punishment, and urges its members to use their professional skills in legislatures and courts to seek a speedy abolition of this form of punishment.

The appropriateness of a professional organization urging its members to take a specific side in a highly contested and very ideologically infused issue may be questioned. Nevertheless, criminologists are people who are supposed to know about such things, but most of them do seem to follow the ASC directive. Criminologists Michael Radelet and Traci Lacock (2009) polled 77 leading criminologists who were eminent members of the ASC by asking them if they believed that the death penalty is a deterrent to further murder; 88.2% agreed or strongly agreed that it was not. Only 6% came to the same "not sure" conclusion as the CDDP. But no matter how eminent the reputations of the surveyed criminologists, we don't know if any of them seriously studied the death penalty issue or how knowledgeable they are about the contrary evidence. Neither can they discard their own ideological baggage that comes with such a highly politicized topic as capital punishment. A survey of American criminologists by Cooper, Walsh, and Ellis (2010) found that 68% of them described themselves as either liberal or radical, and the abolition of capital punishment is part of the social agenda for people on the liberal side of the political divide.

What about the opinion of police chiefs, who are hardly likely to be liberals or radicals, but certainly know crime and criminals? A poll of 500 police chiefs was conducted in 2008 asking them to react to a series of statements about the death penalty (among other issues) as being accurate or inaccurate (Dieter, 2009). The ratings on the accuracy of the death penalty statements are presented in Figure 7.3. Looking at these data, it seems to us that most knowledgeable people on both sides of the death penalty issue would provide the same answers as the chiefs, and only the fourth response ("The death penalty significantly reduces the number of homicides") directly engages the deterrence issue. A lot more police chiefs (37%) than criminologists (5%) considered this an accurate statement. However, a better response option would have been: "The death penalty *as currently practiced* reduces the number of homicides *to some unknown extent*." The qualifying phrase "as currently practiced" reduces the difference between the theory and actual practice of capital punishment. Perhaps the respondents viewed the death penalty as impotent as currently practiced, but that it could serve as a deterrent if applied with more certainty and more swiftly. Replacing "significantly" with "to some unknown extent" removes the confusion and contradictions associated with the term "significant" since it means quite different things to the statistically knowledgeable (for whom it simply means "reliably found," however small or inconsequential the difference) than it does for the person in the street. For the person in the street unfamiliar with statistics and its jargon,

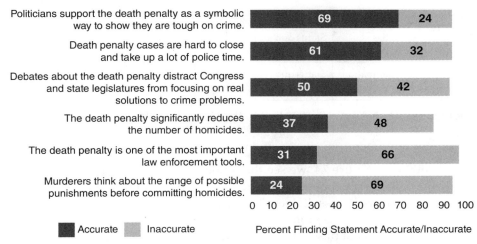

FIGURE 7.3 Responses of Police Chiefs to Various Statements about the Death Penalty
Source: Death Penalty Information Center

even for police chiefs, the word probably implies its dictionary synonyms: "large," "substantial," or "important."

PASCAL'S WAGER: A "LAST DITCH" EFFORT

If the members of the CDDP are correct that the use of statistical science has led to inconclusive results and that decisions on the death penalty should not therefore rely on them, on what are we to rely to make that decision? One "last ditch" strategy employed by proponents of the death penalty is to rely on simple rational argument using **Pascal's wager**, otherwise known as the "best bet" argument.

Blaise Pascal was a seventeenth-century mathematician, physicist, and philosopher with a deep interest in spiritual matters. Pascal was a religious man who admitted to the uncertainty of God's existence, but who also said that in the face of such uncertainty the "best bet" is to wager that he does and to live accordingly. God either exists or he doesn't; this is the way it is, so the only thing that determines an outcome for a person is what he or she chooses to believe. The rational person will always bet on the existence of God based on a cost–benefit analysis of the two choices available. Note that this argument applies only to conditions of uncertainty in which the probabilities are one-half each (God either exists or he does not; he cannot exist just a little bit or only now and again).

	God Exists			Death Penalty Deters	
Believe	Yes	No	**Execute**	Yes	No
Yes	Eternal bliss	Status quo	Yes	Innocent lives saved	Status quo
No	Eternal damnation	Status quo	No	Innocent lives lost	Status quo

FIGURE 7.4 Pascal's Wager Applied to the Death Penalty

Referring to Figure 7.4, we see that under conditions of uncertainty about God's existence, if we choose to believe that he does, and if he indeed does, we stand to gain eternal bliss. It doesn't matter what religion we are talking about since all theistic religions promise a blissful afterlife, and even religions such as Buddhism that do not posit a monotheistic God promise a pleasant afterlife (or at least a more pleasant reincarnation) and eventual Nirvana (the profound peace of mind when liberated from all desires) if one follows its prescriptions and proscriptions. If God exists and we choose not to believe this, we risk eternal damnation. If God does not exist, what we choose to believe makes no difference to our fate after death (status quo).

Death penalty proponents apply Pascal's reasoning to the death penalty debate under the assumption that rational people will consider the death penalty the "best bet." This version of the argument also accepts the uncertainty about the central issue (the deterrent effect of the death penalty) and says that we have to live with this uncertainty. We do as a society, however, get to make a choice in the face of this uncertainty based on what we stand to lose versus what we stand to gain. If the death penalty deters some unknown number of murders and we choose to use it, we have saved innocent lives. If the death penalty deters and we choose not to use it, we are in some sense a party to the loss of those innocent lives that would not have been lost had we chosen otherwise. If it does not deter, then we have neither lost nor gained anything in terms of innocent lives whichever choice we make. Indeed, law professors Cass Sunstein and Adrian Vermeule (2005) argue that the death penalty is "morally required" if it deters more killings than it inflicts.

Opponents of capital punishment may have several objections to this argument. They may find the very idea of gambling with lives repugnant, and object to placing "status quo" in the upper-right-hand column of Figure 7.4. They would say that lives are lost, even if those lives are the lives of murderers. Some of these alleged murderers may have been wrongfully convicted, so in this case "innocent lives" were lost in the false gamble that capital punishment deters. Some anti–death penalty individuals may well be persuaded by the "best bet" argument that it would be prudent to execute murderers if by doing so we as a society possibly can prevent at least some future murders. However, pro–death penalty philosopher Ernest van den Haag points out that many anti–death penalty advocates consider execution so morally repugnant that "asked whether they would execute murderers if each execution were to deter ten murders, thereby saving innocent lives, all abolitionists I have questioned answer in the negative" (2003, p. 239).

Thus, as we mentioned in the opening paragraph of this chapter, the deterrence argument is irrelevant for those whose vision of morality finds state killing repugnant under any circumstance, even if it may prevent any number of murders. We also said that deterrence was irrelevant for those whose morality leads them to defend the death penalty as morally required in the name of justice, regardless of whether it does or does not prevent further murders. Thus, three positions on the death penalty exist, all based on different conceptions of morality. We have the practical morality of consequentialism based on the trade-off that taking the lives of murderers will save the lives of innocents. Then we have the two non-consequentialist positions for which the deterrence argument is irrelevant. Both positions maintain that we should do something if it is the moral thing to do (the categorical imperative) regardless of any consequences, but they differ by 180 degrees about what that moral imperative is. Such are the conundrums faced by those wishing to argue the merits of capital punishment on the basis of deterrence.

SUMMARY

This chapter looks at the concept and assumptions of deterrence. For punishment to be effective as a deterrent, it must be certain, swift, and severe to be taken seriously. Furthermore, deterrence is a concept that is rationally based; without rational decision-makers, the concept holds no validity. We saw that only a small number of murders are death-eligible, and that only about 15% of murderers sentenced to death since 1976 have been executed. Under such violations of deterrence theory assumptions, it is difficult to study the deterrent effect of capital punishment.

Nevertheless, hundreds of studies have been conducted to do precisely that. We saw that states with the death penalty generally had higher homicide rates than states without it, but also that we cannot claim any "causal" direction for this. We also noted that economists and sociologists and criminologists typically come to different conclusions in their studies, with the former almost always claiming a deterrent effect, and the latter almost always claiming no deterrent effect. Some possible reasons for this divide were provided. The studies of both economists and sociologists/criminologists have been used in U.S.

Supreme Court decisions to either deny or affirm the deterrent effect of capital punishment.

Some sociologists/criminologists have even asserted that capital punishment has a brutalizing rather than deterrent effect. Economists do not agree with this position, and neither do the majority of criminologists. The authors of this book see little merit in the brutalizing effect, although it is possible that some deranged individual may perceive a state execution as a license to engage in murder.

The Committee on Deterrence and the Death Penalty was formed to examine the issue of deterrence. This committee concluded that at present we cannot know from the empirical studies whether it does or does not deter. The committee further recommended that deterrence studies not be used in judicial deliberations about the death penalty, and also provided recommendations for future death penalty deterrence studies.

We examined the opinions of criminologists and police chiefs on the deterrence issue. Predictably, most (88.2%) criminologists believed that the death penalty is not a deterrent, and police chiefs were not too convinced of it either. We argued that the criminologists' opinions could be viewed in terms of both the ideological position (liberal) of most criminologists and the "official" position of the American Society of Criminology. The responses of the police chiefs could well be the responses of even ardent supporters of capital punishment given the way the questions were worded.

Finally, we examined moral arguments with reference to Pascal's wager. This is a "best bet" argument that maintains that under conditions of uncertainty in which the probabilities are exactly 50-50, rational individuals will always choose the alternative that provides the best outcome. Pascal applied his famous argument to the existence of God, but death penalty proponents have applied it to the existence of a deterrent effect for the death penalty. We cannot currently know whether or not the death penalty is a deterrent, so we as a society must make a choice based on a cost–benefit ratio. Opponents of the death penalty may rebut this argument on certain grounds, but for strong opponents, it is simply irrelevant since they would not support the practice even if they knew it would save innocent lives. On the other side, supporters of the death penalty would support the practice on moral grounds even if it didn't deter.

DISCUSSION QUESTIONS

1. Explain the assumptions of deterrence theory. Do you believe them?
2. Do death penalty states generally have a higher homicide rate because they have the death penalty or have the death penalty because they have high

homicide rates, or are other factors responsible for a state's decision to retain or abolish the death penalty?
3. Do you think the death penalty would be a deterrent if it were applied with a lot more certainty and swiftness than is now the case?
4. Explain why the Committee on Deterrence and the Death Penalty concluded that at present we cannot know whether or not the death penalty deters.
5. What is the role of ideology (conservative, moderate, liberal, radical) in the death penalty debate?
6. Explain Pascal's wager as it applies to the death penalty. Is it convincing to you?
7. Assuming you do not support the death penalty on moral grounds, if it could be conclusively shown that each execution saved five innocent lives, would you change your mind? Why or why not?

GLOSSARY

Brutalizing effect: The assumption that executions are perceived by some as saying that it is all right to kill people who have offended us, and that a segment of those who perceive the situation this way will act on that perception, with executions thus increasing the number of homicides.

Contrast effect: The distinction between the conditions of the threatened punishment and the conditions of the everyday lives of those being punished.

Pascal's wager: Otherwise known as the "best bet" argument, states that under conditions of either/or uncertainty, the rational option is always the one that logically provides the best outcome for the gambler.

REFERENCES

Bailey, W. (1980). Deterrence and the celerity of the death penalty: A neglected question in deterrence research. *Social Forces, 58,* 1308–1333.

Bailey, W. (1998). Deterrence, brutalization, and the death penalty: Another examination of Oklahoma's return to capital punishment. *Criminology, 36,* 717–733.

Baze v. Rees. (2008). 553 U.S. 35.

Beccaria, C. (1963/1764). *On crimes and punishment.* Trans. H. Paulucci. Indianapolis: Bobbs-Merrill.

Berk, R., A. Li, and L. Hickman. (2005). Statistical difficulties in determining the role of race in capital cases: A re-analysis of data from the state of Maryland. *Journal of Quantitative Criminology, 21,* 365–390.

Boudon, R. (2003). Beyond rational choice theory. *Annual Review of Sociology, 29,* 1–21.
Bushway, S., and P. Reuter. (2008). Economists' contribution to the study of crime and the criminal justice system. *Crime and Justice, 37,* 389–451.
Cameron, S. (1994). A review of the econometric evidence on the effects of capital punishment. *Journal of Socio-Economics, 23,* 197–214.
Clarke, R., and D. Cornish. (1985). Modeling offenders' decisions: A framework for research and policy. In *Crime and justice annual review of research,* ed. M. Tonry and N. Morris, pp. 145–187. Chicago: University of Chicago Press.
Cochran, J., M. Chamlin, and M. Seth. (1994). Deterrence or brutalization? An impact assessment of Oklahoma's return to capital punishment. *Criminology, 32,* 107–134.
Cooper, J., A. Walsh, and L. Ellis. (2010). Is criminology ripe for a paradigm shift? Evidence from a survey of American criminologists. *Journal of Criminal Justice Education, 21,* 332–347.
Cornish, D., and R. Clarke. (1986). *The reasoning criminal.* New York: Springer-Verlag.
Death Penalty Information Center. (2010). "States without Death Penalty Have Had Consistently Lower Murder Rates." http://www.deathpenaltyinfo.org/deterrence-states-without-death-penalty-have-had-consistently-lower-murder-rates.
Dieter, R. (2009). *Smart on crime: Reconsidering the death penalty in a time of economic crisis.* Washington, DC: Death Penalty Information Center.
Ehrlich, I. (1975). Deterrence: evidence and inference. *Yale Law Journal, 85,* 209–227.
Federal Bureau of Investigation. (2014). Crime in the United States, 2013. Washington, DC: National institute of Justice.
Garland, D. (2014). Peculiar institution: America's death penalty today. In *Die Sinnprovinz der Kriminalität,* ed. H. Schmidt-Semish and H. Hess, pp. 233–244. Wiesbaden, Germany: Springer Fachmedien.
Gerritzen, B., and G. Kirchgässner. (2013). "Facts or Ideology: What Determines the Results of Econometric Estimates of the Deterrence Effect of Death Penalty? A Meta-analysis." Discussion paper no. 2013-03, School of Economics and Political Science, University of St. Gallen, Switzerland.
Hargrove, T. (2010). "Unsolved Murder Rate Increasing." http://www.newsnet5.com/dpp/news/crime/unsolved-murder-rate- increasing#ixzz2Vjwsqtps.
Keel, T., J. Jarvis, and Y. Muirhead. (2009). An exploratory analysis of factors affecting homicide investigations. *Homicide Studies, 13,* 50–68.
Kirchgässner, G. (2011). Econometric estimates of deterrence of the death penalty: Facts or ideology? *Kyklos, 64,* 448–478.
Langan, P., and D. Farrington. (1998). *Crime and justice in the United States and England and Wales, 1981–1996.* Washington, DC: Bureau of Justice Statistics.

Manski, C. (2011). Policy analysis with incredible certitude. *Economic Journal, 121*, 261–289.

Nagin, D., and J. Pepper, eds. (2012). *Deterrence and the death penalty.* Washington, DC: Committee on Law and Justice, National Academies Press.

Paternoster, R. (2010). How much do we really know about criminal deterrence? *Journal of Criminal Law and Criminology, 100*, 765–823.

Peterson, R., and W. Bailey. (2003). Is capital punishment an effective deterrent for murder? An examination of social science research. In *America's experiment with capital punishment,* ed. J. Aker, R. Bohm, and C. Lanier, pp. 251–282. Durham: University of North Carolina Press.

Radelet, M., & T. Lacock. (2009). Do executions lower homicide rates? The views of leading criminologists. *Journal of Criminal Law and Criminology, 99*, 489–508.

Radzinowicz, L., and J. King. (1979). *The growth of crime: The international experience.* Middlesex, UK: Penguin Books.

Rosenfeld, R. (2000). Patterns in adult homicide. In *The crime drop in America,* ed. A. Blumstein and J. Wallman, pp. 130–163. Cambridge, UK: Cambridge University Press.

Sellin, T. (1967). *Capital punishment.* New York: Harper & Row.

Sharp, D. (1997). "Death Penalty and Sentencing Information in the United States." http://www.prodeathpenalty.com/dp.html.

Shepherd, J. (2005). Deterrence versus brutalization: Capital punishment's differing impacts among states. *Michigan Law Review, 104*, 203–256.

Snell, T. (2011). *Capital punishment, 2010: Statistical tables.* Washington, DC: Bureau of Justice Statistics.

Spelman, W. (2000). The limited importance of prison expansion. In *The crime drop in America,* ed. A. Blumstein and J. Wallman, pp. 97–129. Cambridge, UK: Cambridge University Press.

Stohr, M., and A. Walsh. (2015). *Corrections: The essentials,* 2nd edition. Thousand Oaks, CA: SAGE.

Sunstein, C., and A. Vermeule. (2006). Is capital punishment morally required? Acts, omissions, and life-life tradeoffs. *Stanford Law Review, 58*, 703–750.

Van den Haag, E. (2003). Justice, deterrence and the death penalty. In *America's experiment with capital punishment,* ed. J. Aker, R. Bohm, and C. Lanier, pp. 233–249. Durham, NC: Carolina Academic Press.

CHAPTER 8

THE DEATH PENALTY AND SPECIAL POPULATIONS

Race, Gender, Age, and Mental Capacity

On June 16, 1944, just 83 days after the alleged crime, a very frightened 5-foot 1-inch, 95-pound black boy named George Junius Stinney Jr. was led by guards to the execution chamber in South Carolina and electrocuted. He was apparently so small that the large Bible he carried to the execution site had to be placed on the execution seat, so his head could reach the electrodes, and the adult-sized mask flew off his face with the first jolt of electricity. At age 14, Stinney was the youngest person to be executed in the United States in the twentieth century.

Stinney was convicted of murdering two white girls aged 11 and 8 whose crushed skulls were found on March 23, 1944, the day after they disappeared. Police arrested Stinney after he told a member of the search party that he had spoken to the girls the previous day. The police claimed that, during his interrogation, Stinney confessed to the murders, indicating that he had killed both girls because he wanted to have sex with the older one. Stinney's trial lasted three hours and commenced in a highly charged racial atmosphere on April 24. Following ten minutes of deliberation by an all-white jury (despite three-quarters of the county population being black), Stinney was found guilty. The only evidence produced at the trial was Stinney's alleged confession and the fact that he had spoken to the two girls on the day of their disappearance. It did not help matters that a lawyer who had never worked on a criminal case before was appointed as his counsel and that the attorney called no witnesses on Stinney's behalf.

Over the years, there have been numerous claims that Stinney was innocent and that a member of a prominent white family later made a deathbed confession, but these have yet to be substantiated. More than 70 years after the boy's execution, a coalition of civil rights advocates petitioned the courts to either retry or exonerate Stinney posthumously. In December 2014, Circuit Judge Carmen T. Mullen vacated Stinney's sentence, stating that Stinney's execution was a "truly unfortunate episode in our history" and "This Court finds fundamental, Constitutional violations of due process exist in the 1944 prosecution of George Stinney, Jr. and hereby vacates the judgment."

LEARNING OBJECTIVES

- Understand the changing pattern of capital punishment in terms of race.
- Understand race-of-defendant and race-of-victim discrimination charges.
- Know the legal and scientific reasoning behind the abolition of the juvenile death penalty.
- Understand why women are underrepresented on death row and among people executed.
- Know the difference between mental disability and mental illness, and how these impairments impact death penalty decisions.

George Stinney's case starkly illustrates a number of issues addressed in the chapter. Is the death penalty biased against black defendants? If it is not biased against black defendants in general, is the punishment nonetheless biased against black defendants who murder whites, particularly white females? Is there a bias in favor of white female victims, or even in favor of female murderers in the sense that they are less likely to receive the death penalty than male murderers? Then one must consider the issue of the execution of juveniles. Although no longer permitted in the United States, what were the arguments presented against this practice, and are they the same as those used in debates today over the execution of the mentally ill or individuals with intellectual disabilities (formerly referred to as the "mentally retarded")? These are the primary issues discussed in this chapter.

Throughout American history, representatives of all races, ethnicities, nationalities, religions, genders, ages, and intellectual competencies have been executed. There have even been several elephants executed for killing human beings, including one hung by a crane in 1916. This chapter concentrates on issues surrounding the death penalty involving race, gender, age, and mental competency. These issues do not necessarily address the appropriateness of the death penalty per se, but rather they engage questions pertaining to issues specific to these categories of people. One such question is "Is the death penalty administered in an unbiased way?" This question addresses issues of race and gender. For instance, would the Stinney case have moved from crime to execution in just 83 days if the alleged murderer was white, or if Stinney had been accused of murdering a black victim? Another question is "Are there certain categories of individuals who should be exempt from the death penalty because of certain characteristics?" This question addresses issues of age and mental competency and mental illness. Should we hold juveniles such as Stinney (assuming he was actually guilty) to the same level of culpability as an adult, or how about someone with a very low IQ or someone who is suffering from a mental illness such as schizophrenia? We begin with the most contentious of these categories, which is indisputably the issue of race.

RACE AND THE DEATH PENALTY

When we speak of race in the United States, we are almost always speaking of matters pertaining to African Americans. The history of race relations in this country is painfully disturbing to say the least. No one doubts that African Americans have been treated badly from the time that the first African slaves landed in America in 1619 until relatively recently. Aside from the loathsome practice of slavery itself, after emancipation blacks were subjected to the Black Codes, Jim Crow laws, disenfranchisement, "separate but equal" statutes, literacy tests, vicious stereotypes, and lynch mobs (Walsh & Hemmens, 2014). And surely the *Stinney* case reveals how the rights of African Americans have historically been blatantly ignored. There is a tendency for many individuals to examine modern racial issues in this historic context, and they thus find it difficult to imagine that the death penalty can be administered in a racially neutral way. For those who think this way, racial bias in capital cases is taken for granted. Others contend that history is just that—history—and that in this modern age the situation has changed dramatically in the United States. Some scholars maintain that death penalty opponents raise the racial issue not out of any special concern for African Americans or for racial bias issues, but because they abhor the penalty itself for moral reasons and use race to center their arguments (McAdams, 1998).

RACIAL DISPROPORTIONALITY IN CAPITAL PUNISHMENT

There is no doubt that African Americans have historically been convicted of capital crimes and executed in greater numbers than whites. Robert Bohm

(2012) provides a blizzard of statistics to demonstrate this, a sampling of which is presented here:

1. In 1856, slaves in Virginia could be convicted of 66 crimes carrying the death penalty, while only murder carried the death penalty for whites.
2. The attempted rape of a white woman was a capital crime for blacks until the mid-twentieth century in seven Southern states.
3. Although making up about 11% of the population during the period examined, 50% of all people executed in the United States from 1800 to 2002 were African American.
4. Between 1930 and 1980, 53% of persons executed were black.
5. A 1990 U.S. General Accounting Office report that examined the results of 28 studies found that 75% of them had concluded that black defendants were more likely than white defendants to receive the death penalty.

Augmenting the above is Elliot Cramer's (2009) testimony before the House Select Committee of North Carolina on the death penalty, in which he indicated that from 1910 to 1961, 133 blacks and 36 whites were executed in North Carolina. However, he also indicated that since 1984 the situation has changed dramatically, with 13 blacks and 28 whites being executed in the state. Nevertheless, nationwide there are still proportionately more blacks than whites on death row and proportionately more blacks than whites have been executed since 1976 when the moratorium on the death penalty was lifted. This is indicated in Figure 8.1 based on information from the Death Penalty Information Center (DPIC) (2013). African Americans have represented between 11% and 13% of the U.S. population between 1976 and 2012, but have constituted 35% of the executions. Likewise, blacks make up 41% of current U.S. death row inmates. Thus, since the resumption of executions in 1976, blacks have been overrepresented relative to their proportion of the general population by roughly 3 to 1 in terms of executions and as death row residents. Such statistics are taken by many as clear evidence that the death penalty is still biased against African Americans.

Claims of disproportionality cannot be evaluated by comparing the percentages of each race executed or on death row with their proportion of the general population. To assess this claim logically, we have to compare each race's proportion of *murderers* with its proportion of executed prisoners or those on death row. Blume, Eisenberg, and Wells (2004) did just this with data from the 31 states that sentenced 10 or more individuals to death from 1977 through 1999 (5,953 death sentences), comparing the proportion of black murder offenders in each state with the proportion of black inmates on death row. In California, Nevada, and Utah, blacks were overrepresented on death row relative to their proportion of murders in those states; in all other 28 states, they were underrepresented. For example, in Nevada the proportion of black

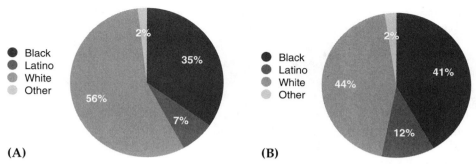

FIGURE 8.1 (A) Race of Defendants Executed from 1976 to 2012. (B) U.S. Death Row Population by Race
Source: Death Penalty Information Center

murder offenders in the state during that same 22-year period was 0.302, and the proportion of blacks on death row in Nevada was 0.331. In Utah, the respective proportions were 0.086 and 0.105, and in California, they were 0.338 and 0.353. As opposed to these miniscule differences, in most of the remaining 28 states, blacks were underrepresented to a large degree. In Tennessee, African Americans committed 60.4% of murders in the state, but their percentage on death row was 33.3%. In Mississippi, the respective percentages were 77.9% and 59.0%, and in Missouri, they were 62.6% and 41.1%. Blume, Eisenberg, and Wells (2004) found that one explanation for these results is that black-on-black murders are significantly more common and underrepresented on death row, while black-on-white murders are less common and overrepresented on death row. We will visit the issue of offender–victim race in much more depth shortly.

In 2013, 52.2% of individuals arrested for murder in the United States were African Americans and 47.8% were white (Federal Bureau of Investigation [FBI], 2014). Because the FBI places Hispanics and non-Hispanic whites into a single "white" category (93% of Hispanics-Latinos are defined as white) in its Uniform Crime Reports (UCR), we cannot make direct black/white comparisons between UCR and DPIC statistics. The inclusion of Hispanics in the white category inflates white numbers because Hispanics have a higher crime rate than Anglos (Steffensmeier et al., 2011). Steffensmeier and his colleagues tell us that when Hispanics are taken out of the white category, the black homicide rate is 12.7 times higher than the white rate (2011, p. 209). A comparison of homicide and execution/death row data thus leads to the conclusion that "although they are overrepresented among death row populations and executions relative to their share of the U.S. population, Blacks are underrepresented based on their arrests and convictions for murder" (Robinson, 2008, p. 191). We should remember, however, that only a tiny fraction of homicides are death-eligible, and an even smaller proportion (about 2% to 6%, depending on jurisdiction) actually receive a death sentence (Berk, Li, & Hickman, 2005; Streib, 2003).

It seems from these data that white murderers are proportionately more likely both to receive a death sentence and to be executed for death-eligible homicide. For instance, an early post-*Furman* study (Kleck, 1981) found that from 1930 onward in Northern states whites were more likely to receive the death penalty, and that the discrimination evidenced against blacks in death penalty cases of earlier years in the South dissipated in later years. Greenfeld and Hinners (1985) examined the cases of 1,405 prisoners under sentence of death and found that 15.8 per 1,000 white murderers were sentenced to death versus 11.6 per 1,000 black murders. A large study by Gross and Mauro (1989) looked at death sentences in over 14,000 cases and found that whites received a death sentence in 26.5% of the cases involving felony circumstances and in 1.4% of the cases with non-felony circumstances. On the other hand, 17.2% of blacks convicted in felony circumstances and 0.4% in nonfelony circumstances received a death sentence (calculated by McAdams [1998] from Gross and Mauro's data). A 2001 U.S. Department of Justice study of federal death-eligible cases reached a similar conclusion with regard to federal murder cases:

> United States Attorneys recommended the death penalty in smaller proportions of cases involving Black or Hispanic defendants than in those involving White defendants; the Attorney General's capital case review committee likewise recommended the death penalty in smaller proportions of involving Black or Hispanic defendants. . . . In the cases considered by the Attorney General, the Attorney General decided to seek the death penalty for 38% of the White defendants, 25% of the Black defendants, and 20% of the Hispanic defendants.

Why we should see bias (if indeed it is bias) against whites in death penalty cases is an open question. In the days when African Americans were disproportionately charged, convicted, and executed for capital crimes, it was relatively easy to explain: racism. Yet the Southern states—considered the bastions of racism—are the states in which blacks are most underrepresented on death row relative to the number of murders they commit. One explanation is that Southern states have large African American populations, and African Americans have been shown to be less likely to favor the death penalty than whites (Blume, Eisenberg, & Wells, 2004). With a fair proportion of blacks on a jury, prosecutors may decide not to seek the death penalty, or black jurors may refuse to convict if the death penalty is on the table. Another view is that perhaps prosecutors, judges, and juries are more careful in handling minority cases in an attempt to convince themselves they are being impartial with their treatment of minorities in an attempt to avoid the dreaded "racist" label.

THE ISSUE OF VICTIM'S RACE

On the other hand, the literature consistently shows that killers of whites (regardless of the killer's race) are more likely to receive the death penalty than killers of other racial groups. Perhaps the primary reason whites are more likely to receive the death penalty is because homicide is overwhelmingly intraracial (whites typically kill whites and blacks typically kill blacks). Prosecutorial reluctance to seek the death penalty for blacks might reveal a devaluation of black victims vis-à-vis their white counterparts, and a perception that black-on-black crime is not a threat to the white power structure. Thus, the race issue in death penalty discourse remains alive and well, but it has done something of a U-turn. McAdams contends that now a greater proportion of condemned whites are executed than condemned blacks, capital punishment opponents who:

> first adopted an offender-centered concept of justice . . . turned on a dime and adopted a victim-centered concept of justice (when the data in fact showed that too many Whites are being executed). Had they maintained a philosophical consistency, the opponents might have lauded the current situation on the ground that a sort of affirmative action was being employed. That is, against an historic background of harsh treatment of Black people in most aspects of public policy, Black offenders are getting favorable treatment from the criminal justice system. (1998, p. 160)

By a "victim-centered concept of justice," McAdams means that the focus has now moved from bias against black *defendants* to bias against black *victims* or, conversely, bias in favor of white victims, particularly white female victims. In other words, the reason that whites are more likely to receive a death sentence and to be executed than blacks is that whites overwhelmingly kill whites, and blacks overwhelmingly kill blacks. Thus, when we see fewer blacks receiving a death sentence and being executed than whites, it is not because of any bias in favor of black defendants, but rather bias in favor of white victims. Moreover, the charge made today is that the death penalty is most often sought when the victim is white and the perpetrator is black.

Before controlling for aggravating and mitigating factors, all studies show that killers of whites (regardless of the race of the killer) are more likely to receive the death penalty than killers of blacks. In the Gross and Mauro data (1989), 28.8% of blacks who killed whites under felony circumstances received a death sentence versus 6% of blacks who killed other blacks under similar circumstances. Whites who killed blacks under felony circumstances received a death sentence 18.2% of the time. Thus, whites who kill blacks are more likely to receive the death penalty than blacks who kill blacks, although this must be viewed in light of the fact that whites only commit about 5% of interracial murders, with blacks killing whites in about 95% of all interracial murders (Robinson, 2008).

More recent data from three independent teams commissioned by the National Institute of Justice examined the role of race in the application of the death penalty in federal cases. These data are summed up in a 209-page report in which Klein, Berk, and Hickman write:

> When we look at the raw data and make no adjustment for case characteristics, we find the large race effects noted previously—namely, a decision to seek the death penalty is more likely to occur when the defendants are White and when the victims are White. However, these disparities disappear when the data coded from the AG's [Attorney General's] case files are used to adjust for the heinousness of the crime. For instance, B&H [Berk & He] concluded, "On balance, there seems to be no evidence in these data of systematic racial effects that apply on the average to the full set of cases we studied." The other two teams reached the same conclusion. KF&B [Klein, Freedman, & Bolus] found that, with their models, after controlling for the tally of aggravating and mitigating factors, and district, there was no evidence of a race effect. "This was true whether we examined race of victim alone . . . or race of defendant and the interaction between victim and defendant race." Schonlau reported that his "analysis found no evidence of racial bias in either USAO [U.S. Attorney's Office] recommendations or the AG decisions to seek the death penalty." (2006, p. xvii)

A more recent study is that of Hemant Sharma and colleagues (2013) who examined all first-degree murder convictions in Tennessee from 1976 to 2007. They noted that prosecutors sought the death penalty for 76% of white defendants and 62.6% of black defendants, and that 37.3% of white defendants for whom the death penalty was sought received this sentence versus 23.6% of black defendants. Prosecutors sought the death penalty in 64% of the cases where the victim was white, and in 33% of the cases where the victim was black. When controlling for a variety of aggravating and mitigating factors, as well as demographic and evidentiary variables, they found that the killing of a law enforcement officer, history of prior violent offenses, and all evidentiary (scientific, co-perpetrator testimony, confession, and strong eyewitness testimony) variables were by far the strongest predictors of a death sentence for defendants of any race. The victim's race did not play any significant independent part, but a victim's sex (female) did. The racial makeup of the crime (black offender/white victim; white offender/white victim, etc.) had no significant independent effect, but the race of the defendant did, with whites being 2.26 times more likely to receive the death penalty than blacks over the 30-year period.

Another study of 1,163 capital cases found an additional complication (Bjerregaard et al., 2015). This study found that blacks who killed whites in "high severity" circumstances (multiple aggravating "heinous, atrocious, and cruel" factors) had an increased probability of a death sentence, but blacks who killed whites at lower levels of severity (such as a shooting death in the process of a robbery) had decreased probabilities of receiving the death penalty. Under low severity circumstances, a black defendant who kills a white victim had almost half the odds of receiving a death sentence than a black defendant who kills a black victim or a white defendant who kills either a white or black victim. This is an extremely odd finding that is difficult to explain, and the authors did not try to. The average number of aggravating factors in black defendant/white victim cases was 2.20 (23.4% of the cases) while the white defendant/black victim cases (3.6% of the cases) were 1.47. The average number of aggravating factors in black/black cases (30.9% of cases) was 1.96, and for white/white (42.1% of cases) it was 1.84. This supports the earlier Katz (2005) study that black defendant/white victim cases are more likely to have multiple aggravating factors.

DUELING STATISTICIANS REDUX

According to the previously cited studies, what are the characteristics of a case that make racial disparity "disappear"? In *McCleskey v. Kemp* (1987), law professor David Baldus and his colleagues (1990) basically argued that with zero or one aggravating factor and little risk of a death sentence, there was no racial discrimination regardless of the racial makeup of the victim/offender dyad. Similarly, with multiple aggravating factors (such as multiple victims, a prior homicide conviction, child victims, torture, etc.), there was no discrimination and the risk of a death sentence was high regardless of the racial makeup of the victim/offender dyad. However, Baldus and colleagues claimed that it is in the middle range of aggravating circumstances where the "correct" sentence is less clear that racial disparities appear. On the other hand, in the U.S. Department of Justice study (2001) discussed earlier, not only was the death penalty sought at lower rates for blacks and Hispanics than for whites, but this was also true "both in 'intraracial' cases, involving defendants and victims of the same race and ethnicity, and in 'interracial' cases, involving defendants and victims of different races or ethnicities."

In an analysis of the same Georgia data on which Baldus and colleagues relied, statistician Joseph Katz (2005), who was statistician for the state in the *McCleskey* case, examines all aggravating and mitigating circumstances. In a sample of 1,082 homicide defendants, 141 cases involved a white victim and a black perpetrator. In 67.1% of white victim/black perpetrator cases, the victim was killed in the course of a robbery compared to 7.4% in black victim cases, and in 70.6% of the white victim cases the victim was a stranger compared with 9.6% of black victim cases. Katz also indicated that "white victim homicides show a greater percentage of mutilations, execution-style murders, tortures, and beaten victims, features which generally aggravate homicide and increase the likelihood of a death sentence" (2005, p. 405). Katz cites a number of other studies finding similar results in 10 different states; that is, once the full array of aggravating and mitigating factors are considered, there is little or no discrimination evident in white victim/black perpetrator cases that is not accounted for by aggravating circumstances and other legally relevant variables. As Cassell explains the nature of the relationship: "Black-defendant-kills-white-victim cases more often involve the murder of a law enforcement officer, kidnapping and rape, mutilation, execution-style killing, and torture—all quintessential aggravating factors—than do other combinations" (2008, pp. 23–24).

A study by criminologists Paternoster and Brame (2003) that looked at 1,130 death-eligible homicide cases in Maryland found no race-of-defendant bias, but significant race-of-victim effects. That is, cases in which the offender was black and the victim was white were about 3.5 times more likely than any other offender/victim dyad to receive a death sentence. Statisticians Berk, Li, and Hickman looked at the same data and arrived at the opposite conclusion: "When race surfaces, cases with a Black defendant and White victim or 'other' racial combinations are *less* likely to have death sentences imposed" (2005, p. 381). Berk and colleagues thus conclude: "For both capital charges and death sentences, race either played no role or a small one that is difficult to specify" (2005, p. 386).

A particularly sophisticated study of the "white victim effect" addressing this issue that warrants extended discussion is that of Wesley Jennings and colleagues (2014). These researchers looked at every death-eligible case ($N = 1,356$) prosecuted in North Carolina from 1977 to 2009. After surveying a number of other studies with contradictory findings (but mostly supporting the white victim effect), they applied a particularly sophisticated research design and statistical tool called propensity score matching (PSM). PSM is a technique that attempts to overcome a demonstrated effect determined by simply comparing a particular "treatment"—race of the offender/victim dyads in this case—between those who received a death sentence and those who received a life without parole (LWOP) sentence by introducing other factors that predict the same outcome by matching cases, thus rendering them more comparable. In other words, PSM allows for a statistical approximation of a quasi-experimental design by removing systematic differences between cases prior to comparing the outcome of interest—death versus LWOP.

Jennings and his colleagues first estimated the white victim effect using traditional statistical (logit regression) models controlling for 50 legal and nonlegal factors and found, regardless of the offender's race, that there was a significant effect with an odds ratio of 1.393. In effect, this means that the odds of receiving a death sentence if the victim was white is 1.393 times greater than the odds of a death sentence if the victim was of any other race. When the same researchers looked at black offender/white victim dyads, the odds ratio was 2.834. After applying PSM to the data, however, both effects were close to zero; that is, neither the race of the victim nor the racial makeup of offender/victim dyads had any independent effect on whether or not a defendant received the death penalty. The authors conclude the "'white victim effect' on capital punishment decision-making is better considered a 'case effect' rather than a 'race effect'" (2014, p. 384). In other words, each case is unique in that it contains a multitude of case characteristics (aggravators and mitigators) and evidentiary qualities that have to be considered. Given the ability to case-match (albeit imperfectly), this quasi-experimental approach is currently the best method we have to tease out any discriminatory effects that may be present in sentencing.

Despite the growing sophistication of our methodological and statistical tools, we still have a situation similar to the deterrence issue with studies making conflicting claims with "incredible certitude." Of course, something may be true in one jurisdiction but not in another, or true in the same jurisdiction at one time but not at another time. However, the Georgia and Maryland analyses discussed above were made by separate teams examining the *exact same data* and arriving at different conclusions. In death penalty studies involving race, we are often confronted with dueling statisticians just as we see psychiatrists for the state and for the defense making contrary claims about the same defendant. Which of the conflicting claims made by psychiatrists we believe might depend on our opinion of psychiatry, but isn't mathematics the ultimate of dependable objectivity and "truth"? Numbers do not lie, of course, but people lie with numbers (either inadvertently or knowingly) in order to support their position on something, particularly if it is a deeply emotional issue for them such as the death penalty. Just as sociologists and criminologists butt heads with economists over the deterrence issue, sociologists and criminologists seem to butt heads with mathematical statisticians over the race-of-victim issue. The race issue, then, may be just as intractable as the deterrence issue for the time being. Another way of looking at the apparent impasse is offered by Scheidegger, who writes, "Many academics who do research on the death penalty reliably produce results that favor one side, raising a suspicion of partisan bias" (2012, p. 161). This is similar to Gerritzen and Kirchgässner's (2013) contention regarding deterrence studies discussed in Chapter 7—ideology, thinly disguised within various statistical assumptions, plays a huge role in the discourse on capital punishment.

Part of the trouble with contradictory findings is that we expect too much from limited data, especially when such an emotional issue as the death penalty is the focus. As statistician Elliot Cramer (2009) points out: "Given the large number of possible relevant variables and the small number of homicides in each judicial district, I do not see the possibility of any statistical study being able to adequately draw conclusions about racial disparities in administration of the death penalty." Cramer does not mean that we cannot reach conclusions about the race of the perpetrator or victim, or who does or does not receive the death penalty; we hardly need sophisticated statistics to tell us that. Rather, the problem is whether or not the death penalty is warranted after adjusting for aggravating and mitigating circumstances and the strength of the evidence.

For those who believe in the death penalty, those upon whom it is imposed deserve it, and the only answer to the sentencing equity issue is to indict African Americans for death-eligible offenses at the same rate as whites, and also execute more of them until the data on that race attain parity with those for whites convicted of similar crimes who are executed. For individuals who oppose the death penalty, the only answer to the issue is to execute no one.

JUVENILES AND THE DEATH PENALTY

Although George Stinney was the youngest person to be executed in the twentieth century, the youngest person ever to be legally executed was 12-year-old Hannah Ocuish, a Pequot Indian girl with an intellectual disability, who was convicted of killing a six-year-old white girl in 1786 in Connecticut (Streib, 1987). As far as is known, the first juvenile to be executed in territory that was to become part of the United States was a 16-year-old boy named Thomas Graunger (or Granger), who was hanged in 1642 for committing bestiality with a variety of farm animals, many of whom were executed along with him (Brown, n.d.). In the three and one-half centuries that have passed since then, Streib (2003) states that 365 juveniles have been executed in the United States, and from 1973 to 2003, a total of 22 were executed in the United States, with most of those executions occurring in the late 1990s and early 2000s.

According to Linde (2011), this spike was the result of public outrage at the high violent crime rates of the 1980s and 1990s when the 15- to 19-year-old age group had the second highest homicide rate (after the 20- to 24-year-old age group). One particularly nasty example was that of Scott Hain, the last person to be executed before the juvenile death penalty was ruled unconstitutional. Hain was 17 when he and an accomplice carjacked an automobile in Tulsa, Oklahoma, in 1987. The car was occupied by a man and a woman whom Hain and his companion robbed, and then locked in the trunk of the car. Hain subsequently set fire to the car, resulting in the man and woman being burned alive. He was executed by lethal injection in 2003.

The perception that punishments designed for adults were inappropriate for juveniles led to the establishment of the first separate court for juveniles in Chicago in 1899. These courts operated under then English common law doctrine of *parens patriae*, which translates literally as "father of his country" but loosely and practically as "state as parent." This doctrine confers the right of the state to intercede and act in the best interest of the child, and means that the state and not parents have the ultimate authority over children. *Parens patriae* was supposed to be a paternalistic doctrine that always operated "in the best interests of the child," and as such, the juvenile courts operated with little concern with the procedural rights afforded adults. This began to change with the rights revolution in the early 1960s (Walsh & Hemmens, 2014) as juveniles slowly accumulated most of the rights of adults. However, this proved to be a double-edged sword because it also precipitated a trajectory toward treating juveniles like adults as they gained adult procedural rights. Thus, many more juveniles who committed serious crimes were referred ("waived") to adult court for trial and punishment (Sarkar, 2007).

The death penalty has been applied to juveniles as it is to adults; that is, to those who have murdered in particularly heinous and depraved ways. It was the judicial review of such cases that eventually led to the abolition of the death penalty for juveniles in 2005. For instance, in 1977, 16-year-old Monty Lee Eddings and several companions stole an automobile. They were stopped in the stolen vehicle by an Oklahoma highway patrol officer, whom Eddings shot and killed as the officer approached the car. At Eddings's sentencing hearing, the state presented three aggravating circumstances to warrant the death penalty, but the judge only allowed Eddings's age to be used as a factor for mitigation. In *Eddings v. Oklahoma* (1982), the Supreme Court vacated Eddings's death sentence, ruling that in death penalty cases the courts must consider all mitigating factors (Eddings had been a victim of abusive treatment at home) when considering a death sentence. This was the first time that the Supreme Court viewed age as an important factor in determining a death sentence (Robbers, 2007). As Justice Lewis Powell wrote in the majority opinion:

> Youth is a time and condition of life when a person may be most susceptible to influence and to psychological damage. Our history is replete with laws and judicial recognition that minors, especially in their earlier years, generally are less mature and responsible than adults. Particularly during the formative years of childhood and adolescence, minors often lack the experience, perspective, and judgment expected of adults.

As we will see in Chapter 9, Justice Powell's insight into the immaturity of adolescence has been vindicated by modern neuroscience.

Another such case in the evolution leading to the abolition of the juvenile death penalty was *Thompson v. Oklahoma* (1988). This involved 15-year-old William Thompson, who was one of four young men charged with the murder of his former brother-in-law. All four were found guilty and sentenced to death. Thompson appealed to the Supreme Court, claiming that a sentence of death for a crime committed by a 15-year-old is cruel and unusual punishment. The Court agreed, and using the "evolving standards of decency" principle, it drew the line under which execution was not constitutionally permissible at age 16.

One year later, a similar case before the Court in *Stanford v. Kentucky* (1989) involved even more heinous circumstances surrounding a murder (see Chapter 3). Kevin Stanford, age 17, and his accomplice repeatedly raped and sodomized a female cashier during and after their robbery of a gas station, following which they drove her to a secluded area, where Stanford shot her in the face and in the back of her head. In a 5-4 decision, the Supreme Court ruled that if states choose to execute juveniles who were 16 or 17 at the time of the commission of their crimes, it is constitutionally permissible. The *Thompson* and *Stanford* cases taken together thus set the minimum age for the execution of juveniles at 16.

There were certain indications in *Stanford* that some of the justices were eager to revisit the juvenile death penalty issue again as soon as possible and that their intention was to eventually rule it unconstitutional. Their opportunity came 16 years later, when they heard *Roper v. Simmons* (2005) and the Court redrew the age line under which it was constitutionally impermissible to execute anyone at age 18, thus abolishing the juvenile death penalty (see Chapter 4). Christopher Simmons was 17 when he and two younger accomplices broke into a home, kidnapped the owner, beat her, and threw her still alive from a bridge into the river where she drowned. Simmons had told many of his friends before the crime that he wanted to commit a murder, and he bragged to them about it afterward. His crime was a "classic" death penalty case—premeditated, deliberate, and cruel, and Simmons appeared to be unremorseful. Nevertheless, his sentence drew condemnation from around the world, with *amicus curiae* briefs filed in favor of Simmons by many organizations, including the European Union, the American Bar Association, and the American Medical and Psychological Associations. This case led to the commutation of sentences for 72 death row inmates who had committed their crimes while juveniles (Linde, 2011).

In a 5-4 opinion, Justice Anthony Kennedy noted that the United States was the only country in the world that gives official sanction to the juvenile death penalty (in other words, the only country to officially acknowledge it). He also noted the growing body of evidence from neuroscience on the immaturity of the adolescent brain. The majority opinion also cited *Atkins v. Virginia* (2002) (see Chapter 4). In noting that the Court in *Atkins* had ruled the execution of intellectually disabled individuals to be cruel and unusual punishment because of the lesser degree of culpability attached to the mentally challenged, it reasoned that such logic should be applied to juveniles. The Court also pointed out that the plurality of states (30) either bar execution for juveniles or have banned the death penalty altogether, thus citing state legislation as part of the impetus behind its decision.

There is nothing natural about the age of 18 that turns a juvenile into an adult overnight. Under English common law, a child under the age of 7 was presumed absolutely incapable of committing a crime, as were children aged 7 to 14, unless the prosecution could prove the child fully understood what he or she did was wrong. Thus, the age of criminal responsibility has shifted with the times. Today, 18 is the legally defined age of adulthood and consequently of adult responsibility. This decision to lower the age from 21 was made during the Vietnam War era, when 18-year-olds were being drafted to fight. The reasoning was that if these young men were old enough to engage in combat, they were old enough to vote and to take on other adult responsibilities. Because evidence from neuroscience tells us that the human brain is not fully mature until the mid-twenties (see the discussion of this subject in Chapter 9), perhaps the Supreme Court will one day hear a case claiming that a 22-year-old defendant convicted of a capital crime should not be executed, with the Court perhaps redrawing the red line under which it is not permissible to execute anyone younger than 25, a much more "natural" age to define adulthood if brain maturity is to be regarded as the benchmark.

WOMEN AND THE DEATH PENALTY

The first woman executed in territory that was to become part of the United States was Jane Champion, executed in the Virginia colony in 1632 for murdering her illegitimate infant (Bohm, 2012). The first woman to be executed in the United States by the federal government was Mary Surratt, convicted as a conspirator in the assassination of President Abraham Lincoln (see Figure 8.2). She was hanged in July 1865 (Cashin, 2002). Women have constituted only about 2% of persons executed in the United States since the inception of the death penalty (Robinson, 2008). As of

FIGURE 8.2 Mary Surratt
Source: Wikipedia, public domain

December 2014, there were 59 women on death row, or 1.94% of the total death row population of 3,125 persons, and women have accounted for only 15 (0.9%) of persons (11 white, 4 black) actually executed since 1976 (see the listing in the subsection that follows). Women constitute 50% or more of the population, which means they have been and are massively underrepresented as persons executed or on death row. Is this indicative of pro-female bias? It would be if females committed approximately the same number of death-eligible homicides as males, but they consistently commit only about 10% of all homicides each year. Many of these homicides are committed against spouses and lovers in self-defense situations, and only rarely do we find women committing the heinous kinds of murders that draw down the death penalty (Walsh, 2011). However, Bohm (2012) estimates that 4% to 6% of women murderers would receive death sentences "if women and men were treated equally [and if] no factor other than the offense was considered" (p. 211). We will discuss these "other" factors later, but for now we present thumbnail sketches of the 15 women executed since 1976 whose offenses were indeed heinous.

Women Executed Since 1976

1. The first of the 13 women executed since 1976 was Velma Barfield. Barfield was a drug addict who poisoned her lover with rat poison in North Carolina in 1984. She apparently did so because she was afraid that he would find out she was forging his checks to pay for her addiction. Barfield confessed to three previous murders, and was suspected in another as well as arson and insurance fraud. She was 45 at the time of the crime for which she was convicted, and 52 when executed.
2. Karla Faye Tucker, a rock groupie, prostitute, and drug abuser, was the next woman to be executed. Tucker was convicted in 1984 of the pickaxe murder of a man and a woman in Texas when she was 23. She was executed in Texas in 1998. Tucker's case garnered extensive coverage in the United States and international press because of the many pleas for clemency by noted pro–death penalty advocates because she had become a "redeemed" born-again Christian while in prison.
3. Judy Buenoano was executed in 1998 in Florida at age 54 for the 1971 murder of her husband. She was also convicted for the 1980 murder of her son and the 1983 attempted murder of her fiancé. She also confessed to the 1978 murder of a boyfriend in Colorado, and was convicted of multiple counts of arson and insurance fraud.
4. Betty Lou Beets was executed in Texas in 2000 at the age of 62 for the murder of her husband in 1983. Betty Lou was married five times; she shot her second husband in the head and tried to run over her third with her car. The remains of another former husband were found buried in Beets's garage.

5. Christina Riggs was executed in 2000 in Arkansas for the 1997 murder of her two children, ages 2 and 5. Riggs had tried to commit suicide and left a note saying that she didn't want her children to be a burden on anyone. Riggs was unusual in that she demanded the death penalty and would not allow any appeals. She was executed just two years after her crime.
6. Wanda Jean Allen was executed at the age of 41 in Oklahoma in 2001 for the 1989 murder of her lesbian lover, whom she had met in prison while serving time for the murder of a previous alleged lesbian lover. She was the first African American women executed in the United States since 1954.
7. Marilyn Plantz was executed at the age of 40 in Oklahoma in 2001 for the 1988 murder of her husband. Plantz often prostituted herself to pay for hard-core drugs. She hired her teenage boyfriend and another teenager to kill her husband for life insurance money. The men beat Planz's husband with a baseball bat and then burned his body in a remote location. Planz's boyfriend was executed in 2000.
8. Lois Nadean Smith was executed in Oklahoma in 2001 at the age of 61 for the 1982 murder of her son's ex-girlfriend, whom she shot nine times and stabbed in the throat. Smith and her son taunted the victim, and after Smith shot her, she jumped on her chest while the son was reloading the gun. Smith claimed that she was trying to protect her son and was under the influence of alcohol and drugs at the time.
9. Lynda Lyon Block was executed in Alabama in 2002 (the last person to be electrocuted in Alabama) for the 1993 shooting death of an Alabama police officer after he and Block's boyfriend got into a gunfight outside a Walmart store. At the time, she and her boyfriend were on the run from a Florida assault charge against her ex-husband.
10. Aileen Wuornos was executed at the age of 46 in Florida in 2002 for the murders of 6 men (she admitted to killing 7) beginning in 1989. Wuornos was a lesbian, drug abuser, and prostitute whom many think of as America's first "real" female serial killer (i.e., a person who kills more than three victims over a period of time with no ulterior motive such as financial gain). She claimed that all her victims had tried to rape her.
11. Frances Newton was executed at age 40 in Texas in 2005 for the 1987 murder of her husband and her 7-year-old son and 21-month-old daughter, allegedly to collect on a $100,000 life insurance policy. She was the first black woman to be executed in Texas since the resumption of the death penalty. Newton claimed that a drug dealer killed all three because her husband was in debt to him, but the murder weapon was found in her handbag, and there was gunpowder residue on her skirt.
12. Teresa Lewis was executed at the age of 41 in Virginia in 2010 for the 2002 murder of her husband and stepson. Lewis hired two of her illicit lovers to commit the murders so that she could claim life insurance money.

13. Kimberly McCarthy, a 52-year-old crack addict and former wife of the founder of the New Black Panther Party, was executed in 2013 in Texas for the robbery and murder of Dorothy Booth in 1997. McCarthy bludgeoned and stabbed Booth to death and cut off her fingers to get her rings. On the basis of DNA evidence, McCarthy was also indicted, but not tried, for the 1988 robbery and murders of two other elderly women. She is the third black woman to be executed since 1976.
14. Suzanne Basso, 59, was executed in Texas in February 2014; she became the 14th woman to be executed in the United States since the resumption of capital punishment. Basso was executed for the 1998 slaying of 59-year-old Louis Musso, a mentally disabled man whom Basso married in order to receive his Social Security benefits. Basso, her son, and one other accomplice later brutally tortured and murdered Musso for his life insurance money.
15. Lisa Coleman, 38, was executed in Texas in September 2014 for the torture-murder of her lesbian lover's 9-year-old son Davontae Williams. At the time of his death, Davontae was found to have over 250 wounds on his body and was severely emaciated.

The Chivalry Explanation in Female Capital Cases

All 15 cases just enumerated had multiple aggravating circumstances—murder for hire, murder for profit, multiple victims, prior murder conviction, cruelty, child victims, et cetera—that made their murder convictions death-eligible. What are the extralegal factors Bohm refers to that supposedly save any number of other female murderers from the death penalty in circumstances that would probably guarantee male murderers received it? The most obvious one is the chivalrous or paternalistic attitudes about women that tend to still prevail in society, leading to a reluctance to impose the death penalty on women—society's "most valued members"—convicted of crimes that would bring down such a penalty on men. For instance, Reza (2005) cites the example of a petition to the governor of California signed by male inmates of San Quentin State Prison in 1941 to prevent the execution of Ethel Spinelli, a career criminal, ex-wrestler, and knife thrower, who murdered a gang member she feared would inform on her. Such an execution, they wrote, would be "a blot on the reputation of the state and repulsive to the people of California because of *her sex and her status as a mother*" (p. 183, emphasis added).

Such chivalry remains in evidence today. The pending execution of Karla Faye Tucker in 1998 produced a spate of protests from unlikely pro–death penalty sources. Voicing his opposition to her execution, Colonel Oliver North exclaimed, "I don't think chivalry can ever be misplaced" in pleading for clemency, and TV personality Geraldo Rivera said: "Please don't let this happen. This is—it's very unseemly. Texas manhood, macho swagger. . . . What are ya' going to kill a lady? Oh jeez. Why?" (in Robinson, 2008, p. 205). Reza (2005) cites the case of Susan Smith, who in 1994 strapped her two sons, ages 3 years and 14 months, into their car seats and rolled the car into a lake, drowning them both. Smith was attempting to reunite with her lover, who had ended their relationship because of her children. Smith was sentenced to life for the cold-blooded killings because, according to Reza, she was viewed by the jury as a jilted victim "and loving mother with severe emotional issues" (2005, p. 188).

The Evil Woman Explanation in Female Capital Cases

What then of women who are sentenced to death and actually executed? Enter the "evil woman" counterpart to the chivalry hypothesis. Both Tucker and Smith were fairly good-looking young women who came across to TV audiences as matching the stereotype of femininity and "sweetness," despite having committed heinous acts. The evil woman hypothesis avers that females who in any number of ways defy traditional gender roles by not enacting a feminine identity invite the wrath of male actors in the criminal justice system (Reza, 2005). Such women tend to be "unladylike" in their general demeanor and very much out of their proscribed gender roles by acting "manly" and being "man hating," such as Wanda Jean Allen, Aileen Wuornos, and Lisa Coleman, all of whom were lesbians. And according to Clinton Duffy, warden of the prison housing Ethel Spinelli, she departed from her gender role expectations in many ways. He called her the "coldest, hardest character, male or female" and added that she was very unattractive, "a hag, evil as a witch, horrible to look at" (in Shatz & Shatz, 2011, p. 2).

If female murderers on the whole are treated more leniently on the basis of their sex, then men are being discriminated against, and for abolitionists, it is yet another indication of the unfairness of the death penalty in a system that claims fairness and neutrality. For supporters of the death penalty, this makes males no less deserving of a death sentence, and the unfairness lies in our double standards for males and females. Victor Streib, an opponent of the death penalty, warns that if women want to be treated as men's equals, then if men are eligible for the death penalty, women should be, too: "Otherwise, women are lumped with juveniles and the mentally retarded as not fully responsible human beings" (2003, p. 322). Similarly, Elizabeth Reza, an apparent supporter of the death penalty, opines:

> When women commit similar [death-eligible] crimes, we should not withhold capital punishment simply because the murderer is a mother, sister, or wife. . . . [T]he American judicial system must equalize the capital punishment system so that all, regardless of gender, are punished in a manner society and the legal system has deemed appropriate to impose on those who callously take the lives of others. (2005, p. 211)

In other words, just as the solution to the race equity issue is to either execute more African Americans or to execute no one, the solution to the gender equity problem is either to execute more women or to execute no one.

THE DEATH PENALTY AND MENTAL ILLNESS

Two bizarre cases engage issues both on race and on mental disability and illness. Two serial killers unknown to one another kidnapped, raped, and tortured women in the same city (Philadelphia) and were arrested five months apart in the same year (1987). Both men lured prostitutes to their homes and imprisoned them in their basements. One killer—Gary Heidnik—was white, and the other—Harrison Graham—was black. Heidnik killed two women, and other victims found in his basement would have doubtless been killed had he not been arrested, and Graham murdered seven. Heidnik had an extensive history of mental illness (schizophrenia) and Graham was mildly mentally retarded (Branson, 2013). Despite having killed five fewer women than Graham, Heidnik was sentenced to death and executed in 1999. Graham was given six death sentences, but they were not to be carried out until his seventh sentence—life without the possibility of parole—was completed, which guaranteed that he would never be executed. As murdering seven victims is more heinous than killing two, is this another instance of racial discrimination in the application of the death penalty, or is it a matter of mental disability being more mitigating than mental illness? Today, states are constitutionally forbidden to execute the mentally disabled (but not the mentally ill), but this was not the case at the time of Graham's trial and conviction.

PERSPECTIVE FROM A CLINICAL PSYCHOLOGIST: CRAIG BEAVER

Dr. Craig Beaver is a clinical psychologist who has been in practice for over 30 years. In addition to his private practice specializing in both clinical and neuropsychology, Dr. Beaver is a clinical instructor at the University of Washington Medical Center in Seattle. He has worked as an expert on numerous death penalty cases across the country. Dr. Beaver has vast experience in clinical diagnoses of capital defendants suffering from mental illness and commonly evaluates their neurocognitive abilities for legal consideration in the courtroom.

FIGURE 8.3 Dr. Craig Beaver

I am not sure any clinician starts out their career anticipating they will spend a significant amount of time crisscrossing the United States going to various jails and maximum security facilities to see death penalty defendants. However, after practicing for about ten years, I was asked to become involved in my first death penalty case. Ultimately, this has led to me being involved in approximately 80 death penalty cases across the United States. I have now been in 22 states dealing with death penalty issues.

States vary as to the specificity of aggravating circumstances for applying the death penalty; they also vary widely with regard to statutorily defined mitigation issues. Often, mitigation is very open-ended. This is largely related to a U.S. Supreme Court decision in 1978 involving the case of *Lockett v. Ohio* (1978) as well as later U.S. Supreme Court rulings that indicated many issues could be considered for mitigation in a death penalty case. Further, mental health professionals could and should be involved (see *Eddings v. Oklahoma*, 1982). Consequently, after the imposition of the death penalty was stopped in *Furman v. Georgia* (1972) and was reinstated in *Gregg v. Georgia* (1976), there has been growing interest in mental health professionals and especially neuropsychologists being involved in the mitigation process of death penalty cases, which is my clinical specialty.

Clinical neuropsychology is the study of brain–behavior relationships. Neuropsychology provides a unique framework for integrating information relevant to the court proceedings in a death penalty sentencing proceeding. Neuropsychology deals with how brain functioning, brain development, and one's environment affect behavior, "state of mind" and judgment. Thus, issues in neuropsychology are of particular relevance with regard to concerns about culpability for individuals and their capacity to understand, appreciate, and control their actions.

The U.S. Supreme Court has designated certain groups of defendants as ineligible for the death penalty. First, juveniles were excluded (*Thompson v. Oklahoma*, 1988). More recently, individuals diagnosed with mental retardation, now defined as intellectually disabled, were also excluded (*Atkins v. Virginia*, 2002). The arguments in both cases focused on each group's inherent limitations in cognitive functioning, reducing culpability for their actions. Neuropsychology, as well as other professional groups, contributed significantly to the understanding of the specific groups' limitations.

In my work as a neuropsychologist, the designation of these groups makes sense on issues of how responsible a person should be for their actions. Juveniles and individuals with developmental disabilities have less neuropsychological capacity to deal with the world. In my involvement in many death penalty cases, the key issue is understanding what the individual is capable or not capable of doing. For example, are they disinhibited because of neurodevelopmental problems or neurological injuries (i.e., frontal head injuries)? Do they have less ability to control or manage their emotions, such as anger or rage, in a situation because of limitations in their neurocognitive skills? Do they, in fact, have less ability to cope and manage significant life stressors? Are they able to weight the consequences of their actions and to anticipate what the consequences might be of actions they take? These issues are of particular relevance in considering what an individual's neurocognitive abilities are. How are they able to process, plan, weigh, and balance choices in their lives? This is clearly affected by one's brain functioning as well as one's own history and life experiences. Thus, neuropsychology has become increasingly important for identifying these special populations that are exempt from the death penalty and communicating to the court a defendant's neuropsychological abilities.

A third population that is not, per se, exempt from consideration of the death penalty but, as a practical matter, often is excluded from death penalty consideration, are individuals considered "insane." This is a legal term, not a clinical term. However, it relates to individuals who have such severe psychological/psychiatric difficulties they do not understand their actions or the world around them to a sufficient degree that they should be held to the same level of culpability as another person. Consequently, the court not only does not allow individuals to go to trial if they are not competent ("insane"), but also does not allow individuals who are considered "insane" to be executed. Much of this hinges on understanding how an individual's mental health issues interfere with their abilities to accurately perceive the world around them, to logically understand their circumstances, to assist in decision-making and problem-solving, as well as to communicate and effectively assist in the legal process, all of which again leads back to the importance of understanding an individual's neurocognitive abilities and, in the case of insanity, how this affects their thinking abilities.

While issues of culpability and neurocognitive capacity provide a framework to present mitigation information to the court, pragmatically it really boils down to one central theme. Successful mitigation depends on how effectively the defendant can be humanized in the eyes of the jury. In most cases, the defendant has committed a truly horrific and unforgivable crime of taking the life of another. With juries now deciding on whether or not a defendant will receive the death penalty, the mitigation process is, in fact, geared toward helping jurors understand who these individuals are, how their history and their strengths and limitations in their abilities have led them to this circumstance. It is not to justify their actions or behaviors, but to provide a human understanding of how such a tragedy could have occurred. The U.S. Supreme Court has now begun to recognize there are, in fact, specific populations (juveniles, individuals with mental retardation, now called intellectual disabilities, and individuals who are, in fact, "insane") that are indeed less culpable and, therefore, cannot be punished at the highest level.

Mental Disability

In Sir William Blackstone's *Commentaries on the Laws of England*, written in 1765, he stated that "in criminal cases, therefore, idiots and lunatics are not chargeable for their own acts, if committed when under these incapacities" (in Dillard, 2012, p. 463). People we once called "idiots" we later referred to as "mentally retarded," and today call *mentally disabled*. People we formerly called "lunatics" we now call *mentally ill*, and to them we affix a specific label such as schizophrenia, the mental condition most strongly linked to homicide (Walsh & Yun, 2013). The primary legal issues the courts have to resolve in terms of both mental deficiency and illness are the following: (a) Is the person under indictment competent to stand trial? (b) Did this person at the time of the crime have the requisite ability to form *mens rea* (guilty mind)? (c) Does the person's mental condition warrant a more lenient sentence than would normally be attached to this crime? (Dillard, 2012).

Mental disability is "a lifelong condition of impaired or incomplete mental development. According to the most widely used definition of mental retardation, it is characterized by three criteria: significantly subaverage intellectual functioning; concurrent and related limitations in two or more adaptive skill areas; and manifestation before age 18" (Mandery, 2005, p. 352). A subaverage level of intellectual functioning is defined as an IQ of 70 or below, a score that puts an individual at the bottom 2% of the general population. Using a standard formula for obtaining mental age using IQ score and chronological age, an 18-year-old with an IQ of 70 is functioning at the mental level of a child 12 to 13 years old. This does not mean that the mentally disabled cannot be held responsible for their actions; it only means that they should be held to a lower level of culpability than persons operating at higher intellectual levels.

This was not always the case. For instance, in 1979, paroled rapist Johnny Penry was sentenced to death for a very brutal rape and murder in Texas. Penry appealed to the Supreme Court on Eighth Amendment grounds that it would constitute cruel and unusual punishment to execute a mentally retarded person. Penry claimed that the jury was not instructed that it could consider his low IQ (between 50 and 63) as mitigating evidence against imposing the death penalty. The Supreme Court held in *Penry v. Lynaugh* (1989) that the jury should have been instructed that it could consider mental retardation a mitigating factor when deciding Penry's sentence, but imposition of the death penalty on a mentally retarded defendant is not per se a violation of the Eighth Amendment. However, in 2008, Penry's sentence was commuted to life imprisonment in light of *Atkins v. Virginia* (2002).

In *Atkins v. Virginia* (2002), the Court overruled itself with regard to executing the mentally disabled. The Court concluded that there was a national consensus (public opinion was again cited) against executing the mentally disabled, and that since such individuals are less capable of evaluating the consequences of their crimes, they are less culpable than the average offender (recall that *Atkins* provided the legal reasoning for ruling the juvenile death penalty unconstitutional in *Roper*). The Court also noted that mentally disabled individuals are more prone to confess to crimes that they did not commit and therefore more prone to wrongful execution. Six of the justices also concluded that the overwhelming disapproval of the world community must be considered a relevant factor in the Court's deliberations regarding the constitutionality of imposing capital punishment on the mentally disabled.

The question of mental retardation in capital cases is supposed to be an objective one—the person is or is not mentally retarded. The lives of many death row inmates depend on what the courts deem the most reliable information from contesting experts. Consider the case of Gerald Pizzuto, a death row inmate who was convicted of killing Berta Herndon and her nephew Del Herndon in 1985. The Herndons were arriving at their cabin in the mountains when Pizzuto approached them with a gun and forced them into the cabin, tied them up, and bludgeoned them to death with a hammer. He later bragged about killing the Herndons to his friends. Pizzuto was convicted and sentenced to die. He still resides on Idaho's death row and is arguing that his sentence ought to be commuted to life because his IQ at the time of the crime was 72, which is only two points above the standard for mental retardation. According to applicable

Idaho law, Pizzuto's IQ must have been 70 or lower during the time of the crime and the retardation must have been established prior to his 18th birthday (a rather difficult thing to prove if the subject was not tested prior to his 18th birthday). Pizzuto argued that his 72 IQ score is subject to a five-point margin of error; thus, his IQ could have been as low as 67. The state applied the same logic and argued that the five-point error could also mean his IQ might have been as high as 77. The 9th U.S. Circuit Court of Appeals agreed with the state and refused Pizzuto's request to have his sentence overturned because of his low IQ, but with the 2014 ruling in *Hall v. Florida* regarding the unconstitutionality of rigid cut-off points, his life may be spared.

Mental Illness

Although it is constitutionally impermissible to execute the mentally disabled, it is still permissible to execute the mentally ill. The logic behind this is that whereas mental retardation is permanent and unalterable (and cannot be faked), mental illness is not. Rarely, if ever, are mental illnesses such as schizophrenia "cured," but like any other chronic disease such as diabetes, it can be managed with medication. In other words, adhering to a correctly prescribed medical regimen, most mentally ill individuals can be restored to sanity and lead meaningful lives.

In English common law and under the U.S. Constitution, the execution of the presently insane is not permitted; as Sir William Blackstone wrote: "Madness alone punishes the madman" (in Dillard, 2012, p. 461). Note that the phrase is "currently insane," and not "insane at the time of the crime." In the not-so-distant past, if a person was insane "at the time of the crime," that person would have been insane "currently" as well because there was no acceptable method of restoring a person to sanity. Now that we have a number of effective antipsychotic medications, new Eighth Amendment and due process issues have arisen (as well as new ethical issues for the medical community).

The first of these issues arose in *Jackson v. Indiana* (1972), although the case had nothing to do with the death penalty per se. Theon Jackson, a deaf-mute with low intelligence, had been arrested for two petty thefts and found incompetent to stand trial. Because of his incompetency, Jackson was involuntarily committed to a psychiatric hospital. If a person is unrestorably incompetent, this effectively means a life sentence for a crime as minor as a petty theft. In *Jackson*, the Supreme Court ruled that it is constitutionally impermissible to commit a defendant for an indefinite period of time based on his or her incompetence to stand trial, and such defendants must either be civilly committed (committed by a noncriminal court) or released from criminal detention. This forced the states to undertake strenuous efforts to restore competency at a time when effective psychotropic drugs were becoming available.

The restorability of sanity became an issue in *Ford v. Wainwright* (1986). This case involved a career criminal named Alvin Ford who coldbloodedly executed a wounded police officer who had responded to a robbery being committed by Ford. There were no competency issues raised during Ford's trial, and he was sentenced to death for a "classic" death penalty homicide. Ford's claim of a descent into insanity while on death row became an issue in 1982. Prosecutors viewed Ford's claim of current insanity as a convenient ploy used just as his appeals were running out, although three of four psychiatrists who examined him concluded that he was psychotic (Mello, 2007). In *Ford*, the U.S. Supreme Court reiterated ancient English common law in holding that the Eighth Amendment prohibits execution of the insane. However, the Court ruled that if Ford was currently mentally incompetent, and thus free of the threat of immediate execution, he would still have to prove (insanity is an affirmative defense in which the burden of proof lies with the defendant) that he was as mentally ill as he claimed to be (Mello, 2007). The Court basically ruled that society's retributive goals (persons must be aware of the punishment they are about to suffer and why they will suffer it) and humanitarian goals (persons should be afforded opportunities to prepare themselves mentally and spiritually for death) must be served, but set forth no procedural standards ensuring due process for defendants asserting their incompetency claims (Sewell, 2010). In Ford's case, it was all moot anyhow; he died of natural causes while still on death row in 1991, some 28 years after his crime.

In *Panetti v. Quarterman* (2007), the Supreme Court went beyond the "mere awareness" standard for sanity set in *Ford* to a "rational understanding" (of why one is being executed) for the requisite competence to be executed (Sewell, 2010). The difference between the two standards is that while one might be fully aware that one is going to be executed ("mere awareness"), that person may believe that God will intervene to prevent it, or perhaps that he or she is being executed because of religious or political views rather than for heinous murders, in which case he or she would be lacking in "rational understanding."

Scott Panetti killed both his mother-in-law and father-in-law in 1992. There was little doubt about Panetti's mental illness because he had a long history of schizophrenic-like behavior for which he was taking medication. Despite his undisputed mental illness, he was found competent to stand trial and to waive legal counsel (he defended himself—quite incompetently). While the U.S. Supreme Court recognized that the Eighth Amendment forbids the execution of the insane, it declined to follow *Atkins* and overturn Panetti's death sentence or to offer guidance for formulating rules for determining mental competence beyond the "rational understanding" mentioned above. Instead, it ordered a stay of execution and remanded the case back to the Texas courts so that they could more fully evaluate Panetti's incompetence claim. On December 3, 2014, less than 12 hours before Texas was to execute Panetti, an appeals court issued a stay, opening the door for his lawyers to again argue that the death penalty was unconstitutional in his case.

The law on competency and execution is still murky and in need of further clarification, but at present it boils down to the fact that defendants can be executed as long as they demonstrate at least "rational understanding" that they are about to die and the rational reason why. Even delusional individuals can grasp these facts at some level. Thus, if someone is deemed currently incompetent to be executed because of mental illness, that person can be rendered competent with medication. The issue then becomes whether the state can forcibly administer antipsychotic drugs to insane inmates facing execution. Neither *Ford* nor *Panetti* touched on this issue, although in *Washington v. Harper* (1990), the Supreme Court ruled that in a prison environment an inmate may be involuntarily medicated "if the inmate is dangerous to himself or others, and the treatment is in the inmate's medical interest" (Sewell, 2010, p. 1292). To the extent that medication is voluntary, the insane on death row are confronted with a horrible choice: madness or execution. To the extent that it is not, prison physicians are presented with an ethical dilemma in that if they medicate someone "in the inmate's medical interests," they are simultaneously rendering the person "sane enough" for execution. Of course, after the execution date is set and approaches, the inmate can choose to go off his or her medication, and the whole bizarre scenario recirculates.

SUMMARY

Some of the most interesting issues in the generic death penalty debate involve its application on special populations, such as racial minorities, juveniles, women, and the mentally disabled and the mentally ill. For decades, one of the most telling arguments against the death penalty was its disproportionate use on African Americans. However, we find today that African Americans are significantly underrepresented both on death row and among those executed in proportion to the number of murders they commit. Now that whites are executed in disproportionate numbers to blacks, the "racial bias" issue has moved to claiming that blacks who kill whites, especially white females, are more likely to be sentenced to death than any other victim/offender dyad. This is true before adjustments are made for the heinousness of the offense, but not after such adjustments are made. We concluded this section by stating that in light of current research which reaches the opposite conclusions from the same data set, we perhaps expect too much from such death penalty data sets.

Individuals who committed murder of a particularly heinous sort while they were juveniles have faced execution in the past. However, in *Roper v. Simmons*, the U.S. Supreme Court ruled the juvenile death penalty unconstitutional. In this case, the Court cited its previous decision in *Atkins v. Virginia* banning the execution of the mentally disabled, but it also took notice of the neuroscientific evidence pointing to the immaturity of the adolescent brain to reason that juveniles should be held to lower standards of culpability than adults.

Women have always been vastly underrepresented among individuals receiving death sentences in the United States. Although they commit about 10% of homicides each year, they represent less than 2% of all people executed. Their underrepresentation was explained (apart from the fact that they commit far fewer homicides than men) by the chivalry hypothesis, and why some women are executed was explained by the evil woman hypothesis.

Ancient English common law forbids the execution of "idiots and lunatics," and executions of individuals with intellectual disabilities are forbidden in the United States today. However, the difficulty lies with determining who does and who does not meet the criteria for conditions that reduce criminal culpability. At present, such a condition is defined as someone having an IQ of 70 or below. In any case, at this time, it is constitutionally forbidden to execute anyone with this level of mental disability (though IQ scores are heavily argued in the courtroom—see Chapter 4). Likewise, states are constitutionally forbidden to execute the currently insane, but advances in modern medicine have made it possible to restore such a person to sanity, thus making him or her "sane enough" to be executed.

DISCUSSION QUESTIONS

1. Given the extensive evidence that whites have been proportionately more likely to be sentenced to death and actually executed than blacks since the resumption of the death penalty in 1976, why do you think we still hear concerns to the contrary?
2. Does the natural brain maturation process that almost all of us undergo without murdering anyone serve as a viable excuse for those who do commit murder?
3. Give reasons why women who commit death-eligible crimes should receive the death penalty at the same rate as men who commit the same crimes. If you are against the death penalty, play devil's advocate on this question.
4. Explain the chivalry and evil woman hypotheses.
5. Why are the mentally ill subject to capital punishment but not the mentally disabled?

6. Assume you are a prison physician responsible for administering antipsychotic medication to a death row inmate. Do you relieve the inmate of his madness by giving him medication and thereby exposing him to execution, or do you refuse to medicate the inmate and abandon him to the hell of insanity?

REFERENCES

Atkins v. Virginia. (2002). 536 U.S. 304.

Baldus, D., G. Woodworth, & C. Pulaski, Jr. (1990). *Equal justice and the death penalty: A legal and empirical analysis.* Boston: Northeastern University Press.

Berk, R., A. Li, and L. Hickman. (2005). Statistical difficulties in determining the role of race in capital cases: A re-analysis of the data from the state of Maryland. *Journal of Quantitative Criminology, 21,* 365–390.

Bjerregaard, B., M. Smith, J. Cochran, J. & S. Fogel, S. J. (2015). A further examination of the Liberation hypothesis in capital murder trials. *Crime & Delinquency,* 0011128715574454.

Blume, J., T. Eisenberg, and M. Wells. (2004). Explaining death row's population and racial composition. *Journal of Empirical Legal Studies, 1,* 165–207.

Bohm, R. (2012). *Deathquest: An introduction to the theory and practice of capital punishment in the United States.* Cincinnati, OH: Anderson.

Branson, A. (2013). African-American serial killers: Overrepresented yet underacknowledged. *The Howard Journal, 52,* 1–18.

Brown, B. (n.d.). "The Case of Thomas Granger." http://legalconstitutionalhistory.sharepoint.com/Pages/CaseofThomasGranger.aspx.

Cashin, J. (2002). *The war was you and me: Civilians in the American Civil War.* Princeton, NJ: Princeton University Press.

Cassell, P. (2008, Summer). In defense of the death penalty. *Journal of the Institute for the Advancement of Criminal Justice,* 14–28.

Cramer, E. (2009, May 27). "Statistical Evidence of Racial Discrimination in the Death Penalty." Testimony before the North Carolina House Select Committee on Capital Punishment. http://www.ourpaws.info/cramer/death/talk.txt.

Death Penalty Information Center. (2013). "Race of Death Row Inmates Executed Since 1976. http://www.deathpenaltyinfo.org/race-death-row-inmates-executed-1976

Dillard, A. (2012). Madness alone punishes the madman: The search for moral dignity in the Court's competency doctrine as applied to capital cases. *Tennessee Law Review, 79,* 461–514.

Eddings v. Oklahoma. (1982). 445 U.S. 104.

Federal Bureau of Investigation. (2014). *Crime in the United States: 2013.* Washington, DC: U.S. Government Printing Office.

Gerritzen, B., and G. Kirchgässner. (2013). Facts or ideology: What determines the results of econometric estimates of the deterrence effect of death penalty? A meta-analysis. Discussion Paper no. 2013-03, School of Economics and Political Science, University of St. Gallen.

Greenfeld, L., and D. Hinners. (1985). *Capital punishment, 1984.* Washington, DC: U.S. Department of Justice.

Gross, S., and R. Mauro. (1989). *Death and discrimination: Racial disparities in capital sentencing.* Boston: Northeastern University Press.

Jennings, W., T. Richards, M. Smith, B. Bjerregaard, and S. Fogel. (2014). A critical examination of the "white victim effect" and death penalty decision-making from a propensity score matching approach: The North Carolina experience. *Journal of Criminal Justice, 42,* 384–398.

Katz, J. (2005). *Warren McClesky v. Ralph Kemp*: Is the death penalty in Georgia racially biased? In *Capital punishment: A balanced examination,* ed. E. Mandery, pp. 400–407. Sudbury, MA: Jones & Bartlett. http://www.ourpaws.info/cramer/death/katz.htm.

Kleck, G. (1981). Racial discrimination in criminal sentencing: A critical evaluation of the evidence with additional evidence on the death penalty. *American Sociological Review, 46,* 783–805.

Klein, S., R. Berk, and L. Hickman. (2006). *Race and the decision to seek the death penalty in federal cases.* Santa Monica, CA: Rand Corporation.

Linde, R. (2011). From rapists to superpredators: What the practice of capital punishment says about race, rights and the American child. *International Journal of Children's Rights, 19,* 127–150.

Mandery, E. (2005). *Capital punishment: A balanced examination.* Sudbury, MA: Jones & Bartlett.

McAdams, J. (1998). Racial disparity and the death penalty. *Law and Contemporary Problems, 61,* 153–170.

Mello, M. (2007). Executing the mentally ill: When is someone sane enough to die? *Criminal Justice, 22,* 30–41.

Panetti v. Quarterman. (2007). 551 U.S. 930.

Paternoster, R., and R. Brame. (2003). *An empirical analysis of Maryland's death sentence system with respect to the influence of race and legal jurisdiction.* Final report, Department of Criminology, University of Maryland.

Penry v. Lynaugh. (1989). 492 U.S. 302.

Reza, E. (2005). Gender bias in North Carolina's death penalty. *Duke Journal of Gender Law & Policy, 12,* 179–214.

Robbers, M. (2007). Death penalty. In *Encyclopedia of juvenile violence,* ed. L. Finley, pp. 55–57. Westport, CT: Greenwood.

Robinson, M. (2008). *Death nation: The experts explain American capital punishment.* Upper Saddle River, NJ: Prentice Hall.

Roper v. Simmons. (2005). 112 S.W. 3rd 397.

Sarkar, S. (2007). Too young to kill? US Supreme Court treads a dangerous path in *Roper v. Simmons. Journal of the American Academy of Psychiatry and the Law, 35,* 364–372.

Scheidegger, K. (2012). Rebutting myths about race and the death penalty. *Ohio State Journal of Criminal Law, 10,* 147–165.

Sewell, M. (2010). Pushing execution over the constitutional line: Forcible medication of condemned inmates and the Eighth and Fourteenth Amendments. *Boston College Law Review, 51,* 1279–1322.

Sharma, H., J. Scheb, D. Houston, and K. Wagers. (2013). Race and the death penalty: An empirical assessment of first-degree murder convictions in Tennessee after *Gregg v. Georgia. Tennessee Journal of Race, Gender, & Social Justice, 2,* 1–39.

Shatz, S., and N. Shatz. (2011). "Chivalry Is Not Dead: Murder, Gender, and the Death Penalty." http://works.bepress.com/steven_shatz/1.

Steffensmeier, D., B. Feldmeyer, C. Harris, and J. Ulmer (2011). Reassessing trends in black violent crime, 1980–2008: Sorting out the "Hispanic effect" in Uniform Crime Reports arrests, National Crime Victimization Survey offender estimates, and US prisoner counts. *Criminology, 49,* 197–251.

Streib, V. (1987). *Death penalty for juveniles.* Bloomington: Indiana University Press.

Streib, V. (2003). Executing women, juveniles, and the mentally retarded: Second class citizens in capital punishment. In *America's experiment with capital punishment,* ed. J. Aker, R. Bohm, and C. Lanier, pp. 301–323. Durham, NC: Carolina Academic Press.

Thompson v. Oklahoma. (1988). 487 U.S. 815.

U.S. Department of Justice. (2001). *The federal death penalty system: Supplementary data, analysis and revised protocols for capital case review.* Washington, DC: U.S. Department of Justice. http://www.justice.gov/dag/pubdoc/deathpenaltystudy.htm.

Walker, E. (2002). Adolescent neurodevelopment and psychopathology. *Current Directions in Psychological Science, 11,* 24–28.

Walsh, A. (2011). *Feminist criminology through a biosocial lens.* Durham, NC: Carolina Academic Press.

Walsh, A., and C. Hemmens. (2014). *Law, justice, and society: A sociolegal introduction,* 3d ed. New York: Oxford University Press.

Walsh, A., and I. Yun. (2013). Schizophrenia: Causes, crime, and implications for criminology and criminal justice. *International Journal of Law, Crime and Justice, 41,* 188–202.

Washington v. Harper. (1990). 494 U.S. 210.

CHAPTER 9

MODERN SCIENCE AND THE DEATH PENALTY

In September 1986, Anna Fowler, an elderly woman, was found dead in her Oklahoma City apartment. The 83-year-old woman had been raped and murdered. A few months later, a 90-year-old woman who lived across the street from Fowler, Zelma Cutler, was raped and murdered also. Police collected semen found at the crime scene of one victim and blood, hair, and saliva from the other. They ran serology tests on the evidence from both crime scenes and concluded that the secretor had type A blood and was more than likely African American. Police scoured the neighborhood asking African American men to provide blood samples.

Police learned that Robert Miller was a type A secretor. They brought him in for questioning and after 12 hours of interrogation, police believed that Miller was guilty of both murders. Miller told police that he had visions of the murders in his dreams and described details of the crime scenes that were accurate; he also provided inaccurate information with numerous inconsistencies. Miller maintained his innocence, but was found guilty at trial and sentenced to death for the murders.

In 1992, new DNA technology allowed for a more sophisticated method of testing semen. Forensic analysts compared Miller's DNA profile to the semen found at the crime scene and concluded that the semen could not have belonged to Miller. In 1995, the Oklahoma Court of Criminal Appeals overturned Miller's conviction and granted him a new trial. There was no need for a new trial, however, because even more advanced DNA testing methods became available during this time and were conducted on the evidence once again; this time, the DNA profile not only excluded Miller, but it matched a man by the name of Ronald Lott. Miller was exonerated and Lott was charged, convicted, and sentenced to death.

Lott was already serving time for the rapes of two other elderly women in Oklahoma City when police tied him to the murders of Fowler and Cutler. Lott was executed in 2013. Anna Fowler's son, Jim Fowler, said that this case completely changed his opinion about the death penalty. He explained: "I used to support the death penalty. I thought it was alright until I found out how many mistakes we have with it and to kill an innocent human being is awful."

LEARNING OBJECTIVES

- Understand the difference between exoneration and mitigation.
- Understand the reasons why some decry the intrusion of science into the death penalty debate.
- Understand the basics of polymerase chain reaction and how it is used in matters of guilt and innocence.
- Understand how brain imaging is used to mitigate punishment.
- Know the problems involved in using science as an error-free tool for determining guilt and innocence.

EXONERATION AND MITIGATION

The huge advances made by the genomic and brain sciences over the past three decades have revolutionized death penalty discourse in the United States. Because science is playing an ever-increasing role in death penalty cases, there have been an abundance of articles in legal journals attempting to explain genetic and neurological methods to those involved in such cases. Many attorneys are active participants in the conversation, and consequently courses are being taught on the basics of genetics and neuroscience in a number of U.S. law schools (Jones & Shen, 2012). It is thus becoming increasingly important for students of criminal justice—or anyone interested in death penalty issues—to develop an elementary understanding of this science. This chapter provides an accessible introduction to the fascinating techniques of DNA testing and brain imaging as these techniques relate to exoneration and mitigation, and what this science may mean for law, justice, and the death penalty in the future.

To successfully prosecute a case, the prosecutor must prove that the defendant committed the guilty act (*actus reus*) intentionally and with a guilty mind (*mens rea*). The defense may counter the prosecutor's claims by asserting that the defendant did not, in fact, commit the criminal act, or if the fact that the defendant committed the act is not in doubt, the defense may offer an affirmative defense. An **affirmative defense** is one in which the act is admitted but a guilty mind is denied, and includes justification defenses (self-defense, victim consent, execution of public duties) and excuse defenses. Excuse defenses include duress, age, or the presence of a rationality defect (essentially, legal insanity or mental disability) at the time when the offense was committed, with the burden of proof squarely on the defense.

Before we explain the science behind exoneration and mitigation in this chapter, we need to be clear on these terms' meanings. **Exoneration** is defined as official legal relief provided to someone from the burden of responsibility, obligation, or punishment (also see Chapter 10). In the case of the criminal justice system, exoneration occurs when a person convicted of a crime is later deemed to be innocent; this engages the *actus reus* concept—he or she never committed the guilty act and the burden of conviction and punishment is thus removed. Recall from Chapter 3 that mitigation refers to the lessening of the degree of responsibility for an act, and thus presumably the severity of the punishment received for committing it. This engages the *mens rea* concept in that the convicted person had some mental defect that prevented him or her from fully appreciating the wrongfulness of his or her act.

No one of conscience would deny the rights of a person such as Robert Miller to use DNA evidence to prove his innocence (at least we hope this would be the consensus) and, thus, exonerate himself. But do you think using DNA evidence, such as that mentioned in the opening vignette in Chapter 1, in an attempt to mitigate the level of *mens rea* and the sentence that Stephen Mobley received for executing a Domino's Pizza manager is a valid use of such evidence? Guilt and responsibility are thus two different issues addressed in this chapter. DNA evidence is used overwhelmingly in issues of guilt and innocence, whereas brain imaging is used solely to address issues of mitigation. We address these two concepts in light of concerns that many scholars have about traditional ideas of justice, responsibility, and human agency.

THE INNOCENCE REVOLUTION

As noted earlier, advances in the genomic and brain sciences have revolutionized death penalty debates. Abolitionist arguments once focused on such factors as morality, fairness, financial cost, constitutional/procedural, and deterrence issues, but the new and more powerful issue now dominating their arguments is innocence. These arguments appear to have penetrated and influenced public opinion far more than other abolitionist arguments, since guilt and innocence have substance and are far more easily grasped than legal arguments about constitutionality, statistical arguments over the deterrence issue, and philosophical arguments about fairness and morality.

As Lawrence Marshall states: "Unlike other challenges to the fairness of capital proceedings, which have failed to stimulate widespread public outrage, evidence of the system's propensity to factual error has the power to open closed minds and trigger reexamination of the costs and benefits of capital punishment" (2004, p. 597). Indeed, arguments surrounding possible innocence were central in the decision not to reinstate the death penalty in New York State in 2004, the repeal of the death penalty in New Mexico in 2009, and Governor George Ryan's clearing of Illinois' death row shortly before leaving office in 2003 (Aronson & Cole, 2009). The specter of executing an innocent person may be the beginning of the end of the death penalty in the United States, although, as we shall see, others think it might lead to a resurgence of pro–death penalty sentiments.

Science has penetrated the American legal system to the core, despite the skepticism and even hostility toward it on the part of some. Judges seem to be especially influenced by expert testimony if it involves biological factors, although it does not appear to influence their opinions about agency and responsibility (see Chapter 1). For instance, 181 judges from 19 states were presented with the hypothetical case of a defendant diagnosed as a psychopath who had robbed a restaurant and pistol-whipped the manager, leaving him brain-damaged (Aspinwall, Brown, & Tabery, 2012). It was found that almost all the justices considered a defendant's psychopathy to be an aggravating factor, but when also presented with neuroscientific explanations for that condition, they tended to mitigate the severity of their sentences. All 181 judges were informed that the defendant was a psychopath, but only a random half were provided with genetic and neurological evidence relating to the causes of the psychopathy, with half of them receiving the evidence from the defense, arguing that it should be mitigating, and half from the prosecution, arguing that it should be aggravating. On the whole, the hypothetical psychopath received a longer sentence (averaged over all judges) than typically meted out for aggravated assault to defendants without psychopathy, but judges who were given biological explanations for psychopathy imposed an average of about one year less than judges who did not get that same information (12.83 vs. 13.93 years).

SCIENCE, AGENCY, GENES, AND CULPABILITY

Science has attained something of the status of a god in Western societies to which we appeal to settle all kinds of dilemmas—including moral ones—that confront human beings. The death penalty is certainly one of the biggest moral dilemmas confronting American society. What was in former times exclusively the domain of philosophers with their moral arguments and social scientists with their statistical models has been somewhat co-opted by geneticists and neuroscientists, who have dragged their big guns into the fray. According to some, in doing so, they have challenged the very foundations on which our civilization rests—the assumption that individual agency underlies our capacity to make moral choices (Morse, 2006). These scholars believe that if the "hard" evidence of science is accepted uncritically by the courts, it will undermine traditional ideas of justice because a wholly scientific approach undermines traditional ideas of human responsibility ("My genes made me do it" or "My defective frontal lobes made me do it"). As Carter Snead argues, neuroscientists are using the "claims of their discipline to overthrow retributive justice as a legitimate justification for criminal sanctions" (2007, p. 1316). Others may welcome these claims as the road to eventual abolition of capital punishment.

Genes are certainly wonderful and powerful mechanisms, but there is no such thing as a "crime gene." Recall from the vignette in Chapter 1 that Stephen Mobley's attorneys unsuccessfully attempted to use a version of the monoamine oxidase A (MAOA) gene to persuade the courts to spare Mobley's life. MAOA is an enzyme responsible for breaking down neurotransmitters (chemicals that send messages between brain cells), particularly serotonin. Serotonin levels are involved in emotion and mood, such as depression, impulsivity, and problems with anger control (Munafo, Brown, & Hariri, 2008).

The MAOA gene comes in five versions, or "repeats," although the three- and four-repeat versions are by far the most common (see p. 222 for an explanation of "repeats"). The version of the MAOA gene that Mobley had is the three-repeat version, the so-called risk version because it evinces low serotonin activity (Baum, 2011). Too little serotonin can lead to impulsiveness and, in conjunction with high doses of testosterone, can facilitate antisocial behavior (Sjoberg et al., 2008). Note the use of the word "facilitate"; low serotonin functioning is a risk factor for impulsive criminal behavior and not a "cause" in any absolute way.

The low-activity version of the gene has been given the catchy but highly misleading moniker of "warrior gene" (Lea & Chamber, 2007). For instance, Kevin Beaver and his colleagues (2010) found that males who carry the low-activity version (MAOA-L) were more likely to join gangs than males with the high-activity version (MAOA-H), and those who did join a gang were four times more likely to use weapons in a fight. Another study of a birth cohort found that MAOA-L had no effect on offending by itself, but when combined with severe childhood maltreatment, it had very large effects (Caspi et al., 2002). For males with MAOA-L who were also maltreated, the odds of a verifiable conviction for a violent crime were 9.8 times greater than the odds for subjects with neither a history of abuse nor MAOA-L having such a conviction. Although MAOA-L + maltreatment males were only 12% of the cohort, they were responsible for 44% of its criminal convictions.

To emphasize that genes are not puppet masters producing the same effects in all people, let us put all this into perspective. In Beaver and colleagues' (2010) study, 440 (42.3%) of the males had the low-activity version of the MAOA gene as opposed to 601 (57.7%) who had the high-activity version. Although much was made of the fact that gang members carrying the MAOA-L gene were about four times more likely to use a weapon in a fight than gang members with the high-activity version, it is instructive to note that 15 out of 33 MAOA-L gang members (45%) said they had used a gun compared to 4 out of 21 MAOA-H gang members (19%). In other words, the MAOA-L genetic variant is quite common, and although it is undoubtedly a risk factor for antisocial behavior, only a very small proportion of males join antisocial gangs; still fewer carry guns and commit serious antisocial acts.

Nevertheless, the MAOA gene is the gene most frequently used (although still extremely rare) as a mitigating factor in murder cases. While the MAOA mitigation claim did not work for Mobley, it saved the life of David Bradley Waldroup. Waldroup was charged with the brutal murders of his wife, Penny Waldroup, and the aggravated kidnapping and first-degree murder of Leslie Bradshaw, Penny's best friend. The jury took note of Waldroup's possession of the MAOA-L gene and his childhood history of abuse, and convicted him of voluntary manslaughter in the matter of Leslie Bradshaw's death rather than first-degree murder, which would have meant a death sentence. Waldroup was sentenced to a total of 32 years fixed for all his crimes (Baum, 2011). According to Baum (2011), this has been the only successful use of MAOA-L (plus childhood abuse) as a mitigating factor in the United States up to the time of his research.

Similarly, while in a kind of mechanical sense our brains are *us* because the brain is the place where genetic dispositions and environmental experiences are integrated and become one, to what extent can we point to images of our brains and say "because of this we won't hold you completely responsible for what you have done"? Because we believe that we have a better understanding of behavior today than was previously the case due to the advances made by genomic science and neuroscience, it leads many of us away from thinking in terms of agency to thinking in terms of causality in an overly mechanistic way.

No one denies that human behavior is the result of causal chains. Humans are natural beings with a nature forged by evolution. This nature is shaped individually by developmental experiences as it interacts with its environment, so we cannot escape the net of natural causality that has destroyed overly strong notions of free will. The growing knowledge about human behavior from genetics and neurobiology may have destroyed the concept of libertarian free will (it was never really a very healthy animal anyway), but this does not necessarily mean that it has destroyed the kind of human agency championed by compatibilists (see Chapter 1) or that it has overturned each individual's duty to live within the bounds of the law and to behave responsibly.

Let us first take a brief look at what genes are and how the CSI technicians that we see on television are able to determine from whose body minute traces of some bodily fluid came. We will then examine the neuroscience of brain imaging and what those images tell us (and don't tell us) about how a person's brain is functioning.

WHAT ARE GENES AND HOW DO THEY MAKE US DIFFERENT?

A **gene** is a segment of deoxyribonucleic acid (DNA) that codes for a protein. Genes simply make proteins: the "stuff" that builds, maintains, and replaces the tissues in your body. Although protein products such as neurotransmitters and hormones have a lot to do with how we behave or feel, they do not *cause* us to behave or feel one specific way or another. They *facilitate* our behavior and our feelings by producing tendencies or dispositions to respond to the environments in one way rather than in another. That is, they incline us rather than compel us.

DNA is found on our chromosomes that are packed into the nucleus of each of the trillions of cells in our bodies. DNA consists of two strings of nucleotides bonded in a chain and twisted around each other to form the familiar double-helix "ladder." The nucleotide bases are aligned as the rungs of the ladder and come in four different types: adenine (A), thymine (T), cytosine (C), and guanine (G). Nucleotides are joined together by bonding with each other in specific ways: C can only pair with G and vice versa, and A can only pair with T and vice versa. The following sequence of bolded and underscored base pairs make up a section of DNA we call a gene: ACGCTTAGC**CTACGGAAATA**CGATGC-TACGT. Real genes, of course, contain many more bases than this.

As you know, we get our genes from our parents, who might provide us with both the same or different version of the same gene called an **allele**. For instance, you may have received a "brown" allele of the "eye color gene" from your father and an allele for blue eyes from your mother. This fact helps us to understand why it is that although every human being has all the same genes that make us human, we can still be differentiated by our alleles.

Alleles typically come in different varieties called polymorphisms. **Polymorphism** refers to the differences in allelic combinations located at the same place on a chromosome. Polymorphisms are thus minor variations on a common theme. About 90% of polymorphisms are single-nucleotide polymorphisms (SNPs) (Altukhov & Salmenkova, 2002). As the term implies, a difference in just one nucleotide is all that differentiates one allele from another allele. Take the following sequence of nucleotide bases as part of a hypothetical gene in Person 1:

TCACCTTGGAATGGGCTA

Compare the above sequence of bases with the sequence below from Person 2:

TCACCTTGGAGTGGGCTA

The bolded and underscored nucleotide is the only one of the 18 that is not identical in the two individuals.

The second type of polymorphism is the tandem repeats of base pairs called "variable number of tandem repeats," or VNTRs. Compare the following repeat sequences for the bases TTA in the following two alleles of a hypothetical gene in which TTA is repeated five times in the top allele and twice in the bottom allele:

Five-repeat Allele: TGGATA**TTA**TTA**TTA**TTA**TTA**ATTATGTA

Two-repeat Allele: TGGATA**TTA**TTA

It is these SNP and VTNR differences that are used to differentiate people by their DNA, and it is these repeats that are being referred to when we hear talk of the three-repeat or four-repeat polymorphism of the MAOA gene, or any other gene.

DNA "FINGERPRINTING" IN A NUTSHELL

When you see detectives on television taking a cigarette butt or an empty soda can into the CSI lab to run DNA tests, you may have wondered how technicians could possibly arrive at those DNA "fingerprints" they compare with DNA taken from suspects from such minute evidence. The answer lies in something called the **polymerase chain reaction (PCR)**. PCR is a technique used to greatly amplify the number of copies of a DNA sample from a crime scene to get enough copies for testing. What follows is an extremely oversimplified "cookbook" explanation of the very complex process involved. Remember, what CSI technicians are looking for are identical patterns in the polymorphic regions of the DNA—the variable regions of the DNA that make us all different, not the conserved regions that are the same for all people.

After the "parent" DNA sample from the crime scene is isolated in a test tube, two strands of nucleic acid synthesized in the lab called "primers" that recognize the DNA region serve as a starting point for the replication of "daughter" strands. The sample DNA is heated to 95° Centigrade (C), which pulls the two strands apart. This process is called "denaturation." The DNA is then cooled to 54°C and primers containing all ATCG bases that are complementary to the target sequence from the sample are added. At 72°C, a special enzyme called DNA polymerase is added that synthesizes the DNA strands. Each of the strands then sets about rebuilding the complementary strand to itself as the free nucleotides attach themselves (annealing), resulting in a new double-stranded daughter molecule of DNA (Overberg et al., 2009). This process is then repeated, and four DNA strands result; then again to produce 8, then 16, 32, 64, and so on as the DNA strands increase exponentially (the 2^{36} in Figure 9.1 results in 68,719,476,736 copies produced in about four hours!). This process is

Chapter 9 MODERN SCIENCE AND THE DEATH PENALTY

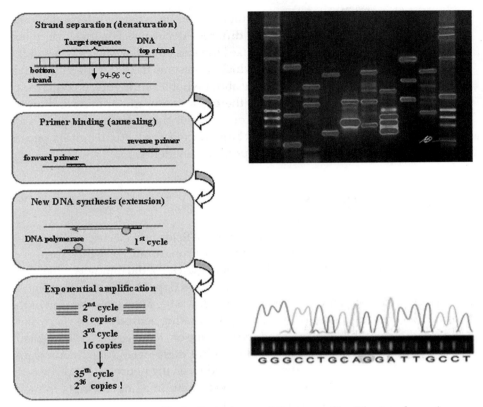

FIGURE 9.1 Polymerase Chain Reaction and Images after Electrophoresis
Source: National Center for Biotechnology Information, http://www.ncbi.nim.nih.gov/projects/genome/prob/doc

illustrated (very simplistically and in compressed form) on the left side of Figure 9.1.

After sufficient copies of DNA are produced, the copies are separated by size by a process called "electrophoresis." The term *phoresis* means "migration," and *electro* pertains to anything having to do with electricity. Thus, **electrophoresis** is the migration ("movement") of the DNA molecules that have been placed in a gel box with an electric power source. Because DNA is negatively charged, it migrates to the positive pole of the gel box when electrical current is applied. Smaller DNA strands move faster through the gel than larger strands, which results in the "barcode" patterns seen in upper right-hand side of Figure 9.1. To be seen like this, the DNA molecules have to be strained and viewed under ultraviolet light.

It should be noted that even slight contamination of the DNA sample may lead to false-positive or false-negative results because of the extreme sensitivity of the technique. Furthermore, the results have to be expertly interpreted, and two different laboratories may make different decisions. For instance, when something called an "allelic dropout" (i.e., the loss of a peak such as one on the graph at the bottom left of Figure 9.1, which represents the DNA information) is found, different decisions can be made about what it represents. It could mean that the DNA was contaminated, that there is a nonmatch, or even that an acceptable or unacceptable margin of error exists (Aronson & Cole, 2009). In such a case, a factually innocent person may be convicted or a factually guilty person may walk free in the absence of other pertinent evidence.

BRAIN IMAGING IN A NUTSHELL

The brain is a living "machine" full of magnetic fields and electric currents produced by the buzzing interaction of billions of neurons (brain cells) that "form over 100 trillion connections with each other—more than all of the Internet connections in the world!" (Weinberger, Elvevag, & Giedd, 2005, p. 5). This communication takes place via tiny electrical signals that run down the axon (an extension of the neuron) like a neon sign. Between each communicating neuron is a tiny gap called a synapse. To cross that gap and send the message on, the message is "translated" from electrical to chemical energy, and chemical messengers called neurotransmitters jump the gap between the sending and receiving neuron. This process requires energy provided by oxygen-rich blood. Brain imaging attempts to make sense of this apparent chaos by transforming it into pictures of areas in the brain activated in response to stimuli presented to the person undergoing a brain scan.

There are a number of brain-imaging techniques used in neurological research and in clinical situations, but those used most frequently in a court proceeding in support of mitigation are magnetic resonance imaging (MRI) and **functional magnetic resonance imaging (fMRI),** the "workhorse" of functional neuroimaging. MRI shows the anatomical structure of the brain and will inform us if certain parts of the brain contain tumors, are damaged or atrophied, or have some other structural impairment as a result of injuries or infections. fMRI allows us insight into the functioning of the brain in real time. As is the case with PCR, whole books have been written about the complexities of fMRI, which involves a lot of physics and mathematics. All this, as well as the interpretation of the data it produces, defies a short description. However, we venture to offer one only so that students will have at least some idea of the science behind the major tool used for the purpose of mitigation. Our explanation is based primarily on the more technical explanations supplied by Jones and colleagues (2009) and Logothetis and Pfeuffer (2004).

To do fMRI scans, you need a very expensive machine that looks like a large cylinder-shaped tube. This machine produces a powerful magnetic field and radiofrequency pulses, all of which are connected to computers. This combination of tools produces computer-generated colored pictures of a person's brain in action. To accomplish this, the person is placed lying down in the fMRI machine and asked to perform a series of relevant mental tasks, or presented with pictures or scenarios on a video screen designed to evoke certain emotions. Subjects respond to questions by pressing buttons on a response box. As the person performs these tasks or emotionally responds to the stimuli, a computer picks up and stores information about the regions of his or her brain that are being used. To be able to do this, the technique takes advantage of the brain's physiology. Like the muscles of the body, the harder the brain works, the more oxygen it requires, so when a particular region is activated, more blood containing oxygen is routed to that region. The basic fMRI procedure uses what is known as the **blood-oxygen-level-dependent (BOLD) contrast.**

To reiterate, when neurons are active, they require more energy supplied by blood. Red blood cells carry a protein substance called hemoglobin that carries the oxygen to active areas. Like every atom in the universe, the atoms in oxygen have positively charged protons in their nuclei (the center of atoms). The fMRI scanner manipulates these protons by applying a strong magnetic field, and when it does, the protons in the blood capillaries align within the field like metal filings attracted to a magnet. The machine then delivers a brief pulse of radio wave energy that knocks the protons temporarily out of alignment, after which they return to their original position. This releases energy that is recorded, amplified, and sent to a computer, where a mathematical algorithm produces detailed pictures of the brain. The more active an area of the brain is, the more the energy released in this process, and the more intense is the color of the image of that area seen on the researcher's screen.

These recordings are possible because of the different magnetic properties of oxygenated and deoxygenated blood. The oxygenated blood that brings energy to neurons in the part of the brain area being activated is virtually resistant to magnetism. On the other hand, the blood that has given off its energy to the neurons becomes deoxygenated and is a lot more magnetic. In other words, the protons in the two kinds of blood have difference resonances (resonance = the tendency to respond; in this case, to magnetism—hence the name of the imaging technique) with the energy supplied by the scanner. This hemodynamic (literally, "blood movement") response produces the BOLD contrast.

BRAIN IMAGING AND THE ABOLITION OF THE JUVENILE DEATH PENALTY

The most far-reaching use of brain-imaging data to date involves its use in challenging the juvenile death penalty. Every parent who has suffered through the teenage years knows that when children hit puberty, sweet sons and daughters often become distant, rude, and even obnoxious. Most teenagers also commit minor, and sometimes serious, antisocial acts that devastate their parents. However, it has long been known that the vast majority of youth who offend during adolescence desist, and that only a small number continue to offend in adulthood (Moffitt, 1993). The 2003 New York Academy of Sciences conference on adolescent brain development provided three key points that help us to understand why and how the hormonal and brain changes of adolescence affect adolescent behavior (White, 2004, p. 4):

1. Much of the behavior characterizing adolescence is rooted in biology intermingling with environmental influences to cause teens to conflict with their parents, take more risks, and experience wide swings in emotion.
2. The lack of synchrony between a physically mature body and a still maturing nervous system may explain these behaviors.
3. Adolescents' sensitivities to rewards appear to be different than in adults, prompting them to seek higher levels of novelty and stimulation to achieve the same feeling of pleasure.

Puberty marks the beginning of the transition from childhood to adulthood and is accompanied by numerous physiological and neurological changes (Walsh & Bolen, 2012). There is a 10- to 20-fold increase in testosterone in males, a hormone linked to aggression and dominance seeking, and the ratio of excitatory to inhibitory neurotransmitters becomes unbalanced as the brain undergoes a period of slowly refining the neural circuitry to its adult form (Collins, 2004; Walker, 2002). For instance, the prefrontal cortex (PFC) is getting its final coat of a fatty substance called myelin to insulate various brain structures that are important for the speedy electrochemical transmission of information. The PFC modulates emotions from the brain's emotional centers in the limbic system and makes judgments and plans, and is the part of the brain that we think of as housing our logical reasoning and our moral conscience.

There are thus *physical* reasons why adolescents do not show the same level of rational judgment that adults do and why they tend to assign faulty attributions to situations and to the intentions of others. A brain on "go slow" superimposed on a hormone-driven physiology on "fast forward" may explain why "teenagers often find it difficult to gauge the meanings and intentions of others and to experience more events as aversive during adolescence than they did as prepubescent children and will do so again as adults" (Walsh, 2002, p. 143). When the brain reaches its adult state in the mid-twenties, more adult-like personality traits emerge, such as becoming more conscientious and agreeable and less irritable and neurotic (Blonigen, 2010). Thus, the adolescent brain is immature, and as neuroscientist Richard Restak put it, "The immaturity of the adolescent's behavior is perfectly mirrored by the immaturity of the adolescent's brain" (2001, p. 76). Thus, regardless of one's stance on the death penalty, we have to agree that neuroscience has shown that a lower level of culpability attaches to juvenile offenders.

This brain immaturity was a major factor in the U.S. Supreme Court's ruling on the unconstitutionality of the juvenile death penalty in *Roper v. Simmons* (2005) discussed in Chapter 4. The Simmons case brought on a blizzard of *amicus curiae* ("friend of the court") briefs, which are written arguments supporting one side in the case presented to the Court by interested parties not directly involved with the case. Parties filing amicus briefs in favor of Simmons included the American Medical and Psychological Associations, which offered extensive brain-imaging evidence relating to the juvenile brain.

In writing the majority opinion, Justice Kennedy noted neurological evidence of the immaturity of the adolescent brain, but stressed that this was not the basis of the Court's decision. Supreme Court decisions must have at least the appearance of being based on constitutional grounds. The Court does not justify its decisions with statements such as "the scientific evidence compels us" or "world opinion demands," because this is politics, not law. Nonlegal statements are considered dicta, which are legally nonbinding explanatory statements. The Court's decision must be based on legal precedent, and thus the *ratio decidendi* (Latin for "reason for the decision") was based on *Atkins v. Virginia* (2002), in which the Supreme Court ruled that executing the mentally retarded (we call people with this affliction developmentally disabled today) constituted cruel and unusual punishment. Few commentators doubted that it was the neurological evidence that won the day, however, even if it had to be relegated to nonbinding dicta for appearance's sake. On the other hand, in *Graham v. Florida* (2010), in which the Court ruled that life in prison without the possibility of parole for juveniles in non-homicide cases is unconstitutional, it explicitly referred to neuroscience as a compelling factor in its majority decision.

PERSPECTIVE FROM A NEUROPSYCHIATRIST: DR. JAMES MERIKANGAS

Dr. James Merikangas is board certified in both neurology and psychiatry, with more than 30 years of experience in the practice of neuropsychiatry. As a founding member of the American Academy of Neuropsychiatry, he established guidelines for the routine evaluation of patients with complex brain disorders in neuropsychiatry made up of neurological examinations, neuroimaging, and neuropsychological evaluations.

FIGURE 9.2   Dr. Merikangas

He has been actively involved in teaching and clinical care in inpatient and outpatient settings and is currently a clinical professor of psychiatry and behavioral science at the George Washington University School of Medicine in Washington, DC.

Dr. Merikangas's primary clinical interest is the evaluation and treatment of patients with complex brain–behavior problems. He has been engaged in forensic evaluations in both civil cases and the criminal justice system, with particular expertise in the neural basis of aggressive and violent behavior. Dr. Merikangas has worked on more than 100 death penalty cases across the country.

My expert witness work began as a natural progression from patient care. My first academic job was to be the neurologist and psychiatrist in the Neurodiagnostic Clinic of the University of Pittsburgh School of Medicine. In that position I worked with a team consisting of myself, a neuropsychologist, a psychiatric nurse, and a psychiatric social worker. We evaluated two patients a day with complete studies including a physical and neurological examination, neuropsychological testing for brain damage, a psychiatric interview, and a social, educational, and occupational history. Each patient also received an electroencephalogram (EEG), a computerized axial tomogram of the brain (a CAT scan, as the MRI was not yet invented), and a battery of blood tests for metabolic derangements, infectious or autoimmune disease, and a screen for drugs. This model was so successful that it is now the standard of care to do a similar evaluation for admission to a psychiatric inpatient service, and for outpatient treatment with medication. The *Diagnostic and Statistical Manual* (DSM-V) of the American Psychiatric Association requires a medical evaluation to be performed before arriving at a psychiatric diagnosis, as many physical, biological brain disturbances result in the symptoms of mental illness. It is now accepted that schizophrenia is a brain disease with genetic and environmental causes and not simply "psychological."

Many of the patients seen for their mental and behavioral problems could thus have their brain pathology diagnosed, and effective treatment could then follow a rational course, rather than a hit-and-miss trial of medications combined with psychoanalytically based interpretations of unconscious conflicts. No longer was autism thought to be the result of "refrigerator mothers," or schizophrenia the result of flawed parenting. This team approach remains the most efficient and effective way to proceed with the discovery of mitigating evidence. Mitigation requires a thorough investigation of family history, birth history, developmental history, and educational history to be factored into the development of a diagnosis. For this I have been aided by social workers, psychologists, and mitigation specialists of various disciplines, as well as by the many dedicated lawyers who do the tedious work required to obtain such information.

Violent behavior, including assault, rape, and murder, may have many causes to the final common pathway. Therefore, to understand a particular behavior requires a look at the brain that produced it. Violence can result from antisocial personality, sometimes referred to as malignant narcissism, from defects in impulse control, from depression, psychosis with delusions or command hallucinations, mental deficiency (formerly mental retardation), or immaturity resulting in bad judgment. It is now unconstitutional to execute children or to imprison them for life without the possibility of parole, but we still kill the mentally ill. The law and the "insanity defense" statutes have not caught up with modern scientific understanding of human psychology.

Mitigating evidence is designed to demonstrate an impairment of the will, a reduction in the degree of guilt that does not rise to the standard for "not guilty by reason of insanity." The definition of insanity differs from state to state and the federal standard is a deviation from a long tradition that one could not be held accountable for acting on a delusion, and does not comport with what is known about the mind in modern neuroscience. The ancient Greeks understood that mental illness excuses moral guilt, and the ancient Romans did not have the death penalty for murder, preferring exile from Rome for its citizens. We, however, have inflexible verdicts of "guilty" or "not guilty." Human behavior is much more complicated than this, and for that reason mitigating factors are presented in an attempt to reduce the degree of guilt. As juries and judges may lack an understanding of psychology, psychiatry, and neuroscience, the facts must be explained in clear and simple terms. Prosecutors will attempt to dispute science with appeals to "common sense," although common sense will tell you the world is flat and atoms do not exist.

An example is the case of a respected banker who at age 60 requested a lewd sex act from a 16-year-old clerk in a 7-Eleven store. He was arrested and charged, but the judge suspected this bizarre change in behavior might have been the result of a psychiatric problem. His psychiatric interview did not suggest any mental illness, and his physical examination was also normal. A CAT scan of the brain, however, disclosed an abnormality of the temporal lobe of the brain suggestive of herpes encephalitis, a viral infection that seemed like a slight cold a few weeks previously. He had survived this often fatal disease with the impairments in judgment and impulse control that resulted in his crime. Treatment with carbamazepine and fluoxetine corrected his behavior and allowed him to return to work. Had it not been for the CAT scan, he would have ended up in prison.

Another case was a serial rapist-murderer whose crimes were stereotypic rituals, always involving slender brunette young women whom he stalked until he could no longer control himself. His PET (positron emission tomogram) scan of the brain demonstrated abnormal function, and the CAT scan demonstrated abnormal anatomy, but the defense team did not present these facts because they did not comport with the obsolete insanity statute. He was executed after the only argument presented was that he should be kept alive "to be studied."

A case where the insanity defense was accepted was that of a Mormon fundamentalist who heard God order him to kill his family, which he did, and who then failed to kill himself with a poorly aimed gunshot to his head. His long history of delusional behavior convinced the court that his acts were insane, and he never had to face a jury.

My studies of the causes of murder have been directed toward finding preventable causes and educating the public and other professionals that mental illness is as real as diabetes or cancer, and not simply a psychological maladjustment or "evil." Persons who lack free will, or are driven by delusions, or the inability to control their impulses because of disease, are not as culpable as those motivated by money or hate, and sick people should be treated for their illness, not punished for a condition beyond their control. The death penalty for those who are sick through no fault of their own is simply wrong.

SOME PROBLEMS WITH DNA TESTING TO CONSIDER

There is an old saying often repeated by professors teaching statistics classes: "Statistics don't lie, but liars lie with statistics." There are numerous examples in the literature of how "experts" have wittingly or unwittingly misused statistics to make all sorts of implausible claims. Similarly, we can say that "DNA doesn't lie, but people can (also wittingly or unwittingly) lie with DNA." We have already seen some of the problems inherent in DNA testing such as the necessity that the DNA sample be meticulously handled so as not to become contaminated, and also the sometimes problematic interpretation of PCR results. But there are problems beyond these technical difficulties involving human errors, incompetence, and downright fraud.

Any number of scholars have argued that despite all the celebrations surrounding the DNA exonerations of numerous inmates (death row and otherwise), the technology may breathe new life into arguments in support of the death penalty. If the fear of executing an innocent person is a major argument against the use of the death penalty, and if the "certainty of DNA" is the tool that prevents it, pro–death penalty advocates can now rely on that same "certainty" and assert that we have removed the major obstacle (the possibility of executing the innocent) and can move forward with a more just death penalty. Thus, the advocacy of DNA as some sort of truth device is a double-edged sword—if it can be used to exonerate the innocent with apparent certitude, it can be used to condemn the guilty with the same apparent certitude. This kind of "certainty" can provide what advocates of the death penalty might describe as a "foolproof" death penalty. This understandably upsets those who oppose the death penalty on moral grounds, regardless of certainty of guilt.

A number of police labs have been accused and found guilty of falsifying and fabricating DNA. Others have been shown to be incompetent in their use of PCR, to be incompetent in interpreting results, and to have cross-contaminated and mislabeled sample DNA (Aronson & Cole, 2009). Many of these occurrences are to be expected when dealing with complicated technical matters, and human beings surely make errors, take shortcuts, and even fudge the data to conform to the desired conclusion. In a police lab, the "desired conclusion" is, of course, a match between the evidence DNA and the accused's DNA.

Even without a biasing context, experts may come to different conclusions. For instance, Dr. Itiel Dror and Dr. Greg Hampikian (2011) presented "mixed" DNA evidence (DNA from two or more sources) from a sexual assault case to 17 different DNA analysts, omitting the biasing contextual criminal case information. Dror and Hampikian found that only 1 of the 17 analysts reached the same conclusion ("defendant cannot be excluded") as the original analysts in the criminal case, while 12 concluded "exclude" and 4 "inconclusive." To be sure, out-and-out fraud is a rarity, but the fact that it happens and the fact that experts often disagree in their interpretations of DNA evidence should be enough to stop us from thinking of DNA as the holy grail of guilt and innocence. However, the consequences of disregarding DNA evidence of someone's innocence are too far-reaching to doubt it, although a healthy skepticism in terms of DNA supplying the sole evidence of someone's guilt is a good thing.

SOME PROBLEMS WITH fMRI TO CONSIDER

Data from fMRI testing are based on aggregating the BOLD responses of a number of individuals. Because fMRI results emerge from data averaged over a group of subjects, they are problematic when applied to specific individuals. As Jones and Shen put it: "Just because a particular pattern of neural activity is associated, on average at the group level, with impaired decision-making, it does not necessarily follow that a defendant before the court whose brain scans produce the same neural patterns necessarily has a cognitive deficit" (2012, p. 356).

Social scientists call this jumping from group data to specific individuals an ecological fallacy. An **ecological fallacy** is thus a mistake in logic made when one makes an inference about individuals deduced from aggregate statistical data derived from the group to which he or she belongs. In other words, an inference about a group may be reliable and valid (e.g., Asian Americans have the highest median household income in the United States), but the inference made on that basis that your new Asian neighbors are well off may indeed be correct, but it may also be totally wrong. So it is with aggregate fMRI data applied to specific individuals.

The neuroimaging evidence relating to which parts of the brain are activated under what conditions, and what parts are responsible for which behaviors, is both consistent and strong. But we must understand that neuroimages are maps of the terrain, not the terrain itself. They are indirect rather than direct evidence of increased neural activity because a conclusion derived from the data is still based on a statistical aggregate forming a correlation between a particular trait, behavior, or brain process, and BOLD responses in a particular brain area. Another truth we learn in statistics is that correlation is not causation, and it still is not. A correlation is a trend in a given direction, and that correlational trend in brain scans is not entirely true of all brains tested, and certainly not in terms of the wide variations in strength of brain responses of different people to identical stimuli. Of course, applying group data to individuals is still a better bet than ignoring such data completely; we are simply saying that it is still statistical, and statistical data are probabilistic by definition.

Even given this, it is a big jump from talking about "impaired judgment" inferred from mistakes subjects make on tasks they are asked to perform in the laboratory and a brutal murder performed in the real world. Just how impaired is the defendant's brain compared to the average level of those subjects said to be impaired, and how many of these subjects similarly impaired have committed murder? Likewise, we may ask if Christopher Simmons's brain is any more or any less immature than those of millions of other adolescents who did not plan, execute, and then brag about committing a horrendous random murder. As Morse comments on *Roper*: "Crimes committed impulsively . . . are still committed consciously and intentionally" (thus, they engage the *mens rea* concept;

2006, p. 406). Although we believe that the U.S. Supreme Court rightly decided *Roper v. Simmons*, to argue that Simmons's crime was in any way a direct result of the normal maturational process that everyone's brain undergoes is surely a logical fallacy.

Another matter is that the imaging of defendant's brains is typically performed many years after the crime was committed. Today's brain is not yesterday's brain, and the images jurors may see in court may be vastly different from what they may have seen shortly after the crime for which the defendant is seeking mitigation. For instance, scans of Brian Dugan's brain (see Box 9.1) were taken 26 years after he raped and killed Jeanine Nicarico. His scans may have unequivocally shown that he is a psychopath, but they tell us little about his state of mind when he committed the crime, nor do they definitively show that he was incapable of controlling his behavior. None of this is meant to say that brain scanning is of little use. It is of tremendous importance in medicine and neuroscience research, but it cannot read minds, particularly mind states that occurred years prior to the scanning. Scanning tells us the probable state of the subject's mind at the time of the scan; therefore, it cannot completely settle matters of legal responsibility.

BOX 9.1

Neuroimaging a Psychopathic Serial Killer: A Case of Successful Exoneration and Failed Mitigation

Brian James Dugan was one of the worst psychopaths ever diagnosed with the condition, scoring 38 out of a possible 40 on the Hare Psychopathy Checklist, which is a standard instrument for assessing psychopathy worldwide. Brian began his life of crime at the tender age of 8 when he and a younger brother burned down his family's garage and burned a cat alive after pouring gasoline on it. He committed numerous other crimes, including burglaries and arsons, while still a teenager. In 1983, 10-year-old Jeanine Nicarico was abducted, raped, and beaten to death. The police initially arrested two Hispanic males, Rolondo Cruz and Alejandro Hernandez, for the murder, both of whom were convicted and sentenced to death.

At the age of 18 in 1984, Dugan raped and murdered 27-year-old Donna Schnorr; in 1985, he raped and murdered 7-year-old Melissa Ackerman, and the same year he raped a 21-year-old woman who survived the attack. Dugan had also previously attempted to abduct and rape other girls and women. He was arrested the day after Melissa Ackerman's murder. The evidence was so overwhelming that he confessed to the murders of

Ackerman and Schnorr, as well as that of Jeanine Nicarico, in exchange for a life sentence in lieu of the death penalty. His confession to Nicarico's murder was not taken seriously because Cruz and Hernandez had already been convicted of the crime. However, in 2002, DNA evidence linked Dugan to the crime and Cruz and Hernandez were exonerated more than 10 years after being convicted. Dugan was indicted for the murder in 2005.

In an effort to save Dugan from the death penalty, his attorneys enlisted the help of neuroscientist Dr. Kent Keihl to scan Dugan's brain. Keihl found that Dugan's brain showed all the classic signs of psychopathy, such as the inability to "tie" together the brain's emotional and rational sides, and a relatively inactive amygdala, the part of the brain that deals with emotions, particularly fear. The inability to engage the emotions typically means that the person will lack empathy, shame, and guilt, and will thus be callously indifferent to the suffering of others. A relatively inactive amygdala signals a relative lack of fear, which leads psychopaths to take risks that most other people would not. The jury, however, was unimpressed and voted to send Dugan to his death in 2009. Patricia Nicarico described the verdict as a relief and added, "We are shedding tears not of sadness, but of joy, but not really very, very joyful because the death sentence is never really a joyful thing. But Brian Dugan is somebody who deserves it, in our minds" (Barnum & Gregory, 2009). However, Illinois Governor Pat Quinn abolished the death penalty in March 2011 (cementing Governor Ryan's 2003 moratorium), and Dugan's sentence was commuted to life in prison.

SUMMARY

This chapter has taken a look at a major turn in the death penalty argument in the form of the science used to exonerate the innocent and to mitigate the punishment of the guilty. Abolitionist arguments have moved away from the old standbys, such as the lack of a deterrent effect and the morality of the death penalty, to embrace innocence. The idea of executing an innocent person has always been a major, and the most powerful, argument in the abolitionist's arsenal, but with a number of individuals being exonerated by DNA evidence, it has taken on vastly greater power. As positive as it is to see innocent people exonerated, the Innocence Revolution may be supplying new ammunition to death penalty advocates. That is, if DNA is foolproof evidence of innocence, it is also foolproof evidence of guilt. There is also the danger that an uncritical acceptance of DNA as an instrument of absolute truth may leave us with an overly mechanistic view of human behavioral causation and upset the values of agency and responsibility that underlie our system of criminal justice.

We looked at the process of making billions of copies of DNA sequences from minute samples through polymerase chain reaction (PCR). Although this is a marvelous tool, it is a very complicated process and requires absolute assiduous concern with every detail from collecting the DNA evidence, preserving its integrity, and interpreting PCR results. We saw how it has been used fraudulently and incompetently, which cautions us again not to think of DNA as "truth medicine" ordered by Dr. Justice.

Much the same can be said of brain imaging via functional magnetic resonance imaging (fMRI). Again, this is a marvelous and very valuable tool when used for the purposes for which it was designed. It is used today in many death penalty cases to mitigate the sentence and to argue for life imprisonment. fMRI shows colorized computer-generated maps of areas of the brain that are active when people perform a specific task or respond emotionally to stimuli. It is measured by blood-oxygen-level-dependent (BOLD) contrasts, and is thus not a direct and unequivocal indicator of actual neuronal activity. These scans can tell us an awful lot about the brain's structure and functioning, but we cannot read minds with this technology. Ultimately, whether or not a brain is considered sufficiently defective or deficient to warrant some degree of exculpation is a matter that the courts will continue to sort out. Some argue that it is a moral issue to be decided by human beings according to their views of morality, agency, and responsibility.

DISCUSSION QUESTIONS

1. In your opinion, is a diagnosis of psychopathy grounds for increasing or decreasing a psychopath's sentence? Can a psychopath help being that way?
2. Have your views relating to the causal "power" of genes on human behavior changed as a result of reading this chapter? If so, or if not, why?
3. Has the exoneration of the innocent by DNA weakened or strengthened the case for capital punishment? Give your reasons for either position.
4. Is evidence of some brain abnormality determined by fMRI (or any other technique) grounds for mitigation? How about a tangible condition such as a brain tumor?
5. Explain the issue of ecological fallacy with respect to fMRI data.

GLOSSARY

Affirmative defense: A defense in a criminal case in which the defendant admits the act, but denies a guilty mind by claiming a justification defense (self-defense, victim consent, execution of public duties) or an excuse defense (acted under duress, mental incapacity).

Allele: An alternate form of the same gene. You get one allele of a gene for a given trait from your mother and another from your father.

Blood-oxygen-level-dependent (BOLD) contrast: The contrast between oxygenated and deoxygenated blood captured as an image on a computer screen when a subject undergoes an fMRI.

Ecological fallacy: A mistake in logic made when one draws an inference about individuals deduced from aggregate statistical data derived from the group to which he or she belongs.

Electrophoresis: A technique that causes DNA molecules in a gel box with an electric power source to move in certain ways so that their "fingerprint" can be read.

Exoneration: Official legal relief from the burden of responsibility, obligation, or punishment.

Functional magnetic resonance imaging (fMRI): A brain-imaging technique that allows researchers to view the functioning of the brain.

Gene A segment of deoxyribonucleic acid (DNA) that codes for a protein.

Polymerase chain reaction (PCR): A technique used to greatly amplify the number of copies of DNA to get enough copies for testing.

Polymorphism: A difference in an allelic combination located at the same place on a chromosome. Polymorphisms are thus minor variations on a common theme that make us different from one another.

REFERENCES

Altukhov, Y., and E. Salmenkova. (2002). DNA polymorphisms in population genetics. *Russian Journal of Genetics, 38,* 1173–1195.

Aronson, J., and S. Cole. (2009). Science and the death penalty: DNA, innocence, and the debate over capital punishment in the United States. *Law & Social Inquiry, 34,* 603–633.

Aspinwall, L., T. Brown, and J. Tabery. (2012). The double-edged sword: Does a biomechanism increase or decrease judges' sentencing of psychopaths? *Science, 337,* 846–849.

Barnum, A., and T. Gregory. (2009, November 12). Jeanine Nicarico murder: Tears of joy as Brian Dugan gets death penalty. *Chicago Tribune.* http://articles.chicagotribune.com/2009-11-12/news/0911111045_1_patricia-nicarico-brian-dugan-penalty.

Baum, M. (2011). The monoamine oxidase (MAOA) genetic predisposition to impulsive violence: Is it relevant to criminal trials? *Neuroethics, 6,* 287–306. DOI: 10.1007/s12152-11-9108-6.

Beaver, K., M. DeLisi, M. Vaughn, and J. Barnes. (2010). Monoamine oxidase: A genotype is associated with gang membership and weapon use. *Comprehensive Psychiatry, 51,* 130–135.

Blonigen, D. (2010). Explaining the relationship between age and crime: Contributions from the developmental literature on personality. *Clinical Psychology Review*, 30, 89–100.

Caspi, A., J. McClay, T. E. Moffitt, J. Mill, J. Martin, I. W. Craig., et al. (2002). Role of genotype in the cycle of violence in maltreated children. *Science*, 297, 851–854.

Collins, R. (2004). Onset and desistence in criminal careers: Neurobiology and the age-crime relationship. *Journal of Offender Rehabilitation*, 39, 1–19.

Dror, I., and G. Hampikian. (2011). Subjectivity and bias in forensic mixture interpretation. *Science and Justice*, 51, 204–208.

Jones, O., J. Buckholtz, J. Schall, and R. Marois. (2009). Brain imaging for legal thinkers: A guide for the perplexed. *Stanford Law Review*, 5–53. Vanderbilt Public Law Research Paper No. 10-09.

Jones, O., and F. Shen. (2012). Law and neuroscience in the United States. In *International neurolaw: A comparative analysis*, ed. T. Spranger, pp. 349–380. Berlin: Springer-Verlag.

Lea, R., and G. Chamber. (2007). Monoamine oxidase, addition, and the "warrior" gene hypothesis. *New Zealand Medical Journal*, 120, 1–6.

Logothetis, N., and J. Pfeuffer. (2004). On the nature of BOLD fMRI contrast mechanism. *Magnetic Resonance Imaging*, 22, 1517–1531.

Marshall, L. (2004). The innocence revolution and the death penalty. *Ohio State Journal of Criminal Law*, 1, 573–584.

Moffitt, T. (1993). Adolescent-limited and life-course-persistent antisocial behavior: A developmental taxonomy. *Psychological Review*, 100, 674–701.

Morse, S. (2006). Brain overclaim syndrome and criminal responsibility: A diagnostic note. *Ohio State Journal of Criminal Law*, 3, 397–412.

Munafo, M. R., S. M. Brown, and A. R. Hariri. (2008). Serotonin transporter (5HTTLPR) genotype and amygdala activation: A meta-analysis. *Biological Psychiatry*, 63, 852–857.

Overberg, L., A. Giulietti, D. Vicks, and C. Mathieu. (2009). Real-time polymerase chain reaction. In *Molecular diagnostics*, ed. G. Patrinos and W. Ansorge, pp. 87–105. London: Academic Press.

Restak, R. (2001). *The secret life of the brain*. New York: Dana Press and Joseph Henry Press.

Sjoberg, R., F. Ducci, C. Barr, T. Newman, L. Dell'Osso, M. Vikkunen, et al. (2008). A non-additive interaction of a functional MAO-A VTNR and testosterone predicts antisocial behavior. *Neuropsychopharmacology*, 33, 425–430.

Snead, C. (2007). Neuroimaging and the "complexity" of capital punishment. *New York University Law Review*, 82, 1265–1338.

Walker, E. (2002). Adolescent neurodevelopment and psychopathology. *Current Directions in Psychological Science*, 11, 24–28.

Walsh, A. (2002). *Biosocial criminology: Introduction and integration*. Cincinnati, OH: Anderson.

Walsh, A., and J. Bolen. (2012). *The neurobiology of criminal behavior: Gene-brain culture co-evolution.* Farnham, England: Ashgate.

Weinberger, D., B. Elvevag, and J. Giedd. (2005). *The adolescent brain: A work in progress.* Washington, DC: National Campaign to Prevent Teen Pregnancy.

White, A. (2004). Substance use and the adolescent brain: An overview with a focus on alcohol. *Alchohol-info.com: Topics in Alcohol Research,* 1–27.

CHAPTER 10

WRONGFUL CONVICTIONS AND THE DEATH PENALTY

Damon Thibodeaux, a 22-year-old, falsely confessed to murdering his 14-year-old half-cousin, Crystal Champagne, in 1996. Champagne was last seen when she left her family's home to walk to a nearby grocery store in Westwego, Louisiana. When she did not return home, family, friends, and law enforcement began searching for her. The search ended when Champagne's body was discovered by a levee in a neighboring city. She had been strangled to death with an extension cord, and there was some indication that she may have been sexually assaulted.

After over eight hours of interrogation by detectives, Thibodeaux confessed to having raped and murdered Champagne. There was a problem, though—his confession was inconsistent with the facts of the case. After being fed information by detectives that the victim had been strangled, Thibodeaux claimed he used white or gray stereo speaker wire from his car to strangle Champagne. What Thibodeaux did not know was that the victim had, in fact, been killed with a red extension cord hanging from a tree next to where the body was found. In addition, no evidence of semen was found in or on the victim's body to indicate that a sexual assault had taken place. Law enforcement officials claimed that the maggots uncovered on the victim's body may have degraded any semen evidence. Prosecutors presented Thibodeaux's confession as the primary evidence in their case. They also presented eyewitness testimony from two witnesses who claimed to have seen Thibodeaux at the crime scene and identified him in a photo lineup. Thibodeaux was convicted of murder and aggravated rape, and sentenced to death.

Ten years later, the Innocence Project and District Attorney's Office collaborated to reinvestigate the crime based on evidence pointing to Thibodeaux's innocence. DNA testing was ordered on the maggots and it revealed the absence of semen evidence, indicating that no rape had occurred. The cord on the tree used to kill Champagne had blood on it that was tested as well.

The blood belonged to a male, but not Thibodeaux. Furthermore, the eyewitnesses had seen Thibodeaux's photo on the news prior to making their identification, claiming to have seen him at the crime scene when he was already in police custody. Thibodeaux was released from prison in September 2012 after serving 15 years on Louisiana's death row, making him the 300th person to be exonerated by DNA testing and the 18th DNA exoneree to serve time on death row (Innocence Project, 2015).

LEARNING OBJECTIVES

- Understand and describe Packer's two models of criminal justice.
- Understand the leading causes of wrongful convictions.
- Be able to identify areas of improvement for our criminal justice system that will serve to reduce the likelihood of wrongful convictions.
- Understand the role of police officers and prosecutors and how their actions can both lead to and prevent wrongful convictions.
- Understand how the government compensates the wrongfully convicted.

EXONERATION AND FACTUAL INNOCENCE

Though cases like Damon Thibodeaux's are not common, there have been six innocent people exonerated from death row in Louisiana alone (Innocence Project, 2015). Recall that since the death penalty was reinstated in 1976 (see Chapter 3), over 1,200 people have been executed in the United States and more than 150 released from death row (Amnesty International, 2015); 20 of these were DNA exonerations (DNA revealed that the convicted person could not have committed the crime). As we learned in Chapter 5, Governor George Ryan of Illinois commuted the death sentences of the state's entire death row population (167 inmates), explaining: "The facts that I have seen in reviewing each and every one of these cases raised questions not only about the innocence of people on death row, but about the fairness of the death penalty system as a whole" (*New York Times*, 2003).

The conviction of a factually innocent person is a grave injustice that not only violates that individual's rights, but also undermines our confidence in the criminal justice system. Furthermore, when we convict the wrong person, we allow the actual perpetrator(s) to escape justice. It is important to note, however, that the term "exoneration" is not necessarily the same as "innocent." Exoneration is a wrongful conviction if the exoneree is factually innocent, but exoneration does not always have to do with factual guilt or innocence (Zalman, Smith, & Kiger, 2008). Recall from the last chapter that exoneration is to officially relieve someone of the burden of responsibility, obligation, or punishment. The relief granted by the courts does not necessarily mean that the convicted individual is innocent of the charges that led to the imposition of the burden in the first place. Put otherwise, exoneration means legal innocence and not necessarily factual innocence (though they are typically one and the same). As we shall soon see in our discussion of the due process model of criminal justice, the law purposely puts obstacles in the way of "truth seeking" that benefit defendants in order to minimize the possibility of convicting an innocent person. This is particularly true of death penalty cases.

Although we can never really know how often wrongful convictions occur, we do know that they happen too frequently. The unsettling notion of a person being wrongfully convicted is no longer an abstract concept. Wrongful convictions are a reality that has played out before us in popular media headlines for the last several decades. We now know what it looks like for a person to be wrongfully convicted of a crime because we see their faces plastered across our television sets and are able to readily access their stories on countless social media and Internet sites. There are also numerous databases that track data on those who have been wrongfully convicted. For instance, the National Registry of Exonerations (NRE) (2015), part of the University of Michigan Law School, tracks both DNA and non-DNA exonerations. The NRE reports over 1,550 exonerations from 1989 to the present (see Figure 10.1). Another organization that tracks exonerations is the National Innocence Project (Innocence Project, 2015). Its website allows visitors to browse through the 325 postconviction DNA exoneration profiles, dating back to 1989. Twenty of the 325 exonerated defendants served time on death row. More than 75% of exonerations have occurred since 2000 (the first DNA exoneration occurring in 1989); therefore, we loosely characterize the turn of the twenty-first century as the **Innocence Movement** (Innocence Project, 2015).

Hollywood has capitalized on the national attention garnered by the Innocence Movement. A fairly recent movie depicting a miscarriage of justice, *Conviction,* is a true story starring the critically acclaimed actor Hilary Swank. Swank plays the part of Betty Anne Waters, a small-town waitress turned attorney for the sole purpose of freeing her brother Kenneth Waters, who was convicted of a murder that he did not commit. Unable to get adequate legal assistance for her brother, Waters decides to go to law school and becomes an attorney herself, eventually securing her brother's freedom with DNA evidence. It took 18 years of fighting the legal system to gain Waters' freedom. *The Hurricane* is another Hollywood wrongful conviction movie based on actual events; it stars Denzel Washington as the former world-class middleweight boxing champion "Hurricane" Carter, who was convicted in a triple-murder case and sentenced to life in prison. Nearly 20 years later, he was freed

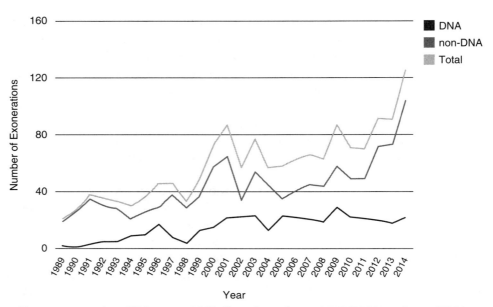

FIGURE 10.1   As of February 2015, there have been 1,552 DNA and non-DNA Exonerations since 1989
Source: National Registry of Exonerations (2015)

following an immense struggle to clear his name. Other box-office hits offering fictional portrayals of the falsely accused include *The Shawshank Redemption, The Fugitive,* and *My Cousin Vinny.*

Unfortunately, the reality of wrongful convictions is all too real. Although we can never know with any real degree of accuracy how often these convictions occur, we may assume that any number, no matter how small or large, is more than we are willing to accept. In a 2005 study examining hundreds of exonerations, Samuel Gross and colleagues predicted that it is plausible for there to be thousands, if not tens of thousands, of other wrongful convictions that we do not know about, although only hundreds have been uncovered thus far. Keep in mind, however, that wrongful convictions related to violent crimes (like those that we test DNA for) tend to be the ones uncovered, not the less serious crimes that may indeed lend credibility to the prediction of higher numbers. Former U.S. Supreme Court Justice Souter referenced the probability of the frequency of exonerations when he wrote:

> Today, a new body of fact must be accounted for in deciding what, in practical terms, the Eighth Amendment guarantees should tolerate, for the period starting in 1989 has seen repeated exonerations of convicts under death sentences, in numbers never imagined before the development of DNA tests. (*Kansas v. Marsh*, 2006)

Now that we are certain of their existence, we want to know why miscarriages of justice happen. Moreover, how can a person be convicted, sentenced to death, and possibly executed for a crime that he or she did not commit? We will begin exploring this issue by examining Herbert Packer's (1968) theoretical models of justice as a starting point.

DUE PROCESS VERSUS CRIME CONTROL MODELS OF CRIMINAL JUSTICE SYSTEMS

Herbert Packer, a Stanford University law professor, formulated two idealistic and contrasting models of criminal processing: the *due process* and *crime control* models. These models are what sociologists call "ideal-type" models, or pure models that accentuate and exaggerate differences between them for illustrative purposes. That is, the various elements said to make up these models form a continuum that shifts back and forth with the times, and probably nowhere in the world does either of these models exist in a pure or absolute form.

The U.S. criminal justice system operates under a **due process model** that assumes the most critical function of the criminal justice system is to protect defendants' civil liberties by providing due process under the law. Due process is essentially a set of instructions informing agents of the state how they must proceed in their investigation, arrest, questioning, prosecution, and punishment of individuals who are suspected of committing crimes. Therefore, the primary focus of this model is on the defendant, rather than the victim and the community. Recall that the Bill of Rights sets forth protections for individuals who find themselves accused by the government of breaking the law. A key to Packer's due process model is the idea that the government should not be allowed to convict a person solely on the findings of fact; rather, a person may be found guilty only if the government follows the legal procedures required of it during the fact-finding process. Packer (1968) compared the due process model to an obstacle course because this model requires procedural safeguards or *obstacles* at nearly every level of the criminal justice process to protect all defendants whether factually innocent or guilty. One such procedural safeguard is that discretionary police powers ought to be limited in order to maintain the integrity of an individual's rights.

In contrast, the main function of the **crime control model** is to repress crime by prioritizing the swift handling of factually guilty defendants with as few obstacles as possible. Packer (1968) likens this model to an assembly line/conveyor belt because of the efficiency with which offenders are processed through the system. It emphasizes community protection from criminals, and maintains that civil liberties can only have real meaning in a safe, well-ordered society. This system thus concentrates much more on victim and community rights than those of the defendant and is centered around discovering the truth, rather than strictly on efforts to protect the legal process. Consequently, this model allows for expanding discretionary police powers and limiting the legal technicalities that hinder police investigations. In theory, if the police arrest someone, then the accused should be presumed guilty because the fact-finding process by police and prosecutors is thought to be largely reliable.

Given what we know about Packer's models, one might conclude that a defendant is presumed innocent until proven guilty under the due process model and guilty until proven innocent under the crime control model; thus, the burden of proof seemingly lies with the government in the due process model and with the defendant for the crime control model once a suspect has been arrested. This assumption would be wrong, however. Remember, we are talking about ideal types here, and Packer does not want us to think of a presumption of guilt as the conceptual opposite of the presumption of innocence. As Packer himself puts it, "Reduced to its barest essentials and operating at its most successful pitch," the crime control model consists of two elements: "an administrative fact-finding process leading (1) to the exoneration of the suspect, or (2) to the entry of a plea of guilty" (1968, p. 5).

Which model do you prefer? Which model do you think best exemplifies the ideals of justice? It is clear that both models have their faults as well as their strengths. The danger of a runaway crime control model is a return to the days when due process was nonexistent. The danger of a runaway due process model is that truth and justice may get lost in a maze of legal ritualism. But as we said earlier, these are ideal-type models that do not exist in pure form anywhere in the world where the rule of law is respected. Given the swift justice ideals of the crime control model, we might assume that there is a stronger likelihood of an innocent person being wrongfully convicted since it happens in our due process justice system, with all of the "obstacles," much too often. To choose one model as being superior to another is a matter of deciding which values are most important, but the point we wish to make is that despite the numerous procedural safeguards that are supposed to prevent wrongful convictions in our system, they still happen.

THE BLACKSTONE RATIO

English jurist William Blackstone once remarked that it is "better that ten guilty persons escape than one innocent suffer" (Laufer, 1995, n. 17). This quote became known as the **Blackstone ratio**. Blackstone proposed that the "error-ratio of false acquittals to false convictions" ought to be very high—10 to 1 (Allen & Laudan, 2013, p. 11). He believed that a system which is able to secure this ratio would be *just* and minimize occurrences of wrongful convictions. Jeremy Bentham (1829), another well-known jurist and philosopher, warned that the sentiment underlying Blackstone's ratio may jeopardize the overall goal of a criminal justice system to seek justice for those who are guilty. Bentham cautions:

> We must be on guard against those sentimental exaggerations which tend to give crime impunity, under the pretext of insuring the safety of innocence. Public applause has been, so to speak, set up to auction. At first it was said to be better to save several guilty men, than to condemn a single innocent man; others, to make the maxim more striking, fix the number ten; a third made this ten a hundred, and a fourth made it a thousand. All these candidates for the prize of humanity have been outstripped by I know not how many writers, who hold, that, in no case, ought an accused person to be condemned, unless evidence amount to mathematical or absolute certainty. According to this maxim, nobody ought to be punished, lest an innocent man be punished. (Bentham, 1829, p. 198)

Bentham believed that although it may be preferred to err on the side of "acquitting the guilty versus convicting the innocent," they are both "great evils," with the latter being the greater of the two (Laufer, 1995). Most of us would agree there is no question that wrongful convictions are contrary to the fundamental tenets of our system of justice.

Perhaps the only event more egregious than a wrongful conviction would be the wrongful conviction of a person sentenced to death. As we learned in Chapter 3, our system in a post-*Furman* era embraces the sentiment that "death is different" (a phrase used by the U.S. Supreme Court) and, therefore, requires extra procedural safeguards to prevent executing an innocent person. We know that there are many factors that lead to erroneous convictions, but there are six major *causes*.

THE "BIG SIX"

Eyewitness Misidentification

Though many procedural safeguards distinguish our criminal justice system, wrongful convictions happen and there are several reasons why. Let us explore the issue of eyewitness error first. Eyewitness misidentification is the leading cause of wrongful convictions. It has been found to play a major role in approximately 75% of all DNA exoneration cases (Innocence Project, 2015). It most certainly played a key role in Damon Thibodeaux's case that we learned about at the start of this chapter. The victims, both of whom identified Thibodeaux, were

FIGURE 10.2 Bobby Poole and Ronald Cotton
Source: Burlington Police Department/Associated Press

certain that he was the attacker, and yet DNA evidence proved otherwise. Were the victims maliciously lying about their accusations or were they merely mistaken?

Consider the case of Ronald Cotton (see Figure 10.2). While Cotton's case is not a capital one, it is a great example of how fallible eyewitness identification can be. Cotton is an African American man from North Carolina who was 22 years old when he was convicted of raping Jennifer Thompson, a 22-year-old white college student. Thompson said that she made a point of studying her attacker's face during the crime so that she could later identify him if given the opportunity. Thompson got her chance when police put together a group of lineup photos based on the composite sketch she helped police to create. Thompson picked Cotton's photograph (police had Cotton's mug shot from a juvenile conviction), and he was subsequently convicted and sentenced to life in prison, plus 54 years for the crime.

Thompson identified the wrong man. After 10 years of imprisonment for a crime that he did not commit, Cotton was freed when the DNA evidence pointed to another man, Bobby Poole (who was previously identified by another victim raped that same night, and who served time in the same prison with Cotton for a series of brutal rapes). In a strange turn of events, Thompson and Cotton are now friends who have become advocates for reforming eyewitness identification protocols. They have also co-authored a bestselling book entitled *Picking Cotton*, which provides a detailed account of their story.

Few would accuse Thompson of intentionally identifying the wrong man. Indeed, Ronald Cotton bears some resemblance to Bobby Poole (see the comparison photo here). But, Thompson is like many victims whose memories are not reliable when it comes to recalling specific details about their attackers.

Eyewitness misidentification in capital cases is especially disconcerting if it is the primary evidence used to convict a defendant. One notable example is that of Troy Davis, whose case received worldwide attention when he was executed in 2011 by the state of Georgia. Davis was convicted of murdering a police officer in 1989 based on eyewitness testimony. Because the murder took place in a crowded Burger King parking lot, there were 34 witnesses for the prosecution and 6 for the defense. Seven of the nine individuals who testified that they witnessed Davis kill the officer recanted their story some 20 years later (*New York Times*, 2011). Furthermore, three jury members from Davis's trial reported that they would not have agreed to sentence him to death if they had known of the reliability issues associated with eyewitness testimony.

Davis had numerous supporters who vocalized their belief in his innocence and actively sought to help with exoneration efforts. Among Davis's advocates were former President Jimmy Carter and death penalty supporter William Sessions (former director of the FBI). Unfortunately, Davis's team was unable to save him from execution. Davis maintained his innocence until his last breath when he told the victim's family, "I did not personally kill your son, father, brother. . . . All I can ask is that you look deeper into his case so you really can finally see the truth" (Severson, 2011). While we may never know for certain that Davis was innocent, his case gives pause when contemplating the problems with eyewitness testimony.

There is little debate about the fallibility of eyewitness testimony. As early as 1908, Hugo Munsterberg, a German psychologist and former president of the American Psychological Association, warned of the effects of eyewitness error as it pertains to trial outcomes. Since then, a plethora of social science research has confirmed that our memory is both malleable and highly unreliable, especially as time passes. Modern research on the topic of eyewitness identification began in the 1970s and took shape during the 1980s (with the advent of DNA evidence and testing) (Wells, 1993), though we know more about it today than ever before. U.S. Supreme Court Justice William Brennan was clearly concerned about the unreliability of eyewitness testimony and its impact on juries: "All the evidence points rather strikingly to the conclusion that there is almost nothing more convincing than a live human being who takes the stand, points a finger at the defendant, and says 'That's the one!'" (*Watkins v. Sowders*, as cited in Loftus, 1979, p. 19).

Why is eyewitness identification so unreliable? Essentially, there are four general explanations for eyewitness error. First, a witness may not be telling the truth. Second, the witness's perception may not be accurate. Third, the witness's memory may be inaccurate. Fourth, the witness's recollection may have been influenced by outside suggestion (Hunt, 2011). Wells (1978), a renowned expert on eyewitness testimony, categorized these variables into two groups: system and estimator variables. **System variables** are variables that are linked to the investigative phase and its impact on a witness's memory. These variables include improper lineups and suggestive interview techniques. **Estimator variables** refer to variables that occur outside of the investigative process having to do with the circumstances surrounding the offense and witnesses' observations. Estimator variables include environmental variables such as lighting, proximity of a witness to the crime, weather, and other like variables. The impact of these variables can be estimated and taken into consideration when determining the reliability of a witness's information (Wells, 1978). Munsterberg was particularly concerned with the correlation between the influence of suggestion and memory (system variables) and commented that "one factor more than anything else devastates memory and plays havoc with our best intended recollections: that is the power of suggestion" (1908, p. 67).

One of the authors of this book (Hatch) has experience working on wrongful conviction cases.[1] One of these involved several eyewitness misidentifications, some of which stemmed from suggestive lineup procedures by police during their investigation. In one particular case, the victim of a horrific crime made questionable lineup identifications. To provide some brief background, the victim had been brutally stabbed, beaten, and then left to die by multiple attackers on a roadside in a northwestern state. Police had few leads and made little progress in solving the case for nearly two years. Surely, they felt immense pressure to locate, apprehend, and bring the perpetrators to justice. Indeed, they enlisted the help of a popular crime show, *America's Most Wanted*, in hopes of attracting leads. A detective working on this case presented the victim/witness with photo lineups and instructed the victim to choose the person who looked "most like" her attacker. Another curious identification made in this case occurred when the victim admitted to selecting a photo of a person that she thought was her attacker based on her memory of the actor portrayals on the *America's Most Wanted* segment.

Consider why the instructions by the detective during the lineup would breach effective procedure recommendations, as supported by the research. If you were the victim in this case and were asked to look at a photo array and

---

[1]Hatch worked on an Innocence Project case for which *Dateline NBC* produced a segment titled *One Summer Night*. See: http://www.nbcnews.com/watch/dateline/one-summer-night-part-1-303030851782.

then pick the person who most closely resembled the individual who attacked you, then you might feel compelled to choose someone so long as he or she resembled your attacker (or looked most *like* the attacker), right? And you might not even question such a request because you, like most Americans, trust the police and believe that they know what they are doing, right? Or, perhaps you do not even notice the flaw in the instructions given to you; you might subconsciously respond by picking someone from the lineup without even giving the instructions from the police a second thought.

It probably comes as no surprise that the victim in this case repeatedly selected people from the lineups who were not her attackers. On one of these occasions, the victim was informed (by police) that she had selected an individual whom the police believed was the *wrong* suspect. This is another obvious error—police administering lineups should not know if the suspect's image is present or not in the photos that they show to witnesses. Without always knowing it, police may bias witness selections if they know that a prime suspect is in the lineup. This issue is avoided when a **double-blind lineup** procedure is used. This procedure involves a "blind" administration by which neither the witness nor lineup administrators know if the suspect will appear in the lineup.

The above case is only one of many other eyewitness misidentification cases, but it illustrates the critical need for police to utilize best practices when collecting eyewitness evidence. There are numerous ways to improve the practice of eyewitness identification procedures. The Innocence Project, a national nonprofit legal organization dedicated to freeing the wrongfully convicted, explains: "witness memory is like any other evidence at a crime scene; it must be preserved carefully and retrieved methodically, or it can be contaminated" (Innocence Project, 2015). If witnesses are to be treated like any other type of evidence, then we must evaluate what practices best preserve eyewitness evidence.

A few of the major changes known to increase the reliability of eyewitness identification are focused on lineup procedure reform. There is no question that lineup identifications are vital for investigators to narrow their suspect pools. To begin, the administrator should notify the witness that the suspect may or may not be in the lineup. Recall that it is important to utilize the double-blind method. Also, investigators should move away from the traditionally used simultaneous (side-by-side) photo lineups. Research dictates that sequential lineups are much more effective because the witness views photos one at a time and, therefore, is not simultaneously comparing the characteristics of individuals in some of the photos with those of individuals in other photos (Wells & Lindsay, 1985; Steblay, Dysart, Fulero, & Lindsay, 2001). Additionally, the "fillers" (nonsuspects included in a photo array) should closely resemble the suspect if he or she is going to be included in the lineup. Once an identification has been made, administrators should then ask the witness to identify the degree of certainty with which he or she has picked the correct suspect (Bond-Fraser, Fraser, & Ready, 2012).

Other reform efforts have been focused on legislative remedies. Historically, eyewitness testimony has been given a lot of weight in the courtroom (consider Justice Brennan's comment above). It is not uncommon for courts to uphold convictions even if they are based on botched lineups and questionable eyewitness testimony (*Manson v. Brathwaite*, 1977). In response to these issues, there have been recent legislative changes in states such as Maryland and New Jersey. In 2009, the state of Maryland created legislation requiring prosecutors to have DNA evidence linking the defendant to the crime, a recorded confession of the suspect, or a videotape of the crime in order to seek the death penalty (Porter, 2009). As of 2012, the Supreme Court of New Jersey requires judges to provide jury instructions on the reliability of eyewitness identification in cases with such evidence; the Court outlined specific factors that can influence an eyewitness (e.g., witness stress, lighting, cross-racial identification, lineup procedures used by law enforcement, etc.) and remarked that a jury should be fully informed when making decisions about the credibility of eyewitness testimony (New Jersey Courts, 2012). Despite these efforts, the issue of eyewitness error continues to be a serious problem in our criminal justice system.

False Confessions

Munsterberg (1908) wrote extensively about his experiences with false confessions and the power that they have in the courtroom. He believed that erroneous confessions are relatively normal and are brought on by unusual circumstances. Consider the famously unsolved murder case of Jon Benet Ramsey in 1996. Ramsey was a 6-year-old beauty pageant queen who was found dead in the basement of her home. Her attacker raped and strangled her to death. Nearly ten years later, Jon Mark Karr, an American teacher living in Thailand, confessed to the crime. DNA evidence found at the crime scene, however, revealed that Karr could not have been the killer (*New York Times*, 2006).

It is hard to imagine that an innocent person would willingly admit to a crime that he or she did not commit, but we know this happened in approximately 27% of DNA exoneration cases (Innocence Project, 2015). Recall that Damon Thibodeaux (from the opening vignette) provided detectives with a false confession. Prosecutors in Thibodeaux's case stated that they believed he confessed because the threat of the death penalty intimidated him (Innocence Project, 2015). According to Leo and Ofshe (1998), false confessions are powerful—"a confession is universally treated as a damning and compelling evidence of guilt" (p. 429).

There are three general types of false confessions: voluntary, compliant, and internalized. **Voluntary confessions** are those provided by people without prompting by police (Kassin, 2008). John Michael Karr contacted authorities claiming to be Jon Benet Ramsey's killer. No one has ever been able to figure out exactly why Karr confessed to a murder that he did not commit. Kassin (2008) explains that there are numerous explanations for voluntary confessions. For example, one might have delusional guilt or a pathological desire to seek attention. There is speculation that Karr suffers from mental illness after claims that he fantasized about Jon Benet surfaced; he reportedly thought that she loved him. Or, maybe he just wanted the attention and notoriety that come with high-profile cases. Another plausible explanation for a voluntary confession may be that a person is willing to "take the rap" to protect someone who is guilty. **Compliant confessions** are those prompted by highly stressful police interrogations. In such cases, a person may be willing to seek short-term relief by confessing to a crime that he or she did not commit in order to be removed from the stressful environment. Sometimes the confessor will perceive a benefit or reward for telling the police what they want to hear (e.g., the suspect will be allowed to go home, given permission to take a smoke break, etc.). The suspects in the infamous 1989 case of the "Central Park jogger" (jogger was brutally raped and left for dead) serve as an example of a compliant confession. Four of the five teens who were interrogated by police confessed to raping the jogger and were subsequently convicted. More than ten years later (2002), another man came forward claiming that he was, in fact, the rapist. Authorities verified his story with DNA tests. It turns out that the five teens could not have been responsible for the attack, yet they claimed to have committed the crime. When later asked why they provided police with confessions, each of the convicted men indicated that after lengthy interrogations, he had believed the police would allow him to go home if he simply confessed to committing the crime. While seemingly odd to consider that anyone of sound mind would do such a thing, this case illustrates how powerful the perceived reward of being allowed to leave a stressful police interrogation can be (Kassin, 2008).

One of the authors of this book (Hatch) worked on a murder case for the Innocence Project that involved a false confession. The suspect in this case, a teenager, admitted to the rape and murder of a young woman after nearly 40 hours of intensive police interrogations over the course of several days. The teen was subjected to suggestive and blatantly improper police interrogations during the time of his "confession." After numerous attempts to explain that he did not commit the crime of which he was accused, he was fed key information about the crime by his interrogators, which ultimately resulted in a polished and seemingly legitimate confession. Moreover, there was DNA evidence (semen) on the body of the victim that conclusively proved the defendant could not have committed the rape and murder. So why did this young man confess to the crime? When asked his reasons for providing police with a confession, he explained that he just wanted to be left alone and free to go home. It is difficult to imagine that a rational person would believe he or she could simply walk free after confessing to a murder, so why does this happen?

Those who study false confessions often cite the problems associated with the **Reid technique** used by police as playing a role in inducing false confessions. Police in the United States commonly utilize this technique when interrogating suspects, and it has come under intense scrutiny in recent years. This technique involves the use of intensive interrogation tactics that include intimidating suspects by sometimes providing false information to support the interrogator's accusation of guilt (e.g., claiming that police have DNA to link the suspect to the crime or that a witness has come forward with evidence that the suspect is guilty). Another approach is minimizing the seriousness of the crime and the consequences that a suspect may suffer if he or she admits to committing the crime. Often, this requires the interrogator to pretend that he or she can identify with, and wants to help, the suspect (Kostelnik & Reppuci, 2009). Police-induced confessions often result when "a suspect's resistance to confession is broken down as a result of poor police practice, overzealousness, criminal misconduct, and/or misdirected training" (Leo & Ofshe, 1998, p. 440). Police interrogators are sometimes so confident they have found the correct suspect that they fail to investigate other suspects or alternate scenarios (in other words, they suffer from tunnel vision). Instead, the investigation typically ends once the confession is made and police will often focus their efforts on working with prosecutors to secure a conviction against the defendant (Leo & Ofshe, 1998). The last type of false confession, **internalized confessions**, occurs when a vulnerable suspect confesses to a crime that he did not commit and becomes convinced that he actually committed the crime. A number of factors can cause a person to believe that he actually committed the said crime. These confessions typically follow highly suggestive police interrogations (Kassin, 2008).

Kassin (2008) identifies three significant problems with confession evidence. First, police are unable to tell the difference between those who tell the truth and those who are lying in many cases. Second, there are some interrogation practices that put innocent people at risk for confessing, especially vulnerable populations (e.g., those who are mentally impaired, of a young age, etc.). Third, both judges and juries trust confessions, even when clear evidence suggests that a confession has been coerced.

Despite the growing concerns with false confessions, little has been done to improve the interrogation practices that often contribute to this problem. This is largely because the police are poorly trained in interrogation techniques and the methods that might reduce the likelihood of eliciting false confessions. Leo and Ofshe (1998) recommend that all police interrogations be recorded in order to maintain objectivity and the integrity of confession evidence. Judges and juries may then review recordings when the reliability concerns arise. Currently, 18 states require police to record interrogations of suspects (Innocence Project, 2015).

PERSPECTIVE FROM AN INNOCENT MAN AND FORMER DEATH ROW INMATE: CHARLES FAIN

Daralyn Johnson was 9 years old when she was abducted in Nampa, Idaho, in February 1982 while walking to her elementary school. Three days later, her body was found by fishermen near the Snake River. Medical examiners determined that Daralyn had been raped and then drowned by her attacker. Charles Fain was tried, convicted, and sentenced to death for her murder. After nearly 18 years of being confined to a small prison cell on Idaho's death row, and coming within three days of execution on one occasion, Fain's lawyers were able to prove his innocence with DNA testing. Mitochondrial DNA tests were conducted on pubic hairs recovered from the victim's body. This type of testing was not available when Fain was tried. The results excluded Fain as the attacker and he was freed from prison in 2001.

FIGURE 10.3 Charles Fain

I lost almost 18 years of my life while in prison, both of my parents died and I never got to say goodbye. They died not knowing that I was freed. I had no idea how exactly it would happen, but I knew I would walk free someday because I knew a secret that [the government] didn't—I was innocent. When I was released, it was weird to be able to walk more than six steps forward and three from side-to-side. It seemed that the world had changed because everyone looked so young and I looked old. The first thing I wanted to do was pet a cat because I love animals and it had been so long since I was able to pet one. My sister picked me up from the prison and took me to dinner. When she asked me what I wanted to eat, without thinking I said, "Whatever is on the tray." We actually ate at a restaurant that had trays and she took mine from me and said, "You aren't eating on a tray tonight." After I was released, I had plans to move back to Oregon, but realized that I could not board a plane with my prison identification card which read "Death Row Inmate"! I had no other form of identification, so we decided that it would be best to drive to Oregon.

> There were many unfair things that happened in my case that led to my wrongful conviction. The worst was that the prosecutor let a man who was facing 230 years in prison testify that I confessed to him in jail. He only spent four years in prison after only 20 minutes of lying in the courtroom. He got a great deal. No one should get the death penalty on the word of a snitch. Also, there was a FBI agent who testified that the pubic hairs found on the little girl's body were "unique and unusual" and could have belonged to me. Years later, mitochondrial DNA testing on the hairs proved that they could not have belonged to me. And it turns out that they were not so "unique and unusual" after all.
>
> Assuming that offenders are guilty, I believe in the death penalty. I have lived with men on death row who have killed lots of people and I think they deserve to die. Some people do things that are so terrible that society has to send a message that we won't put up with it. However, no man should be executed if he is innocent. I would not be for the death penalty if it weren't for the long appeals process for death row defendants because it gives the defendant time to prove his innocence. In fact, I would not be free if not for being on death row because I had all kinds of attorneys wanting to help me during the appeals process.
>
> Many people ask me how I survived living on death row knowing that I was innocent. It's simple—God got me through this. I became a Christian five days after I was arrested. I frequently read the Bible and am still an active Christian today.
>
> *Charles Fain is now a married man who is gainfully employed, enjoys spending time with his family, and fishes for fun. Remarkably, he bears no resentment toward police, prosecutors, and others whose actions (or inactions) may have prevented this tragedy. Charles is one of only 20 people in the United States to be exonerated by DNA after having served time on death row.*

Informant/Snitch Testimony

Testimony by informants/snitches (the terms are used interchangeably) is an age-old problem linked to miscarriages of justice. The first documented case of a wrongful conviction involving a snitch occurred in 1819. Two brothers were accused of murdering their brother-in-law in Vermont when one of the brothers was placed in a jail cell with a snitch who claimed that that brother confessed to the killing. The snitch's testimony ultimately led to the conviction and death sentence of both brothers. They were freed, however, when authorities discovered that the brother-in-law was not dead and was actually living in New Jersey!

Snitch testimony has been a key issue in more than 15% of DNA exoneration cases (Innocence Project, 2015). Of the first 111 post-*Furman* death penalty exonerations, though, informant testimony was at issue in approximately 46% of the cases, thereby classifying snitch testimony as the leading cause for wrongful convictions in capital cases (Center on Wrongful Convictions, 2005). The percentage of snitch testimony is probably higher in non–death penalty cases given the extra safeguards that are supposed to be in place in capital cases.

Snitch testimony, also known as *incentivized testimony*, is inherently flawed due to the motivations that underlie an informant's desire to fabricate information. Keep in mind that informants are frequently serving time for their own crimes when they provide information to police. They are often in jails awaiting trial or sentencing and, therefore, in a position to help themselves when provided with the opportunity. Essentially, snitches have nothing to lose and everything to gain by conjuring up stories to support a prosecutor's case. If the prosecutor chooses not to utilize a snitch for testimony, then the snitch is in no worse position, but if the prosecutor offers the snitch a deal, then he or she may have hit the jackpot. Recall that Charles Fain's conviction and death sentence was largely predicated on snitch testimony (see the Perspective feature in this chapter). The snitch in Fain's case, Ricky Chilton, was facing 230 years in prison for armed robbery, fraud, escape, and kidnapping when he testified that he overheard Fain confessing to the murder. Chilton was handsomely rewarded for his testimony, with a sentence reduction of 226 years. Ultimately, Chilton served just four years in prison while Fain was on death row fighting for his life.

It is common practice for snitches/informants to be paid or receive a deal for their cooperation. Deals take on many forms and typically include charge dismissal or reduction, sentence reduction, or promise of future consideration. Although many states require the prosecution to disclose if a formal deal has been made in exchange for testimony, much of the deal-making can be accomplished informally and thus never known to jury members or judges. The U.S. Federal Court of Appeals for the 9th Circuit warned about the dangers of informant testimony:

> The need for disclosure is particularly acute where the government presents witnesses who have been granted immunity from prosecution in exchange for their testimony. . . . We said that informants granted immunity are by definition . . . cut from untrustworthy cloth, and must be managed and carefully watched by the government and the courts to prevent them from falsely accusing the innocent, from manufacturing evidence against those under suspicion of crime, and from lying under oath in the courtroom. . . . Accordingly, we expect prosecutors and investigators to take all reasonable

measures to safeguard the system against treachery. (*Carriger v. Stewart*, 1997, sec. 479)

The incentive for snitches to improve their own circumstances is sometimes so great that they will devise creative scams to obtain the information needed to help prosecutors. Leslie Vernon White is a notorious snitch who agreed to be interviewed on the popular television news show *60 Minutes* to explain how he was able to dupe the Los Angeles Prosecutor's Office into believing that he had knowledge of key evidence in numerous cases. He fabricated testimony in at least a dozen cases; in a 36-day period, he provided prosecutors with testimony in three murder cases and a burglary case. White explained in detail how he was able to obtain the information that he needed. He began by asking his cellmates what they had been charged with and would then call the courthouse from jail posing as a prosecutor or police officer in order to obtain details about the cases that were not known by the public. White would then claim that the defendants in each of these cases revealed to him key details about the crimes of which they were accused (Bloom, 2002). He shared some popular snitch slogans, such as: "Don't go to the pen, send a friend" and "If you can't do the time, just drop a dime."

Despite numerous wrongful convictions that have revealed the problems with snitches, prosecutors and police continue to utilize such testimonies with little to no verification in many cases. In one shocking display of informant recruitment in the Albuquerque area, police placed an ad in the city's newspaper seeking informants for hire in 2008. The ad read:

> **WANTED:** People who hang out with crooks to do part-time work for the Albuquerque Police Dept. Make some extra cash! Drug use and criminal record OK. Must be willing to work odd hours. Give us a call and we can work out the details. Confidentiality GUARANTEED!!! (Associated Press, 2008)

While it is certainly logical to assume that snitch/informant testimony can be a valuable tool for police and prosecutors to investigate crimes and solve cases, research suggests that more procedural safeguards need to be in place to prevent informants from providing false information. For instance, wiring snitches so that their conversations with accused suspects are recorded would eliminate any doubt as to whether the snitch is fabricating conversations with the accused. Recording the exchanges of law enforcement officers when they meet with snitches may also be valuable to promote transparency. Also key to improving problems with snitch testimony would be to require prosecutors to disclose if snitches have been compensated or rewarded in any way or form, as many states now practice. Although such requirements may not result in detecting "off-the-books" rewards, they are certainly a move in the right direction (Center on Wrongful Convictions, 2005).

Bad Science

The use of improper or invalidated forensic science to convict innocent persons is an issue that has contributed to more than 50% of DNA exoneration/wrongful conviction cases (Innocence Project, 2015) (see Figure 10.4). We must remember, however, that prior to the start of DNA testing (in the 1990s), law enforcement had little to work with in terms of forensic science. With few options, investigators utilized questionable methods to solve their cases out of necessity. Now we know quite a bit more about the validity (or lack thereof) of fingerprint evidence, hair comparison/analysis, arson analysis, and other forensic practices that have since been labeled as "junk science."

Fingerprint analysis is not as conclusive as we once thought. Gould and colleagues (2012) extensively studied the causes of wrongful convictions for the National Institute of Justice and found that the "science" of fingerprinting lacks adequate testing and standards for determining matches. We have long assumed that each of us has fingerprints that are unique and our assumptions are correct; no two humans share identical prints, but they can be quite similar. Given that they can be close, but not identical, print analysis may be problematic when the prints are compared manually to one another. Yes, we have sophisticated computer technology that is both quick and efficient at matching prints in various law enforcement databases, but these programs require "good" fingerprints (point standards, etc.) in order to work. Contrary to popular belief, fingerprints that are lifted by police at crime scenes are not always sufficient for analysis via these computer programs. (Yes, we know that it only takes seconds for fingerprint scans to solve crimes on popular crime television shows; if only this were true!) This is not to say that partial prints are not usable, just that they will require manual comparisons. This process involves a fingerprint technician (hopefully one with advanced training) having to visually compare prints to decipher if they match the prints belonging to the suspect(s). When prints are partial or smudged, technicians begin examining them by comparing their ridge characteristics (the width of the ridges and the spacing of oil pores). Technicians will be asked in court about their level of certainty that the print in question matches the print of the suspect taken during the booking process. And to make matters more complicated, there are few standards or guidelines for analysts to rely on when drawing their conclusions. Even an experienced print analyst might incorrectly reach conclusions that prints match when they, in fact, do not. Sometimes reports from multiple analysts conflict with one another, leaving the matter up to the courts to decide. As you might imagine, each side (prosecution and defense) manages to find and present expert testimonies with findings that "fit" their own theories. Essentially, judges and/or juries are tasked with determining which expert analysis is most credible.

When working with fingerprint experts on one of her Innocence Project cases, Hatch discovered that fingerprints deemed to lack value by one expert were found to have value by another. Ultimately, just about every fingerprint can be compared differently, depending on who is assessing its "value." As one fingerprint expert explained to Hatch, "Fingerprint analysis is more like an art than a science."

Hair comparison and analysis are other examples of "bad" science. Before DNA testing was available, investigators examined hair evidence under a microscope and compared it with hair belonging to potential suspects. Today, if the root is still attached to a hair sample, there is a good chance that mitochondrial DNA (mDNA) testing may be utilized for determining matches. Without the root, however, we must return to manual comparisons. The same problem exists with manual comparison of hair that exists with fingerprint analysis—expert subjectivity. Fain's innocence would not have been realized if not for DNA testing to refute the testimony of the FBI agent who compared Fain's hair to the hairs found on the murder victim's body. Recall that the

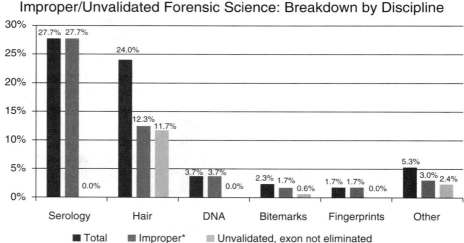

FIGURE 10.4 DNA Exoneration and Forensic Science
Source: The Innocence Project, http://www.innocenceproject.org/causes-wrongful-conviction/FSBreakdownDiscipline.pdf

agent testified the hair collected from the body was likely Fain's. The agent made a visual comparison that was clearly inaccurate. That mistake, combined with the snitch testimony, nearly cost Fain his life. The Law Enforcement Assistance Administration Laboratory Proficiency Testing Program, which reviewed over 235 crime labs in the United States, found hair analysis to be the "weakest of all forensic laboratory techniques tested, with error rates as high as 67% on individual samples and the majority of laboratories reaching incorrect results on four out of five hair samples analyzed" (Gould et al., 2012, p. 17).

What can be done to fix "bad" or "junk" science? While there have been numerous improvements, training and informative expert testimony in the courtrooms are key to meaningful reform efforts. Training police departments and crime analysts on best practices will minimize error. Consider all of the eyewitness reform efforts of late and how much they have improved our criminal justice system. Training defense attorneys and prosecutors is also beneficial because the more that these professionals understand the strengths and limitations of the various sciences, the more likely they will be to critically evaluate the merits of expert testimony. Providing statistics in expert testimony is crucial for juries when they assign weight to the probabilities of subjective analyses. For example, it would have been much more instructive for the FBI agent in Fain's case to cite statistics on the likelihood of Fain's "unusual" hair matching the hairs found at the crime scene (e.g., by giving the percentage of statistical probability when compared to others in the population) rather than providing such vague descriptors as "unusual."

We now have DNA testing to replace some of these "junk" sciences, but DNA testing is expensive and not always available. According to Gould and colleagues (2012), even large departments like the New York City Police Department, which has its own crime lab, uses DNA testing in only 7% of its murder investigations because of the exorbitant costs. Cost concerns have resulted in police turning to DNA testing as a last resort, thereby forcing them to rely on less accurate forms of forensic analysis (Gould et al., 2012). Consider that DNA testing is an option in less than 10% of serious felony cases because most cases do not have testable evidence (Innocence Project, 2015). Unfortunately, many of the older cases (prior to the 2000s) that included collected evidence occurred during a time when most states were not required to keep evidence beyond a defendant's last appeal. This means that many of the defendants whose cases had evidence that would now be eligible for modern DNA testing methods to prove innocence (in mostly rape and murder cases) may never have their day in court. Much like the "dark figure of crime" that we talk about in criminal justice studies, the "dark figure of wrongful convictions" is something we continue to investigate.

Ineffective Defense Counsel

The right to counsel is a key constitutional protection for criminal defendants via the Sixth Amendment. The U.S. Supreme Court has determined that this fundamental right includes more than just the mere assignment of counsel, however. We have the right to effective assistance of counsel and take it from us—there is a difference! A person who has been accused of a crime is not likely to be skilled in the art of law and therefore needs an attorney to defend his or her rights; without such, that person is at risk for unequitable treatment and, in the worst case scenario, wrongful conviction. A Columbia University study that examined death penalty appeals over a 23-year period discovered that ineffective defense attorneys were the "biggest contributing factor to the erroneous conviction or death sentence of criminal defendants in a capital cases" (Gould et al., 2012, p. 20).

The problem of inadequate defense counsel is largely an issue associated with the poor. This is because defendants with lower socioeconomic statuses are assigned court-appointed counsel who typically find themselves overworked, underpaid, and devoid of resources. Approximately 80% of criminal defendants require court-appointed counsel because they cannot afford to hire an attorney (Williams, 2002). In a study looking at indigent criminal defense programs in the largest 100 counties in the United States, it was found that public defenders handled 82% of all criminal cases (Bureau of Justice Statistics, 2000). And in death penalty cases (where one really needs a good attorney), 90% of capital defendants are indigent (Cawley, 2007). A Harris County, Texas, study examined the impact of legal counsel on prosecutors' decisions to seek the death penalty by comparing defendants with privately hired counsel to those with court-appointed counsel ($n = 504$) and found that defendants with court-appointed counsel were significantly more disadvantaged than those able to obtain private counsel. More specifically, the study concluded that defendants who hired counsel were significantly less likely to be sentenced to death (Phillips, 2009).

The issue of poor defendants routinely receiving deficient counsel to represent them is rarely disputed in research (Dripps, 1998; Bright, 1999; Levinson, 2001; Reiman, 2007). The likelihood that a defendant will be assigned inadequate counsel largely depends on the level of training and resources provided to counsel by the state in which the attorney is employed. Levinson compares getting defense counsel for the poor from jurisdictions that do not provide the proper resources as analogous to "getting brain surgery from a podiatrist" (2001, p. 149). The unfortunate reality is that a person who finds himself or herself in the criminal justice system is more likely to obtain qualified and competent defense counsel if he or she has financial resources; if a defendant can afford good counsel, his or her chances of keeping the system "honest" are increased (Reiman, 2007). There are countless examples of defense attorneys who fail to meet minimum standards, such as thoroughly investigating their clients' cases and meeting filing deadlines. More egregious examples of poor representation include instances of attorneys sleeping in court and appearing before the court intoxicated.

One tragic example is that of a death penalty defendant in Alabama. Horace Dunkins was convicted of raping and killing a 26-year-old mother of four. Dunkins's attorney failed to inform the jury that his client had an IQ equivalent to that of a 6-year-old child, though he was well aware of this fact. This omission, along with other mitigating evidence that was not presented, resulted in the jury imposing a death sentence. After Dunkins was executed, members of the jury came forward and asserted that they would not have imposed the death penalty if they had been provided with information on the accused's extremely low IQ (Levinson, 2001). It appears that the shortcomings of Dunkins's attorney may have very well cost Dunkins his life. Another example is a 1995 capital case of a defendant convicted of murder in Texas. It involved a court-appointed defense attorney who slept through the majority of his client's trial and missed entire witness testimonies. When asked why he slept during the court proceedings, the attorney explained that he was bored (Bright, 1999). The trial judge assigned to this case gave the following explanation when attempting to rationalize the attorney's performance, or lack thereof: "The Constitution doesn't say the lawyer has to be awake" (Bright, 1999, p. 26). Perhaps even more bizarre is a case from Idaho, *Charboneau v. Klauser* (1997), involving a defendant who unsuccessfully argued that his attorney's actions resulted in an unfair trial outcome. Charboneau's attorney held a seance by which he reported communicating with Charboneau's murdered ex-wife (*The Federal Reporter*, 1997). As you may have guessed, the jury did not buy the thoughts and version of events attributed to the wife. Charboneau worried that his attorney's actions may have influenced the jury's verdict. Can you blame him?

What can a defendant do when he or she is confronted with issues such as these (or hopefully those less egregious than the ones we mentioned)? Recall that we have a constitutional right to effective counsel. If a defendant receives *ineffective* assistance of counsel (IAC), he or she may file an appeal based on a Sixth Amendment rights violation. The **Strickland standard** is a standard set by the courts to determine whether counsel has been deficient in representing a defendant. This standard resulted from the U.S. Supreme Court decision in *Strickland v. Washington* (1984). The Strickland test requires that two prongs be met in order for an IAC claim to prevail. First, the defendant must demonstrate that counsel's performance was deficient. Deficiency in legal representation is subjective because the courts allow quite a bit of discretion for attorneys and their defense "strategies." Second, the error(s) made by counsel must be prejudicial. This essentially means that the defendant did not receive a fair trial and, but for the errors of his attorney, the trial outcome would have been different. The second prong is the more difficult to meet because the defendant must make a persuasive argument that a jury would not have chosen to convict if the said error(s) had not occurred. Consider the *Charboneau* case. No one would question that Charboneau had a solid argument to satisfy the first prong—the attorney should not have called a seance. It is illogical to conclude that a good defense attorney would summon the dead for interviews. Meeting the second prong would prove much more challenging. Charboneau had to show that no other evidence would have resulted in a guilty verdict if the seance had never happened. In other words, if there was other evidence that the jury relied on when reaching its verdict, then the seance would not have constituted prejudicial error; the jury would have found the defendant guilty regardless of the seance. The courts call this "harmless error."

The *Strickland* decision has been highly criticized for the ambiguity in its language that allows most actions taken (or not taken) to fall within acceptable legal boundaries for defense attorneys. Indeed, none of the case examples just given fully satisfied the Strickland test requirements. It is hard to imagine that a sleeping defense attorney representing a death penalty defendant would not be classified as ineffective counsel (the prosecution must have really had an airtight case!). It makes sense, however, that our courts will not grant new trials to every defendant who argues that his or her attorney erred. Our system simply could not function if this were the case. As a matter of necessity, courts can only grant new trials for those who might actually obtain different outcomes; otherwise, we are wasting our system's already limited and precious resources. There are still many critics, however, who believe the Strickland standard is much too difficult to meet.

Dripps attempts to describe the feeling among defense attorneys regarding the minimal scrutiny for IAC claims: "The test of ineffective assistance of counsel is said to be whether counsel can fog a mirror" (1998, p. 249); if counsel can breathe, he or she is fit to pass the test for effectiveness. Former U.S. Supreme Court Justice Harry Blackmun criticized the standards set forth in *Strickland* in a compelling dissent (to deny certiorari for an IAC case): "My 24 years of overseeing the imposition of the death penalty from this Court have left me in grave doubt whether this reliance is justified and whether the constitutional requirement of competent legal counsel for capital defendants is being fulfilled" (Rigg, 2007, p. 4).

When reviewing defense attorney errors made in DNA exoneration cases, the Innocence Project found other attorney errors that likely would have changed the outcome of the case: failure to investigate a defendant's alibi, failure to call forensic experts when necessary, failure to be present at important court proceedings, and failure to present opening and closing statements at trial, to name a few (Innocence Project, 2015). Perhaps the most salient issues underlying poor representation by defense counsel is lack of resources/funding, "an absence of quality control, and a lack of motivation" (Gould et al., 2012, p. 20). With that said, it appears total structural reform of our public defender system is needed if we hope to reduce the likelihood of wrongful convictions.

Government Misconduct

We contend that prosecutors and police are mostly honest and try their best to get the "bad guys" off the streets in a lawful manner, but this is not always the case. We know from wrongful conviction research that prosecutorial and police misconduct occurs far too often. Some cases involve mere mistakes, but others involve instances of police and prosecutors becoming so intent on securing a conviction that they lose sight of their other duties and, in some cases, go out of their way to sidestep justice.

Police misconduct is closely connected to four of the "Big Six" leading causes of wrongful convictions—*false confessions, snitch testimony, eyewitness error*, and *government misconduct* in general. There is no question that a few "bad apples" can have devastating consequences for our entire justice system. Alton Logan, from Chicago, knows too well the effects of police misconduct. He was awarded $10.25 million from the city of Chicago in 2013 after he spent 26 years in prison for a crime committed by another man. Logan and Edgar Hope were accused of shooting and killing an off-duty police officer at a McDonald's restaurant. Police arrested Logan and Hope after a witness identified them as the shooters. The witness was right about Hope but wrong about Logan. Hope revealed to his defense attorneys that police arrested the wrong accomplice and that he had committed the crime with a man by the name of Andrew Wilson. Indeed, a few days after the murder, Andrew Wilson was charged with murdering two other Chicago police officers in an unrelated case. Hope's attorneys even contacted Wilson's attorneys and told them that Hope had implicated Wilson in the earlier shooting. Wilson's attorneys then confronted Wilson and he admitted to committing the first murder with Hope. Unfortunately, Wilson's attorneys were faced with an ethical dilemma—they could not breach their attorney–client confidentiality agreement by disclosing what Wilson had shared with them. The attorneys chose to write notarized affidavits about their client's confession and safeguard them in a lockbox until their client died. When Wilson passed away in prison in 2007, his attorneys immediately came forward and with their secret and Logan was released from prison (Spielman, 2013). A special investigation into allegations of police misconduct by prosecutors revealed that a police commander was instrumental in cover-ups of other cases, which led to numerous wrongful convictions, not just Logan's. The commander was convicted in 2010 of perjury and obstruction of justice when he lied about his knowledge of the alleged torturing of suspects by other officers for decades. Logan alleges that the commander also knew that when Wilson was arrested for the other police officers' murders, he was in possession of a sawed-off shotgun that had been linked to the crime of which Logan was accused. Furthermore, police knew that witnesses had implicated Wilson, but such information was never disclosed to his defense team. The police commander is currently serving a four-and-a-half-year prison sentence for his actions in this case. To compensate Logan and other victims, the city of Chicago has paid over $56 million in settlement fees.

Although police error and misconduct can have devastating consequences for the wrongfully accused, the ultimate decision to move forward with charging defendants of crimes belongs to prosecutors. Prosecutors are arguably the most powerful actors in our justice system because they alone get to decide if a defendant will be charged with a crime. Bohm notes that prosecutors "are the most powerful people in the capital punishment process. They are the gatekeepers of this process and alone decide whether to charge a suspect with a capital crime. . . . Prosecutors are the first authorities to determine who among those arrested is fit to live and who should die" (Bohm, 2012, p. 226).

Given this immense amount of power that prosecutors hold, it would seem logical that strong checks and balances exist to ensure that these individuals act with integrity and in accordance with the rule of law. Sadly, this is not always the case, as evidenced by numerous exonerations. In one study of 88 post-*Furman* death penalty exoneration cases, prosecutorial misconduct was found to be at issue in 31% of the cases. More specifically, approximately half of the cases of prosecutorial misconduct involved the withholding of exculpatory evidence; other cases involved perjury and the improper use of evidence (Bohm, 2012). **Exculpatory evidence** is evidence that is favorable to the accused (or has potential to be) and must be presented to the defense by the prosecutor. In some cases, the exculpatory evidence may be powerful enough to clear a defendant. Prosecutors are bound by law to disclose all exculpatory evidence (*Brady v. Maryland*, 1963). In a report on Illinois death penalty cases, it was found that prosecutorial misconduct was the cause for 21% of reversal cases. In another study of Ohio death penalty cases, it was discovered that 14 of 48 capital cases involved ethical violations by prosecutors (Johns, 2005).

Despite clear evidence of prosecutorial misconduct in wrongful conviction cases, prosecutors are rarely held accountable for their involvement in unethical behavior(s) (Johns, 2005). In a study reviewing 381 murder convictions that were reversed due to police or prosecutorial misconduct, not a single prosecutor was held criminally responsible or disbarred for his or her conduct, even in cases where it was discovered that a prosecutor deliberately withheld evidence of innocence (Bohm, 2012).

How can a prosecutor break the law and not be held accountable for his or her actions (or inactions)? Prosecutors enjoy the protection of **absolute** and **qualified immunity**. The type of immunity to be applied in each case depends on which capacity the prosecutor was acting in when the misconduct was alleged. If the prosecutor is acting as an advocate, then he or she is granted complete immunity (no criminal charges may be filed) from criminal charges, even when there is proof that the prosecutor has acted "intentionally, in bad faith, and with malice" (Johns, 2005, p. 54). In cases where prosecutors act in investigative or administrative roles, their conduct falls under qualified immunity review. This means that if their actions rise to a level that clearly violates the law, then they may not be protected by immunity and, therefore, may be criminally liable if it can be shown that they *should* have known their actions were not lawful. Johns (2005) opines that "absolute prosecutorial immunity should be reconsidered. . . . The supposed checks on prosecutorial misconduct fail to deter or punish misconduct or to protect the wrongfully accused" (p. 149).

POST-EXONERATION COMPENSATION

We have learned how it is possible for wrongful convictions to occur, but what happens after exoneration? Just because someone has received legal acknowledgment of innocence does not mean that individual's struggles have ended. Exonerees are not immune from the significant disadvantages that guilty offenders experience upon release (joblessness, housing problems, lack of education, need for drug and/or mental health treatment, etc.). Charles Fain (see this chapter's Perspective feature) was released from death row with nothing more than some clothing, a bus ticket, and his prison identification card; the state of Idaho does not have compensation statutes for the wrongfully convicted. Fain recalls wanting to fly to visit his family in another state upon his release, but having only his prison ID card, which read "Death Row Inmate." (He figured that it would be best to hitch a ride to see his family rather than attempt to board an airplane with that ID.)

How can states begin to reconcile the damage that has been done to those who have suffered years of wrongful incarceration? Post-exoneration compensation is one approach offered by some states to help relieve the burdens of wrongful conviction. Twenty-seven states, the District of Columbia, and the federal government have statutes to compensate these individuals (Mandery et al., 2013). Most compensation states have statutes that take into account the amount of time that the wrongfully accused served when calculating the monetary amount to offer, but few provide additional compensation for those who spent time on death row. The federal government, however, pays $50,000 per

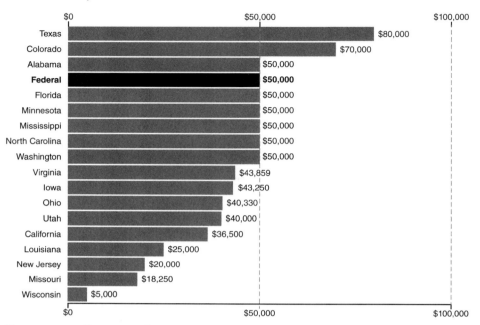

FIGURE 10.5   Exonoree Compensation
Source: The Innocence Project

year for a "normal" year in prison and an additional $50,000 per year for time spent on death row. Figure 10.5 shows compensation amounts for states that pay a set amount for each year a person is wrongfully convicted. Not all states have the ability to pay exonerees (sometimes millions of dollars), which results in lawsuits that can drag on for years. The state of Connecticut cleverly awarded compensation to one man, who spent 18 years in prison for a rape that he did not commit, with money from an unclaimed lottery ticket (Poitras, 2007).

The unfortunate reality is that many exonerees are at great risk for offending after their release from prison. Mandery et al. (2013) conducted a study of 118 exonerees and tracked their postrelease status. They discovered that those who were awarded more than $500,000 "commit offenses at a significantly lower rate" than those who were compensated less or not at all (Mandery et al., 2013, p. 553). Consider that while these men and women were locked away in prison, their family and friends moved on with their lives and built futures for themselves. When the exonerees leave prison, they basically have to start over; many of them are older and lack the skills needed to secure meaningful jobs. Postrelease compensation is, therefore, critical to the successful reintegration of these individuals back into society.

Of course, it would be ideal to avoid wrongful convictions altogether in our system, and changes have been proposed and implemented to reduce the likelihood of these occurrences. One such recommendation is for each state to form an investigative commission tasked with implementing improvements in each of the "Big Six" areas: making recommendations and overseeing the use of evidence-based practices to reduce instances of wrongful convictions. To date, eleven states have formed such commissions. For example, the state of North Carolina has created its own innocence commission, the North Carolina Actual Innocence Commission, at the direction of the chief justice of its state supreme court. The commission's work has been effective and deemed a national model for reform (Innocence Project, 2015).

SUMMARY

It would be unrealistic to believe that we can avoid all error in our criminal justice system, but there is always room for improvement. The only sure way to avoid executing an innocent person is to eliminate the death penalty entirely, and it does not appear that we are quite ready to do that (see Chapter 5 on public opinion), though some indications suggest that the Innocence Movement could be the catalyst for abolition in the future.

In this chapter, we have discussed the major factors that lead to wrongful convictions, along with the proposed reform efforts in each area, and exoneree compensation. But there are many other consequences for our criminal justice system when we calculate the damages associated with wrongful convictions, beyond the problem of innocents serving prison time for crimes that they did not commit. The costs resulting from miscarriages of justice can be astronomical when we consider exoneree compensation and the money spent to retry cases, which is an extremely costly process, especially when the death penalty is involved (see Chapter 11 on costs).

DISCUSSION QUESTIONS

1. In your opinion, which of Packer's models of criminal justice processes better supports the goals of justice? Explain your choice.
2. What do you think about the Blackstone ratio? Is a system that allows ten guilty people to go free in order to avoid one innocent person being convicted a good one? Explain your response.
3. Which of the "Big Six" errors do you believe is the most egregious? Explain your answer.
4. Do you believe that the Strickland standard is sufficient for judging whether a defense attorney is "effective"? If not, what suggestions do you have for improvement?

5. Do you think that prosecutors and other government officials should be allowed to act with absolute immunity? Explain your answer.
6. Would you allow snitch testimony in death penalty cases if you were a judge?
7. Do you believe that states should compensate the wrongfully convicted? If so, what do you think is a fair amount? How would you calculate the amount?

GLOSSARY

Absolute immunity: Immunity that protects prosecutors from criminal liability if they are accused of misconduct while acting in an advocacy role.

Blackstone ratio: Sir William Blackstone's proposition that the error ratio of false acquittals to wrongful convictions ought to be high (10 to 1) in order to achieve a just system that protects the innocent.

Compliant confessions: Confessions that are prompted by highly stressful or coercive police interrogations.

Crime control model: Herbert Packer's model of justice that seeks to repress crime by prioritizing the swift handling of factually guilty defendants with as few obstacles as possible. This model is likened to an assembly line/conveyor belt because of the ease with which offenders are processed through the system.

Double-blind lineup: This procedure involves a "blind" administration by which neither the witness nor lineup administrators know if a suspect is in the lineup.

Due process model: Herbert Packer's model of justice that assumes the most critical function of the criminal justice system is to protect defendants' civil liberties by providing due process under the law. This model is often referred to as an obstacle course because of the procedural safeguards that are present at nearly every level of the criminal justice process in order to protect all defendants whether factually innocent or guilty.

Estimator variables: Variables that occur outside of the investigative process having to do with the circumstances surrounding the offense and witnesses' observations. Such variables include environmental variables like lighting, proximity of a witness to the crime, weather, and other like variables.

Exculpatory evidence: Evidence that is favorable for the accused (or has the potential to be) and must be presented to the defense by the prosecutor. In some cases, this type of evidence may be powerful enough to clear a defendant's guilt.

Innocence Movement: The period categorized by the majority of DNA exonerations due to advances in technology (late 1990s to current).

Internalized confessions: Confessions that occur when a vulnerable suspect admits to a crime that he or she did not commit and becomes convinced he or she actually committed the crime.

Qualified immunity: A form of limited immunity that allows prosecutors to be prosecuted for misconduct if they acted unlawfully and played an investigative or administrative role in a case.

Reid technique: An interrogation technique commonly utilized by police when interviewing suspects that involves the use of intensive tactics.

Strickland standard: The two-pronged standard set forth in the U.S. Supreme Court case of *Strickland v. Washington* (1984) that is used by the courts to determine whether defense counsel has been deficient in its representation of a client.

System variables: Variables that are linked to the investigative phase and its impact on a witness's memory. These variables include improper lineups and suggestive interview techniques.

Voluntary confessions: Confessions that are provided by people without prompting by police, sometimes driven by a pathological desire to seek attention or delusional guilt.

REFERENCES

Allen, R., and L. Laudan. (2013). "Deadly Dilemmas." University of Texas Law, Public Law Research Paper No. 141. http://papers.ssrn.com/sol3/papers.cfm?abstract_id=1150931. Public Law Research Paper No. 141, University of Texas Law School.

Amnesty International. (2012). "Death Penalty Facts." http://www.amnestyusa.org/pdfs/DeathPenaltyFactsMay2012.pdf.

Associated Press. (2008). "Albuquerque Police Want Ad: We Need Snitches." http://www.nbcnews.com/id/27859436/.

Bentham, J. (1829). *Principles of judicial procedure, with the outlines of a procedure code.* London, England: Edinburgh.

Bloom, R. (2002). *Ratting: The use and abuse of informants in the American justice system.* Westport, CT: Praeger.

Bohm, R. (2012). *Deathquest: An introduction to the theory and practice of capital punishment in the United States.* Boston: Anderson.

Bond-Fraser, L., I. Fraser, and E. Ready. (2012, Fall). To legislate or not to legislate: Encouraging the law to recognise advances in the science of eyewitness testimony. *Perspectives 15,* 3–15.

Brady v. Maryland. (1963). 373 U.S. 83.

Bright, S. (1999). Neither equal nor just: The rationing and denial of legal services to the poor when life and liberty are at stake. *New York University of School of Law Annual Survey of American Law, 1997,* 1–53.

Bureau of Justice Statistics. (2000). "Indigent Defense Services in Large Counties, 1999." http://www.bjs.gov/content/pub/pdf/idslc99.pdf

Carriger v. Stewart. (1997). 132 F.3d 463.

Cawley, W. (2007). Raising the bar: How *Rompilla v. Beard* represents the Court's increasing efforts to impose stricter standards for defense lawyering in capital cases. *Pepperdine Law Review, 34*(4), 1–15.

Center on Wrongful Convictions. (2005). "The Snitch System: How Snitch Testimony Sent Randy Steidl and Other Innocent Americans to Death Row, a Center on Wrongful Convictions Survey." http://www.innocenceproject.org/docs/SnitchSystemBooklet.pdf.

Dripps, D. (1998). Ineffective assistance of counsel: The case for an ex ante parity standard. *Journal of Criminal Law and Criminology, 88*(1), 242–302.

The Federal Reporter. (1997). *Charboneau v. Klauser, 107F.3d15.* http://bulk.resource.org/courts.gov/c/F3/107/107.F3d.15.95-35277.html.

Gould, J., J. Carrano, R. Leo, and J. Young. (2012). Predicting erroneous convictions: A social science approach to miscarriages of justice. National Institute of Justice. https://www.ncjrs.gov/pdffiles1/nij/grants/241389.pdf.

Gross, S., K. Jacoby, D. Matheson, N. Montgomery, and S. Patil. (2005). Exonerations in the United States 1989–2003. *Journal of Criminal Law and Criminology, 95*(2), 523–560.

Innocence Project. (2015). The Cases: DNA Exoneree profiles. http://www.innocenceproject.org/cases-false-imprisonment

Hunt, S. (2011). The admissibility of eyewitness-identification expert testimony in Oklahoma. *Oklahoma Law Review, 63,* 511–551.

Johns, M. (2005). Reconsidering absolute prosecutorial immunity. *Brigham Young University Law Review,* 2005(1), 53–149.

Kansas v. Marsh. (2006). 548 U.S. 163.

Kassin, S. (2008). False confessions: Causes, consequences, and implications for reform. *Association for Psychological Science, 17*(4), 249–253.

Kostelnik, J., and N. Reppuci. (2009). Reid training and sensitivity to developmental maturity in interrogation: Results from a national survey of police. *Behavioral Science and the Law, 27,* 361–379.

Laufer, W. (1995). The rhetoric of innocence. *Washington Law Review, 70*(17), 487–530.

Leo, R., and R. Ofshe. (1998). The consequences of false confessions: Deprivations of liberty and miscarriages of justice in the age of psychological interrogation. *Journal of Criminal Law and Criminology, 86*(2), 429–496.

Levinson, J. (2001). Don't let sleeping lawyers lie: Raising the standard for effective assistance of counsel. *American Criminal Law Review, 38*(1), 147–178.

Loftus, E. F. (1979). *Eyewitness testimony.* Cambridge, MA: Harvard University Press.

Mandery, E., A. Shlosberg, V. West, and B. Callaghan. (2013). Criminology: Compensation statutes and post-exoneration offending. *Journal of Criminal Law and Criminology, 103*(2), 553–584.

Manson v. Brathwaite. (1977). 432 U.S. 98.

Munsterberg, H. (1908). *On the witness stand: Essays on psychology and crime*. New York: Doubleday.

National Registry of Exonerations. (2015). http://www.law.umich.edu/special/exoneration/Pages/about.aspx.

New Jersey Courts. (2012). "Supreme Court Releases Eyewitness Identification Criteria for Criminal Cases." http://www.judiciary.state.nj.us/pressrel/2012/pr120719a.htm.

New York Times. (2003, January 12). "Citing Issues of Fairness, Governor Clears Out Death Row in Illinois." http://www.nytimes.com/2003/01/12/us/citing-issue-of-fairness-governor-clears-out-death-row-in-illinois.html.

New York Times. (2006, August 30). "Reflection and Red Faces after the Ramsey Storm." http://www.nytimes.com/2006/08/30/arts/television/30media.html?ref=johnmarkkarr.

New York Times. (2011, September 20). "A Grievous Wrong." http://www.nytimes.com/2011/09/21/opinion/a-grievous-wrong-on-georgias-death-row.html. Packer, H. (1968). *The limits of criminal sanction*. Stanford, CA: Stanford University Press.

Phillips, S. (2009). Legal disparities in the capital of capital punishment. *Journal of Criminal Law and Criminology, 99*(3), 717–755.

Poitras, C. (2007, May 16). "Another Plan Emerges to Compensate Man." http://articles.courant.com/2007-05-16/news/0705160949_1_mr-tillman-rival-bill-james-c-tillman.

Porter, N. (2009). "The State of Sentencing 2009: Developments in Policy and Practice." http://www.capps-mi.org/pdfdocs/State%20of%20Sentencing%202009.pdf.

Reiman, J. (2007). *The rich get richer and the poor get prison*, 8th ed. Boston: Pearson.

Rigg, R. (2007). The T-rex without teeth: Evolving *Strickland v. Washington* and the test for ineffective assistance of counsel. *Pepperdine Law Review, 35*(1), 77–106.

Severson, K. (2011, September 21). "Davis Is Executed in Georgia." *New York Times*. http://www.nytimes.com/2011/09/22/us/final-pleas-and-vigils-in-troy-davis-execution.html?pagewanted=all.

Spielman, F. (2013). "Chicago to Pay $10.25 Million in Another Burge Case." http://www.suntimes.com/news/metro/17576309-418/city-to-pay-1025-million-in-another-burge-case.html.

Steblay, N., J. Dysart, S. Fulero, and R. Lindsay. (2001). Eyewitness accuracy rates in sequential and simultaneous line-up presentations: a meta-analytic comparison. *Law and Human Behavior, 25*(5), 459–473.

Strickland v. Washington. (1984). 466 U.S. 668.

Watkins v. Sowders. (1981). 449 U.S. 341, 352.

Wells, G. (1978). Applied eyewitness-testimony research: system variables and estimator variables. *Journal of Personality and Social Psychology, 36*(12), 1546–1557.

Wells, G. (1993). What do we know about eyewitness identification? *American Psychologist, 48*(5), 553–571.
Wells, G., and R. Lindsay. (1985). Methodological notes on the accuracy-confidence relation in eyewitness identifications. *Journal of Applied Psychology, 70*(2), 413–419.
Williams, M. (2002). A comparison of sentencing outcomes for defendants with public defenders versus retained counsel in a Florida circuit court. *Justice System Journal, 23*(2), 249–257.
Zalman, M., B. Smith, and A. Kiger. (2008). Officials' estimates of the incidence of "actual innocence" convictions. *Justice Quarterly, 25,* 72–100.

CHAPTER 11

THE FINANCIAL BURDEN OF THE DEATH PENALTY AND OTHER COLLATERAL COSTS

The case of serial killer Charles Chi-Tat Ng is unique in at least three ways. First, he is the only known Asian American serial killer of the twentieth century; second, he and his partner, Leonard Lake, were one of the few documented serial killing teams in history; and third, his death penalty prosecution was the costliest state capital prosecution in U.S. history, costing the taxpayers of the state of California almost $11 million.

Ng was born in 1960 to wealthy Chinese parents in Hong Kong, but his entire childhood was troubled by antisocial behavior, particularly stealing. He was expelled from a number of schools, including a boarding school in England, for stealing. He immigrated to the United States and joined the U.S. Marines, but shortly thereafter he was charged with stealing machine guns and desertion and served three years in the brig. Ng moved in with Lake, another ex-Marine, after being dishonorably discharged, and the two began a campaign of kidnapping, rape, torture, and murder of as many as 25 victims.

The pair's orgy of murder ceased when Ng's compulsive stealing saw him arrested in 1985 for shoplifting. Through a series of events, Ng's arrest eventually led to the arrest of Lake (who committed suicide). Meanwhile, Ng fled to Canada, where his stealing once again led to his downfall after he was arrested for shoplifting and wounding a security guard, and subsequently sentenced to prison. While in Canadian custody, the state of California embarked on a legal battle to extradite Ng to the United States. Canadian authorities argued that it would be in breach of Ng's human rights to send him back to the United States only to face the death penalty, and refused to do so. Ng finally lost the battle, and in 1991 he was shipped across the border. He was convicted in 1999 of the murders of six men, three women, and two infants and sentenced to death. As of October 2014, he is still on San Quentin's death row.

Ng's is a "classic" death penalty case. His murders were horribly cruel, heartless, and remorseless. His guilt was never in doubt; he has never attempted to deny any of the murders he committed, and has even boasted about them. Having been returned to American custody in 1991 and convicted of almost a dozen murders in 1999, why is he still alive after California paid close to $11 million to see him executed? Many believe that we should not execute him or anyone else regardless of the heinousness of their crimes; others believe that execution is the only response to such evil, but may nevertheless object to the death penalty for financial reasons.

LEARNING OBJECTIVES

- Understand the extensive costs of the death penalty and why they exist.
- Compare and contrast these costs with the costs associated with life without parole (LWOP).
- Know why the costs of the death penalty are less in Texas than in California.
- Understand the promises of the Antiterrorism and Effective Death Penalty Act (AEDPA) and why they have not been realized.
- Appreciate why it is important to hear the voices of victims' and defendants' families, as well as the voices of the condemned.

DEATH PENALTY: A YELLOW BRICK ROAD

The financial and other costs of the death penalty are a rare consideration in the debate about capital punishment. These very concrete costs tend to take a back seat to such debating points as deterrence, retribution, innocence, justice, and a variety of legal and moral issues. When the cost argument does come up among laypersons, we frequently hear statements that go something like this: "Why should the taxpayer board and feed these evil creatures for life—just execute them and be done with it and save your tears for their victims and their victims' families." However, the reality is that the cost of a capital case from arrest to execution far exceeds the cost of pursuing a life without the possibility of parole (LWOP) sentence in the same case, even if the inmate spends 50 years in prison. We will see in this chapter that the costs of pursuing the death penalty rather than LWOP are many times greater, add much more time to the process, and prolong the suffering of the families of victims who look to execution for some closure. Like the yellow brick road in *The Wizard of Oz*, the death penalty is a very expensive road that rarely takes a state that practices it to the intended destination.

The Ng case presented in the opening vignette aptly demonstrates that the ladder from crime to the gallows is costly, very tall (often taking years to climb), and ever-expanding. In pre-*Furman* days, the ladder was cheap, short, and swiftly climbed. A case in point was that of a Florida man, Walter "Doc" Williams, an African American who was arrested for raping a white woman 12 days after the crime and executed just 33 days later on October 8, 1934. The story of his execution warranted only 98 words in the *Bradford County Telegraph*, which reported Williams's final remarks: "I only ask the Lord to have mercy on my soul." The total cost to Florida for the 33 days from arrest to execution was roughly estimated at around $4,000, or $71,037 in 2014 dollars according to the U.S. Treasury Department's inflation calculator. We estimated the cost of Williams's execution based on the costs of incarceration per day, the salaries of the judge and the prosecution for the one-day trial (there's no indication that he had a defense lawyer since this was long before the state was required to provide one), the salaries of guards, and the costs of electrocution based on today's estimates. Such swift "justice" was not at all uncommon in those days and was unceremoniously carried out in a manner much like the old Wild West's "frontier justice."

What has led to the situation in which we have gone from 33 days from arrest to execution at a cost of about $71,000, as in the Williams case, to 24 years and counting for Ng's case to be finally resolved, and at a cost of approximately $11 million? We saw in Chapter 3 that the *Furman* and *Gregg* decisions resulted in the dramatic expansion of due process in capital cases because of the Supreme Court's "death is different" principle. Rapid frontier no-frills justice has evolved into today's "super due process" justice. Super due process has resulted in so many hoops for states to jump through and so many loopholes for defendants to wiggle through that the death penalty in the United States has become an inordinately expensive "super farce." Before we examine the particulars that led to this situation, we want to examine a very important federal case that was supposed to lead to reforms resulting in "a more efficient death penalty"—the Timothy McVeigh case.

THE TIMOTHY MCVEIGH FEDERAL MURDER TRIAL

Although Ng's battle against extradition from Canada and the cost of his trial and appeals made his the costliest state death penalty case in U.S. history, the trial of Timothy McVeigh in federal court was even more costly. On April 19,

1995, McVeigh detonated a massive bomb that destroyed the Alfred P. Murrah Federal Building in Oklahoma City, killing 168 people and injuring 680 others. McVeigh was arrested just 90 minutes after the explosion by an Oklahoma state trooper, who stopped him for driving without a license plate, and discovered that McVeigh was carrying an unlawful weapon. Forensic evidence subsequently linked McVeigh to the bombing of the federal building.

Timothy McVeigh never really denied his guilt. He wanted a trial so that his attorneys could present a "necessity defense," which would give him a soapbox to air his grievances against the federal government before the jury and before the rest of the world. McVeigh believed he might convince at least some members of the jury that the bombing was designed to deter further government crimes, and thus was justifiable. The government "crimes" McVeigh was particularly upset about were federal actions taken at Ruby Ridge, Idaho, and Waco, Texas. Both had resulted in the deaths of people who were antigovernment like himself. McVeigh's attorneys, however, decided against a necessity defense since this would require them to prove that the government had placed McVeigh in imminent danger, and they knew that such a circumstance could not be shown. Instead, his lawyers decided on a strategy that would paint him as a "designated patsy" (someone who takes the blame for others) in a larger conspiracy since the bombing was far too complex an operation for McVeigh to have conceived and carried out alone.

Jury selection in the McVeigh case began on March 31, 1997, and after three weeks, a seven-man, five-woman jury was chosen. Over the course of the trial, the prosecution presented 137 witnesses and the defense 25, although they could not come up with a single alibi witness and knew their case would be impossible to win. The jury took twenty-three hours to deliberate and returned a verdict of guilty on eleven counts of murder. The jury deliberated for an additional two days on the penalty phase and came back with a sentence of death, which was duly imposed on June 13, 1997 (Jones, 2001). McVeigh was executed on June 11, 2001, in the federal prison in Terre Haute, Indiana, just two days shy of four years after being sentenced. His execution was the first carried out by the federal government since Victor Feguer had been hung for kidnapping in 1963.

The McVeigh trial cost U.S. taxpayers $13.8 million, including $6.7 million for 19 lawyers, $3 million for defense experts, $1.5 million for support staff for the attorneys, $1.5 million for housing and security, almost $2 million for investigators, and $541,885 in travel expenses (Jones, 2001). Court personnel, lawyers, expert witnesses, investigators, and hoteliers made a pretty penny on McVeigh's horrible crime, and on top of all the human suffering and the hundreds of millions of dollars in damage caused by the bombing, the American taxpayer forked out nearly $14 million to safeguard his rights. This case gave major impetus for congressional legislation called the Antiterrorism and Effective Death Penalty Act (AEDPA) that was supposed to make the death penalty more rapid and efficient and less costly. We will explore the AEDPA more thoroughly later in this chapter.

THE FINANCIAL BURDEN OF THE DEATH PENALTY

Examining the financial costs of the death penalty is difficult because there are no standardized data across states to make comparisons. Thus, our examination will concentrate on the state with both the largest population and the largest number of convicts on death row: California. We will contrast California primarily with Texas since California and Texas are arguably at the extremes among death penalty states. According to Price and Byrd, while the liberal state of "California reluctantly executes capital punishment," the conservative state of "Texas rigorously implements the death penalty" (2008, p. 207). Moreover, Texas state courts enjoy support from the more conservative 5th Federal Circuit Court than California state courts do from the liberal 9th Federal Circuit Court, although the 9th Circuit has been less hasty to override "the will of the people" since Chief Justice Rose Bird and two other justices were voted out of office in 1986 for overturning 90% of California's death sentences (see Chapter 5). Texas also has a court of criminal appeals that hears *only* criminal appeals, so cases move much faster there. Additionally, the 5th Circuit is not as overburdened with cases in general (not just death penalty cases) as the 9th Circuit, where a case may take years to make its way through the appeals process (Spohn & Hemmens, 2012).

Both of these states have very large death rows and sentence numerous murderers to death each year, but Texas typically executes more people each year than California has in total since 1992 (Price & Byrd, 2008). According to the Death Penalty Information Center (DPIC) (2014), California has the largest death row with 743 inmates, Florida is second with 404, and Texas is third with 276. Texas has always had a death penalty, but California reintroduced it by popular demand after a 25-year moratorium in 1992 (Price & Byrd, 2008). Lieberman (2000) conservatively estimated the cost per execution in 1985 dollars to be $2.3 million in Texas ($5.08 million in 2014 dollars) and $5 million in California ($11.05 million in 2014 dollars). Much of the cost difference results from the speedier and more efficient processing of death penalty cases in Texas.

THE FINANCIAL COST OF COURT PROCEEDINGS: DEATH PENALTY VERSUS LWOP

As shown in Figure 11.1, according to DPIC, the overall cost of the death penalty in California has been over $4 billion since 1978. As you can see in the chart, most of these costs are accounted for in the pretrial and trial phases.

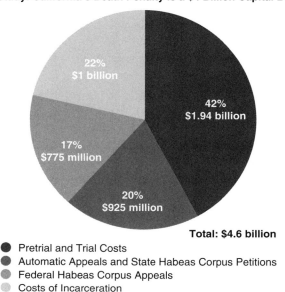

FIGURE 11.1   Cost of California's Death Penalty, 1978–2011
Source: Death Penalty Information Center (2011) http://www.deathpenaltyinfo.org/california-cost-study-2011

We previously learned that Charles Ng's prosecution cost California taxpayers nearly $11 million in the pursuit of the death penalty. Had California alternatively sought LWOP, Canada would have extradited Ng without multiple legal suits and the legal costs incurred at all stages of the prosecution would have been much less. Despite all these costs, Ng's execution will probably never happen.

In a historic and sweeping capital punishment ruling, Federal District Court Judge Cormac Carney (a George W. Bush appointee) vacated the death sentences of Ernest Jones and 747 other California death row inmates. Jones was convicted of raping and killing his girlfriend's mother, Julia Miller, in 1992 (*Jones v. Chappell*, 2014). In his ruling, Justice Carney noted that of the 900 people who were sentenced to death in California since the reinstitution of the death penalty in 1976, only 13 people (or 1.4%) had actually been executed, the last one in 2006. If we break down the $4 billion per execution during that time period, California's taxpayers would have doled out approximately $308 million for each execution. Judge Carney stated in his opinion:

> Inordinate and unpredictable delay has resulted in a death penalty system in which very few of the hundreds of individuals

sentenced to death have been, or even will be, executed by the State. It has resulted in a system in which arbitrary factors, rather than legitimate ones determine whether an individual will actually be executed. And it has resulted in a system that serves no penological purpose.

In effect, Judge Carney ruled that the very delays caused by the system for the defendant's benefit create uncertainty in the mind of the defendant as to when (or whether) he or she will actually be executed. The assertion was that systemic delay creates an uncertainty that constitutes cruel and unusual punishment. Furthermore, even if a person convicted of a capital crime is executed, it will occur so long after the crime that it serves neither retributive nor deterrent purposes. Carney's ruling is not the last word because his ruling can be appealed to the U.S. 9th Circuit Court of Appeals and, if upheld there, to the U.S. Supreme Court.

If the issue does go to the Supreme Court, it is worth noting that in 2006 the Court denied *certiorari* (meaning that the Court declined to hear the case and thus left the ruling of the lower court in place) in *Allen v. Ornoski* (2006), which was also a California case. It involved the appeal of Clarence Ray Allen, who had been on death row for 23 years at the time (two years longer than Ernest Jones) for organizing the murder of three fellow inmates in California's Folsom Prison while serving a life sentence with the possibility of parole for the 1974 murder of Mary Sue Kitts, his son's girlfriend. Because of the Supreme Court's denial of *certiorari* in this case raising the same issue, it is possible that Judge Carney's ruling will be overturned. Only time will tell. Allen was executed on January 17, 2006, at the age of 76, becoming the second-oldest inmate to be executed in the United States since 1976. The oldest person executed (after 19 years on death row) since the death penalty was reinstated in 1976 was John Nixon, executed in Mississippi in 2005 at the age of 77 for the murder-for-hire of Virginia Tucker in 1985 (Maningo, 2014).

If the voters of California continue to want the death penalty, they need to be aware of its costs and what else can be done with that money if LWOP is substituted. According to Alarcon and Mitchell,

> Recent studies reveal that if the current system is maintained, Californians will spend an additional $5 billion to $7 billion over the cost of LWOP to fund the broken system between now and 2050. In that time, roughly 740 more inmates will be added to death row, an additional fourteen executions will be carried out, and more than five hundred death-row inmates will die of old age or other causes before the state executes them. (2002, p. S1)

The DPIC (2011) cites a 2011 California study showing that if the sentences of all prisoners on California's death rows were commuted to life without parole, a savings of $130 million per year would result. The American Civil Liberties Union (ACLU) (2012) also provides some shocking information about the financial costs of pursuing the death penalty in California. The ACLU reports that there was a $1.1 million difference between the least expensive death penalty prosecution and trial (*People v. Saurez*), which cost $1.8 million, and the most expensive non–death penalty murder prosecution and trial (*People v. Franklin*), which cost $661,000.

Given such costs and assuming that the public is made aware of them, why do death penalty states continue to invest so many taxpayer dollars in such a poor proposition? Professor Frank Zimring's answer to this question is: "What we are paying for at such great cost is essentially our own ambivalence about capital punishment. We try to maintain the apparatus of state killing and another apparatus that almost guarantees that it won't happen. The public pays for both sides" (cited in Tempest, 2005, p. B1). The money spent pursuing or chasing something perhaps we don't really want to catch would be better allocated to other criminal justice practices designed to protect the public from the activities of criminals. Think of how many public safety employees California could hire with the money it spends pursuing a goal it knows will be thwarted in all but the tiniest fraction of instances.

Although it is indisputable that the costs associated with the "upfront" prosecution of capital cases are far higher than in LWOP cases, some believe that the overall cost savings are inflated. LWOP costs after prosecution are much higher than they are for other inmates for a number of reasons. Costs per year of incarceration are typically calculated by dividing the total costs of running the prison system by the number of inmates regardless of the length of their individual sentences or security level. But because of their status, LWOP inmates are housed in more secure areas, significantly increasing security costs. Furthermore, while most inmates are young and will be released while still relatively young, LWOP inmates are in prison for life and will incur the health problems and attendant costs that all aging citizens incur. As Reams and Putnam explain: "Prisoners who are serving LWOP have much higher total costs, such as medical costs associated with geriatric care, medical care for chronic health issues and 'end of life' care" (2011, p. 22). Of course, death row inmates also require housing in more secure units, and given the length of time spent on death row and the greater likelihood of them dying of old age rather than execution, they incur the same housing and care costs.

Chapter 11 THE FINANCIAL BURDEN OF THE DEATH PENALTY

COURT COSTS

One of the biggest differences in expenses between a death penalty trial and one in which the prosecutor seeks LWOP involves the number of court days. After the preliminary hearing is held to determine if sufficient evidence exists to charge the defendant, court proceedings begin with a series of pretrial hearings. These hearings consist of motions filed by prosecutors and defense lawyers for argument before a judge and are the tools that set boundaries for the trial (what can or cannot be said, done, or introduced) before it even takes place. For example, the defense may file a motion arguing that certain evidence should be excluded, that the defendant is not mentally competent to stand trial, that certain individuals should not be allowed to testify, or that the case should be dismissed. In a case where the prosecutor is asking for the death penalty, it is estimated that pretrial hearings take, on average, 85.2 days of court time versus 14 days for an LWOP trial (Marceau & Whitson, 2013).

The next stage is jury selection or the *voir dire* process. The French verbs *voir* and *dire* mean "to see" and "to say," respectively, and taken together essentially mean that jurors should "speak the truth" when asked questions by the prosecution or defense teams. Theoretically, the *voir dire* exists to empanel an impartial jury, but in reality both sides are looking for a jury likely to favor their side. This is why what seems like the simple task of picking 12 people out of a jury pool can take such a long time. The estimated average number of days required to pick a jury in a capital case is 26 versus 1.5 in an LWOP case (Marceau & Whitson, 2013). This is because of the extensive vetting of jurors, and may even include hiring jury consultants, who are typically behavioral scientists with expertise in picking the "right" jurors for the desired outcome and in developing trial strategies designed to shape juror perceptions, leading to a favorable verdict for their clients.

Having chosen a jury, the next step is the trial itself. The average time for a death penalty trial is 19 days versus 8.2 for an LWOP trial, and for the sentencing phase, it is 21 days in a capital case and 0.78 days in an LWOP case. Adding all these stages together, the estimated average number of court days taken by a death penalty trial is 147.6 days (that's nearly 5 months) versus 24.48 days for an average LWOP trial (Marceau & Whitson, 2013).

While all of these court proceedings take place, additional costs are being incurred in further investigating the alleged crime in preparation for the trial or for post-trial appeals if the original trial has already occurred. The investigation of murders, particularly the kind of murders that render the perpetrator eligible for the death penalty, can take as long as the case is

PERSPECTIVE FROM A POLICE CHIEF: JAMES P. ABBOTT

FIGURE 11.2   Police Chief James P. Abbott

Police Chief James P. Abbott has worked in law enforcement for the city of West Orange, New Jersey (located approximately 15 miles from Manhattan), for nearly 35 years. He obtained his bachelor's degree from Kean University and a master's degree from Seton Hall University. The West Orange Police Department is internationally accredited through the Commission on Accreditation for Law Enforcement Agencies (CALEA) and is considered a flagship agency that utilizes best practices. In 2006, Chief Abbott was appointed to serve on a special committee tasked with studying capital punishment in New Jersey, which ultimately resulted in the state abolishing the death penalty.

In 2007, New Jersey's legislature and governor replaced the death penalty with a sentence of life in prison without parole. The measure has been hailed as a historic moment across the country. I guess that makes sense, because no state had legislatively abolished its death penalty in more than 50 years. As a police chief and proud Republican who had long supported the death penalty, I was asked to serve on the capital punishment committee, in part to ensure its balance. We had a variety of members which included a reverend, prosecutors, judges, defense attorneys, and representatives of crime victims.

It was clear that the capital punishment system was broken; some people wanted to fix it, while others wanted to abolish it. I never imagined that I would find myself siding with the latter group after listening to testimony from a variety of experts on the subject. I have dedicated my life to protecting the public and making our streets safer. Believe me, sympathy for killers is nowhere in my vocabulary. In fact, if we had to vote to keep or abolish the death penalty on the first day of our committee meeting, I would have voted to keep it. But that is not what happened. What I learned in the following year shocked me.

Chapter 11 THE FINANCIAL BURDEN OF THE DEATH PENALTY

While there are a number of valid considerations for abolishing the death penalty, two struck me as particularly important. First is the issue of cost. Financially, the death penalty is a drain on our system. There is no doubt that it is more costly than life without parole, yet many people still believe that it is less expensive. I learned that the death penalty throws millions of dollars down the drain. In New Jersey, we spent $250 million on the death penalty over a 25-year period and we never even used it! It just does not make sense to use such a practice when budgets are tight and resources are scarce. That money could have been used to provide victims with crucial services to help them heal, or funding law enforcement and preventing crimes in the first place through the use of better technology. The prosecutors who sat on the commission with me confirmed through direct experience that capital cases deplete their resources more than any other type of case. Studies in other states found the same thing. As a police chief, I find this use of state resources offensive. The death penalty is supposed to help me fight crime? I say: Give a law enforcement professional like me $250 million, and I'll show you how to reduce crime. The death penalty isn't anywhere on my list. The second issue that I found compelling was wrongful convictions. There were a few testimonies from men that have had a profound impact on me. One was from a man, Kirk Bloodsworth, who spent time on death row before being exonerated by DNA evidence. Another was from a prosecutor in Texas who worked on Cameron Todd Willingham's case. Willingham was convicted of killing his family in a fire and executed, but was later found to have been innocent. The prosecutor in that case spoke to our committee and explained to us that he has to go to bed each night knowing that he played a part in executing an innocent man.

I also learned that capital punishment drags the families of victims through a long and torturous process that only exacerbates their pain. I want to share what I learned from the families whose loved ones were lost, because I believe their untold stories are the shameful, hidden secret of the death penalty. One by one they came before me—mothers, fathers, children, and spouses. Their cries of pain were devastating. The judicial process sentences victims' families to an indeterminate time in legal limbo, waiting for the day that the offender will be executed. For most of them, it never will be. The death penalty was supposed to help families like these. Virtually everything I heard told me that the process was tearing them apart.

At the conclusion of our study, all but one of the committee members voted to abolish the death penalty. I don't think the vote was historic at

> all—it was just plain common sense. Before serving on the committee, I had a narrow view of the death penalty. I focused strictly on retribution, but I learned that there are so many other viable issues. It is easy to support the death penalty when you watch the news and see the images of the victims. In my heart I still feel that the death penalty is justified in some cases, but you cannot have a penalty under these special circumstances—you have to look at the big picture. As a whole, society is much better without the death penalty.

actively under appeal. The defense may raise any amount of exculpatory or mitigating evidence that the prosecution must investigate and defend against. The defense may also hire private investigators (at state expense) who may charge anywhere up to $200 per hour. Because the person writing the checks is normally the state treasurer, normal market forces operating on financial transactions are not present. The money is coming out of the taxpayers' pockets, not the treasurer's, so there is less incentive for anyone to monitor expenditures the way he or she otherwise would.

EXPERT WITNESSES

Operating based on the same "Hey, it's not your money" foundation, expert witnesses often command fees many times greater than they could under market principles. A case in point is a $3.5 million bill presented to the state of Connecticut by a legal scholar for six years of investigating discriminatory processes in capital cases within the state. The state refused to pay the bill, although no one denied the researcher had not done significant work. Typically, a scholar employed by a research university would be overjoyed just to get his or her hands on the data and publish articles from them—that's what university professors get paid for. Anyway, the state finally agreed to pay the researcher $1.75 million, although the governor had to approve emergency funding to do so (Holloway, 2014). That much money for six years of work comes to almost $292,000 a year, or about 2.5 times more than the average salary a full professor receives. We do not know if this amount was on top of the researcher's university salary or whether it was a grant, in which case the university received the lion's share of the money.

The 2012 federal trial of Brian Richardson highlights the high cost of expert witnesses (Rankin, 2012). The 49-year-old Richardson was already serving life for a series of armed robberies when he viciously murdered his

60-year-old cellmate in 2007. Since Richardson and his cellmate were locked in their cell and his cellmate was dead and Richardson wasn't, you would think the case might have been a slam dunk, but under super due process nothing is. The U.S. Attorney's Office deemed it necessary to assign eight prosecutors to the case and to fly in and pay fees to, and expenses for, victims of crimes that Richardson had committed years beforehand. It also appointed 20 private attorneys at $125 an hour to represent inmates who testified against Richardson, and rewarded them with reduced sentences for cooperation. The four-year-long prosecution and nine-week trial did not get the government what it wanted; instead, Richardson received an LWOP sentence. In other words, $3.5 million bought Richardson the same sentence he was already serving.

Expert witness costs in the Richardson case included $150,000 to mental health experts who, although prevented by the judge from testifying on a technicality, were nevertheless paid (the defense claimed Richardson had mental health problems that had not been addressed). Other expenses came to around $200,000. As one of Richardson's lawyers remarked: "This was a colossal waste of taxpayer money. Brian was willing to plead guilty in exchange for a life sentence from day one. This entire episode could have been avoided." For its part, the prosecution defended its decision to seek the death penalty because of Richardson's previous prison violence (he had splashed bleach in one guard's face and stabbed other inmates), and the prosecutors were convinced he would kill again (Rankin, 2012).

There is no denying that seeking LWOP rather than the death penalty would save taxpayers an enormous amount of money better spent elsewhere. There are people, however, who are outraged at the thought of vicious serial killers living a long life in a warm cell, with three meals a day, and even cable television while their victims lie beneath the cold ground. Such people ask why the death penalty costs so much and why a country that put people on the moon with great efficiency cannot put its most heinous criminals on the execution gurney with the same efficiency while still preserving due process. In other words, these people assert that rather than using the cost of the death penalty as a reason to get rid of it, why can't we reform the system to make it more cost-efficient? In a country operating under a crime control model, we could indeed proceed from sentence to execution more efficiently. For instance, juries in France (there is no death penalty in France) are chosen by the simple drawing of lots, and judges decide if expert witnesses are needed and employ them at fixed costs, and these witnesses are neutral rather than partisan (Walsh & Hemmens, 2014). The United States, on the other hand, eschews efforts aimed at bringing swift closure to cases, especially cases involving capital punishment.

However, there have been serious efforts to curtail the costs and time delays of capital cases by attempting to restrict habeas corpus rights. We now turn to these attempts.

HABEAS CORPUS PETITION VERSUS DIRECT APPEAL

We cannot understand why enormous costs are incurred in death penalty cases without understanding the concept and practice of habeas corpus. **Habeas corpus** is a Latin term that literally means "you have the body." It is a civil law process that challenges the legality of a person's confinement and is a court order requiring that an arrested person be brought before a judge to determine the legality of his or her detention. If a judge decides that the individual is imprisoned without legally sufficient reason(s), he or she may order the individual be freed. This does not necessarily mean that that the individual is innocent; it only means that sufficient legal grounds do not exist to hold the person, or if the person has already had a trial and was found guilty, there are issues with the way the trial was conducted that may have affected the trial's outcome and/or the punishment handed down.

Habeas corpus is a very important concept in common law. It has been called the "Great Writ" and was formally codified into English common law by the Habeas Corpus Act of 1679 (Walsh & Hemmens, 2014). Indicative of the respect in which habeas corpus was held by the Founding Fathers is that it is only one of three individual rights mentioned in the U.S. Constitution (the other two are the prohibition of bills of attainder—imposing punishment without trial—and the prohibition of ex post facto laws—legislation making some acts criminal after the fact). The other individual rights that Americans enjoy were formalized in the first ten amendments to the Constitution (the U.S. Bill of Rights), almost as an afterthought.

A habeas corpus petition and an appeal are quite different in many respects. An ordinary appeal is a direct appeal that is almost always limited to issues already addressed in the criminal trial. Such appeals are related to what has already happened in the trial court, with the defense asking the appeals court to review the legal procedures and decisions made prior to the judgment of guilt. Direct appeals do not typically allow for the introduction of new arguments or evidence relevant to the appellant's possible innocence.

On the other hand, as mentioned above, a petition for habeas corpus is a civil action against a state agent (typically, a prison warden) holding the petitioner in custody regarding the legality of a person's confinement or the conditions of confinement. It is an indirect appeal challenging the legal grounds for holding a person in custody based on a state's constitution or the U.S. Constitution.

Any number of claims can be made in a habeas petition, such as a claim that the petitioner was denied "effective legal counsel." Habeas petitioners may also introduce new evidence and new arguments that point toward their innocence. Habeas petitions filed in state court are often arguments pertaining to some fundamental legal error, such as the manner in which the trial was conducted, the inclusion of evidence that the defense asserts should have been excluded, or the way the petitioner's defense was presented. Up to this point, it is much like an ordinary direct appeal; however, there are unique differences between habeas and direct appeals. Within a habeas petition, which, remember, is a civil law matter even though the issues pertain to criminal matters, a petitioner is not restricted to the trial record, as is the case of a direct appeal, providing him or her with an opportunity to raise a variety of new claims.

INTRODUCTION OF THE ANTITERRORISM AND EFFECTIVE DEATH PENALTY ACT

Habeas petitions filed in federal court to appeal a state conviction, on the other hand, often involve layers of additional complications that must be surmounted or requirements that must be met because of the **Antiterrorism and Effective Death Penalty Act (AEDPA).** AEDPA was passed with broad bipartisan support in Congress, by a vote of 91 to 8 with 1 abstention in the Senate and 293 to 133 with 7 abstentions in the House of Representatives, and was signed into law by President Bill Clinton in 1996 (Orye, 2002). Two primary events led to the passage of AEDPA: the crime control–oriented Republican Party majority in both the Senate and the House, and the bombing of the Alfred P. Murrah Federal Building in Oklahoma City by Timothy McVeigh, which came on the heels of the first bombing of the World Trade Center by Islamic terrorists in 1993. The American public was also growing tired of, and outraged by, the interminable appeals filed by convicted murderers, costing the nation multiple millions of tax dollars, and wanted some guarantee of finality in capital cases. According to the language of AEDPA, its goal is "to deter terrorism, provide justice for victims, [and] provide for an effective death penalty" (Orye, 2002, p. 441).

Prior to AEDPA's passage, there was no statute of limitations on filings (petitions could be filed at any time) and no limit to their number (Orye, 2002). Appeal after appeal was filed up and down state and federal court systems with virtually no end in sight. There was also no requirement that separate claims be consolidated into one appeal, so one minor issue was frequently broken down into several even smaller issues and filed at different times. Needless to say, under this system, death rows across the country were increasingly and rapidly becoming deadlocked.

AEDPA imposed a number of limitations on the up until that point practically unlimited access to habeas corpus petitions. First, the still-existing law imposes a strict one-year statute of limitations on them. Second, a petitioner can no longer file successive petitions unless a federal court of appeals approves it. Third, habeas relief is available only if a state court's ruling is deemed contrary to, or unreasonably applied to, established federal law as determined by the U.S. Supreme Court. In other words, defendants now have one shot at habeas corpus and all relevant appeal issues must be consolidated in that one petition. Figure 11.3 illustrates the place of habeas corpus in the process of seeking the death penalty in the state of Tennessee, from the initial prosecutorial decision to the possibility of gubernatorial action.

ALL BARK AND LITTLE BITE

With the passage of AEDPA with its one-year statute of limitations, consolidation of issues, and promise of expedited federal review, death penalty proponents celebrated the end of interminable delays to the imposition of "the people's will." But as Figure 11.4 shows, AEDPA has more bark than bite because the average time from sentencing to execution has increased five years from the date of its passage in 1996 (130 months) to 2012 (190 months), rather than decreased. What went wrong? After all, the United States Supreme Court has upheld the constitutionality of the Act on more than one occasion.

Lawyers, like philosophers, can find many holes in any written document (just the summary version of the AEDPA is a 56-page, single-spaced document full of titles, subtitles, sections, and subsections requiring the patience of Job to read and the legal mind of Justice Antonin Scalia to properly understand). Because of this, AEDPA's statutory language has led to numerous interpretive splits in different federal appeals courts (Blume, 2006). There are other, more concrete, reasons that AEDPA has not lived up to its hype. First of all, the United State Supreme Court ruled in *Horn v. Banks* (2002) that the Act is not retroactive, so the hundreds of pre-AEDPA cases can still proceed as before. More importantly, the Act was not automatically applied to the 50 states; they had to fulfill certain requirement in order to qualify. In order for a state to opt in to AEDPA, the Act requires that states establish certain mechanisms and adhere to strict standards and procedures that, in effect, shift the financial burden from the federal government to the states. The major stumbling block is that states must provide fully competent and adequately compensated counsel in order to avail themselves of AEDPA's reforms; no state has done so thus far (Spohn & Hemmens, 2012). The state of Texas did try to opt in but failed to do so when the 5th Circuit ruled that it had failed to meet the requirement to

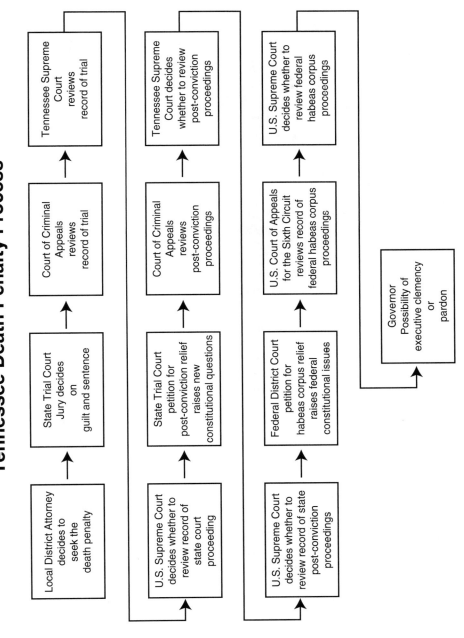

FIGURE 11.3 Habeas Corpus in Death Penalty Cases
Source: http://www.tncourts.gov/sites/default/files/docs/history_of_capital_punishment.pdf

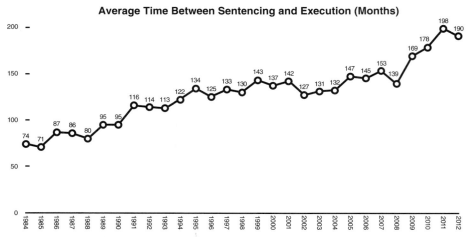

FIGURE 11.4 Failure of AEDPA: Increase in Time (per year by %) between Sentencing and Execution
Source: Death Penalty Information Center (2013)

provide competent attorneys (as defined by AEDPA) for defendants (Kannenberg, 2009).

Attorneys who meet the stringent competency requirements of AEDPA are hard to find. They must have either represented defendants in at least seven felony appeals, including a murder appeal, or completed five appeals including two death penalty appeals (Alarcon, 2007). If attorneys competent at this level are available, they are compensated to the tune of "only" $140 to $163 per hour in California (Alarcon, 2007). Although this might sound like a fortune to someone laboring at one-tenth that hourly sum, such attorneys can command from $250 to $540 per hour in civil litigation (Alarcon, 2007). These attorneys have done the math and decided their best interests lie in more lucrative pastures than those where habeas petitions grow, and states are understandably reluctant to match the princely sums available to them elsewhere.

COLLATERAL COSTS: VICTIMS' AND DEFENDANTS' FAMILIES

An even more neglected topic in the death penalty debate than its financial costs is the collateral impact on those most affected by it—the families of victims and of defendants, as well as the condemned themselves. Perhaps the most common complaint of crime victims and their families is that they are practically ignored by the criminal justice system. One notable exception is the day of execution. Close family members of the victim are typically invited to the execution, and both victim's and offenders' family members are eagerly sought out by members of the press for their thoughts and opinions following the execution. The opinions of such family members (whether they are related to the victim or the offender) about the execution and what it means to them are naturally suffused with emotion, especially if relatives offer their remarks immediately after the execution. Such thoughts and opinions hardly provide adequate insight into the horrible circumstances families on either side have had to endure for so many years while the courts were deciding the case, but their voices do deserve to be heard.

Analyses of newspaper stories reveal that the comments of victims' family members are remarkably diverse, although some sentiments are more often expressed than others. Perhaps the sentiment most frequently expressed is that of closure. When Governor George Ryan of Illinois was deciding to grant clemency to all death row inmates, upon hearing the opinions of victims' families, he remarked: "To a family they talked about closure.... They pleaded with me to allow the state to kill an inmate in its name to provide the families with closure" (cited in Bohm, 2013, p. 67). Closure signifies for victims' families an end, a conclusion, a finality to the seemingly endless business of seeking justice for their murdered loved ones. They want the press to know the pain they have suffered and to gain some recognition at a time when most attention is being directed toward the condemned. The execution brings closure to many of the victims' families in the form of relief—they never have to read about the condemned person in the newspaper again, never have to again report for yet another court hearing, or never have to fear that a judge will someday free the condemned person on a technicality.

Closure definitely does not mean the end of the pain that victims' family members suffer, but many "express confidence that it will come eventually, or that the execution is one step along the path" (Gross & Matheson, 2003, p. 491). Other family members believe that closure is impossible, and some even find it insulting to suggest that execution affords them closure. As one family member put it: "I get sick when death penalty advocates self-righteously prescribe execution to treat the wounds we live with.... Those who hold out an event—execution—as the solution to pain have no understanding of healing. Healing is a process, not an event" (cited in Bohm, 2013, p. 68). Nevertheless, many family members of homicide victims do appear to regard execution as at least the beginning of the closure process (Gross & Matheson, 2003).

Other victims' family members express the simple opinion that the execution means justice has been done. A number of people in this category have suggested that they would have preferred to kill the executed person themselves, or that the condemned person's death was too quick and painless and therefore an insufficient form of revenge: "The penalty was carried out, but this is by no means justice. He went to sleep. Kim [the offender's victim] suffered a violent death" (cited in Gross & Matheson, 2003, p. 496). Others who speak of justice and retribution and who believe that death row inmates suffer pangs of guilt oppose the death penalty because they believe it cuts short murderers' suffering. Some victims' families that have opposed the death penalty for the perpetrator have offered other reasons: wanting to avoid prolonged contact with the criminal justice system, a preference for the finality that a more timely LWOP sentence would offer, the hope that the offender will someday feel remorse, or even moral opposition to the death penalty (Bohm, 2013). The more religious among victim family members may indeed express opposition to the death penalty ("Vengeance is mine, sayeth the Lord"), pray for the condemned person, and express compassion for him or her. They are also more likely to pray for and express compassion for the offender's family, knowing that they, too, have been living a nightmare for years. Although their hurt is certainly not of the same magnitude as that inflicted on victims' families, offenders have still brought a considerable amount of pain on their own families through their own actions.

As Robert Bohm (2013) points out, however, violence, abuse, and neglect are common in the families of capital offenders, and these circumstances are thus partially responsible for their offspring's actions. It is difficult to imagine members of such families, who may have long ago abandoned their offspring, being overly concerned with what happens to them. However, some families of capital murderers provided them with a decent upbringing and may be sickened and deeply ashamed by what their relatives did to the victims and their families, to themselves, and to their own family. Such families have also been victimized by years of knowing that one of their children may be executed, and by neighbors, and even friends and other family members, who stigmatize, shame, and harass them. It is not uncommon for some family members to disown a murderer, particularly if they are convinced of his or her guilt, if the victim was another family member or a child, or if multiple acts of murder were involved. As one mother of a death row inmate reported: "Most people just flat out said I had raised the devil himself. This came from friends, family, and complete strangers" (cited in Bohm, 2013, p. 113). Of course, had the offender been sentenced to LWOP rather than the death penalty, the hurt, shame, and humiliation would still be there, but the fear, anxiety, and feelings of hopelessness knowing that someday a loved one will be executed would not haunt them.

SUMMARY

This chapter has examined the financial burden of taxpayers and other costs of the death penalty on the families of victims and defendants. We have seen how the time has grown from just a few weeks and a cost of around $71,000 to execute a capital offender to an average of around 16 years and millions of dollars. This is the result of the U.S. Supreme Court's "death is different" super due process in effect today. We noted how the federal trial of Timothy McVeigh was costlier than Charles Ng's state trial but was brought to finality much more quickly, and how the McVeigh trial was part of the impetus leading to the Antiterrorism and Effective Death Penalty Act (AEDPA).

Our examination of the financial burden of the death penalty focused on California because it has the largest number of death row offenders in the United States. We saw that the cost of the death penalty since 1978 for California taxpayers is estimated to be over $4 billion, and that the state has spent all that money to execute only 13 offenders. It was also noted that in 2014 a federal judge struck down California's death penalty as unconstitutional. The judge reasoned that the long delays between sentence and execution cause death row offenders mental anguish, and this constitutes cruel and unusual punishment.

The costs incurred prosecuting a death penalty case were explored. The upfront costs include pretrial investigations and hearings, and jury selection. All of these costs greatly exceed costs for the same procedures in an LWOP case. The extraordinary costs for so-called expert witnesses are also a major financial drain.

The concept and practice of habeas corpus and how it differs from ordinary direct appeals was examined. Habeas corpus is a civil action challenging the legality of a person's confinement. It differs from a direct appeal in that it is not confined to the trial record, and a wide variety of issues, such as evidence of innocence, can be raised. Offenders convicted prior to the passage of AEDPA in 1996 could file almost limitless appeals by breaking any issue into numerous small ones and then presenting them at different times. AEDPA was supposed to prevent this by requiring the consolidation of all issues into one and placing a one-year limit on the filing of any appeal. AEDPA has not lived up to its promise of a faster and more efficient death penalty, primarily because of its strict requirements with regard to the provision and competency of death penalty attorneys.

We completed the chapter by looking at the impact of the death penalty on the families of both victims and offenders. Victims' families suffer unimaginable pain when they lose a loved one, and the execution of the offender is supposed to bring closure. It appears to offer a certain amount of relief, but never closure. Some victims' families actually oppose execution for a variety of reasons. The offenders' families can also be deeply affected by the death penalty, but it was pointed out that frequently the circumstances within such families may have actually helped set the offender on a path of crime.

DISCUSSION QUESTIONS

1. If you were pro–death penalty prior to reading about its costs, have you changed your mind?
2. Discuss realistic ways to reduce the costs of seeking the death penalty if we as a country are determined to retain it.
3. Regardless of your stance on the death penalty, what do you think of the reasoning behind Judge Cormac Carney's ruling that California's death penalty was unconstitutional?
4. What could be done to curb the excessive costs of expert witnesses, and the practice of both the prosecution and defense calling their own conflicting experts?
5. Do you agree or disagree with what AEDPA tried to accomplish?
6. Why has AEDPA not lived up to its promise?
7. Does the criminal justice system pay enough attention to the concerns of families of murder victims? If not, how far should those concerns go?

GLOSSARY TERMS

Antiterrorism and Effective Death Penalty Act (AEDPA): A congressional act designed to speed up the process from sentence to execution by requiring consolidation of habeas appeals and imposing a one-year limit on filing.

Habeas corpus: A civil law process that challenges the legality of a person's confinement. It is a court order requiring that an arrested person be brought before a judge to determine the legality of his or her detention.

REFERENCES

Alarcon, A. (2007). Remedies for California's death row deadlock. *Southern California Law Review, 80,* 697–752.

Alarcon, A., and P. Mitchell (2012). Costs of capital punishment in California: Will voters choose reform this November? *Loyola of Los Angeles Law Review, 46,* S1–S35.

Allen v. Ornowski. (2005). 435 F.3d 946.

American Civil Liberties Union. (2012). Frequently asked questions about the cost of California's death penalty. https://www.aclunc.org/issues/criminal_justice/deathpenalty/frequently_asked_questions_about_the_costs_of_california's_death_penalty.shtml.

Blume, J. (2006). AEDPA: The "hype" and the "bite." *Cornell Law Review, 91,* 259–302.

Bohm, R. (2013). *Capital punishment's collateral damage.* Durham, NC: Carolina Academic Press.

Bradford County Telegraph. (1934, October 12). Negro gets "hot seat" Monday for criminal assault on white woman, p. 1.

Death Penalty Information Center. (2011). "California Cost Study 2011." http://www.deathpenaltyinfo.org/california-cost-study-2011.

Death Penalty Information Center. (2013). "Time on Death Row." http://www.deathpenaltyinfo.org/time-death-row.

Death Penalty Information Center. (2014). "Death Row Inmates by State." http://www.deathpenaltyinfo.org/death-row-inmates-state-and-size-death-row-year.

Gross, S. R., and D. J. Matheson. (2003). What they say at the end: Capital victims' families and the press. *Cornell Law Review, 88,* 486–516.

Holloway, C. (2014). "Death Penalty Discrimination Expert Witness Receives $1.75 Million." http://blog.expertpages.com/expertwitness/death-penalty-discrimination-expert-witness-receives-1-75-million.htm.

Horn v. Banks. (2002). 536 U.S. 266, 272.

Jones v. Chappell. (2014, July 16). No. 2:09-cv-02158-CJC (C.D. Cal.).

Jones, S. (2001). *Others unknown: Timothy McVeigh and the Oklahoma City bombing conspiracy.* New York: Public Affairs.

Kannenberg, C. (2009). Wading through the morass of modern federal habeas review of state capital prisoners' claims. *Quinnipac Law Review, 28,* 107–182.

Lieberman, J. (2000). The overproduction of death. *Columbia Law Review, 100,* 2030–2156.

Maningo, M. (2014). *The executioner's toll, 2010: The crimes, arrests, trials, appeals, last meals, final words and executions of 46 persons in the United States.* Jefferson, NC: McFarland.

Marceau, J. F., and H. A. Whitson. (2013). The cost of Colorado's death penalty. *University of Denver Criminal Law Review, 3,* 145–163.

Orye, B. (2002). Failure of words: Habeas Corpus reform, the Antiterrorism and Effective Death Penalty Act, and when a judgment of conviction becomes final for the purposes of 28 USC 2255 (1). *The William & Mary Law. Review, 44,* 441–485.

Price, J., and G. Byrd. (2008). Capital punishment in Texas and California: A comparison. *Applied Psychology in Criminal Justice, 4,* 206–227.

Rankin, B. (2012, August 13). "Costs Questioned in Failed Death-Penalty Case." http://www.ajc.com/news/news/local/costs-questioned-in-failed-death-penalty-case-1/nRBbs/.

Reams, J., and C. Putnam. (2011, Summer). The costs of capital litigation. *New Hampshire Bar Journal,* 21–23.

Spohn, C., and C. Hemmens. (2012). *Courts: A text/reader.* Thousand Oaks, CA: Sage.

Tempest, R. (2005, March 6). Death row often means a long life; California condemns many murderers, but few are ever executed. *Los Angeles Times,* p. B1f.

Walsh, A., and C. Hemmens. (2014). *Law, justice, and society: A sociolegal introduction,* 3d ed. New York: Oxford University Press.

CHAPTER 12

THE DEATH PENALTY

The Federal, Military, and International Perspective

In 1984, 21-year-old Niu Yuqiang was sentenced to death in Beijing, China. His "horrible crimes" were stealing a cap and public brawling, something for which he may have spent 30 days in jail in the United States. This harsh sentence for such a minor crime was justified under a campaign against disruption of the social order, which covered a number of crimes subsumed under the catch-all name of "hooliganism" (hooliganism was eliminated as a crime in 1997).

Niu Yuqiang was later resentenced to life and, in 1990, he was granted medical parole because he had tuberculosis. Medical parole lasts only as long as the person is sick; when the person recovers, he or she is returned to prison. When Niu Yuqiang recovered, officials never sought to return him to prison and Niu assumed he was a free man, especially since hooliganism no longer existed as a crime. In the meantime, Niu married and had a son. However, 14 years after his release, the police turned up and took him into custody to serve the remainder of his sentence. It seems the bureaucracy simply overlooked Niu, who never failed to report to his probation officer. The **South China Post** *reporter who filed a story on Niu has indicated that he must serve out his sentence because of China's "abiding authoritarian aversion to admitting mistakes."*

Even worse than China's promiscuous use of the death penalty is the use of the death penalty in North Korea and in many Islamic countries. For instance, Raif Badawi, a Saudi Arabian blogger, was imprisoned in June 2012 for violating the Saudi anti-cybercrime law and sentenced to seven years of imprisonment and 600 lashes. However, it was later recommended that he instead be tried for insulting Islam and apostasy (although there is no evidence that Raif ever converted to any other religion). He was tried by a higher court, found guilty of apostasy, and sentenced to death in December 2013. In common with China, Saudi Arabia seeks to stifle any discussion of issues, via brutal intimidation, that the government deems off-limits.

LEARNING OBJECTIVES

- Know the primary reason why the United States retains the death penalty.
- Identify the features of each country discussed here that have led to their high execution rates.
- Recognize the importance of an independent judiciary to a country's respect for human rights.
- Know why the rule of law is such an important foundation for justice.
- Understand the political nature of the death penalty in the countries discussed here.
- Know why the death penalty in some Islamic countries cannot be appealed by anyone.

This final chapter is meant to accomplish two tasks: first, to examine the federal and military death penalty systems and how they differ from the typical state system, and second, to provide a comparative perspective on the death penalty as it exists in other countries. A comparative perspective always sheds new light on the familiar by illuminating the unfamiliar. We provide an international perspective on the death penalty in the belief that it is beneficial to examine a familiar subject from different perspectives. It has been said that if you only know your own culture, you don't know your own culture. This statement may be a little exaggerated, but as anyone who has lived in another culture for some time or has tried to learn a foreign language knows, experiencing another culture and language leads to a greater, more nuanced understanding of one's own culture and language. Understanding the use of the death penalty in other cultures should thus help us to gain further perspective on the U.S. death penalty. But first we must ask why the United States still retains this form of punishment.

WHY DOES THE UNITED STATES RETAIN THE DEATH PENALTY?

As of 2014, only 58 of the 192 sovereign nations in the world (about 30%) retained the death penalty. Many overseas observers are surprised to learn that the United States is among that 30%, given that it is the only Western democracy among them. Perhaps part of the wonder stems from the fact that the United States prides itself on being a world leader in civil and human rights, and many consider the use of the death penalty as being contradictory to these values. The case of José Medellin may help to explain.

On August 5, 2008, Mexican national José Medellin was executed in Texas for the 1993 gang rape and murder of 14-year-old Jennifer Ertman and 16-year-old Elizabeth Pena as part of his initiation into a violent street gang. The Mexican government sued the United States in the International Court of Justice (the principal judicial court of the United Nations designed to settle legal disputes in accordance with international law) on behalf of 51 other Mexican nationals on death row, asserting that the United States had violated international law requiring that local authorities inform foreign nationals that they have the right to consult with their country's officials, as required by a treaty to which the United States is a signatory. The Court ruled that the United States erred in sentencing these foreign nationals to death without having informed their consulate. Texas asserted that the Mexican government had no standing to bring such a suit, essentially disregarding the International Court of Justice, and carried out Medellin's execution.

This case illustrates the primary reason why the United States has not followed the majority of nations and eliminated the death penalty. The United States is not a "unified" country in the same way that, say, France is, whereby all decisions about important issues are made by a central government. The federal government is certainly more powerful than the government of any single state, but the United States is a federation of states that places value on local autonomy and limited government. Barring a ruling of unconstitutionality by the U.S. Supreme Court, each state retains the right to decide for itself whether to retain or abolish the death penalty. In suing the U.S. government, Mexico was essentially suing an impotent entity as far as the issue at hand was concerned. The United States did not sentence these foreign nationals to death; the various states in which they committed their crimes had.

Unlike other nations, the U.S. government does not have the legal power to impose a nationwide abolition of capital punishment because, for the most part, the U.S. Constitution allocates power over criminal law to the states (unless, of course, the U.S. Supreme Court were to find capital punishment unconstitutional). No county, state, or province in any other Western democracy can do what Texas did—decide a policy issue for itself regardless of the wishes of the central government. When other nations have repealed the death penalty, they have done so regardless of whether or not a majority of its citizens supported the practice. For instance, Canada does not have the death penalty despite a 2013 opinion poll showing that 63% of Canadians favored the death penalty versus only 30% who were opposed (Angus Reid Opinion Poll, 2013). In the United States, the political system makes it more difficult for elected officials to disregard the will of its citizens. The majority of U.S. citizens still support capital punishment, although that percentage is declining (see Chapter 5 on public opinion). Thus, fearing electoral reprisal, elected officials are reluctant to thwart popular will regardless of their personal views on the death penalty. Writing for the U.S. Embassy's series "Got a question about the U.S.?," David Garland (2012) succinctly sums up why the United States retains capital punishment as a form of punishment:

> Liberal democracies—unlike authoritarian or theocratic nations—are committed to limiting government power and protecting individual liberties. The result is that the death penalty has been used less often, eventually disappearing throughout most of the democratic world. But each nation works out the practical balance between "liberalism" and "democracy" for itself. America's distinctive emphasis on the value of local popular democracy—together with the Supreme Court's interpretation of the meaning of liberty—explains why the United States still has capital punishment.

FEDERAL DEATH PENALTY

The federal government provides the death penalty for murder under a wider array of circumstances than any of the states. Despite broader statutes, federal government executions are rare compared to state executions. According to the Death Penalty Information Center (DPIC) (2015), at the end of 2014 there were 61 males and 1 female on federal death row. Male death row inmates are held at the Federal Prison in Terre Haute, Indiana, and women are held at the Federal Medical Center in Fort Worth, Texas. The DPIC states: "Since the reinstatement of the federal death penalty in 1988, 74 defendants have been sentenced to death, of whom 3 have been executed and 10 have been finally removed from death row. Three other defendants have had a jury recommendation for death, but no death sentence by the judge."

Like the death penalty states, the federal government suspended its death penalty in 1972 after the *Furman v. Georgia* decision. Unlike those states, however, the federal government did not take steps to reinstate the death penalty by following the specific guidelines outlined in *Gregg v. Georgia* (1976) until 1988. As the DPIC states above, the **Anti-Drug Abuse Act** of 1988 reinstated the death penalty in federal law in an effort to control drug trafficking. As we have seen, the first federal execution after the Anti-Drug Abuse Act was signed into law was that of Timothy McVeigh in 2001. Drug kingpin Juan Raul Garza was executed for drug-related killings one week after McVeigh, and Louis Jones Jr. in 2003 for the kidnapping, rape, and murder of a woman on a U.S. Air Force Base. The federal government's interest in prosecuting and then executing McVeigh is obvious given that he blew up a federal building and killed many federal employees, and Jones's crime took place on U. S. property, but Garza's crimes were committed in Texas and could have been prosecuted there with much the same outcome, but apparently the federal government wanted to demonstrate that its "drug kingpin" law had bite. Most recently, the federal government sentenced Tamerlan Tsarnaev to death for acts of terrorism in the Boston Marathon bombings (see Box 12.1).

The **Federal Death Penalty Act** of 1994 (part of the Violent Crime Control and Law Enforcement Act of 1994) is another important way station in the resurgence of the federal death penalty. This Act established constitutional procedures for imposition of the death penalty for 60 offenses under 13 existing and 28 new federal capital statutes. These 60 offenses fall into three broad categories: (1) homicide offenses; (2) espionage and treason; and (3) non-homicidal narcotics offenses. Almost all offenses fall into the homicide category and specify a wide variety of particular circumstances in which a homicide is eligible for a death sentence, such as "murder committed at an airport serving international civil aviation," "civil rights offenses resulting in death," and "the murder of a member of Congress, an important executive official, or a Supreme Court Justice." No prosecutor has sought the death penalty for a non-homicidal narcotics offense, nor is it likely that any prosecutor will.

BOX 12.1

The Boston Marathon Bombing

On April 15, 2013, Dzhokhar and Tamerlan Tsarnaev, brothers living in the Boston area, placed two backpacks stuffed with pressure-cooker bombs in the streets of Boston during the city's annual marathon. The bombs were strategically placed in crowds of spectators and were set to go off during the race just before 3:00 pm. When the bombs detonated, three people were killed and 260 were injured. The scene was gruesome—blood and body parts were spewed all over the streets. Two young women, both in their twenties, and an eight-year-old boy died from the explosion, while sixteen people lost their legs.

FIGURE 12.1 Dzhokhar Tsarnaev

After the attack, the Tsarnaev brothers attempted to flee Boston. They hijacked a car and took the driver hostage (the hostage later escaped when they stopped for gas). The hostage notified police and they were able to

FIGURE 12.2   Boston Marathon Bombing

locate the suspects, who then took police on a high-speed chase. The chase ended after the brothers shot at law enforcement and threw explosives out of the car; the older brother, Tamerlan Tsarnaev, was killed during the gunfight. Dzhokhar Tsarnaev was shot multiple times but eluded police. He was found by a local resident hiding inside a boat parked at the resident's home. Tsarnaev was soaked in blood from the gunshot wounds to his neck, head, legs, and hand.

Dzhokhar was charged, federally, with 30 crimes related to the bombing, 17 of which were capital crimes. Most of the charges were related to terrorism and use of weapons of mass destruction. Dzhokhar was represented by high-profile defense attorney Judy Clarke, who has represented several other notable federal death penalty defendants, such as Eric Rudolph, Ted Kaczynski (aka "the Unabomber"), Susan Smith, and Jared Loughner.

A lengthy trial took place whereby Tsarnaev's defense team argued that Tamerlan Tsarnaev was the mastermind behind the attack and, therefore, Dzhokhar Tsarnaev should receive life without the possibility of parole for working under his brother's direction. The jury disagreed: in May 2015, Dzhokar Tsarnaev was sentenced to death by lethal injection after nearly 14 hours of jury deliberation. He is now housed at a federal prison awaiting his execution date.

Although we have said that the United States is a federated rather than unified nation, the federal government can, and does, insert itself into the business of the states in certain instances. The federal judiciary does so frequently when matters pertaining to the U.S. Constitution involving a state issue are brought before it, but the federal legislative and executive branches have played a very limited role in the administration of states' criminal matters. Some readers may remember the beating of African American parolee Rodney King by four white police officers after they had pulled him over following a 20-minute, high-speed car chase. The officers were tried for assault with a deadly weapon and the use of excessive force in a California state court and acquitted after the defense convinced the all-white jury that the officers had followed department procedure by exercising whatever force was necessary to make the arrest. The public outcry—including the riots in Los Angeles that left 53 people dead—following the acquittal led the federal government to indict the officers on civil rights violations to right the alleged wrongs of the California jury. In this second trial in 1993, two of the officers were found guilty and imprisoned, and the other two acquitted.

Why were these officers tried again for the same set of actions after being acquitted, when the double jeopardy clause of the Fifth Amendment protects defendants from being twice put in jeopardy "of life and limb" for the same offense? They were re-tried because the double jeopardy guarantee is counteracted by the doctrine of *dual sovereignty*. Many Americans are not aware that they hold dual citizenship; that is, they are under the protection of two "sovereigns," the United States and the particular state in which they reside, and are responsible for behaving in accordance with the laws of both. It is because of this doctrine that the act of indicting and trying a case that has already resulted in an acquittal in state court is perfectly legal, even if it looks, smells, and quacks like double jeopardy, as one defense lawyer is reputed to have said. Thus, an act defined as criminal by both national and state governments is an offense against both and may be punished by each (Connor, 2010).

The law is fairly well settled that the federal government can prosecute offenders accused of violations of federal law even if an act (e.g., the use of "medical marijuana") is not a crime in the state in which the offender resides, and the state cannot do anything to prevent it. However, in most cases in which the federal government steps in to prosecute, the states welcome such action. It has been said that the federal death penalty is a "safety valve" for the prosecution of heinous killers in states with no death penalty (Mysliwiec, 2010). That is, when confronted with a case of extraordinary callousness and brutality, prosecutors in non–death penalty states may not only welcome federal intervention, but also invite it. As Mysliwiec points out: "In fact, it is common practice for state or local prosecutors to bring a case to the attention of their federal counterparts when they believe sufficient sentences cannot be achieved under the state or local statutes in light of the totality of the circumstances of the crime and the offender" (2010, p. 260).

An example of this is the federal prosecution of Ronell Wilson, the alleged leader of a violent drug gang called the Stapleton Crew, for the execution-style murders of two undercover New York City police officers in 2003. Wilson was quickly arrested and charged with two counts of capital murder, but New York's death penalty statute was overturned by its highest court in 2004. The Staten Island District Attorney then met with his federal counterpart to persuade her to prosecute the case federally (Connor, 2010). Wilson was subsequently charged federally with two counts of capital murder "in furtherance of racketeering" and sentenced to death. He was still on death row as of March 2015. According to Mysliwiec (2010), the public response to Wilson's death sentence was overwhelmingly positive.

Mysliwiec (2010) also points to the 2001 case of Gary Lee Sampson, sentenced to death in federal court for two counts of carjacking resulting in death. The federal government enacted a special anti-carjacking statute in 1992, but Massachusetts, where the killings took place, also had such a statute, but with no death penalty attached. The public response to Sampson's death sentence was more mixed in Massachusetts than it was in New York, with a number of protests taking place accusing the federal government of encroaching on the state's repudiation of the death penalty. A series of court battles resulted in Sampson receiving a February 2015 death penalty retrial date, but on December 23, 2014, a federal judge postponed the order until September 2015, "outraging the families of his victims who say they have waited too long for a resolution of the case" (Valencia, 2014).

Another way in which the federal government is legally able to take a case out of the hands of a state is through the so-called commerce clause of the U.S. Constitution. The U.S. Constitution gives Congress the power "to regulate Commerce with foreign Nations, and among the several States, and with the Indian tribes." The clause was put into the Constitution to provide the federal government with the power to prevent states from erecting barriers to free commerce, such as levying taxes on goods from other states, or otherwise hindering domestic free trade among the various states, foreign nations, and Indian tribes (Walsh & Hemmens, 2014). To apply such a simply worded clause to the death penalty seems quite a stretch, but when you have the muscle that the federal government has, you can stretch anything in any direction you please.

Mannheimer (2011) provides us with an example of the use of the commerce clause to remove a case from the jurisdiction of the state of Vermont, which does not have the death penalty and happily relinquished it. The case involved Michael Jacques, who kidnapped, raped, and murdered his 12-year-old niece Brooke Bennett in 2008. Jacques enlisted the help of another young girl whom he had been regularly molesting; he convinced her via emails and text messages that a mysterious organization he called "Breckenridge" had singled out Brooke for "termination." His young accomplice sent out text messages inviting Brooke to a party at the Jacques residence. Jacques picked Brooke up on the night in question and raped and killed her. All these events took place exclusively within the boundaries of Vermont, and prior to 2006, kidnapping resulting in murder was a federal crime only if the victim was transported across state lines. From this short description of the case, can you guess how the feds were able to use the commerce clause to charge Jacques with a capital crime? Yes, the use of text messages and emails, and the car driven by Jacques to pick Bennett up, constituted "instruments of interstate commerce" regardless of whether they were used entirely within the boundaries of one state (Mannheimer, 2011). Jacques pleaded guilty to Brooke's murder in 2014 (escaping the death penalty by doing so) and was sentenced to life in prison, plus 70 years (Hemmingway, 2014).

The availability of another source of prosecution may indeed serve states without the death penalty as a safety valve to quiet public outrage. It may also be a factor behind decisions not to reinstate the death penalty in states such as New York, since they can always turn to the federal government, with its vastly greater resources, to fill the void for them. Other people, whether they applaud a particular outcome resulting from federal intervention in a state case or not (as in any of the cases discussed), may view it as an egregious overreach of federal power and a danger to our system of state governments.

THE U.S. MILITARY DEATH PENALTY

The U.S. military also has a separate death penalty under the **Uniform Code of Military Justice (UCMJ)**, which establishes a standard set of procedural and substantive criminal laws for the U.S. military services that is separate from civilian law. The UCMJ defines punishable acts and provides procedural safeguards for the accused that are identical to those guaranteed by civilian criminal law, such as the right to be represented by counsel, the right to be informed of the exact nature of the charge, the right to remain silent, and the right to be informed of these protections. Although executions in the military are even rarer than in the federal civilian system, the UCMJ (2014) lists 14 capital offenses, 10 that can be imposed at any time (the first 10) and the last 4 only during time of war (we have inserted brief explanatory terms where meanings are not obvious):

1. Mutiny or sedition
2. Misbehavior before the enemy
3. Subordinate compelling surrender (anyone other than the ranking officer persuading others to surrender)
4. Improper use of countersign (a kind of password for gaining access to vital areas)
5. Forcing a safeguard (perform acts in violation of the protection of some person, place, or property)
6. Aiding the enemy
7. Espionage

8. Improper hazarding of vessel (to willfully put a vessel in danger of loss or damage)
9. Murder (premeditated and felony murder)
10. Rape
11. Desertion
12. Assaulting or willfully disobeying a superior commissioned officer
13. Lurking as a spy or acting as a spy
14. Misbehavior of a sentinel or lookout

Prior to the mid-1950s when the UCMJ was introduced, U.S. military justice was contained in the Articles of War, which were largely copied from British articles of war, which were likewise essentially the same articles that governed the behavior of the Roman legions (Myren, 1988). Robinson (2008) tells us that at least 267 personnel were executed by the Union (no figures are available for the Confederacy) during the Civil War, and that 169 were executed (most during the World War II years) between 1942 and 1961. Although quite a number of death-eligible offenses are listed in the UCMJ, there have been no military executions since the execution of John Bennett, hanged at Fort Leavenworth in 1961 for the rape and attempted murder of an 11-year-old Austrian girl (Koener, 2008).

The U.S. military suspended the use of death statutes after the *Furman* decision and applied them again when the various states did. The military's death penalty was struck down as unconstitutional in 1983 by the Armed Forces Court of Appeals (*U.S. v. Matthews*). The U.S. Court of Appeals for the Armed Forces (USCAAF) is composed of five civilian judges appointed for 15-year terms by the president with the advice and consent of the Senate. The USCAAF exercises final appellate jurisdiction over members of the armed forces and other persons subject to the UCMJ. In *Matthews,* the "Court held that the death penalty procedures of the military justice system did not satisfy the constitutional requirement that the court members must make specific findings of individualized aggravating circumstances" (Judge Advocate General's Corps, 1983, p. 7). The administration of President Ronald Reagan quickly got to work to right the deficiencies noted by listing 11 aggravating factors that qualify a defendant for a death sentence, and the military once again had a death penalty system that passed constitutional muster.

When members of the armed forces are accused of committing a crime or some infraction of the military code of justice, they are subject to a court-martial. Depending on the offense, it can be a summary (one that does not require a judge and results in minor penalties), special (one that mirrors a civilian criminal trial and carries more severe penalties), or general court-martial. A general court-martial prosecutes the most serious offenses, including those that carry a possible death sentence. In such instances, the case is heard by a panel of

12 members who decide the facts and the verdict. Panel (jury) members typically are commissioned officers from a different unit and of a higher rank than the accused. Panel members are not selected by the same process as civilian jurors, but rather by the convening authority, who can be anyone from the president of the United States to the immediate superior of the commanding officer initiating the court-martial. If the accused is found guilty, the presiding military judge may impose the appropriate sentences according to UCMJ guidelines. A death sentence requires unanimity; if there is only one dissenting vote, the offender is sentenced to life imprisonment. If the accused is convicted, he or she may appeal the outcome of a court-martial to the military court of appeals; in death penalty cases, the court-martial verdict is automatically appealed. Although the USCAAF is the court of final appeals in the military, in certain circumstances, its decisions are subject to direct review by the U.S. Supreme Court.

The U.S. Military's Current Death Row Population

Despite the large number of death-eligible offenses listed in the USMJ, only 6 inmates—3 African Americans, 2 whites, and a Palestinian American—reside on death row in Fort Leavenworth, Kansas, as of early 2015. All inmates committed particularly heinous crimes that likely would have resulted in the prosecutor of any death penalty state seeking the death penalty. We offer a brief description of each, based on information available at the DPIC website and from various newspaper articles:

Ronald Gray U.S. Army cook Ronald Gray, an African American, was sentenced in 1988 on 14 charges, including 4 counts of murder, 1 count of attempted murder, and 8 counts of rape. Gray's appeal to the U.S. Supreme Court was denied a hearing, and in 2008 President George W. Bush approved his execution. Two weeks before his scheduled execution, a federal judge issued a stay, and the case has been making the rounds in federal court ever since.

Dwight Loving U.S. Army Private First Class Dwight Loving, an African American, was sentenced in 1989 for the premeditated murders of two cab drivers, two counts of robbery, and several other felonies. One of the cab drivers was a fellow soldier moonlighting as a cab driver, and the other a retired U.S. Army sergeant.

Hasan Akbar U.S. Army Sergeant Hasan Akbar (born Mark Kools), an African American and Muslim convert, was convicted of two counts of premeditated murder and three counts of attempted premeditated murder of 16 U.S. soldiers in a grenade and shooting attack that killed 2 and wounded 14 other soldiers in Kuwait in 2003.

Andrew Witt U.S. Air Force Senior Airman Andrew Witt, a white man, was convicted of two counts of premeditated murder and one count of attempted premeditated murder for stabbing another airman and his wife to death. He also seriously injured a friend who tried to intervene. Witt's death sentence was overturned by an appellate court on grounds of ineffectiveness of counsel, but it was reinstated by the Air Force Court of Appeals in 2014.

Timothy Hennis Former Master Sergeant Timothy Hennis, a white man, was convicted in 2010 for the murder of Kathryn Eastburn and two of her daughters in 1985. Hennis had quickly become a suspect in the case; he was arrested, tried, and sentenced to death in a North Carolina state court in 1986. In 1989 Hennis won the right to a new trial and was acquitted. Had Hennis been a civilian, that would have been the end of the story because of the double jeopardy clause of the Fifth Amendment, but the Fifth Amendment does not prohibit a court-martial for the same offense. Hennis retired from the U.S. Army in 2004 but was recalled to active duty in 2006 and arrested on three counts of murder. DNA evidence based on technology that was not available during his earlier trials showed that semen found in Kathryn's body was Hennis's, and a military court subsequently sentenced him to death. Hennis is the only person in U.S. history to have been tried three times for the same offense.

Nidal Hasan U.S. Army Major Nidal Hasan, a Palestinian American, was sentenced to death in 2013 for killing 13 fellow soldiers and wounding many others at Fort Hood, Texas, in 2009 in what has been described as "the worst terrorist attack on American soil since 9-11." In court, he defended himself and sought the death penalty or martyrdom. Hasan had exchanged emails with al-Qaeda in which he asked whether those who attacked fellow soldiers were true martyrs.

THE DEATH PENALTY ON THE INTERNATIONAL STAGE

As we noted earlier, only a minority of countries (at least "officially") retain the death penalty. We are able to only examine a small number of these given space constraints, so our discussion here will focus on the countries (omitting the United States) that, according to Amnesty International (2014), utilized the death penalty most liberally in 2013—China, Iran, Iraq, Saudi Arabia, and North Korea. We will see that the death penalty in these nations is applied swiftly, efficiently, and often cruelly for a variety of offenses that are considered minor (or even non-offenses) in the United States. In these countries, death sentences are imposed in many cases with little concern for evidence or trials. If trials are held, the judiciary is bound to abide by state requirements and court decisions are made accordingly. Of the countries that retain the death penalty, only 22 of them "officially" executed anyone in 2013. We say "officially" because we cannot rely on official figures, as the plus signs that Amnesty International has applied to the government-supplied numbers in Figure 12.4 attest. Four of the 22 countries that executed prisoners in 2013—Indonesia, Kuwait, Nigeria, and Vietnam—resumed the practice after a hiatus of a few years. Other countries then engulfed in violent turmoil, such as Syria and Egypt, doubtless saw many executions, but Amnesty International could not confirm any and thus did not report on them.

PERSPECTIVE FROM A FORENSIC DNA EXPERT: GREG HAMPIKIAN

Dr. Greg Hampikian is a renowned forensic DNA expert and professor of biology and criminal justice. Dr. Hampikian is known for his DNA expertise on Innocence Network cases around the world, including that of Amanda Knox. He has helped with more than a dozen exonerations, and worked on hundreds of cases. He also works with police to solve cold cases, and recently worked with French police, solving a ten-year-old case using a novel DNA technique. Dr. Hampikian is the founder and director of the Idaho Innocence Project and has helped establish such projects in Ireland and France. He has held research and teaching positions at the Yale University Medical School (New Haven, CT), the Worcester Foundation for Developmental Biology (Shrewsbury, MA), Emory University (Atlanta, GA), La Trobe University (Melbourne, Australia), and the Centers for Disease Control (Atlanta, GA).

FIGURE 12.3   Dr. Greg Hampikian

The great benefit of working on international cases is learning that justice and criminality are always locally defined. Taking the witness stand in

Crete, I was introduced as "the son of Aram Hampikian, baptized into the Armenian Orthodox Church," which is not my usual professional title (I prefer Ph.D.). I was then asked if I swore to tell the truth by the Bible or my conscience, to which I answered, "Yes." But the judge looked puzzled and inquired, "Which one?" Seeing the Bible under glass at the witness stand and the large cross on the wall behind the judge, I answered, "the Holy Word, your Honor."

In London, the barrister who brought me to court put on his long wig and heavy gown before entering the courtroom, which was chilled to comfort those in formal regalia (and to shiver the rest of us). In France, the prosecutor, victims, and journalists all sat together at an elevated table to the judge's right, while the defendant and his attorney were alone at a low table on the left. In Italy, I was baffled by the unfamiliar mix of judges and jurors who deliberated together, and by the completely contradictory outcomes we faced in five different Italian courts during Amanda Knox's case. However, in all these places there was one common element of justice: the death penalty was outlawed and considered barbaric.

If Italy had the death penalty, Amanda Knox would surely have been a candidate for it. However, no country in Europe has a death penalty, and extradition treaties with non-death penalty countries generally bar the transfer of those who may face capital punishment. In one of my transnational cases, I learned that Canada would never extradite a prisoner who might face a U.S. death penalty. Any other penalty is acceptable, even though current U.S. prison sentences appear draconian compared with those in many other countries. To many reformers the death penalty is just the most extreme example of U.S. "leadership" in many prison statistics, including incarceration rates, sentences, sex-offender registry numbers, and the paucity of education and reintegration programs.

Fortunately, the state-mandated destruction of life is becoming rarer in the modern world, and thus more "unusual." If the trend continues, it may begin to seem cruel to the U.S. Supreme Court, fulfilling its final requirement for constitutional restraint. Until then, arguments over errors (153 people exonerated from death row since 1976), costs to county governments (usually over $1,000,000), and the use of expired, medically-unapproved drugs will fuel countless editorials. There is no consensus on this issue because Americans, although astonished over foreign beheadings, seem reluctant to judge their own government's terminal retribution. Perhaps we have been sedated by our use of lethal injectables. I wonder if groups like ISIS would be so shocking if they used expired veterinary drugs to kill.

In my own state, Idaho, Charles Fain spent almost 18 years on death row for the kidnapping, rape, and murder of a 9-year-old girl. DNA finally proved his innocence, and the state in its compassion compensated him with a jacket, pair of dungarees from the prison laundry, and money for a bus fare. While this final insult demonstrates the government's inability to deal with its errors, it could have been worse—the system could have worked efficiently and Fain's final gift would have been a pine box, rather than state denim.

The argument that the court needs finality to resolve cases, and thus issue death warrants, rings hollow when one considers the compensation for wrongful killing. Death is not a penalty. It is a mystery. We do not know where spirits go, and we cannot call them back for posthumous exonerations (like those in Texas and Ireland, for example). The state has no authority over death.

In order to enter the European Union, governments must agree that they will not kill their own citizens, and in the United States each year more states independently come to the same conclusion. Given this trend, perhaps the prohibition on court-ordered killing will soon be another common element of justice throughout the civilized world.

THE DEATH PENALTY IN THE COMMUNIST WORLD

People's Republic of China

We see from Figure 12.4 that the People's Republic of China is the leader in the number of persons executed in 2013. China is an authoritarian Communist state governed by a single political party and is the most populous country in the world. It operates under socialist law, which is a low-tolerance crime-control model. The socialist attitude toward crime, criminals, and capital punishment is exemplified by a statement made by Marxist Karl Pearson in 1887 that still resonates strongly in Communist societies:

> The legislation or measures of police, to be taken against the immoral and a antisocial minority, will form the political realization of Socialism. Socialists have to inculcate that spirit which would give offenders against the State short shrift and the nearest lamp-post. Every citizen must learn to say with Louis XIV, *L'état c'est moi!* (as cited in Walsh, 2009, pp. 244–245)

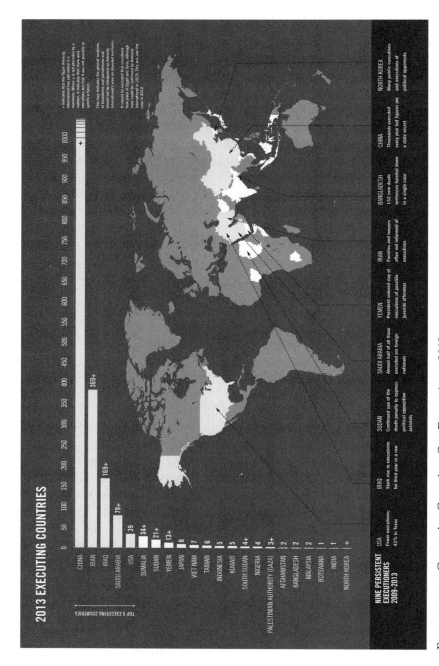

FIGURE 12.4 Countries Carrying Out Executions, 2013
Source: Amnesty International (2014), Reprinted with permission

The French expression *L'état c'est moi* means "I am the state," which in turn means that in a socialist society, the state and the laws that support it are supposed to "wither away," and whatever might be construed as the "state" thereafter would theoretically become at one with the individual. If the state and the individual are considered inseparable entities, the notion of individual rights and procedural protections against state power are meaningless because each person theoretically *is* the state. Thus, offenders have no rights of procedural protections and can be given "short shrift" and summarily led to "the nearest lamp-post" and hanged.

For most of its history, the Chinese have taken this idea seriously in terms of the number and swiftness of their executions. The Chinese system did not operate under the presumption of innocence until relatively recently. Under codes enacted in 1996, the notion of the assumption of innocence was introduced, but the Chinese still stress voluntary confession, contrition, and reintegration back into the community (Liu et al., 2012). According to the Northwestern Law Center for International Human Rights (NLCIHR) (2011), however, torture is still sometimes used in China as a means of obtaining confessions, which obviously casts doubt on the voluntariness of any confession.

The Chinese have lower crime rates and few chronic offenders relative to Western societies. Some believe that this is due to China's frequent use of the death penalty, which is likely imposed on repeat offenders with the greatest frequency (Deng, Zhang, & Cordilia, 1998). The death penalty may be applied for an incredible 55 different offenses in China (down from 68 offenses prior to 2011), although few death sentences are imposed for many of these offenses. Death-eligible offenses include murder, rape, economic crimes committed by high-level officials, and counter-revolutionary offenses, which include a smorgasbord of possible offenses (Liu et al., 2012). According to the Chinese human rights organization Dui Hua (2011), based in the United States and Hong Kong, there were at least 4,000 executions in China in 2010, but because the actual number is a state secret, it may be many more. Amnesty International (2013) writes: "Thousands of people were executed in China in 2011, more than the rest of the world put together. Figures on the death penalty are a state secret. Amnesty International has stopped publishing figures it collects from public sources in China as these are likely to grossly underestimate the true number." The closest to an "official" estimate is 8,000 executions in 2005, calculated by scholars at the Law Institute of the Chinese Academy of Social Sciences (Bezlova, 2006).

Such embarrassingly huge numbers led to a government policy called "kill fewer, kill carefully." The policy was implemented by the Chinese Supreme People's Court when it claimed the right to review each death sentence imposed by lower courts. Xiao Yang, President of the Supreme People's Court, announced that a series of new measures would be implemented to avoid wrongful executions: "As of July 1, 2006, all second-instance trials [appeals] of death-sentence cases shall be heard in open court," said Xiao (Bezlova, 2006). The Supreme People's Court overturned about 15% of the death sentences imposed in the first half of 2008, and the Chinese courts purportedly handed down 30% fewer death sentences in 2007 compared with 2006, when the review process began (Fan & Cha, 2008).

There are two types of death sentences in China: immediate and delayed. A delayed sentence is a two-year suspension of sentence during which defendants must show that they are reformed. A person convicted of murder and certain kinds of rape or robbery is not eligible for a delayed sentence. If a person is considered rehabilitated, the sentence is usually commuted to a long period of incarceration; if not, he or she is executed. An immediate sentence is carried out within seven days of a failed review of the penalty by the Chinese Supreme People's Court. Such a sentence is imposed when in the court's opinion the defendant is beyond rehabilitation.

Execution was traditionally carried out by a single shot at the base of the skull, or more recently by lethal injection (Dui Hua, 2011). China uses the same three-drug cocktail as the U.S. federal government and most U.S. states. The Chinese government claims that this switch in execution methods was motivated by humanitarian concerns, but others (Dui Hua, 2011) suggest that it was motivated by economic gain. China has a highly profitable organs-for-transplant industry, and many bodily organs are "harvested" from executed prisoners and sold. According to the NLCIHR (2011):

> China profits from its executions—65% of organ transplants originating from China are harvested from executed prisoners. Human rights organization Dui Hua speculates that the shift from firing squad execution to lethal injection may have been motivated by the ability to better preserve criminals' organs through lethal injection. The cost of a single dose of lethal injection is also cheaper—at 300 yuan (about $48)—than the 700 yuan (about $113) price tag of a firing squad, and scholars point to this factor, profit, ease of secrecy, and reduction of family complaints (due to cabbaging caused by shots to the back of the condemned's head) as likely factors motivating the switchover to lethal injection.

One of the unique features of the Chinese death penalty is that it is meted out most often in specially equipped "death vans" that shuttle from town to town plying their deadly trade. Death vans are used to save money for poorer localities that cannot afford to construct their own execution facilities, and are also supposed to provide a deterrent effect by executing the condemned locally. The combination of lethal injection and mobility greatly facilitates the speedy removal and quick delivery of undamaged organs. According to MacLeod

(2006): "Corpses are typically driven to a crematorium and burned before relatives or independent witnesses can view them."

Democratic People's Republic of Korea (North Korea)

Another Communist state that regularly performs executions is North Korea. It is a Communist dictatorship that has been ruled by a single family (the Kim family) since the division of the Korean peninsula into North and South Korea in 1946. The Economist Intelligence Unit (2013), a private company that provides research, analysis, and advisory services to governments and businesses, offers a "democracy score" annually for each sovereign country on a scale of 1 to 10. This score is based on the weighted average scores of a number of experts on 63 different factors, such as public political participation and respect for civil rights, and helps us to understand why countries with low scores use the death penalty so promiscuously. In 2013, Norway had the highest democracy score at 9.80 and North Korea the lowest at 1.08 (see Table 12.1). North Korea has consistently rated at the bottom since the democracy index was devised.

China may lack transparency in divulging information regarding the number of executions it carries out, but the situation in North Korea is an almost total blackout. Practically all information coming out of North Korea derives either from government propaganda or from the lucky few who manage to escape to South Korea. Note that Amnesty International does not provide any execution figures for North Korea in Figure 12.4 because the organization was

TABLE 12.1   2013 Executions in Top Five Death Penalty Countries and Their Scores on the Democracy Index Compared with the United States

Country	Population*	Executions**	Rate[†]	Ratio[‡]	Democracy Score
Iraq	33,000,000	169	5.120	41.29	4.10
Iran	77,000,000	369	4.790	38.63	1.98
North Korea	25,000,000	95	3,958	31.92	1.08
China	1,385,000,000	4000	2,889	23.30	3.00
Saudi Arabia	29,000,000	79	2,724	21.28	1.71
United States	314,000,000	39	0.124		8.11

*   2014 population to closest million.
** Executions supplied by Amnesty International (2014); North Korean estimate per Northwestern Law Center for International Human Rights (2013a); Chinese 2009 estimate per Dui Hua (2011).
[†] Rate per million population.
[‡] Ratio of a country's rate of execution to U.S. rate.

unable to gain any kind of official access to figures. However, according to the NLCIHR (2013a): "The media reported a total of 95 executions in 2013, but the real number is likely much higher." Even this minimal estimate still gives North Korea an execution rate almost 32 times higher than that of the United States (see Table 12.1).

South Korean sources indicate that North Korea conducts many public executions, making it the only non-Islamic nation to do so (Iran, Saudi Arabia, Somalia, Syria, and Yemen are the countries that regularly carry out public executions). According to a South Korean newspaper, at least 80 people were publicly executed simultaneously in seven cities in November 2013 for offenses such as watching South Korean movies, possessing a Bible, sexual misconduct, and distributing pornography (Lee, 2013). According to Lee's report, the regime of Kim Jung-un is trying to transform certain cities into tourist destinations and is busily constructing vacation hotels, an airport, and a ski resort, and "the idea that executions would be held simultaneously on a weekend in seven cities suggests an extreme measure by the central government to stamp out public unrest or capitalistic zeal accompanying its development projects."

Unlike the Chinese criminal justice system, the North Korean one makes no pretense of any commitment to a consistent rule of law. Its judicial process is more completely controlled by the ruling Communist party than is China's. The lack of an independent judiciary allows the government to execute individuals without going through the "messy" and expensive process of trials and appeals. Appeals can be heard for non-capital cases, but not for capital cases. This is probably because the government finds many acts for which the death penalty is applied to be dangerous political acts (e.g., passing out Bibles) that threaten the stability of the regime. Only prisoners suspected of non-capital crimes are permitted defense lawyers; this is never the case for those suspected of a death-eligible crime. However, in North Korea, any crime may potentially be a capital crime if the government deems it to be such, depending on the circumstances and the political climate at the time (U.S. Department of State, 2010). Many ordinary crimes may become death-eligible if they are defined as "especially serious," a phrase that itself is not defined. For instance, "In a particularly vague provision, even by North Korean standards, an 'especially serious' case of being a 'scoundrel' is punishable by death" (NLCIHR, 2013a). Such looseness of language thus makes it possible to execute almost anyone for almost anything while still calling the execution legal. The North Korean criminal code is thus extremely broad, extremely vague, and extremely dependent on the whims of government officials. According to the NLCIHR (2013a):

> Offenses in North Korea are defined more broadly and subjectively than in any other nation in the world, and the executive may dictate

judicial outcomes, resulting in the application of the death penalty for a wide range of political offenses and arbitrary application or expansion of the death penalty over time. It is impossible to predict what kinds of "offenses" will be prosecuted as death-eligible, or indeed what legal provisions lead to convictions and death sentences. For instance, intelligence data submitted to Yoon Sang-hyun of the South Korea National Assembly's Foreign Affairs, Trade and Unification Committee indicated that Kim Chol, North Korea's Vice Minister of the People's Armed Forces, was executed by a firing squad in January 2012. He had been convicted for drinking alcohol during the mourning period for former leader Kim Jong-il.

THE DEATH PENALTY IN THE ISLAMIC WORLD

Kingdom of Saudi Arabia

The Islamic world is a harsh and brutal one for anyone who violates the law. The democracy scores supplied by the Economist Intelligence Unit (2013) for the three countries examined (shown in Table 12.1) attest to their lack of concern for human rights. We also see that Iraq performs executions at a rate that exceeds the U.S. rate by more than 41 times, Iran at a rate 38 times greater, and Saudi Arabia at a rate more than 21 times greater.

There are three key factors that distinguish Islamic law from common law. First, it claims to be based on direct revelation from God and, as such, is unchangeable and binding on all people, Muslim and non-Muslim alike. Second, it attempts to regulate the behavior and thought processes of the individual on practically all matters. Unlike common law, which typically attempts to regulate public behavior only, Islamic law contains regulations for personal hygiene, diet, sexual conduct, and child rearing, as well as prescribing specific rules for prayers, fasting, alms-giving, and numerous other religious matters. Islamic law is thus a theocratic (religious) system as opposed to the secular nature of common and socialist legal systems. Islamic law requires total and unqualified submission to the will of Allah as it is laid out in the Qur'an (Koran), Islam's holy book. Third, it neither requires nor finds it desirable to achieve uniformity of law. The lack of recourse to generalized principles of law has led some to consider it a system of ad hoc justice akin to informal dispute resolution rather than a rational and predictable system of law as exists in Western nations (Walsh & Hemmens, 2014).

The Kingdom of Saudi Arabia is an oil-rich country of 25 million people ruled by the House of Saud as an absolute monarchy since the founding of the state in 1932. Muslim countries vary to the extent that they strictly follow Islamic law (known as Shar'ia—"the path to follow"), but the Qur'an functions as Saudi

Arabia's constitution, and thus it expects strict adherence to it. A 26-page publication entitled "Information Pack for British Prisoners in Saudi Arabia" that the British embassy in Saudi Arabia issues to British nationals arrested there tells a chilling story of Saudi justice. It is a publication informing prisoners what the British government can and cannot do for them and how to apply for a transfer to a British prison. The two sentences below deal with the punishment individuals may expect if convicted:

> Criminal law punishments in Saudi Arabia include public beheading, stoning, amputation and lashing. The Saudi courts impose a number of severe physical punishments. The death penalty can be imposed for a wide range of offences including murder, rape, armed robbery, repeated drug use, apostasy, adultery, witchcraft and sorcery and can be carried out by beheading with a sword, stoning or firing squad, followed by crucifixion. (British Foreign Office, 2013, p. 9)

According to Amnesty International, Saudi Arabia "officially" executed 79 people in 2013, although it is suspected that many secret executions also take place. From Table 12.1, we see that this rate of 2.724 executions per million is over 21 times the U.S. rate of 0.124. Even official figures thus show the Saudis to be far more promiscuous in their use of the death penalty that the United States. Contrary to these semi-official figures and calling Saudi Arabia's justice system "farcical," Ali Alahmed (2013) reports that:

> hundreds of people are executed in Saudi Arabia every year—because some executions are carried out in secret, no one knows the real numbers. In 2007, the newspaper *Arab News* reported that 400 people remained on death row in the province of Makka alone. There are 12 other regions in the kingdom, so the total number of people awaiting execution could easily reach several thousand.

Crimes in Islamic countries are categorized according to the punishments they elicit. There are three categories of crime, each of which can carry the death penalty: *hudud, quesas,* and *ta'zir* (there are various other English spellings of these words). *Hudud* crimes have fixed punishments prescribed by the Qur'an; *quesas* crimes are retribution, "eye-for-an-eye" crimes; and *ta'zir* crimes are crimes that carry discretionary penalties. The death penalty is prescribed for three *hudud* crimes—adultery, highway robbery, and apostasy. However, the evidentiary requirements to prove these crimes make it extremely difficult to obtain convictions.

Circumstantial evidence (evidence relying on an inference from something specific such as fingerprints or DNA and connecting it to a reasoned conclusion of guilt) is not permitted. Only direct evidence (the least reliable form of evidence) is. Direct evidence is given in the form of witnesses and/or confessions. Furthermore, if the condemned withdraws his or her confession, and does so four times, the punishment cannot be applied (Peiffer, 2005). *Hudud* crimes are thus least likely to result in the death penalty, so similar acts may be tried as a *quesas* or *ta'zir* crime to better assure conviction and punishment.

Whether the crime is a *quesas* or *hudud* offense depends on the circumstances. Murder would be punished as a *hudud* if it was committed during the commission of some other *hudud* crime such as a robbery or an act of terrorism, because terrorism is "waging war against God and his Apostle" and making or spreading "corruption on earth." Homosexual behavior and adultery can also be judged death-eligible crimes: homosexuality is a capital crime for men but carries a penalty of 100 lashes for females; married adulterers can receive the death penalty, while unmarried partners receive 100 lashes (El-Awa, 1982). Execution and amputations are carried out in Riyadh, Saudi Arabia's capital city, in Dira Square, which has been nicknamed "Chop Chop Square" by foreigners living there (see Figure 12.5).

Saudi Arabian judges typically have degrees in Shar'ia law and sometimes a postgraduate qualification from the Institute of Higher Judiciary in Riyadh. The legal education of these judges is entirely religious (based on the Qur'an and collections of religious saying of the prophet Muhammad called the *Hadith*), with no reference to any kind of secular procedural and evidentiary concerns (Walsh & Hemmens, 2014). Neither blacks (10% of the Saudi

FIGURE 12.5 Dira Square (also known as Chop Chop Square by expatriates), in Riyadh, the Capital City of Saudi Arabia, the Site of Public Amputations and Beheadings
Source: Taken by BroadArrow in 2007

population) nor women can be judges (Alahmed, 2013). Death penalty cases are tried before a three-judge panel known as the General Court; there is no jury system. Due to the lack of generalized principles of law, Saudi judges have almost unlimited discretion to render decisions based on their own distillation of the facts and the principles of religion. They are not bound by the precedents of higher courts as American courts are, and are not even bound by their own precedents. In murder cases, however, they are bound by the wishes of victims' families, who can demand execution or can "forgive" the defendant in exchange for blood money.

Death penalty sentences are appealable unless the sentence was handed down for a *hudud* or *quesas* crime, and appeals must be filed within 30 days following conviction. Because *hudud* crimes and their punishments are prescribed by the Qur'an, they are in theory not subject to interpretation, although pardons and stays have been granted by the king. However, even the king cannot reduce the punishment for a *hudud* crime; pardons are based only upon doubt about guilt. The death sentence for a *quesas* murder may be appealed to a victim's family only, and the family may then "pardon" the offender in exchange for blood money; there is no possibility of a government-issued pardon for *quesas* crimes. This leaves only death sentences for *ta'zir* crimes. *Ta'zir* crimes carrying the death penalty are mostly drug-related crimes (the death penalty is mandatory for drug smuggling) and terrorism but also include sorcery, heresy, or "spying for infidels."

Because there is little uniformity in Islamic law, judges have the discretion to ignore the *hudud/ta'zir* distinction in order to impose any sentence they want. Peiffer (2005) points to one case involving robbery, which is a *hudud* crime for which amputation is prescribed as a punishment. In this case, the judge sentenced two robbers to death by treating the robbery as a *ta'zir* crime, even though no one was hurt and the money stolen was returned. The Appellate Court must review these sentences but does not review either the law or the facts; rather, it "merely ensures that the judge paid sufficient attention to the point of objection" (Peiffer, 2005, p. 521).

Islamic Republic of Iran

Like Saudi Arabia, Iran is an Islamist state with a legal system based on the Qur'an and Shar'ia. Its law is slightly different than Saudi Arabia's because Iran follows Shia Islam, while the Saudis follow Sunni Islam. Prior to the Islamic Revolution led by Ayatollah Khomeini in 1979, Iran was a secular semi-democratic monarchy with a civil law code similar to the law in place in most European countries (Nayyeri, 2013). Today, it is a theocratic authoritarian state with power concentrated firmly in the Islamic clergy. At the top of the hierarchy is the supreme leader who is an ayatollah (a very high-ranking Shi'ite cleric), followed by the Guardian Council, which consists of 12 jurists who decide if legislation is permissible under Islamic law and who may run for president or parliament. After the Council comes the Assembly of Experts, which consists of Islamic scholars who supposedly oversee the activities of the supreme leader, and then the Expediency Council, which operates in an advisory role to the supreme leader. It is not until this point in the hierarchy that anything resembling secular authority emerges in the office of the president, who is totally subordinate to the supreme leader.

The criminal code in Iran is extremely harsh, and as in the case of North Korea and Saudi Arabia, it is often subject to political and/or judicial whims. MacEoin (2006) provides a particularly egregious example of a 16-year-old girl who was publicly hanged in 2004 for having unmarried sex (a *hudud* crime). In this case, it was judicial capriciousness rather than a strict interpretation of Islamic law that led to her sentence because Shar'ia law mandates execution only for married adulterers; unmarried sex is fornication, for which 80 lashes is the typical punishment. Her "real crime" is that she had talked back to the judge, "who later remarked that he would not have ordered her execution had it not been for her 'sharp tongue'" (p. 1). MacEoin (2006) provides a number of other examples, including the public hanging of two boys—one 18 and the other 16—for homosexual acts, also a *hudud* crime. The existence of both these "crimes" (unmarried and homosexual sex) and the execution of juveniles are contrary to international human rights laws (Nayyeri, 2013). However, Islamic governments see such rights as weakness and "oppose the notion of human rights as a Western or Zionist evil" (MacEoin, 2006, p. 11).

Because *hudud* crimes and their punishments are prescribed by the Qur'an, there is little or any difference between Saudi and Iranian practices with respect to them. Iranians are more likely to be executed by hanging than beheading, however, and adulterers may be stoned to death—a punishment still available in the new Islamic penal code of 2012 (Nayyeri, 2013). People convicted of robbery often have the fingers of their right hand amputated publicly prior to hanging (Iran Human Rights [IHR], 2014). Another difference is that for a murder charged as a *quesas*, members of the family of the victim are encouraged to carry out the execution (IHR, 2014). As in Saudi Arabia, the criminal can be forgiven by the family on the payment of blood money, but the state may then impose a prison sentence (but not a death sentence) if it believes that the murder may have public order consequences, such as the murder of a police officer or public official (IHR, 2014).

The *ta'zir* category of crimes is the most important category for administering punishment from the state's point of view, even though such crimes often carry less severe punishments. This is because the punishments for *hudud* crimes are prescribed by God and thus immutable and their evidentiary requirements difficult to meet; in the case of *quesas,* the state is more like a referee and must acquiesce to victims' wishes. *Ta'zir* crimes are thus offenses that are defined by the state and whose punishment is prescribed by the state. This state prerogative led to the death sentence for a 20-year-old student for throwing three stones during a protest. The court reasoned that a rock is a weapon and throwing one was an act of war against God. This was its interpretation of a statute from the code that reads: "Any person who resorts to a weapon to cause terror and fear or disruption of public safety will be considered a *mohareb*" [a person who wages war against God] (in Nayyeri, 2013, p. 13).

The new Iranian penal code indirectly encourages the murder of individuals belonging to certain disfavored groups by private Iranian citizens (Nayyeri, 2013; IHR, 2014). The following persons or situations exempt people who kill others from *quesas*:

> Father and paternal (not maternal) grandfathers of the victim
> Killing someone who has committed a *hudud* crime punishable by death
> Killing a rapist
> Killing a wife and her lover caught in the act of adultery
> Muslims who kill followers of unrecognized religions or nonprotected persons

A "nonprotected person" is a member of a non-Muslim faith or anyone considered a terrorist and an enemy of Iran. Although Amnesty International (2014) reports "only" 369 executions in Iran in 2013, according to the IHR (2014), there were "at least" 687 confirmed and 130 unconfirmed executions in 2013, and 142 in the first two months of 2014. Also according to the IHR (2014), most (48%) of executions were for drug offenses, followed by murder (22%), rape/sexual assault (8%), and *mohareb* (5%), and 17% were for unknown offenses. The IHR also stresses: "It is important to emphasize that the lack of due process of law, unfair trials, forced confessions, the use of torture and the political nature of the Iranian judicial system are all major problems that must be kept in mind when analysing the use of the death penalty in Iran" (2014, p. 9).

Republic of Iraq

The Republic of Iraq is defined in its 2005 constitution as a democratic, federal, Islamic republic composed of executive, legislative, and judicial branches with political power residing with a president and a prime minister. Passed during the American occupation, the initial Iraqi constitution had a decidedly Western flavor. However, as Shi'ite Islamists have come more to the fore in government, they have looked to impose Shar'ia law on Iraqi society and to eliminate all Western influences in the constitution. The 2005 constitution enshrined women's rights regarding marriage, inheritance, and child custody, and is viewed as the most progressive in the Middle East (Brown, 2005). However, in 2014, the Iraqi cabinet voted in favor of Shi'ite Islamic jurisprudence in personal status affairs and permits the marriage of girls as young as 9, automatically awards child custody to fathers, and allow husbands to demand sex from their wives whenever they wish (al-Salhy, 2014). Given the movement toward Shar'ia in personal status matters, the criminal code may also revert to Shar'ia in the near future. This has already happened in the parts of Iraq that are in the hands of ISIS (the Islamic State of Syria and Iraq) as of March 2015. It is indeed ironic that the Iraq War, which was initiated by President George W. Bush and was supposed to lead to democracy, has resulted in a more Islamified and brutal Iraq than was the case under the leadership of the secular Saddam Hussein.

From Table 12.1, we see that Iraq led the world in the rate of executions in 2013, with a rate over 41 times higher than that of the United States. Iraq is in a unique situation, however, in that it is currently caught up in the middle of serious violent sectarian conflicts (including mass terrorist bombings) between Sunni and Shi'ite factions of Islam, and in particular with ISIS, a vicious Sunni group intent on establishing a modern-day caliphate in the region. Most of the executions in Iraq are for terrorist or drug-related activities in support of terrorism (NLCIHR, 2013b), but ISIS itself executes any person of another religious faith who refuses to convert to its brand of Islam in the territories under its control. Indicative of the increasing influence of Islamic principles in Iraqi society, there have been reports of individuals being executed for consensual homosexual activity, although these executions were carried out by militias and were therefore extra-judicial executions; that is, they were not officially sanctioned by a legal Iraqi government (Jakes, 2012).

Theoretically, defendants facing the death penalty in non-ISIS–controlled Iraq have access to lawyers, but lawyers are scarce in Iraq, the quality of representation is poor, and lawyers who defend death-eligible defendants open themselves to threats and intimidation—lawyers have actually suffered detention, torture, and even death at the hands of various militias (U.S. Department of State, 2013). Few death penalty cases actually go to a trial, with almost all convictions being the result of confessions, often obtained through torture or threat of torture. Amnesty International (2013) provides many examples of these practices in its publication "Iraq: A Decade of Abuses." Many people have been sentenced to death as the result of such questionable confessions, even with the court noting allegations of torture.

Death sentences are appealed to the Court of Cassation (cassation means "to quash"; i.e., to reverse the decisions of lower courts), and both the president and prime minister have the power to pardon a defendant. One appeal is allowed and must be heard within a month following the verdict. Again according to Amnesty International (2013), lawyers are rarely available to defendants at appeal, and if the appeal fails or an executive pardon is not forthcoming, the death sentence must be enforced within 30 days of the final verdict (NLCIHR, 2013b).

SUMMARY

This chapter began by asking why the United States, alone among Western democracies, retains the death penalty. When most scholars answer this question, they do so in terms of public opinion and the fear of electoral reprisal for politicians who thwart the public will, which still favors capital punishment.

The federal government has its own death penalty separate from that of individual states, although it hasn't executed anyone since 2003. Because American citizens are citizens of both the United States and their state of residence, it is possible for them to be re-tried, after an acquittal at the state level, in a federal court because of the principle of dual sovereignty. The federal government can take on the legal prosecution of a state case with or without the state's consent, but in many instances, states are willing to have the federal government do so, and may even request this course of action if they believe the state punishment for the crime in question is inadequate.

The U.S. military also has an independent death penalty, although it has not executed anyone since 1961. Despite the large number of offenses (14) that possibly carry the death penalty in the military, only six inmates currently sit on its death row, all for particularly heinous crimes that would result in the death penalty in any capital punishment state.

We then took a look at the death penalty from an international perspective, under the assumption that a comparative view results in a deeper level of insight into the familiar. We first examined the use of the death penalty in China, a country that executes far more people than any other nation, although its rate of execution is less than that of Iraq, Iran, or North Korea. As of 2015, China permitted the death penalty for 55 different offenses. There are few procedural rules governing trials and appeals for crimes in China, but there are a modicum of rights available now that were not applicable previously. Today, China executes most of its condemned via lethal injection, and accusations have been made that the organs of executed persons are frequently harvested and sold.

North Korea is "officially" the least democratic country in the world. It is a very secretive society that executes numerous individuals for almost any offense that the government deems threatening to the stability of the nation. One can even be executed for something as vague as "being a scoundrel," without representation by an attorney. Estimates of North Korea's rate of execution put it at about 32 times greater than the U.S. rate.

Saudi Arabia is another country with a complete disregard for human rights. It is a theocratic state that uses the Qur'an as its constitution. It has nothing like the Western notion of law as a uniform set of principles applicable across the board and relies on ad hoc decisions made by judges trained in religion rather than law. Saudi Arabia carries out barbaric punishments for *hudud* crimes as prescribed by the Qur'an. Murder is not a *hudud* crime and can be forgiven by the payment of blood money. The Saudis often find it more convenient to charge crimes as *ta'zir* offenses, even though they may fall under the rubric of a *hudud* or *quisas* crime because they are not bound by the strict evidentiary rules of a *hudud* crime, nor can they be forgiven by offended parties through the payment of blood money.

Iran is also an Islamic country with a legal system based on the Qur'an. It, too, applies the death penalty for a variety of crimes, including premarital sex and homosexuality. As in all the comparison countries examined, torture is often used to obtain confessions from suspects. Because of the lack of a uniform system of laws, judges have almost unlimited discretion as to the sentences they impose. In 2013 Iran had an estimated execution rate almost 39 times the U.S. rate.

Finally, we looked at the place of capital punishment in Iraq. It was once believed by a number of optimists that Iraq would become a beacon of democracy in the Middle East following the Iraq War and the enactment of a U.S.-inspired constitution. However, with the premature withdrawal of American troops in 2011, the nation rapidly became more Islamified than it was under Saddam Hussein. Many rights in the constitution were simply withdrawn, and as of 2015, the future of Iraq is far from clear. Even before the barbarism of the Islamic State of Iraq (ISIL) became apparent, Iraq was executing people at a high rate (41 times higher than the U.S. rate) without even a semblance of due process.

DISCUSSION QUESTIONS

1. What is an alternative view of why the United States retains the death penalty?
2. Should the federal government have interfered with the jury verdict acquitting the police officers who beat Rodney King? Why or why not?
3. Should the federal government have removed the case of Ronell Wilson from the state of New York? If you think the federal government was right in its decision to take on this case but wrong in the *King* case (or vice versa), give your reasons for the contradictions.
4. Should the U.S. military retain the death penalty for nonhomicide cases given its special needs and concerns?
5. Give your opinion about the "harvesting" of vital organs from executed criminals in China.
6. Would you rather be on trial for murder in China or Saudi Arabia?
7. Some Islamic countries favor public executions. What are their reasons for this? What might be the reaction in the United States if we resumed public executions?

GLOSSARY

Anti-Drug Abuse Act: The act of legislation that reinstated the death penalty in federal law in an effort to control drug trafficking.

Federal Death Penalty Act: The act of legislation establishing constitutional procedures for the imposition of the death penalty for 60 offenses under 13 existing and 28 new federal capital statutes.

Uniform Code of Military Justice (UCMJ): The code establishing a standard set of procedural and substantive criminal laws for the U.S. military services.

REFERENCES

Alahmed, A. (2013, March 15). "The execution of the Saudi seven." *Foreign Policy*. http://www.foreignpolicy.com/articles/2013/03/15/The_execution_of_the_Saudi_Seven.

al-Salhy, S. (2014, March 8). "Iraqi women protest against proposed Islamic law in Iraq." http://www.reuters.com/article/2014/03/08/us-iraq-women-islam-idUSBREA270NR20140308.

Amnesty International. (2013). "Iraq: A Decade of Abuses." https://www.amnesty.org/en/documents/MDE14/001/2013/en/ http://www.amnesty.ch/de/laender/naher-osten-nordafrika/irak/dok/2013/ein-jahrzehnt-der-menschenrechtsverletzungen/iraq-a-decade-of-abuses-91-p.

Amnesty International. (2014). "Death Sentences and Executions: 2013." http://www.amnestyusa.org/research/reports/death-sentences-and-executions-2013.

Angus Reid. (2013). Three in five Canadians would bring back death penalty. http://angusreidglobal.com/wp-content/uploads/2013/03/2013.03.20_Death_CAN.pdf

Bezlova, A. (2006, March 31). "China to 'Kill Fewer, Kill Carefully.'" *Asia Times*. http://www.atimes.com/atimes/China/HC31Ad01.html.

British Foreign Office. (2013). "Information Pack for British Prisoners in Saudi Arabia." https://www.gov.uk/government/.../saudi-arabia-prisoner-pack.

Brown, N. (2005). *Debating Islam in post-Baathist Iraq*. Washington, DC: Carnegie Endowment for International Peace.

Connor, E. (2010). The undermining influence of the federal death penalty on capital policymaking and criminal justice administration in the states. *Journal of Criminal Law and Criminology, 100*, 149–211.

Death Penalty Information Center (2015). Women on death row. http://www.deathpenaltyinfo.org/women-and-death-penalty

Deng, X., L. Zhang, and A. Cordilia. (1998). Social control and recidivism in China. *Journal of Contemporary Criminal Justice, 14*, 281–295.

Dui Hua. (2011). "Dui Hua Estimates 4,000 Executions in China, Welcomes Open Dialogue." http://duihua.org/wp/?page_id=3874.

Economist Intelligence Unit. (2013). "Democracy Index 2012." http://www.eiu.com/public/topical_report.aspx?...DemocracyIndex201.1.

El-Awa, M. (1982). *Punishment in Islamic law: A comparative study.* Indianapolis, IN: American Trust.

Fan, M., and A. Cha. (2008, December 23). "China's Capital Cases Still Secret, Arbitrary." *The Washington Post.* http://www.washingtonpost.com/wp-dyn/content/article/ 2008/12/23/AR2008122302795.html.

Garland, D. (2012). "Why Does the U.S. Have Capital Punishment?" *Embassy of the United States of America.* http://photos.state.gov/libraries/amgov/133183/english/P_You_Asked_WhyCapitalPunishment_English.pdf.

Hemmingway, S. (2014, May 21). "Family Confronts Jacques as Killer Sentenced to Life." *Burlington Free Press.* http://www.burlingtonfreepress.com/story/news/local/2014/05/20/jacques-sentencing-niece-murder/9319095/.

Iran Human Rights. (2014). "Annual Report on the Death Penalty in Iran: 2013." http://www.abolition.fr/sites/default/files/rapport_iran_2014-gb-040314-hd.pdf.

Jakes, L. (2012). "Iraq Emo Killings Raise Alarm." http://www.huffingtonpost.com/2012/03/11/iraq-emo-killings-gay_n_1337427.html.

Judge Advocate General's Corps. (1983). "Annual Report of the U.S. Court of Military Appeals." http://www.loc.gov/rr/frd/Military_Law/pdf/Annual-report-USCMA-FY1983.pdf.

Koener, B. (2008, November). "When Do Soldiers Face Execution?" *Slate.* http://www.slate.com/articles/news_and_politics/recycled/2008/11/when_do_soldiers_face_execution.html.

Lee, Y. (2013, November 11). "Public Executions Seen in 7 North Korean Cities." *JoongAng Daily.* http://koreajoongangdaily.joins.com/news/article/article.aspx?aid=2980240.

Liu, J., R. Zhao, H. Xiong, & J. Gong. (2012). Chinese legal traditions: Punitiveness versus mercy. *Asian Pacific Journal of Police & Criminal Justice, 9,* 17–33.

MacEoin, D. (2006, Fall). Why do Muslims execute innocent people? *Middle East Quarterly, 13,* 15–25.

MacLeod, C. (2006, June 15). "China Makes Ultimate Punishment Mobile." *USA Today.* http://usatoday30.usatoday.com/news/world/2006-06-14-death-van_x.htm.

Mannheimer, M. (2011). Developments in criminal and evidentiary law: Self-government, the federal death penalty, and the unusual case of Michael Jacques. *Vermont Law Review, 33,* 131–161.

Myren, R. (1988). *Law and justice: An introduction.* Pacific Grove, CA: Brooks/Cole.

Mysliwiec, P. (2010). Federal death penalty as a safety valve. *Virginia Journal of Social Policy and Law, 17,* 257–280.

Nayyeri, M. (2013). "Gender inequality and discrimination: The case of Iranian women. Iran Human Rights Documentation Center." http://iranhrdc.org/english/publications/legal-commentary/1000000261-gender-inequality-and-discrimination-the-case-of-iranian-women.html

Northwestern Law Center for International Human Rights. (2011). "The Death Penalty Worldwide: China." http://www.deathpenaltyworldwide.org/country-search- post.cfm?country=China.

Northwestern Law Center for International Human Rights. (2013a). "The Death Penalty Worldwide: North Korea." http://www.deathpenaltyworldwide.org/country-search-post.cfm?country =North+Korea.

Northwestern Law Center for International Human Rights. (2013b). "The Death Penalty Worldwide: Iraq." http://www.deathpenaltyworldwide.org/country-search-post.cfm?country=Iraq.

Peiffer, E. (2005). The death penalty in traditional Islamic law as interpreted in Saudi Arabia and Nigeria. *William and Mary Journal of Women and the Law, 11,* 507–539.

Robinson, M. (2008). *Death nation: The experts explain American capital punishment.* Upper Saddle River, NJ: Prentice Hall.

Uniform Code of Military Justice. (2010). "Uniform Code of Military Justice." http://www.gpo.gov/fdsys/pkg/USCODE-2010-title10/pdf/USCODE-2010-title10-subtitleA-partII-chap47.pdf.

U.S. Department of State. (2010, March 11). "Human Rights Report: Democratic People's Republic of Korea." http://www.state.gov/g/drl/rls/hrrpt/2009/eap/135995.htm.

U.S. Department of State. (2013, April 19). "2012 Human Rights Report: Iraq." http://www.state.gov/j/drl/rls/hrrpt/2012/nea/204362.htm.

United States v. Matthews. (1983). 16 M.J. 354, 380 (C.M.A.).

Valencia, M. (2014, December 23). "Judge Postpones Death Penalty Trial of Convicted Killer: Decision Angers Families of Sampson Victims." *Boston Globe.* https://www.bostonglobe.com/metro/2014/12/23/judge-postpones-death-penalty-trial-convicted-killer-gary-lee-sampson/7zXtgKo1aMpFcIwHBDD8xJ/story.html.

Walsh, A. (2009). *Biology and criminology: the biosocial synthesis.* New York: Routledge.

Walsh, A., and C. Hemmens. (2014). *Law, justice, and society: A sociolegal introduction,* 3d ed. New York: Oxford University Press.

EPILOGUE

LIBBY THE LIBERAL AND CONRAD THE CONSERVATIVE DEBATE THE DEATH PENALTY

This "wrap-up" section features a conversation between Libby the Liberal and Conrad the Conservative on the pros and cons of the death penalty, reiterating a number of points raised in chapters of this book. We have, of course, stereotyped liberals as opposed to capital punishment and conservatives in favor of it to illustrate our points. As we saw in the public opinion chapter, however, 47% of self-identified liberals support the death penalty and 25% of self-identified conservatives oppose it. Thus, there are conservatives who oppose the death penalty as well as liberals who support it. A conservative website even exists devoted to opposing the death penalty called Conservatives Concerned About the Death Penalty. The following statement appears there: "Conservatives Concerned about the Death Penalty is a network of political and social conservatives who question the alignment of capital punishment with conservative principles and values." Conservatives tend to mistrust the government and believe that it cannot do anything right, so some oppose capital punishment for this reason. Libby and Conrad are simply reflections of the views on the death penalty held by the many people who define themselves as liberal or conservative.

Both Libby and Conrad are nontraditional students with B.A./B.S. degrees (Libby in social work and Conrad in criminal justice) returning for M.A./M.S. degrees in criminal justice. Libby has worked as a social worker for the past eight years, and Conrad as a police officer for the past 10 years. At the moment they are classmates in Criminal Justice 503: Ethics in Criminal Justice. Although they are in the same program, this is the first class the two have shared, and previous to this conversation, they have not spoken beyond exchanging pleasantries. They sit down and after a few nervous preliminaries start to discuss the ethics class. The class involves the study of the great philosophers on a variety of ethical issues, including issues of justice, punishment, and the duty of human beings to their fellow human beings. As criminal justice M.A. candidates, they find this format stimulating and a welcome change of pace from how such issues are usually discussed in their other criminal justice classes. The following is a transcript of their hypothetical conversation.

	CONRAD, LIBBY, AND THE DEATH PENALTY
Conrad	So, Libby, what did you think of Dr. Jackson's class today?
Libby	I thought it was very stimulating, but I'm upset at what he said about Kant's justification of the death penalty because on the whole I agree with his deontological ethics—that if something is done with good intentions, and out of a sense of duty, it is morally right. But the death penalty is immoral, no matter what ethical standards we might use to justify it.
Conrad	Not sure if I agree wholeheartedly with Kant. After all, don't they say that the road to Hell is paved with good intentions? But, on the issue of the death penalty, Kant is absolutely right. By killing another human being, according to Kant, the criminal is condoning such behavior, and therefore the state has a right to execute him by his own standards of morality. Doing otherwise would be to disrespect his autonomy.
Libby	Disrespecting his autonomy? Please don't forget that the criminal is not choosing to be executed. Capital punishment is a barbaric anachronism that the United States shares with such authoritarian countries as China and Iran. All other democracies except Japan and South Korea have abolished it. Why are we in the company of countries like China, Saudi Arabia, and Iran instead of Britain, France, and Germany? Indeed, I learned in our corrections class that according to Amnesty International in 2005, China, Iran, Saudi Arabia, and the United States accounted for 94% of the world's known executions. China, Iran, and Saudi Arabia have always shown a lack of respect for the dignity of human life, and our sense of decency should prevent us from being associated with such countries in any way. After all, Conrad, don't we want a state that is better than its people, specifically those who commit heinous crimes?
Conrad	There's a heck of a difference between executions in the United States and in those other countries. People are executed in those countries for all kinds of things, such as homosexuality, converting to another religion, and nonviolent economic crimes, with no, or very few, procedural guidelines. Criminals in the United States are executed only for the most brutal acts of murder, and then only after passing through multiple appeals are they executed many years later.

Libby	Yes, that's true, but the end result is still the killing of another human being by the state in the name of the people. Well, I'm "the people" too, and I find it morally repugnant that the state murders people in my name—or anyone else's. Recall Beccaria's warning that state killings may perpetuate tyranny and desensitize society to death.
Conrad	Libby, you said "murder," but that's an attempt to put what the state does on the same moral ground as what the murderer did.
Libby	Murder is defined as the intentional killing of another, right? Killing is killing, isn't it?
Conrad	Well, let me first say that the moral equivalency of physically equivalent acts is not automatically valid. If, let's say, Dr. Jackson restricts your freedom, binds you, and forcibly transports you his home and locks you in his basement, what he has done it is called "kidnapping." Kidnapping you is a crime. If I, as a police officer, did the same thing to you because you were driving drunk, it is called "arrest." Police officers are legitimate holders of legal authority who represent society's moral order, and they act in its name. The same holds for those who administer the death penalty. Arrest is a moral and legitimate social reaction to some immoral harm done to society. The death penalty is also a moral and legitimate social reaction to an immoral act.
Libby	So what you are saying is that because it is legal today in this country that it is morally right? I'm sure you would agree with me that the Holocaust and slavery were wrong. In both of these cases, the police were enforcing morally wrong laws. If laws were not changed to reflect changing societal values, I still wouldn't have the right to vote as a woman. Admit it, Conrad, our society has evolved . . . but you obviously have not.
Conrad	I am saying that the moral difference between arrest and kidnapping is the same as the moral difference between execution and murder.
Libby	OK, I understand what you are saying, but hear me out. I am saying that the only thing that is separating execution from murder are the current laws of our states where the death penalty is legal. In states that have abolished the death penalty, if those state officials executed a convicted criminal, they would be arrested for murder, right?

Conrad	The state kills—if you absolutely insist I use that word—to protect society and to reinforce its moral norms. The U.S. Supreme Court has found the death penalty to pass constitutional muster for good reason.
Libby	You have the U.S. Supreme Court on your side and I have the rest of the Western world on mine. We will have to agree to disagree on this.
Conrad	Come on, Libby, we have to have some serious punishment mechanism in place for heinous murderers so that others don't think it is OK for them to do it. This has long been recognized as a justification for execution—to deter others from doing it, and that's one of the reasons we execute—sorry, "kill"—murderers.
Libby	Are you trying to tell me that capital punishment deters crime, despite all the evidence to the contrary? I read an article once that said something like 88% of police chiefs say that capital punishment does not deter crime.
Conrad	No one claims that capital punishment deters crime in general. Only a cop on every corner, and then we would need someone to watch them, could possibly deter crime. I'm only claiming that capital punishment deters some instances of capital murder.
Libby	OK, but even Dr. Jackson says there is no sound evidence that it is a deterrent. It may be a deterrent in societies where it is used frequently, mercilessly, and without much legal ado, but not in this country where it is rare, controversial, and takes place many years after conviction. In light of this, and if deterrence is the only rationale for capital punishment, maybe we should join other democracies and rid ourselves of this draconian practice.
Conrad	I agree that there have been few convincing studies demonstrating a deterrent effect of capital punishment in the United States, but, to turn your argument around, if the death penalty were imposed with greater certainty and frequency, we may be able to demonstrate such an effect. There are just too few executions to be able with any degree of certainty to claim a deterrent effect, but by the same token, no study can claim that it is not a deterrent under the current conditions.

Libby	Maybe so, but I'd rather believe the vast majority of criminologists who claim that the death penalty it is not a deterrent.
Conrad	Yes, but most criminologists are academics and have never had to deal with criminals. They may claim that it is not a deterrent, but that's a long way from proving that it's not. The deterrence studies typically examine all homicides, which is a bit of a cheat, since the vast majority of homicides are crimes of passion for which the death penalty does not apply. Studies should be conducted only on the effect of capital punishment on homicides committed with deliberation and premeditation. These homicides are by definition crimes that the perpetrators have thought about (premeditated) and so presumably have thought about the penalty for committing it.
Libby	You are ignoring the fact that states without the death penalty have no fewer murders than states with it. If the death penalty deterred, we would see that death penalty states had lower murder rates, wouldn't we?
Conrad	We might if the death penalty was carried out more frequently and swiftly, but as I said before, it is difficult to discover an effect when it is used so infrequently.
Libby	Conrad, you want to kill—sorry, "execute"—more people to show society that killing is wrong?
Conrad	Yep, if it means saving innocent lives, I do.
Libby	But you've taken the argument back to deterrence, which we have agreed is something we cannot prove or disprove.
Conrad	That's right. We don't know, but under conditions of uncertainty regarding either/or questions—the death penalty either deters or it does not—we can only place our bet on the option that promises the most advantageous outcomes. Let's say for the moment that the death penalty does deter but we can't demonstrate it. If it deters and we choose to use it, we prevent the death of innocent victims. If we do not choose to use it, we'll be party to the murders of those victims.
Libby	What if it does not deter and we use it? We haven't saved anyone's life and we have taken the lives of others.

Conrad	Yes, if it does not deter and we choose to use it, we have gained nothing, and the only cost we have sustained are the lives of those who deserved to die anyway. This cost–benefit assessment, what society stands to lose or gain under these conditions, places the burden of proof squarely on the shoulders of those who wish to abolish the death penalty, not on its proponents. In other words, society stands to gain more by retaining the death penalty if it deters than it stands to gain if the death penalty does not deter and we abolish it. I argue that the onus is on those who wish to deprive society of this alleged protection to prove their case more convincingly.
Libby	This "best bet" argument is all very fine as a hypothetical, but what you are doing is gambling with lives, and I find that objectionable.
Conrad	Well, Libby, either side of the argument is gambling with lives. The difference is that the "execute" side is gambling only with the lives of murderers. The "don't execute" side is gambling with the lives of potential victims. Gambling with the lives of potential victims is what I find objectionable.
Libby	But Conrad, what about the possibility that some people we execute are factually innocent? Didn't Blackstone say that it is better to free 10 guilty men than to see one innocent man suffer?
Conrad	If we were talking 25 years ago, I would agree that the risk of executing the innocent is not worth the retention of the death penalty, but now with multiple safeguards and DNA evidence, we can be reasonably sure of a "reasonably" error-free death penalty.
Libby	But not all death penalty cases hinge on DNA evidence. Many people are sentenced to death based on a whole host of other issues, such as eyewitness misidentification, false confession, and much more. Your argument holds no weight when considering non-DNA cases. As long as there is any possibility of a wrongful execution, we should oppose the death penalty. Did you hear about the man executed in Oklahoma after a new drug combination had him writhing and clenching his teeth on the execution gurney before he died of a heart attack? That's absolutely barbaric and has no place in a civilized society.

Conrad	I would save your sympathy for the woman he raped, shot, and buried alive while she was bleeding out. Who had the worse death: him or her? We should all die as easily as a murderer executed by lethal injection. Why do all you liberals have more sympathy for brutal murderers and rapists than their victims?
Libby	I don't have more sympathy for murderers than for their victims. Only the murderer, as a private citizen, is responsible for the death of his victims, and he should pay for it. If the state kills or executes him, however, I and every other member of society is a party to his death. It is this I object to—killing someone in my name—the murderer didn't do that.
Conrad	Yes, I can see your point on that and can only reply that I'm happy that the state extracts revenge in my name.
Libby	What about that federal judge in California who recently ruled that California's death penalty is unconstitutional? He said that the average person on death row in the state spends 25 years awaiting execution and that's cruel and unusual punishment. He also said that of the 900 inmates on death row since 1977, only 13 have been executed. This supports the notion that the death penalty was administered in an arbitrary and capricious way. The judge said that you couldn't predict who would and who would not get the death penalty based on the nature of the crimes they committed. As Dr. Jackson explains, these concerns mimic the *Furman* decision.
Conrad	I don't know whether to laugh or cry at this one! The courts create the problem of long delays for the benefit of the offender and then call long delays unconstitutional. This reminds us of the old joke about the woman who murdered her husband pleading with the judge for mercy on the grounds that she is a widow. Furthermore, did he examine the records of those who were executed to see if they were more deserving of it than others? I know of one murderer executed in California who raped and killed at least 13 boys and young men.
Libby	That I don't know. But can you imagine sitting on death row for 25 years or more wondering when or if your your time will come? The great French philosopher Camus once wrote that "a man is undone by waiting for capital punishment well before he dies." When we wait 25 years to execute someone, are we really executing the same person? No, we are often not. We have given them the time and opportunity to reform, which only makes the death penalty that much more despicable.

Conrad	Sure, waiting to die for 25 years with three hot meals and a cot and cable TV is so much worse than being already dead at the hands of the evil offender awaiting his fate. And it makes me sick to think about how much we pay for these criminals while they sit awaiting their execution day! The whole lengthy wait on death row debate is either a comedy or a tragedy—don't know which.
Libby	Since you are talking about costs, Conrad—you conservatives are always talking about fiscal responsibility and balancing the budget, but the death penalty has been known to bankrupt some smaller counties with nothing to show for it except a retributive sense of satisfaction for those who think that way. Did you see where the book says that some death penalty cases have cost up to $13 million?
Conrad	I agree with you here, Libby. The costs of pursuing justice in a capital case are prohibitive. I have long ago concluded that either we put an end to interminable appeals or get rid of the death penalty.
Libby	That AEDPA act that we read about was supposed to do that, but I'm glad it didn't work out. Do we really want a more rapid and "efficient" death penalty like Iran or Saudi Arabia or China? I don't think even the most conservative of conservatives would want that, do they?
Conrad	No, we don't want that. We just want justice for victims and their families, and I believe that can be delivered faster than we do now without becoming like Iran. If we cannot do that, then I'm for getting rid of the death penalty and spending the money we will save on other crime control measures.
Libby	Way to go, Conrad, it's about time you've finally come to your senses.
Conrad	Well, I don't know about that, but it sure is an interesting debate. Let's go grab coffee and we can discuss something safe, like religion.
Libby	Ha! Why don't we just play it safe and talk about the weather?

APPENDIX

Wilkerson v. Utah, 99 U.S. 130 (1878)
In re Kemmler, 136 U.S. 436, 447 (1890)
Louisiana ex rel. Francis v. Resweber, 329 U.S. 459 (1947)
Furman v. Georgia*, 408 U.S. 238 (1972)
Gregg v. Georgia*, 428 U.S. 153 (1976)
Woodson v. North Carolina, 428 U.S. 280 (1976)
Coker v. Georgia*, 433 U.S. 584 (1977)
Lockett v. Ohio*, 438 U.S. 586 (1978)
Bell v. Ohio, 438 U.S. 637 (1978)
Eddings v. Oklahoma, 455 U.S. 104 (1982)
Enmund v. Florida, 458 U.S. 782 (1982)
Lockhart v. McCree, 476 U.S. 162 (1986)
Ford v. Wainwright, 477 U.S. 399 (1986)
Turner v. Murray, 476 U.S. 28 (1986)
McCleskey v. Kemp*, 481 U.S. 279 (1987)
Thompson v. Oklahoma, 487 U.S. 815 (1988)
Penry v. Lynaugh, 492 U.S. 302 (1989)
Stanford v. Kentucky*, 492 U.S. 361 (1989)
Payne v. Tennessee, 501 U.S. 808 (1991)
Walton v. Arizona, 497 U.S. 639 (1990)
Apprendi v. New Jersey, 530 U.S. 446 (2000)
Ring v. Arizona*, 536 U.S. 584 (2002)
Atkins v. Virginia*, 536 U.S. 304 (2002)
Tennard v. Dretke, 542 U.S. 274 (2004)
Miller-El v. Dretke, 545 U.S. 231 (2005)
Roper v. Simmons*, 543 U.S. 551 (2005)
Panetti v. Quarterman, 551 U.S. 930 (2007)
Snyder v. Louisiana, 552 U.S. 472 (2008)
Baze v. Rees*, 553 U.S. 35 (2008)
Kennedy v. Louisiana, 554 U.S. 407 (2008)
Hall v. Florida, 572 U.S. ___ (2014)
Glossip v. Gross, 576 U.S. ___ (2015)

---

*Foundational cases discussed in Chapters 3 and 4 are in bold.

INDEX

AAIDD. *See* American Association on Intellectual and Developmental Disabilities
ABA. *See* American Board of Anesthesiology
Abbott, James P., 282f, 282–84
abolition, 40, 164, 217. *See also* innocence
    abolitionist movement, 38–42, 110, 151
    "best bet" argument and, 176–77
    family of victims and, 284
    finances and, 283
    gender and, 201
    in Illinois, 234
    for juveniles, 195–96
    public opinion and, 119–20
    society and, 284
    wrongful convictions and, 283
absolute immunity, 265
accountability, 12
AC electricity, 130
Ackerman, Melissa, 233
actus reus. *See* guilty act
administration, of prison, 45–47
adolescence, 226–27
adultery, 4, 29–30, 319, 321
AEDPA. *See* Antiterrorism and Effective Death Penalty Act
affirmative defense, 216
African Americans, 185, 186, 188, 194
afterlife, 176
age, 74, 183–85, 197
agency, 13–14
aggravating factors, 60, 89, 95, 190–91, 192, 208, 306
Akbar, Hasan, 307
Alabama, 39
ALI. *See* American Legal Institute
Allah, 317
allele, 221–22
Allen, Clarence Ray, 279
Allen, Floyd, 59
Allen, Wanda Jean, 199, 201
Allen v. Ornoski (2006), 279
alpha males, 8
altruism, 7
American Association on Intellectual and Developmental Disabilities (AAIDD), 93
American Board of Anesthesiology (ABA), 149
American Legal Institute (ALI), 59–60

American Psychiatric Association (APA), 83
American Society for the Abolition of Capital Punishment, 40
American Society of Criminology (ASC), 173–74, 178
America's Most Wanted, 248
amicus curiae, 196, 227
Amnesty International, 118, 308–9, 318, 322, 323
amputation, 318–21
amygdala, 234
anarchy, 6, 57, 106
ancestors, 6–7
Anti-Drug Abuse Act (1988), 300
anti-gallows movement, 109–10
antiquity, 30–31
Antiterrorism and Effective Death Penalty Act (AEDPA), 276–77, 287–89, 290f, 293
APA. *See* American Psychiatric Association
apostasy, 297–98
Apprendi v. New Jersey (2000), 91
Arab Islamic states, 11
Arizona, 42, 89–90
Articles of War, 306
Asbury, Heather, 113f, 114
ASC. *See* American Society of Criminology
ASCAAF. *See* United States Court of Appeals for the Armed Forces
Atkins, Daryl Renard, 83–84
Atkins v. Virginia (2002)
    back-story of, 83–84
    concurring opinions in, 84–85
    dissenting opinions in, 85–87
    Eighth Amendment and, 92, 118–19
    mental retardation and, 118–19, 196–97, 206, 210, 227
    ruling, 95, 101t
    Supreme Court justices in, 83f, 84–87
attitudinal model, 108–9
attorneys, 262, 290. *See also* counsel
autonomy, 20
autoregressive integrated moving average, 166

Badawi, Raif, 297
Bailey, Billy, 128–29
Bailey, William, 165
Baldus study, 69, 70, 71
Barfield, Velma, 198

Basso, Suzanne, 200
Batson v. Kentucky (1986), 72
Baze, Ralph, 98
Baze and Bowling v. Reez (2008)
    back-story of, 98
    concurring opinions in, 99–100
    deterrence and, 166
    dissenting opinions in, 100
    ruling, 101*t*
    Supreme Courts justices in, 99*f*, 99–100
beatings, 192
Beaver, Craig, 202*f*, 203–5
Beaver, Kevin, 219
Beccaria, Cesare, 10, 38, 109, 120, 159
Beets, Betty Lou, 198
behavior
    adolescent, 226–27
    contrast effect, 158–59
    control, 8
    criminal, 15
    factors contributing to, 14
    genes and, 221
    primate, 8
    rational, 12–13
    rational choice theory, 156–58
    violent, 229
beheading, 310, 321
belief systems, 105
Bell v. Ohio (1978), 66
belly chains, 46
Benjamin, Charles, 94–95
Bennett, Brooke, 304–5
Bennett, John, 306
Bentham, Jeremy, 12, 172
bestiality, 194
Bill of Rights, 90, 243, 286
Bird, Rose, 277
Blackmun, Harry, 58, 61, 67, 71, 74–75, 262
Blackstone, William, 205, 207, 244–45
Blackstone ratio, 244–45
Blackwelder, John, 155, 168
Block, Lynda Lyon, 199
blood atonement, 142–43
blood money. *See diyya*
blood-oxygen-level-dependent (BOLD) contrast, 225, 232, 235
Bloodsworth, Kirk, 283
"Bloody Code," 33
Bohm, Robert, 106
BOLD. *See* blood-oxygen-level-dependent contrast
Booth, Dorothy, 200
Boston Marathon bombing, 173, 301, 302*f*
Bounds, Dallen, 113–14
Bowling, Thomas, 99
brain
    amygdala, 234
    BOLD, 225, 232, 235
    CAT scans, 230
    development in adolescents, 226–27
    emotion and, 4
    fMRI, 224–25, 232–33, 235
    function of, 224
    genes and, 220
    hemoglobin, 225
    imaging, 216, 224–30, 232–33, 233–34, 235
    imaging, juveniles and, 225–27
    mental illness and, 228
    MRI, 224
    neurons, 225
    neuropsychiatrist's perspective, 227–30
    neuropsychology, 202–5
    neuroscience, 216, 218, 219, 220, 229
    neurotransmitters, 219
    oxygen and, 225
    PFC, 226
    reward centers of, 8
    testing, 232
Branch v. Texas, 56
Brennan, William, 57–58, 61, 64, 71, 74–75, 247
Brewer, Lawrence Russell, 150–51
British Bill of Rights, 54
Britton, James, 29
brutalizing effect, of punishment, 167–69, 178
Buenoano, Judy, 198
Burdell, Michael, 125
Burger, Warren, 58, 59, 61, 64
Bush, George W., 307, 323

California, 107, 107n1, 277, 278*f*, 279–80, 293
Canada, 120
Carney, Cormac, 160, 278–79
Carter, Jimmy, 108, 247
Carver, Allen, 63
Carver, Elnita, 63
case effect, 193
categorical imperative, 19
CAT scans, 230
causation, 232
CDDP. *See* Committee on Deterrence and the Death Penalty
"Central Park jogger," 251
certainty, of punishment, 159–60, 171–72
certiorari, 279
Champagne, Crystal, 239–40
Champion, Jane, 197
Chapman, Jay, 144–45, 146
Charboneau v. Klauser (1997), 261–62
childhood, effect on juveniles, 81
Chilton, Ricky, 255
chivalry, 200–201, 210
Christianity, 3, 5
chromosomes, 221
civil rights movement, 42, 184, 299, 301
Clarke, Judy, 302
classical school, 12
clemency, 40, 47, 107, 291
Clinton, Bill, 287
closure, for family members, 172, 291
Code of Hammurabi, 38

co-evolution, 5–8
Coker, Ehrlich Anthony, 62–63
Coker v. Georgia (1977)
    back-story of, 63
    concurring opinions in, 63–64
    dissenting opinions in, 64–65
    ruling, 76t
    Supreme Court justices during, 62f, 63–65
Coleman, Lisa, 200, 201
collateral costs, 290–92
collective conscience, 3
Colonial law, 34
Colwell, Daniel, 155, 168
Commentaries on the Laws of England (Blackstone), 205
Committee on Deterrence and the Death Penalty (CDDP), 168–70, 178
communism, 311–15
community
    death sentencing and, 173
    juries and, 90
    offenders and, 32
    protection, 243–44
    punishment and, 173
    solidarity, 34
compassion, 31
compatibilism, 13–15
competency, 183–85, 208–9
compliant confessions, 251
compound pharmacies, 149
concurring opinions
    in *Atkins v. Virginia*, 84–85
    in *Baze and Bowling v. Reez*, 99–100
    in *Coker v. Georgia*, 63–64
    in *Furman v. Georgia*, 56–58
    in *Gregg v. Georgia*, 61
    in *Lockett v. Ohio*, 67
    in *McCleskey v. Kemp*, 70–71
    in *Ring v. Arizona*, 89–90
    in *Roper v. Simmons*, 96–97
    in *Stanford v. Kentucky*, 74
confessions
    compliant, 251
    false, 250–54
    internalized, 252
    mental disabilities and, 206
    Reid technique, 252
    torture and, 313
    voluntary, 250–51
Connecticut, 284
conscience, 157
consequentialism, 15, 177
Constitution, U.S., 71–72, 299. *See also specific Amendments*
    commerce clause, 304–5
    deterrence and, 161–62
    framers of, 63, 107–8
    international opinion and, 86
    lethal injection and, 99–100
    rights in, 286

contract killings, 173
contrast effect, 158–59
control behavior, 8
Conviction, 241
correlation, 232
corruption, 3
costs. *See* finances
Cotton, Ronald, 246f, 247
counsel, 260–63, 290
court costs, 281, 284
court-martial, 306–7, 308
Court of Cassation, 323
Cramer, Elliot, 186
crime
    control model of criminal justice, 243–44, 285
    degree of, 39
    elements of, 90
    interracial, 72
    local aspect of, 310
    motivations for, 157, 171
    prevention of, 22
    rate, 42, 111, 111f
    slavery and, 186
    types of crimes in Islamic law, 318–19, 320, 321, 324–25
    wave, 42
Crime Control Act (1990), 111
criminal justice
    Blackstone ratio, 244–45
    due process and crime control models of, 243–44, 285
criminologists, 165–66, 173–74, 178
Crook, Shirley, 94–95
cruel and unusual punishments, 71, 310. *See also* Eighth Amendment
    evolving standards of decency and, 92, 105
    execution methods and, 126–27
    Furman v. Georgia and, 44
    juveniles and, 73–74, 75, 119
    lethal injection and, 99–100
    mental disability and, 206
    Stewart on, 57
Cruz, Rolondo, 233–34
culpability, 85, 96, 97, 185, 227
culture, 298
Currie, Elliot, 16
Cutler, Zelma, 215

Darrow, Clarence, 14
Davis, Allen Lee, 133f
Davis, Troy, 247
Dawson, Bill, 144
DC electricity, 130
deal-making, 255–56
death, 3
Death Penalty Information Center (DPIC), 186–87, 277, 300
Death Penalty Resources, 167

death sentencing
    community and, 173
    first, 30
    mandatory, 62
    motivation of crime and, 171
    in People's Republic of China, 314
    racial discrimination and, 47–48
    until execution, time from, 288, 290f
"death vans," 314
debates, 61, 105, 161–64
decency, 32
defendants. *See also* family members
    characteristics of, 67
    Eighth Amendment and, 67
    race of, 187f, 188, 192–93
    racial discrimination and, 69–72
    socioeconomic status of, 260
defense counsel. *See* counsel
Delaware, 128–29
democracy, 120, 300, 315t
Democratic People's Republic of Korea (North Korea), 297, 315–17, 324
denaturation, 222
Dershowitz, Alan, 155
"designated patsy," 276
determinism, free will and, 13–15, 23
deterrence, 127, 193
    assumptions about, 156–58, 177
    autoregressive integrated moving average, 166
    Baze and Bowling v. Reez and, 166
    brutalizing effect and, 167–69, 178
    CDDP, 168–70, 178
    certainty of punishment and, 159–60, 171–72
    Constitution, U.S. and, 161–62
    contrast effect, 158–59
    criminologists and, 165–66
    debates and, 161–64
    demonstration of, 169–70
    economists and, 165–66
    effect of, 155–56, 166, 168
    Furman v. Georgia and, 164
    general, 35, 158–59
    Gregg v. Georgia and, 164
    history of, 162
    IIDs and, 85
    justification and, 16, 19, 22t, 35–37, 166
    Marshall on, 164
    morality and, 176–77
    organized crime and, 173
    pain and, 166
    principles of punishment and, 159–61
    rational choice theory and, 156–58
    research and experimentation, 169–70
    Schroeder's perspective on, 171–73
    severity of punishment and, 159–61, 172
    sociologists and, 165–66
    specific, 35, 158–59
    swiftness of punishment and, 159–60, 171
    theory, 85, 177

two-stage least squares regression, 166
    in U.S., 35–37
    vector autoregression, 166
Dew, Nathan, 66
Diagnostic and Statistical Manual of Mental Disorders (DSM-V), 83, 228
Diaz, Angel, 146–48
dignity, 138–41
Dira Square, 319f
direct appeals, 286–87
director of corrections perspective, 138–41
discretion, 70–71, 91
dissenting opinions
    in *Atkins v. Virginia*, 85–87
    in *Baze and Bowling v. Reez*, 100
    in *Coker v. Georgia*, 64–65
    in *Furman v. Georgia*, 58
    in *Gregg v. Georgia*, 61–62
    in *Lockett v. Ohio*, 68
    in *McCleskey v. Kemp*, 71–72
    in *Ring v. Arizona*, 90–91
    in *Roper v. Simmons*, 97–98
    in *Stanford v. Kentucky*, 74–76
diyya ("blood money"), 11
DNA, 1
    certainty, 231
    contamination of, 223–24, 231
    definition, 221
    denaturation of, 222
    electrophoresis, 223f
    evidence, 231, 234
    fabricating, 231
    fingerprinting, 222–24
    informant/snitch testimony and, 255
    interpretation of results, 224
    mitochondrial, 258
    PCR, 222, 223f, 231, 235
    perspective of Hampikian, 309–11
    technology, 172, 215
    testing, 161, 216, 230–31, 242, 259
DNA exonerations
    attorney errors in, 262
    bad science and, 257, 258f, 259
    of Bloodsworth, 283
    eyewitness misidentification and, 245
    of Fain, 253–54, 255, 258–59, 311
    innocence and, 117
    of Miller, 215–17
    problems with, 230–31
    since 1989, 242f
    of Thibodeaux, 239–40, 245–46, 250
dopamine, 6–7
double-blind lineup, 249
Douglas, William, 57
DPIC. *See* Death Penalty Information Center
"drop" method of hanging, 127–28
Drummond, Edward, 53
DSM-V. *See* Diagnostic and Statistical Manual of Mental Disorders
dual citizenship, 303
dual sovereignty, 303, 324

due process, 207, 241
    expansion of, 275
    finances and, 285
    model of criminal justice, 243–44, 285
    super, 44–45, 61–62, 285
Duffy, Clinton, 135
Dugan, Brian, 233–34
Dunkins, Horace, 261
Durkheim, Émile, 3, 10f

Eastburn, Kathryn, 308
ecological fallacy, 232
Eddings, Monty Lee, 195
Eddings v. Oklahoma (1982), 68, 195, 203
Edison, Thomas, 41, 130–31
EEG. *See* electroencephalogram
Egypt, 30
Ehrlich, Isaac, 165
18th century. *See* 17th & 18th centuries
Eighth Amendment, 47–48, 56–57, 62, 73–74.
    See also cruel and unusual punishments; evolving standards of decency
    Atkins v. Virginia and, 92, 118–19
    defendants and, 67
    family members of victim and, 69
    Furman v. Georgia and, 44, 110
    IIDs and, 84, 87, 92–93
    insanity and, 87
    juveniles and, 75, 92, 95, 119
    lethal injection and, 146
    medication and, 207
    mental disabilities and, 206
    mental illness and, 208
    professional associations and, 93
    Sixth Amendment and, 90
    violations, 118–19
electrocution ("electric chair"), 41–42
    botched executions using, 132–33
    chair malfunctions, 132–33
    description of process, 131–32
    Edison and, 130–31
    experiments with, 129
    first man executed by, 131–32
    length of process, 132
    names for execution by, 130
    "Old Sparky," 132f
    popularity of, 133
    since 1976, 129f
    Southwick's role in, 130–31
electroencephalogram (EEG), 228
electrophoresis, 223f
emotions, 3, 5
    brain and, 4
    of family members, 115, 291, 293
    morality and, 4, 8, 31
    negative, 23
    rationality and, 4, 9–10, 23
    religion and, 4
    retribution and, 20–21
empathy, 9, 11

Enlightenment, 109
Enmund v. Florida (1982), 68
environment, 220
equal harm concept, 11
equality, women and, 201–2
Ertman, Jennifer, 299
espionage, 301
estimator variables, 248
ethics, 156. *See also* justification
Europe, 310–11
European Court of Human Rights, 17–18
evidence
    DNA, 231, 234
    exculpatory, 264
    of victims, variables in, 190, 193
evil, 106
evil woman explanation, 201–2, 210
evolutionary origins, 2–3
evolving standards of decency, 63, 74, 84, 96–97, 120. *See also* Eighth Amendment
    cruel and unusual punishments and, 92, 105
    first mention of, 118
    juveniles and, 196
    public support and, 107–8
exculpatory evidence, 264
executioners, 149–50, 161
execution methods, 41–42, 151. *See also* electrocution; firing squads; gas chamber; hanging; lethal injection
    cruel and unusual punishments and, 126–27
    evolution of, 126–27
    executioners, 149–50
    most humane, 131
    new, 127
    in People's Republic of China, 314
    by state in U.S., 127f
executions
    attendance of, 36
    countries carrying out, 312f
    democracy score and international, 315t
    with electricity, 41–42
    first documented, 32
    legal process prior to, 172
    Maine law, 39
    of mentally retarded persons, 84–85, 87, 96, 118–19
    planning of, 36
    preparing for, 46
    prison, 45–47
    protocols, 126
    public, 31, 36, 40–41
    race and, 186, 187f
    reduction of, 42, 43t
    San Quentin execution chamber, 147f
    time from sentencing until, 288, 290f
executive clemency, 40, 47
exoneration. *See also* DNA exoneration
    compensation, post, 265, 266f, 277
    Souter on, 242

Expediency Council, 321
expert witnesses, 284–86
"eye-for-an-eye" principle, 11, 37, 114, 150
eyewitness
    misidentification, 245, 246*f*, 247–50
    reform, 259

Fain, Charles, 253–54, 255, 258–59, 265, 311
fairness, 21, 217
false confessions, 250–54
family members
    abolition and, 284
    closure for, 172, 291
    diversity of, 291
    Eighth Amendment and, 69
    emotions of, 115, 291, 293
    history, 229
    justice and, 291–92
    mitigating factors and history of, 229
    treatment of, 140, 290–91
fatalism, 12
fear, social order and, 11
federal capital statutes, 301
federal death penalty, 300–305, 324
Federal Death Penalty Act (1994), 301
Feguer, Victor, 276
felony-murder rule, 66, 67, 68, 89
5th Circuit Federal Court, 277, 288–89
Fifth Amendment, 100, 303, 308
fillers, 249
finances, 274–75
    abolition and, 283
    AEDPA, 276–77, 287–88
    of attorneys, 290
    burden of, 277, 292–93
    of California, 277, 278*f*, 279–80, 293
    collateral costs, 290–92
    court costs, 281, 284
    due process and, 285
    of expert witnesses, 284–86
    Habeas corpus v. direct appeals, 286–87
    homicide investigation costs, 281
    LWOP and, 277–80, 285
    of McVeigh trial, 276, 287
    of New Jersey, 283
    of Ng's case, 278
    of Texas, 277
    Williams, W., case, 275
fingerprint analysis, 257–58
firing squads, 125, 129*f*, 142*f*, 143
fMRI. *See* functional magnetic resonance imaging
Ford, Alvin, 208
Ford v. Wainwright (1986), 87, 208
forgiveness, 22, 24
fornication, 321
Founding Fathers, 286
Fourteenth Amendment, 56, 57, 62, 67, 70, 72
    IIDs and, 87
    juveniles and, 95

Fourth Amendment, 104
Fowler, Anna, 215–16
Fowler, Jim, 215–16
framers of Constitution, 63, 107–8
France, 285, 299
Francis, Willie, 132–33
freedom, 13
free will, 12–15, 23, 220, 230
functional magnetic resonance imaging (fMRI), 224–25, 232–33, 235
Furman, William Henry, 55–56
Furman v. Georgia (1972), 16–17, 32, 54, 161, 203
    back-story of, 55–56
    concurring opinions, 56–58
    cruel and unusual punishments and, 44
    deterrence and, 164
    dissenting opinions, 58
    Eighth Amendment and, 44, 110
    post, 47–48
    public opinion and, 115
    retribution and, 5–6
    ruling, 76*t*
    super due process and, 44–45, 49
    Supreme Court justices during, 55*f*, 57–58

gallows construction, 128
Gallup poll, 110–11, 112*f*, 113
game theory, 21–22
GAO. *See* General Accounting Office
Gardner, Ronnie Lee, 125–26
Garland, David, 300
Garza, Juan Raul, 300–301
gas chamber
    complex features of, 136–37
    cost of, 136, 144
    description of process, 135–36
    first man executed by, 135
    humane aspect of, 133–34, 137
    last man executed by, 137
    length of time needed in executions by, 135
    physical structure of, 135
    potential risks of, 136–37
    since 1976, 129*f*
    testing, 135
    type of gas used in, 135
    World War I and II implications of, 137
    Wyoming, 134*f*
gender, 183–85, 190, 201
General Accounting Office (GAO), 48
general deterrence, 35, 158–59
genes, 1, 14, 219, 220–22, 235. *See also* DNA
Georgia, 40
gibbet irons, 36*f*
global perspectives, 118–20
Glossip v. Gross (2015), 100
goals, 32, 42
God, 175, 176*f*, 177–78, 230, 317, 319, 322
government misconduct, 263–65
governors, 107
Graham, Harrison, 202

Graham v. Florida (2010), 227
Graunger, Thomas, 194
Gray, Jimmy, 137
Gray, Ronald, 307
Great Depression, 42, 49
Great Law, 37–38
"Great Writ," 286
Greenham, James, 88–89
Gregg, Troy, 59
Gregg v. Georgia (1976), 126, 144, 203, 300
    back-story of, 59
    concurring opinions in, 61
    deterrence and, 164
    dissenting opinions in, 61–62
    ruling, 76t
    Supreme Court justices during, 59f, 61–62
Groundwork of the Metaphysics of Morals (Kant), 19
grudgers, 7
guilt, 37, 60, 217, 231
guilty act (*actus reus*), 216–17
guilty mind (*mens rea*), 216–17

Haag, Ernest van den, 177
Habeas corpus, 286–88, 289f, 290, 293
Habeas Corpus Act (1679), 286
Hain, Scott, 81, 194
hair comparison, 258–59
Hall v. Florida (2014), 87, 91–93, 207
Hall v. United States (2014), 87
Hampikian, Greg, 309–11
hanging, 46, 109–10, 127–28, 129f
happiness, 12
Hare Psychopathy Checklist, 233
Harrington, John, 37
Hasan, Nidal, 308
Haughton, Michael, 81
Hawthorne, Nathaniel, 2–3, 4
Hayden, Karen, 113
healing, 291
Heath, Mark, 145
Hedonism, 12, 13
hedonistic calculus, 13
Heidnik, Gary, 202
hemoglobin, 225
Hennis, Timothy, 308
Hernandez, Alejandro, 233–34
Herndon, Berta, 206
Herndon, Del, 206
hierarchy, 8
high severity circumstances, 191
Hippocratic oath, 149–50
homicide (murder), 17, 38, 39, 48
    felony-murder rule, 66, 67, 68, 89
    investigation costs, 281
    motivation of, 155
    offenses, 301
    punishment and, 169
    race and, 186–91
    rape and, 64
    rates by state in U.S., 162, 163f, 164
    reduction of, 162
    in U.S., 160
    women and, 198
homosexuality, 319, 321, 325
hooliganism, 297
Hope, Edgar, 263
Horn v. Banks (2002), 288
Hospira, 148
hudud crimes, 318–19, 320, 321, 324–25
Humane Death Bill (1921), 135
human nature, 4, 6, 12–13, 166
human rights, 17, 299
Hume, David, 20
The Hurricane, 241–42
Hussein, Saddam, 323, 325

Idaho Department of Correction, 138–41
IIDs. *See* Individuals with an Intellectual Disability
Illinois, 234
immunity, 265
impaired judgment, 232
importation, 148
imprisonment, purpose of, 18
incapacitation, 16–17, 22t
incarceration rates, 161
incentivized testimony. *See* informant/snitch testimony
incredible certitude, 162, 193
Individuals with an Intellectual Disability (IIDs), 82–84, 86–87
    deterrence and, 85
    Eighth Amendment and, 84, 87, 92–93
    Fourteenth Amendment and, 87
    IQ and, 87, 93, 205–7, 210
Indonesia, 309
ineffective defensive counsel, 260–63
informant/snitch testimony, 254–57
informed citizenry, 115–17
innocence
    Blackstone ratio, 244–45
    DNA exonerations and, 117
    factual, 240–43
    revolution, 117, 121, 217–18, 234, 241
Innocence Network, 309
Innocence Project, 249, 251
insanity, 13, 53, 54, 87, 229, 230
intellectual disability, 205
internalized confessions, 252
international opinion, 86
international stage, 308–11, 312f, 315t, 324
interracial crime, 72
investigation costs, 281
Iowa, 40
Iraq War, 323, 325
ISIS (Islamic State of Syria and Iraq), 323
Islamic law (*shar'ia*), 317, 322, 323
    lack of uniformity in, 320
    types of crimes in, 318–19, 320, 321, 324–25

Islamic Republic of Iran, 308, 315*t*, 317, 320–24
Islamic State of Syria and Iraq. *See* ISIS
Italy, 120, 310

Jackson, Roscoe, 41
Jackson, Theon, 207
Jackson v. Georgia, 56
Jackson v. Indiana (1972), 207
Jacoby, Susan, 10
Jacques, Michael, 304–5
Jim Crow laws, 185
Johnson, Daralyn, 253–54
Johnson, Lyndon, 110
Jon, Gee, 135
Jones, Ernest, 160, 278
Jones, Louis, Jr., 300
Jones, William, 83, 86
judges, 106, 171–73, 319–20
juries, 39–40, 47, 49
    aggravating factors and, 60
    community and, 90
    in France, 285
    jury nullification, 39–40, 47, 49, 109
    juveniles and, 97
    laws and, 58
    mental disabilities and, 85–86
    mitigating factors and, 60
    right to, 88
    unbiased, 72
    voir dire process, 281
jurors, 72, 188
justice, 72
    family members and, 291–92
    local aspect of, 310
    offender-centered concept of, 189
    restitutive, 11
    swift, 275
    theoretical models of, 243–44
    vengeance and, 10
    vigilante, 40, 57, 106
justification, 2, 15
    deterrence and, 16, 19, 22*t*, 35–37, 166
    human nature and, 12–13
    incapacitation, 16–17, 22*t*
    key elements of, 22*t*
    morality and, 15, 23
    rehabilitation, 17–18, 22*t*, 114
    reintegration, 18, 22*t*
    retribution as, 18, 20–21, 22*t*
juveniles, 77, 94, 194
    abolition for, 195–96
    adolescence, 226–27
    age and definition of, 197
    brain imaging and, 225–27
    cases, 72–76
    childhood effect on, 81
    cruel and unusual punishments and, 73–74, 75, 119
    culpability of, 96, 97, 185, 227
    differences between adults and, 96
    Eighth Amendment and, 75, 92, 95, 119
    evolving standards of decency and, 196
    Fourteenth Amendment and, 95
    identity of, 96
    in Islamic Republic of Iran, 321
    juries and, 97
    laws about, 74
    mentally retarded persons and, 97–98
    morality of, 96
    parens patriae, 195
    Powell on, 195
    puberty, 226
    public opinion and, 104
    responsibility and, 75
    rights of, 195
    Roper v. Simmons and, 76, 87, 119, 196, 210, 227, 232–33
    separate court for, 195
    ultimate penalty appropriate for, 82
    vulnerability of, 96

Kansas, 42
Kant, Immanuel, 19*f*, 20, 156, 172
Karr, Jon Mark, 250–51
Keihl, Kent, 234
Kemmler, William, 41, 131–32
Kendall, George, 32
Kennedy, Anthony, 196
Kennedy v. Louisiana (2008), 65
Kim Chol, 317
Kim Jong-il, 317
Kim Jung-Un, 316
King, Rodney, 303
Kitts, Mary Sue, 279
Knox, Amanda, 309–10
Kuwait, 309

LaChance, Daniel, 150
Lacock, Traci, 174
LaGrand, Walter, 137
Lake, Leonard, 273
Lambert, Robert, 81
Langley, Christopher, 155
Lara, Jonathan, 113
last meals, 150–51, 171
last words, 150–51
Latham, Mary, 29–30
Law Enforcement Assistance Administration Laboratory Proficiency Testing Program, 259
laws. *See also* Islamic law
    Arizona, 89–90
    Colonial, 34
    free will and, 14
    global, 118n3
    Great Law, 37–38
    Jim Crow, 185
    juries and, 58
    about juveniles, 74
    Maine, 39

modern, 9–11, 14
   of retaliation, 37
   rule of law, 316
The Laws and Liberties of Massachusetts (1648), 33
lawyers. *See* counsel
legal ritualism, 244
legal system, 15, 218
leg irons, 46
legislation, 107
legislatures, 71
lethal injection, 47, 126, 142
   anesthetic for, 145–46
   botched executions using, 146–48
   challenges with, 151
   consciousness during, 145–46
   Constitution, U.S. and, 99–100
   cruel and unusual punishments and, 99–100
   description of process, 143–44
   drugs in, 99, 100, 133, 144, 145–48
   Eighth Amendment and, 146
   first statute of, 144
   improper administration of, 144–48
   in People's Republic of China, 314–15
   San Quentin execution chamber, 147*f*
   since 1976, 129*f*
   three- *vs.* one-drug, 145–48
   toxicology reports, 146
   vein issues in, 147
Lethal Injection Secrecy Act (2013), 149
Lewis, Teresa, 199
lex talionis (law of retaliation). *See* retaliation
liberalism, 300
life without the possibility of parole (LWOP), 111, 112*f*, 117, 192, 274–75, 277–80, 285, 292
Lincoln, Abraham, 197
lineups, 248–50
Lockett, Clayton, 147–48
Lockett, Sandra, 66–68
Lockett v. Ohio (1978), 203
   back-story of, 66–67
   concurring opinions in, 67
   dissenting opinions in, 68
   ruling, 76*t*
   Supreme Court justices in, 65*f*, 67–68
Lockhart v. McCree (1986), 68
Logan, Alton, 263–64
Lott, Ronald, 215
Louisiana, 39, 40, 63
Louisiana ex rel. Francis v. Resweber (1947), 100
Loving, Dwight, 307
LWOP. *See* life without the possibility of parole
lynchings, 40, 185

mafia, 173
magnetic resonance imaging (MRI), 224
Magoch, John, 88
Maine, 39, 40
Maine law, 39
mandatory death sentences, 62
Manski, Charles, 162
MAOA gene, 219–20
marriage, 323
Marshall, Thurgood, 57–58, 61, 64, 67, 71, 74–75, 105
   on deterrence, 164
   hypotheses, 115–18
Maryland, 39, 250
Massachusetts, 304
Massachusetts Bay Colony, 33
McCarthy, Kimberly, 200
McCleskey, Warren, 69–70
McCleskey v. Kemp (1987)
   back-story of, 69–70
   concurring opinions in, 70–71
   dissenting opinions in, 71–72
   racial discrimination in, 191
   ruling, 76*t*
   Supreme Court justices in, 68*f*, 70–72
McDuff, Kenneth, 17
McNaughton, David, 53–54
McVeigh, Timothy, 275–77, 287, 293, 300
Medellin, José, 299
medical parole, 297
medication, 207, 209
memory, power of suggestion and, 248
Menninger, Karl, 14–15
mens rea. See guilty mind
mental competency, 183–85
mental deficiency, 66–67. *See also* Individuals with an Intellectual Disability
mental disabilities, 82
   confessions and, 206
   cruel and unusual punishments and, 206
   Eighth Amendment and, 206
   IQ and, 87, 93, 205–7, 210
   juries and, 85–86
   morality and, 86
mental health, 53
mental illness
   brain and, 228
   competency and, 208–9
   Eighth Amendment and, 208
   insanity, 13, 53, 54, 87, 229, 230
   legal component of, 204, 229
   medication, 207, 209
   psychologist's perspective, 202–5
   rational understanding and, 208–9
   schizophrenia, 54, 205, 207, 228
mentally retarded persons, 87, 205–7
   Atkins v. Virginia and, 118–19, 196–97, 206, 210, 227
   executions of, 84–85, 87, 96, 118–19
   juveniles and, 97–98
Merchant of Venice (Shakespeare), 3
Merikangas, James, 227, 228*f*, 229–30
Michigan, 40
Micki, Lanell, 55

Micki, William, 55–56
Midazolam, 100
military, 305–8
military death row population, 307–8
Miller, Julia, 278
Miller, Robert, 215–17
Miller-El v. Dretke (2005), 72
Minnesota, 42
minorities, 44. *See also* race
Mississippi, 40
Missouri, 41, 42
mitigating factors, 60, 67–68, 74, 77, 89, 190, 229
mitigation, 216–17
mitochondrial DNA, 258
Mobley, Stephen, 1, 2, 12, 217, 219
Model Penal Code, 59–60
modern science. *See* science
morality, 2
    categorical imperative, 19
    consequentialism and, 177
    deterrence and, 176–77
    emotion and, 4, 8, 31
    justification and, 15, 23
    of juveniles, 96
    mental disabilities and, 86
    modern science and, 218–19
    religion and, 3, 5
    retribution and, 15, 19
    universal standards of, 20
Mormons, 142
MRI. *See* magnetic resonance imaging
Muhammad, 319
Mullen, Carmen T., 184
Munsterberg, Hugo, 247, 248
murder. *See* homicide
Musgrove, L. H., 40
Musso, Louis, 200
Mussolini, Benito, 120
mutilations, 192

NAACP. *See* National Association for the Advancement of Colored People
National Academy of Science, 168
National Association for the Advancement of Colored People (NAACP), 43–44
National Registry of Exonerations (NRE), 241
natural selection, 7, 8, 23
Nesbitt, Eric, 83
neuroimaging. *See* brain
neuropsychiatry, 227–30
neuropsychology, 202–5
neuroscience, 216, 218, 219, 220, 229
neurotransmitters, 219
Nevada, 133–35
New Hampshire, 38, 129
New Jersey, 41, 250, 282–84
New Testament, 3
Newton, Frances, 199
New York Death Penalty Commission, 131
Ng, Charles Chi-Tat, 273–74, 275, 278, 293

Nicarico, Jeanine, 233–34
Nigeria, 309
nineteenth century, 38–42
9th Circuit Court of Appeals, U.S., 279
9th Circuit Federal Court, 277
Niu Yuqiang, 297
Nixon, John, 279
Nixon, Richard, 58
noncooperation, 21
non-homicidal narcotics offenses, 301
non-kin, 7
North Carolina, 63, 186
North Carolina Actual Innocence Commission, 267
North Dakota, 42
North Korea. *See* Democratic People's Republic of Korea
Norway, 315
NRE. *See* National Registry of Exonerations

Obama, Barack, 108
objectivity, in punishment, 172
Ocuish, Hannah, 194
offenders, 21
    centered concept of justice, 189
    community and, 32
    culpability of, 85
Ohio, 38, 67, 148
Oklahoma City bombing, 275–77, 287
Old Idaho State Penitentiary, 45–47
"Old Sparky," 132f
Old Testament, 3, 5
On Crimes and Punishments (Beccaria), 38, 159
opposition, 107
Oregon, 42
organ harvesting, 314–15
organized crime, deterrence and, 173
Ott, Sandra, 113
Ott, Timothy, 113
Otter, C. L. ("Butch"), 138
Otterstorm, Melvyn, 125

Packer, Herbert, 243–44
pain, 12–13, 157, 166
Panetti v. Quarterman (2007), 87, 208–9
paranoia, 53
pardons, 107
parens patriae, 195
Parker, Al, 66
parole, 17–18
Pascal's wager, 175, 176f, 177, 178
Paskett, Dave, 45–47
Payne v. Tennessee (1990), 69
PCR. *See* polymerase chain reaction
Pearson, Karl, 311
Peel, Robert, 53
Pena, Elizabeth, 299
penalty phase, 60
penitence, 36–37
Penn, William, 37–38

Pennsylvania, 41
Penrose, Charles, 142–43
Penry, Johnny, 206
Penry v. Lynaugh (1989), 84, 87, 96, 206
pentobarbital, 148
People's Republic of China, 297–98, 308, 311–14, 315*t*, 324
Pepys, Samuel, 31
per curiam decision, 56
PFC. *See* prefrontal cortex
photo lineups, 249
physicians, 149–50
Picking Cotton (Thompson & Cotton), 247
Pizzuto, Gerald, 206–7
Plantz, Marilyn, 199
pleasure, 6–7, 9, 12–13, 156–57
police
    chiefs, 174, 175*f*, 178, 282–84
    informant/snitch testimony and, 256
    interrogations, 251–52
    misconduct, 263–65
    power, 244
    training, 259
political adjustment hypothesis, 108–9
polymerase chain reaction (PCR), 222, 223*f*, 231, 235
polymorphism, 221
Poole, Bobby, 246*f*, 247
Poore, Barbel, 73
post-exoneration compensation, 265, 266*f*, 267
Powell, Lewis, 58, 61, 64, 67, 70, 72, 195
power of suggestion, memory and, 248
prefrontal cortex (PFC), 226
press, 291
pretrial hearings, 281
prevention, of crime, 22
primate behavior, 8
prisons, 45–47
probation sanction, 22
professional associations, Eighth Amendment and, 93
professionalism, 138–41
propensity score matching (PSM), 192–93
propofol, 148
proportionality analyses, 74
prosecutors, 91–93, 106, 264–65
PSM. *See* propensity score matching
psychiatry, 193
psychopathy, 218, 233–34
puberty, 226
public executions, 31, 36, 40–41
public opinion, 58
    abolition and, 119–20
    debates and, 105
    demographics of, 106*t*
    expression of, 109–15
    Furman v. Georgia and, 115
    Gallup poll, 110–11, 112*f*, 113
    jury nullification and, 109
    juveniles and, 104
    Rehnquist on, 105
    Supreme Court, U.S., and, 108, 118
    ups and downs of, 104–6
    witchcraft and, 103–4
public policy, race and, 189
public support, 106–8, 116, 120
punishment. *See also* cruel and unusual punishments; execution methods
    brutalizing effect of, 167–69, 178
    certainty of, 159–60, 171–72
    community and, 173
    deterrence and, 159–61, 171–72
    homicide and, 169
    objectivity in, 172
    pleasure and, 156–57
    principles of, 159–61
    in Saudi Arabia, criminal law, 318
    second- and third-party, 8–9, 12
    severity of, 159–61, 172
    swiftness of, 159–60, 171
Punishment and Culture (Smith), 2
Puritans, 32–33, 34
purpose, 2, 4

al-Qaeda, 308
Quakers, 33, 38
qualified immunity, 265
quesas crimes, 318–19, 320, 321–22, 325
Quinn, Pat, 234
Qur'an, 317–18, 319, 320, 321, 324–25

race, 183–85
    application of death penalty and, 190
    Black Codes, 185
    of defendants, 187*f*, 188, 192–93
    executions and, 186, 187*f*
    homicide and, 186–91
    Jim Crow laws, 185
    of jurors, 188
    public policy and, 189
    racial disproportionality, 185–88
    of victims, 189–94
racial discrimination, 43, 77, 173, 184, 209
    Baldus study, 69, 70, 71
    death sentencing and, 47–48
    defendants and, 69–72
    jurors and, 72
    in *McCleskey v. Kemp*, 191
racial disproportionality, 185–88
racism, 188
Radelet, Michael, 174
Ramsey, Jon Benet, 250–51
rape, 62–65, 77
rational behavior, 12–13
rational choice theory, 156–58
rationality
    emotion and, 4, 9–10, 23
    Hedonism and, 13
    mental illness and, 208–9
    self-interest and, 12–13

Reagan, Ronald, 306
reason, 20
reciprocal altruism, 7
reconciliation, 21–22, 24
reform. *See* abolition
rehabilitation, 17–18, 22*t*, 114
Rehnquist, William, 58, 61, 64, 68, 70, 74, 105
Reid technique, 252
Reinke, Brent D., 138*f*, 139–41
reintegration, 18, 21–22, 22*t*, 24
religion, 292. *See also* Islamic law
    afterlife, 176
    blood atonement, 142–43
    definition of, 3
    emotion and, 4
    God, 175, 176*f*, 177–78, 230, 317, 319, 322
    morality and, 3, 5
    New Testament, 3
    Old Testament, 3, 5
    Pascal's wager and, 175, 176*f*, 177, 178
    Qur'an, 317–18, 319, 320, 321, 324–25
    repentance, 34
    Salem witch trials and, 104
    scripture, 34
    in U.S., 33–35
repentance, 34
reproduction, 6–7, 9
Republic of Iraq, 308, 315*t*, 317, 322–23, 324, 325
reputation, 8–9
respect, 20, 21, 138–41
responsibility, 12, 20, 75, 217
restitutive justice, 11
retaliation, law of, 37
retention elections, 107n1
retribution, 5, 15, 85, 115, 127
    confinement as measure of, 159
    emotion and, 20–21
    Furman v. Georgia and, 5–6
    human nature and, 6
    as justification, 18, 20–21, 22*t*
    Kantian, 19–22
    morality and, 15, 19
    in U.S., 37–38
    vengeance and, 10
revenge, 8, 9–10, 18
Reza, Elizabeth, 201
Rhode Island, 40
Richardson, Brian, 284–85
Riggs, Christina, 199
Ring, Timothy, 88–89
Ring v. Arizona (2002)
    back-story of, 88–89
    concurring opinions in, 89–90
    dissenting opinions in, 90–91
    ruling, 101*t*
    Supreme Court justices in, 88*f*, 89–91
Roper v. Simmons (2005)
    aggravating factors in, 95
    back-story of, 94–95
    concurring opinions in, 96–97
    dissenting opinions in, 97–98
    juveniles and, 76, 87, 119, 196, 210, 227, 232–33
    ruling, 101*t*
    Supreme Court justices in, 94*f*, 96–98
rule of law, 316
Ryan, George, 218, 240, 291

Salem witch trials, 33, 35*f*, 103, 104
salvation, 34
Sampson, Gary Lee, 304
Sanders, Laura, 81
San Quentin execution chamber, 147*f*
Saudi Arabia, 11, 167, 297–98, 308, 315*t*, 317, 324
    British Embassy in, 318
    constitution of, 318
    criminal law punishments in, 318
    Dira Square, 319*f*
    judges in, 319–20
Scalia, 74
Scalia, Antonin, 288
The Scarlet Letter (Hawthorne), 2, 4
schizophrenia, 54, 205, 207, 228
Schlatt, Frank, 69
Schnorr, Donna, 233
Schroeder, Gerald, 171–73
science, 20, 215–16
    common sense and, 229
    fingerprint analysis, 257–58
    genes, 219–20
    hair comparison, 258–59
    legal system and, 218
    morality and, 218–19
    neuroscience, 216, 218, 219, 220, 229
    status of, 218
    wrongful convictions and bad, 257, 258*f*, 259
scripture, 34
second- and third-party punishment, 8–9, 12
Sellin, Thorsten, 163–64
separation of church and state, 32
serial killer, neuroimaging of, 233–34
serotonin, 219
Sessions, William, 247
17th & 18th centuries, 32–33
severity, of punishment, 159–61, 172
sex, 6, 325
Shakespeare, William, 3
shar'ia. *See* Islamic law
Shepherd, Joanna, 165
Shia Islam, 320, 322–23
Simmons, Christopher, 94–95, 196, 232
Sixth Amendment, 68, 88, 89–90, 260, 261
60 Minutes, 256
slavery, 39, 185, 186
Smith, Lois Nadean, 199
Smith, Philip, 2
Smith, Susan, 201
snitch testimony. *See* informant/snitch testimony

Snowden, Raymond, 46
Snyder v. Louisiana (2008), 72
social attachments, 7
social cooperation, 5–8, 21–22
social order, 3–5, 11, 21
social solidarity, 4–5, 10–11, 105–6
society, 9, 284
sodium thiopental, 148
solidarity, 21, 34, 173
South Dakota, 42
southern states, 188
South Korea, 315–16
Southwick, Alfred, 130–31
special populations, 204–5
specific deterrence, 35, 158–59
Spinelli, Ethel, 200, 201
Stanford, Kevin, 72–74, 196
Stanford v. Kentucky (1989), 82, 87, 96, 98, 196
    back-story of, 72–74
    concurring opinions in, 74
    dissenting opinions in, 74–76
    ruling, 76t
    Supreme Court justices in, 73f, 74–76
Stapleton Crew, 304
state-sanctioned revenge, 18
statistics, 230–31
statute of limitations, 288
Stewart, Potter, 6, 44, 57, 67, 164
Stinney, George Junius, Jr., 183–85, 194
Strickland standard, 261–62
Strickland v. Washington (1984), 261
strongest inclination, 14
suicide, 149, 155
Sunni Islam, 320, 323
super due process, 44–45, 49, 61–62, 285
Supreme Court, U.S.
    attitudinal model, 108–9
    justice's perspective, 171–73
    political adjustment hypothesis, 108–9
    public opinion and, 108, 118
    role of, 71
Surratt, Mary, 197f
survival, 6–7, 9
Swank, Hillary, 241
swiftness, of punishment, 159–60, 171
sympathy, 9, 11, 31
system variables, 248

Tafero, Jesse, 133
ta'zir crimes, 318–19, 320, 321–22, 325
Tennard v. Dretke (2004), 87
Tennessee, 39, 42, 289f
terrorism, 301, 319, 323
testosterone, 219
Texas, 277, 288–89
Thibodeaux, Damon, 239–40, 245–46, 250
Thompson, Jennifer, 246, 247
Thompson, William, 196
Thompson v. Oklahoma (1988), 76, 98, 196, 203
torture, 172, 192, 313, 323

treason, 38, 301
trial costs. *See* court costs
Trop v. Dulles (1958), 105, 107, 118
Tsarnaev, Dzhokhar, 301
Tsarnaev, Tamerlan, 301
Tucker, Karla Faye, 198, 200, 201
Tucker, Virginia, 279
Turner v. Murray (1986), 72
20th century, 42–48
two-stage least squares regression, 166

UCMJ. *See* Uniform Code of Military Justice
UCR. *See* Uniform Crime Report
Uniform Code of Military Justice (UCMJ), 305–7
Uniform Crime Report (UCR), 111f, 187
United Kingdom, 120
United States (U.S.). *See also* Constitution, U.S.; Supreme Court, U.S.
    abolitionist movement, 38–42
    African American, 186
    ambivalence of, 31–32
    colonial, 32–33
    democracy score of, 315t
    deterrence in, 35–37
    execution method by state in, 127f
    federal death penalty, 300–305
    federal government of, 299
    homicide rates by state in, 162, 163f, 164
    homicides in, 160
    lynching in, 40
    military death penalty, 305–8, 324
    19th century, 38–42
    reduction of executions in, 42, 43t
    religion in, 33–35
    retribution in, 37–38
    separation of church and state in, 32
    17th & 18th centuries, 32–33
    states without death penalty, 119f
    trade, 304
    20th century, 42–48
    values of, 298–300
United States Court of Appeals for the Armed Forces (USCAAF), 306
"upright jerker" method of hanging, 128
utilitarianism, 15

vector autoregression, 166
vengeance, 9–11, 116
Vermont, 304–5
victims, 8, 11, 22. *See also* defendants; family members
    closure for, 172, 291
    evidentiary variables of, 190, 193
    gender of, 190
    race of, 189–94
    of rape, 65
    rights, 243–44
    W/B cases, 191–92
    white victim effect, 192–93

Vietnam (country), 309
Vietnam War, 197
vigilante justice, 40, 57, 106
violence, 2, 229
Violent Crime Control and Law Enforcement Act (1994), 111
voir dire process, 281
voluntary confessions, 250–51

Waldroup, David Bradley, 220
Waldroup, Penny, 220
Walton v. Arizona (1990), 91
Washington, 42, 129
Washington, Denzel, 241–42
Washington v. Harper (1990), 209
W/B. *See* white victim–black perpetrator cases
Weber, Max, 13
Westinghouse, 41
Westinghouse, George, 130
White, Byron, 57, 61, 67, 70, 74, 161
White, Leslie Vernon, 256
white victim–black perpetrator (W/B) cases, 191–92
white victim effect, 192–93
Wilkerson v. Utah (1879), 100, 118
Williams, Davontae Williams, 200
Williams, Walter "Doc," 275
Wilson, Andrew, 263–64
Wilson, James Q., 16
Wilson, Ronnell, 304
Winsor, Allen, 91*f*, 92–93
Winthrop, James, 29
Wiseman, Bill, 144
witchcraft, public opinion and, 103–4

Witt, Andrew, 308
women, 197
 chivalry explanation for cases of, 200–201, 210
 on death row, 198
 equality and, 201–2
 evil woman explanation in cases of, 201–2, 210
 executed since 1976, 198–200
 homicide and, 198
 Reza on, 201
 rights of, 322
 stereotypes of, 201
Woodson v. North Carolina (1976), 62, 63
writ of certiorari, 56, 59
wrongful convictions, 117, 239–41, 241–42
 abolition and, 283
 bad science and, 257, 258*f*, 259
 Blackstone ratio, 244–45
 eyewitness misidentification, 245, 246*f*, 247–50
 false confessions, 250–54
 government misconduct, 263–65
 ineffective defensive counsel, 260–63
 informant/snitch testimony, 254–57
 post-exoneration compensation, 265, 266*f*, 267
Wuornos, Aileen, 199, 201

Xiao Yang, 313–14

Yoon Sang-hyun, 317

Zimmerman, Michael, 15